T0214067

Lecture Notes in Computer Science   12684

Raian Ali · Birgit Lugrin ·
Fred Charles (Eds.)

Persuasive Technology

16th International Conference, PERSUASIVE 2021
Virtual Event, April 12–14, 2021
Proceedings

 Springer

Editors
Raian Ali 🄔
Hamad bin Khalifa University
Education City, Doha, Qatar

Birgit Lugrin 🄔
University of Würzburg
Würzburg, Germany

Fred Charles 🄔
Bournemouth University
Poole, UK

ISSN 0302-9743   ISSN 1611-3349   (electronic)
Lecture Notes in Computer Science
ISBN 978-3-030-79459-0   ISBN 978-3-030-79460-6   (eBook)
https://doi.org/10.1007/978-3-030-79460-6

LNCS Sublibrary: SL3 – Information Systems and Applications, incl. Internet/Web, and HCI

This Springer imprint is published by the registered company Springer Nature Switzerland AG
The registered company address is: Gewerbestrasse 11, 6330 Cham, Switzerland

Preface

Persuasive Technology (PT) is a vibrant interdisciplinary research field focusing on the design, development, and evaluation of interactive technologies. PT aims at changing people's attitudes or behaviors through persuasion and social influence, but with strong considerations regarding transparency and ethics. The 16th International Conference on Persuasive Technology (Persuasive 2021) brought together international researchers and practitioners from industry and academia who are working in the field of behavior design and persuasive technologies. As a community, we aim at enriching people's lives in various domains such as health, safety, and the environment – by supporting their personal goals to change their behavior.

The Persuasive conference series is the leading venue to meet and discuss cutting-edge theoretical and methodological perspectives and to present recent insights from practice and research. The conference provides a venue for networking between researchers and practitioners from all corners of the world and has been held in previous years in different places such as Chicago, USA; Padua, Italy; Linköping, Sweden; Oulu, Finland; Sydney, Australia; Amsterdam, the Netherlands; Salzburg, Austria; Waterloo, Canada; and Limassol, Cyprus.

Persuasive 2021 was the 16th edition in this conference series and was hosted during April 12–13, 2021, by Bournemouth University in the UK. In this edition, we introduced three special tracks: Persuasion and Education, Persuasive Affective Technology, and Digital Marketing, E-commerce, E-tourism and Smart Ecosystems.

On April 12, two tutorials were delivered, and two workshops were held. The first tutorial on 'Persuasive systems design, evaluation and research through the PSD model' was delivered by Prof. Harri Oinas-Kukkonen from Oulu University, Finland. The second tutorial on 'Digital Addiction and Digital Wellness' was delivered by Prof. Raian Ali from Hamad Bin Khalifa University, Qatar. The two workshops were the 9th International Workshop on Behavior Change Support Systems (BCSS 2021) and the Workshop on Designing Persuasive Technology to Support Mental Health.

During April 13–14, the main conference took place with four single-track sessions, including oral presentations of accepted academic papers. The program also included two keynotes as well as a poster session and a panel session.

This volume contains the accepted papers presented during the main conference. The included papers were reviewed by a board of experts in the field in a double-blind review process. Papers were selected for publication and presentation at the conference based on the review process.

Overall, 68 reviewers were assigned to the papers, excluding conflicts of interest. Each review combined a rating of the paper along with a detailed textual review, which not only provided the Program Chairs with significant insight concerning the individual submissions but also ensured that the authors were provided with high-quality feedback and recommendations for the final versions of their papers.

The Program Chairs and Track Chairs carefully assessed all reviews and all comments made by the reviewers, and based on this, the final list of papers to be presented at the conference was assembled. In total, 62 papers were included in the review process, out of which 17 papers were accepted as full papers (an acceptance rate of 27%) and 8 papers were accepted as short papers, while 37 papers were rejected.

We would like to thank all those who contributed to the success of Persuasive 2021. In particular, we would like to thank the authors from 34 countries who submitted their papers to the conference. We also thank the Program Committee for their help in promoting the conference, submitting papers, and playing a critical role in the review process. We are also thankful to Bournemouth University for the organisation of Persuasive 2021 and Hamad Bin Khalifa University for co-sponsoring the conference.

April 2021

Raian Ali
Birgit Lugrin
Fred Charles

Organization

General Chair

Fred Charles   Bournemouth University, UK

Program Chairs

Raian Ali   Hamad Bin Khalifa University, Qatar
Birgit Lugrin   University of Würzburg, Germany

Doctoral Consortium Chairs

Jaap Haam   Eindhoven University of Technology, the Netherlands
Keith Phalp   Bournemouth University, UK
Harri Oinas-Kukkonen   Oulu University, Finland

Workshops and Tutorial Chairs

Nilufar Baghaei   Massey University, New Zealand
Charlie Hargood   Bournemouth University, UK

Technical Demonstration Chair

Christos Gatzidis   Bournemouth University, UK

Persuasion and Education Track

Dena Al-Thani   Hamad Bin Khalifa University, Qatar
Harri Oinas-Kukkonen   Oulu University, Finland

Persuasive Affective Technology Track

Dirk Heylen   University of Twente, the Netherlands
Iolanda Leite   Royal Institute of Technology (KTH), Sweden

Digital Marketing, eCommerce, eTourism and SMART Ecosystems Track

Dimitrios Buhalis   Bournemouth University, UK
Ioannis Assiouras   ESDES, Lyon Catholic University, France
Elvira Bolat   Bournemouth University, UK

Local Arrangement Chairs

Sarah Hodge	Bournemouth University, UK
Dimitrios Buhalis	Bournemouth University, UK

Web, Publicity and Proceedings Chair

Vedad Hulusic	Bournemouth University, UK

Program Committee Members

Raian Ali	Hamad Bin Khalifa University, Qatar
Mohamed Basel Almourad	Zayed University, United Arab Emirates
Amen Alrobai	King Abdulaziz University, Saudi Arabia
Dena Al-Thani	Hamad Bin Khalifa University, Qatar
Luisa Andreu Simó	University of Valencia, Spain
Emily Arden-Close	Bournemouth University, UK
Ioannis Assiouras	Lyon Catholic University, France
Rodolfo Baggio	Bocconi University, Italy
Nilufar Baghaei	Massey University, New Zealand
Robbert Jan Beun	Utrecht University, the Netherlands
Tom Blount	University of Southampton, UK
Jennifer Boger	University of Waterloo, Canada
Elvira Bolat	Bournemouth University, UK
Anne-Gwenn Bosser	École Nationale d'Ingénieurs de Brest, France
Dimitrios Buhalis	Bournemouth University, UK
Sandra Burri Gram-Hansen	Aalborg University, Denmark
Fred Charles	Bournemouth University, UK
Luca Chittaro	University of Udine, Italy
Jacqueline Corbett	Laval University, Canada
Fabiano Dalpiaz	Utrecht University, the Netherlands
Janet Davis	Whitman College, USA
Boris De Ruyter	Philips Research, the Netherlands
Peter De Vries	University of Twente, the Netherlands
Christos Gatzidis	Bournemouth University, UK
Patrick Gebhard	DFKI GmbH, Germany
Jaap Ham	Eindhoven University of Technology, the Netherlands
Charlie Hargood	Bournemouth University, UK
Dirk Heylen	University of Twente, the Netherlands
Sarah Hodge	Bournemouth University, UK
Vedad Hulusic	Bournemouth University, UK
Stephen Intille	Northeastern University, USA
M. Sriram Iyengar	Texas A &M University, USA
Kirsikka Kaipainen	Tampere University, Finland
Maurits Kaptein	Eindhoven University of Technology, the Netherlands
Pasi Karppinen	University of Oulu, Finland

Randy Klaassen	University of Twente, the Netherlands
Nikolaos Korfiatis	University of East Anglia, UK
Theodoros Kostoulas	University of the Aegean, Greece
Sitwat Langrial	Namal Institute Pakistan, Pakistan
Iolanda Leite	Royal Institute of Technology (KTH), Sweden
Gale Lucas	University of Southern California, USA
Birgit Lugrin	University of Würzburg, Germany
Tom MacTavish	IIT Institute of Design, USA
Panos Markopoulos	Eindhoven University of Technology, the Netherlands
Farhad Mehdipour	Otago Polytechnic, Auckland, New Zealand
Alexander Meschtscherjakov	University of Salzburg, Austria
Cees Midden	Eindhoven University of Technology, the Netherlands
Georgios Mikros	Hamad Bin Khalifa University, Qatar
David Millard	University of Southampton, UK
Alexandra Millonig	Vienna University of Technology, Austria
Harri Oinas-Kukkonen	University of Oulu, Finland
Rita Orji	Dalhousie University, Canada
Keith Phalp	Bournemouth University, UK
Marwa Qaraqe	Hamad Bin Khalifa University, Qatar
Astrid Rosenthal-von der Pütten	RWTH Aachen University, Germany
Peter Ruijten	Eindhoven University of Technology, the Netherlands
Philipp Schaper	University of Würzburg, Germany
Jacqui Taylor-Jackson	Bournemouth University, UK
Piiastiina Tikka	University of Oulu, Finland
Nava Tintarev	University of Maastricht, the Netherlands
Manfred Tscheligi	University of Salzburg, Austria
Lisette van Gemert-Pijnen	University of Twente, the Netherlands
Julita Vassileva	University of Saskatchewan, Canada
Katerina Volchek	Deggendorf Institute of Technology, Germany
Nigel Williams	Bournemouth University, UK
Khin Than Win	University of Wollongong, Australia
Guandong Xu	University of Technology Sydney, Australia
Wajdi Zaghouani	Hamad Bin Khalifa University, Qatar

Contents

Theory and Guidelines

AI and Persuasion

Positing a Sense of Agency-Aware Persuasive AI: Its Theoretical and Computational Frameworks

Roberto Legaspi[✉], Wenzhen Xu, Tatsuya Konishi, and Shinya Wada

KDDI Research Inc., 2-1-15 Ohara, Fujimino-shi, Saitama 356-8501, Japan
{ro-legaspi,we-xu,tt-konishi,sh-wada}@kddi-research.jp

Abstract. The notion of a persuasive technology (PT) that is autonomous and intelligent, and more importantly, cognizant of and sensitive to human sense of agency (SoA), i.e., the subjective feeling or judgement that oneself is in control of situations, remains to be theorized, conceptualized and elucidated. Three important questions have emerged from our investigations: (1) why does SoA matter in the design of PT, (2) what computational principles in artificial intelligence (AI) underlie an adaptive PT, and (3) how can this intelligent PT sense, make sense of, and respond sensibly to dynamic changes in SoA under complex settings? We elucidate in this paper our theoretical and computational frameworks to answer our research queries. For the theoretical aspect, we propose an integration of pertinent theories in the cognitive, social and neurosciences that explain the emergence and disruption of SoA. Using this integration as theory of mind, we propose a computational framework for SoA-aware persuasive AI that integrates methods in cooperative inverse reinforcement learning, causal inferencing, explainable AI planning and generative actor-critic learning.

Keywords: Sense of agency · Persuasive technology · Artificial intelligence

1 Introduction

Sense of agency (SoA) refers to the subjective feeling or judgment of control over one's own intentional actions and their consequential outcomes in the world [1–6]. It is only recent that the scientific literature on SoA has significantly grown, indicative of the heightened attention it is garnering [2]. It has been suggested that SoA underlies the experience of volition and free will, self-awareness, social responsibility for one's own actions, and the understanding of causal structures in the world (see [7] for noteworthy references). Further, disruption of SoA has been shown to characterize certain neurological and psychiatric disorders [1, 8], poor health and decreased quality of life [6], thereby making major implications to well-being [9].

Because of its significance in the human sciences, it is not surprising that computational theorists [7, 10] and applied researchers in Human Augmentics [11], HCI [12], Cognitive Developmental Robotics [13, 14] and Human-AI Interactions [15] have begun investigating the SoA construct with its behavioral science underpinnings. However, the reach of computational SoA research is thus far very limited.

© Springer Nature Switzerland AG 2021
R. Ali et al. (Eds.): PERSUASIVE 2021, LNCS 12684, pp. 3–18, 2021.
https://doi.org/10.1007/978-3-030-79460-6_1

Persuasive Technology (PT) research is no exception, evidenced by its paucity of SoA constructs (e.g., [16]). While we are cognizant of the fact that after Fogg's seminal book [17] several approaches propounding novel tools, media and solutions on persuading users have broadened the scope of the topic (e.g., [18–23]), our objective here is to locate the theoretical and conceptual intersections of SoA, PT and AI. We anticipate quandary in this pursuit. Firstly, evidence suggests that an increase in the degree of automation will diminish SoA [24, 25]. Secondly, an autonomous technology can give the impression that it has intentions (via intentional stance [26] and anthropomorphism [27]) and may intend to control. Combining these two with the notion of an intelligent PT may beget the popular discourse on a dystopic future, the focal point being the AI assuming control over humans. Hence, the influence of human SoA in the design of an artificially intelligent PT needs to be theorized, computed and elucidated.

In their recent paper, entitled *"Synthetic Agency: Sense of Agency in AI"*, Legaspi et al. [15] posit the field of AI is poised to infer and manipulate to improve, rather than deter, human SoA (see also their Bayesian psychophysics model of SoA [7]). Their focus was to elucidate how an AI may possess SoA in itself. Our objective, on the other hand, is an *SoA-aware persuasive AI*. We posit two paradigms in which this AI may interact with humans. First, the human may perceive the AI as controlling, which consequently diminishes SoA (Fig. 1a). To resolve this, being SoA-aware, the AI cautiously plans its next actions to lessen its degree of control, which the human must be able to perceive to improve SoA. The second is that the AI infers the SoA dynamics of multiple humans in joint action with the aim of harmonizing their SoA dynamics. To illustrate, one actor may be imperceptive of another's SoA (Fig. 1b). What the SoA-aware AI does is to persuade the actor to consider the other's SoA (Fig. 1c). The actor then contemplates the other's low SoA (Fig. 1d), and aided by the AI, plans and acts toward empowering the other actor to reach a harmonious joint SoA (Fig. 1e).

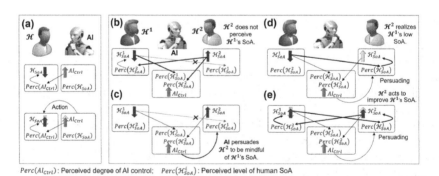

$Perc(AI_{ctrl})$: Perceived degree of AI control; $Perc(\mathcal{H}^i_{SoA})$: Perceived level of human SoA

Fig. 1. Concept of an SoA-aware persuasive AI in single and multiple human interactions

We posit that sensing, making sense of, and responding sensibly to SoA is essential to human-AI interactions. We shall argue with three points in mind. First, SoA is viable in applied research, and pertinently to PT. Second, we propound our theoretical framework that integrates cognitive, social and neuroscience theories on SoA. Lastly, we propose our computational framework for an SoA-aware persuasive AI and reflect on its implications to PT design. We structured this paper following these points.

2 Why Should SoA Matter to Persuasive Technologies?

In 1959, the rental car company Hertz put the slogan "Let Hertz put you in the driver's seat" – a catchphrase that appealed to consumers' natural desire for control. Indeed, giving consumers opportunities to choose proved to increase their SoA. However, the essential question for us from the vantage point of applied research is whether there is added value for technologies, and more pertinently for PT, to be cognizant of SoA. We looked at representative examples to drive the point that it is indeed the case.

Berberian et al. [24] investigated SoA in the complex context of operating an aircraft with diverse degrees of autopilot support. They looked at the important role of automation aids in aviation that can lead pilots to ask if they or the autopilot system is in control. By varying the autopilot settings from minimal to full control, and measuring the pilots' SoA, their results showed that SoA decreased with increasing automation.

Wen et al. [25] posit that if a driver becomes overly reliant on a self-driving car's control, consequently diminishing his SoA, it is very likely that he disengages, or his intervention responses become delayed or even absent. This can hamper resumption of manual control, which in a critical moment can lead to fatality. It is therefore important that the self-driving car is aware when it has become critical to relinquish control to the human to sustain safety. The other effect of low SoA is that a driver, perceiving her control taken away, could withdraw from trusting the self-driving car.

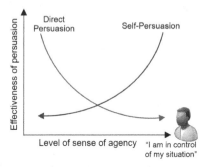

Fig. 2. Relations between SoA and the effectiveness of self- and direct persuasions

A work that is pertinent to PT is Damen et al.'s [28] investigation of the circumstances in which experience as a causal force could motivate oneself to greatly take advantage of any chance for self-driven change. Previous research show that self-persuasion is more effective in shaping attitudes and behavioral intentions than direct persuasions (i.e., arguments presented by others). However, Damen et al. explained that with experiences of low agency, it would be less likely to appraise oneself as a causal force, at the same time heightening vulnerability to endogenous sources.

Hence, direct persuasions may be more effective than self-persuasion when agency experience is low instead of high, and self-persuasion becomes less powerful when agency experience is weak (Fig. 2). Their findings further suggest that even with a small dose or short boost of experienced control, and evading experiences of weakened control, self-driven change can improve one's behavior, cognition, and generally lifestyle.

3 The Phenomenology of Sense of Agency

We have described the relevance of the SoA construct, but have yet to elucidate the theoretical principles that underlie it. There is growing evidence to suggest that SoA is susceptible to any disturbance in the supposed uninterrupted flow of intentional actions to anticipated outcomes [15]. Hence, why and how SoA level changes can be explained by an intention–action–outcome chain with its accompanying elements (Fig. 3).

First, we asked what drives an intentional action. The belief-desire-intention model for agency [29] was developed as a way of constructing future-directed intentions. Belief and desire represent the stored information about the perceived and wanted configurations, respectively, of the world. Further, the theory of planned behavior [30] links belief in one's behavioral control, thus pertinent to SoA, to forming intentions. Intention binds these two and represents the hypothetical actions leading to the desired outcomes in the world. Hence, intention is action specifying and controlling, and can be revised in light of changed belief or desire. Further, SoA is about determining whether intention has been embodied in an action specifically meant to achieve the desired outcome. This is informed by the internal processes of action planning and selection.

Several theories have been forwarded along the intention-action segment alone. It has been shown that SoA increases with the number of alternative actions, with the ability to choose among actions that have different foreseeable aftermaths [31], and choosing freely versus being instructed [31] or coerced [32]. Further, SoA decreases when other intentions emerge that antagonize the about to be executed intention [33].

There are two influential theories from the cognitive neuroscience community on the emergence or disruption of SoA given the intentional action and the resulting outcome. Following Legaspi et al. [15], we put these two together in our framework as their roles fit into a cohesive whole. The comparator model [34] was originally a theory of motor learning and control, but became eventually relevant to action awareness. According to the comparator model, the predicted outcome of an action is compared to the perceived sensory outcome. If the predicted and perceived match, then the outcome is registered in the brain as caused by the self; otherwise, SoA is disrupted. On the other hand, the retrospective inference theory [35] posits that SoA is experienced whenever there is congruence between the outcome that is intended and the outcome that is perceived. Together with the internally generated intentions, other cognitive and perceived factors such as external contextual and social cues are involved in the inference. These theories suggest that when outcomes happen as predicted or intended, a behavior is smoothly executed and thoughts of the behavior lie somewhere at the hem of consciousness (e.g., we are not conscious of our habitual behaviors). However, when an incongruence occurs, one is drawn to consciously answer if her action did or did not cause the outcome.

The disruption of SoA would necessitate adaptation to regain it, and change in behavior (consisting of belief, desire, intention, action and so on) may be required. However, as Damen et al. [28] suggest, individuals show increased attitude to self-facilitated change only if they have a high belief in their ability to control happenings in their life.

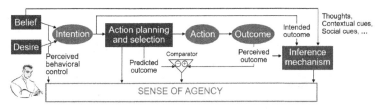

Fig. 3. Components of intention-action-outcome link explain how SoA emerges or is disrupted

4 Computing for a Sense of Agency-Aware Persuasive AI

Our capacity to intuit how the world works, what others think or want, why they act and how they perceive the outcomes of their actions in the world is crucial to our everyday social interactions. Such capacity is called *Theory of Mind* [36, 37] (ToM), which has been posited in cognitive science, both in theory and by experimentation, as fundamental to a broad range of cognitive activities [37]. While our conceptual framework (Fig. 3) outlines the ToM, we detail in this section how our notion of SoA-aware persuasive AI computationally embodies ToM (Fig. 4a). We envision our AI, hereafter $\mathcal{X}$, interacting with a human (or humans), hereafter $\mathcal{H}$, in a partially observable causal world (Fig. 4b). $\mathcal{H}$ and $\mathcal{X}$ jointly formulate action plans and act to maximize a shared reward function within which SoA is a critical component.

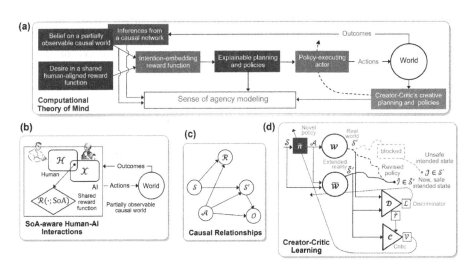

Fig. 4. Computational framework of an SoA-aware persuasive AI.

4.1 Intention-Action Link of a Beneficial and Trustworthy Persuasive AI

$\mathcal{X}$ possesses a belief about a partially observable world that is represented by the set of states $\mathcal{S}$ in the world, set of available action capabilities $\mathcal{A}$, set of conditional transition probabilities $T(s, a, s') = P(s'|s, a)$ between states, set of possible observations $\mathcal{O}$, and set of conditional observation probabilities $\Omega(a, s', o) = P(o|s', a)$. After taking action $a \in \mathcal{A}$ from $s \in \mathcal{S}$, thereby reaching $s' \in \mathcal{S}$, $\mathcal{X}$ observes $o \in \mathcal{O}$. After which, $\mathcal{X}$ may update its belief of the state of the world, which can be calculated using Bayes rule: $b'(s') = \beta\Omega(a, s', o)\sum_{s \in \mathcal{S}} T(s, a, s')b(s)$, with $\beta = 1/P(o|b(s), a)$ as normalizing constant and $b(s)$ denotes the probability that the world is in state s. This configuration is fundamentally of a partially observable Markov decision process (POMDP), which maintains a probability distribution over each possible state of the world.

Further, $\mathcal{X}$ possesses the capability to infer causal structures in the world. The purpose of causal inference is summed up most succinctly by this question: how does a reasoning agent know that one thing causes another? This is fundamental to SoA: one has to know that the desired outcome is self-caused. Our tool will be a causal graph, which is a directed acyclic graphical model consisting of a set of variables $\mathcal{V}$ with directed paths carrying causal semantics, i.e., if there exists a path v_i to v_j, v_i is a potential cause of v_j. A node v may represent state, action, reward or observation (Fig. 4c).

With a causal graph, three aspects become possible for $\mathcal{X}$ that test different kinds of causal reasoning [38, 39]. First, $\mathcal{X}$ may perform associative reasoning, i.e., it observes the world and infer correlations, and depending on the structure of the world, cause and effect, with probability $P(v_j|v_i)$. Second, $\mathcal{X}$ may explore possibilities in the world through interventional reasoning, figuring "What if?" or "What if I do this?", by applying the operator $do(v_i)$ that deletes all incoming edges to v_i and observes the consequences on other variables with probability $P(v_j|do(v_i))$. Lastly, $\mathcal{X}$ may do counterfactual reasoning, i.e., $\mathcal{X}$ imagines and does retrospection by first estimating the causal structures in the world through interventions, and at the last step asks "Why?" or "What if I acted differently?", denoted by the probability $P\left(v_{j_{v_i}} \middle| v_i', v_j'\right)$, which roughly means the probability that it would have been v_j had it been v_i, given that it was in fact v_i' and v_j'. These aspects are referred to consist a causal hierarchy [38]. A causal Bayesian network [40] is sufficient as causal graph implementation for $\mathcal{X}$ to achieve until interventional reasoning, but $\mathcal{X}$ would need a causal structure model [39] to perform counterfactual reasoning. Thus, with a causal graph, $\mathcal{X}$ may discern between causal effects authored by $\mathcal{H}$, itself or other agents. $\mathcal{X}$ may also predict what can happen if variables are intervened. It is also possible for $\mathcal{X}$ to reason backwards, i.e., given a desired outcome, what actions should be intended? All these causal inferencing impact SoA.

We naturally expect $\mathcal{X}$ to collaborate with $\mathcal{H}$ in doing tasks, and more importantly, to prove beneficial to $\mathcal{H}$ by capturing what is desired by $\mathcal{H}$ and acting based on this. A reward function has been used previously to interpret desire (e.g., [37, 41, 42]). However, we want the reward function to be personal to $\mathcal{H}$, and we expect $\mathcal{X}$ to adhere to the same reward function as its pay-off. A recent development in AI research, called cooperative inverse reinforcement learning (CIRL), emphasizes the notion of an AI that aligns itself to what the human values through a shared reward function thereby proving beneficial to the human [43, 44]. CIRL assumes only the human knows the reward function, and optimal solutions that maximize rewards involve the active instruction by the human and active learning by the AI. It has been shown that computing for an optimal policy in CIRL can be reduced to solving a POMDP [43, 44], which critically now includes $\{\Theta, \mathcal{R}\}$, with

Θ as the set of possible reward parameters and the reward function $\mathcal{R}\left(s, a^{\mathcal{H}}, a^{\mathcal{X}}; \theta \in \Theta\right)$ is shared by $\mathcal{H}$ and $\mathcal{X}$.

What is pertinent to our interpretations is θ. With the shared reward function $\mathcal{R}(\cdot; \theta)$, $\mathcal{H}$ is incentivized to teach, and $\mathcal{X}$ to learn, θ. We can imagine θ to parameterize human characteristics that are static (e.g., personality traits and human values) or task-dependent (e.g., preferences). Most important, we can imagine θ to quantify dynamic SoA changes, which can permit both $\mathcal{H}$ and $\mathcal{X}$ to be SoA-cognizant, and if SoA is weighted more than the other parameters, then both agents become SoA-centered.

We have mentioned that intention binds belief and desire, as well as represent hypothetical actions that can produce the outcomes we desire in the world [29]. We suggest intention can be embedded as well in $\mathcal{R}(\cdot; \theta)$. Reward functions have been used previously to quantify not only desires, but also goals and context-specific intentions (see [37]). In CIRL, the intended (or goal) state may be encoded in θ [43]. Thus, intention coherently slides as a component of the shared reward function.

The human-AI interaction proceeds as follows. At each timestep, $\mathcal{H}$ and $\mathcal{X}$ observe the current state s and select their respective actions $a^{\mathcal{H}}$ and $a^{\mathcal{X}}$. Both receive reward $r = \mathcal{R}\left(s, a^{\mathcal{H}}, a^{\mathcal{X}}; \theta\right)$ and observe the outcomes in the world. A state for the next timestep is sampled from the updated transition distribution $\mathcal{T}\left(s, \sigma, a^{\mathcal{H}}, s'\right) = P\left(s', a^{\mathcal{H}}|s, \sigma\right)$, where $\sigma = \left(a^{\mathcal{X}}, v\right)$ is a conditional plan indicative of $\mathcal{X}$'s behavior, v is a mapping from observations to future conditional plans for $\mathcal{X}$ to follow, and the value of a plan σ with belief b (cf. $\mathcal{T}(\cdot)$ and $b(s)$ at the start) is defined as the expected value of the plan across states, i.e., $V_\sigma(b) = b(s)\alpha_\sigma = \sum_{s \in \mathcal{S}} b(s)\alpha_\sigma(s)$ (following [44]). This means that $\mathcal{X}$'s objective is to find the optimal sequence of actions based on its current belief. $\mathcal{H}$ will choose actions that depends on $\mathcal{X}$'s conditional plan, and will convey the most information about θ to $\mathcal{X}$, which consequently influences $\mathcal{X}$'s belief that then influences the future actions of both $\mathcal{X}$ and $\mathcal{H}$. It has been shown in CIRL that the AI's belief about θ is a sufficient statistic for optimal behavior [43].

Based on the above transition-observation dynamics, we can formulate a planning problem Π in terms of a transition function $\delta_\Pi : \mathcal{S} \times \sigma \rightarrow \mathcal{S} \times a^{\mathcal{H}}$, as well as the planning algorithms to solve Π, i.e., $\mathbb{A}^{\mathcal{H}} : \Pi \times \Theta \mapsto \pi^{\mathcal{H}}$ and $\mathbb{A}^{\mathcal{X}} : \Pi \mapsto \pi^{\mathcal{X}}$ for the human and AI, respectively. The objective of both agents is to optimize their policy, $\pi : s \mapsto a$, that maps a specific state to a deterministic action. Eventually, there will exist an optimal policy pair $\left(\pi^{\mathcal{H}*}, \pi^{\mathcal{X}*}\right)$.

The early stages of interactions between $\mathcal{H}$ and $\mathcal{X}$ is a learning phase. Both $\mathcal{H}$ and $\mathcal{X}$ can perform actions that permit $\mathcal{X}$ to learn more about θ. Eventually, $\mathcal{X}$ applies what it learned from $\mathcal{H}$ to maximize the reward without any supervision from $\mathcal{H}$. Two things may emerge from this. First, while dramatic advances in AI indeed promise to produce systems that can sense, make sense and act sensibly on their own, their effectiveness is constrained by their current inability to explain their thought processes that are becoming much more profound, and in certain cases, life-critical. Hence, there is the need for AI-enabled systems to provide explanations of how they arrived at their decisions, to be questioned, and, if needed, challenged when situations are critical. Secondly, if we include SoA in θ then both $\mathcal{H}$ and $\mathcal{X}$ would derive their policies while being cognizant of SoA, and in instances in which $\mathcal{H}$'s SoA is compromised, $\mathcal{X}$ has to explain how its decision-making processes are to $\mathcal{H}$'s best interest that includes her sense of control.

To the above, explainable AI, or simply XAI, is another recent development in AI research that aims to produce more transparent, explainable models to enable humans to comprehend more, appropriately trust, and effectively interact with the AI as responsible partner [45, 46]. We believe such capability makes an AI more effectively persuasive since it is able to explain the rationale for its behavior. Following [47], we adapted two considerations for $\mathcal{X}$ when planning its actions, namely, the inferential capability and mental model of $\mathcal{H}$. When $\mathcal{H}$'s inferential capability or mental model is not aligned with $\mathcal{X}$, then $\mathcal{X}$ must provide explanations to reach alignment. The first consideration includes *inference reconciliation* in which $\mathcal{H}$ has less computational ability than $\mathcal{X}$, i.e., $\mathbb{A}^{\mathcal{H}} < \mathbb{A}^{\mathcal{X}}$, or $\mathcal{H}$'s solution does not lead to $\mathcal{X}$'s policy, i.e., $\mathbb{A}^{\mathcal{H}} : \Pi \times \Theta \nrightarrow \pi^{\mathcal{X}}$. An explanation $\mathcal{E}$ from $\mathcal{X}$ is aimed to reconcile, i.e., $\mathbb{A}^{\mathcal{H}} : \Pi \times \Theta \xrightarrow{\mathcal{E}} \pi^{\mathcal{X}}$. One way to aid the inferential process of $\mathcal{H}$ would be for $\mathcal{X}$ to allow $\mathcal{H}$ to raise specific questions, such as why $a \,\varepsilon\, \pi^{\mathcal{X}}$, why not another plan π', why is the policy $\pi^{\mathcal{X}}$ optimal? $\mathcal{X}$ may then engage $\mathcal{H}$ in explanatory, perhaps persuasive, dialogues to satisfy $\mathcal{H}$'s queries. For the second consideration, i.e., the mental model of $\mathcal{H}$, even if $\mathcal{X}$ comes up with the best plans it could, $\mathcal{H}$ may be evaluating $\mathcal{X}$'s plans with a different mental model. The process of explanation becomes one of *model reconciliation* so that $\mathcal{H}$ and $\mathcal{X}$ can agree, say on the Θ of the plan being made. If $\Pi^{\mathcal{H}}$ is the mental model of the human, the model reconciliation process becomes $\Pi^{\mathcal{H}} + \mathcal{E} \rightarrow \widehat{\Pi}^{\mathcal{X}}$, where $\widehat{\Pi}^{\mathcal{X}}$ approximates $\mathcal{X}$'s mental model such that $\mathbb{A}^{\mathcal{H}} : \widehat{\Pi}^{\mathcal{X}} \times \Theta \mapsto \pi^{\mathcal{H}}$.

We can extend the notations above to accommodate scenarios in which $\mathcal{X}$ interacts with multiple human actors $\{\mathcal{H}^i\}$, each with their own set of actions $\mathcal{A}^{\{\mathcal{H}^i\}}$, and sharing the same reward function $\mathcal{R}\left(s, a^{\{\mathcal{H}^i\}}, a^{\mathcal{X}}; \theta\right)$. Each will have a planning algorithm $\mathbb{A}^{\mathcal{H}^i} : \Pi \times \Theta \mapsto \pi^{\mathcal{H}^i}$ to solve $\delta_\Pi : \mathcal{S} \times \sigma \rightarrow \mathcal{S} \times a^{\mathcal{H}^i}$. Given these, and recalling our example in Fig. 1(b–e), $\mathcal{X}$ can show bias to one of two human actors, $\mathcal{H}^1$, by reconciling the other actor $\mathcal{H}^2$'s plans to $\mathcal{H}^1$'s through explanation, i.e., either by $\mathbb{A}^{\mathcal{H}^2} : \Pi \times \Theta \xrightarrow{\mathcal{E}} \pi^{\mathcal{H}^1}$, or $\Pi^{\mathcal{H}^2} + \mathcal{E} \rightarrow \widehat{\Pi}^{\mathcal{H}^1}$ and then $\mathbb{A}^{\mathcal{H}^2} : \widehat{\Pi}^{\mathcal{H}^1} \times \Theta \mapsto \pi^{\mathcal{H}^2}$.

The mechanisms we have just outlined can have major implications in PT. First, a persuasive AI becomes transparent to the user of its plans and inferences and allows the user to pose questions or challenge them. We believe this makes an AI more effectively persuasive, being able to explain and make more comprehensible the rationale for its behavior. This may also improve its relationship with the user as it is perceived as trustworthy. The AI can also be perceived as empathetic as it explains to the user its understanding of user behavior. Lastly, we hypothesize that co-producing with the AI the plans and inferences in decision-making processes would increase the user's SoA.

4.2 Action-Outcome Link of a Creative Causal Inferencing AI

Armed with a policy, the actor executes an action given by the policy. The actor can be $\mathcal{H}$ ($\pi^{\mathcal{H}}(s) = a^{\mathcal{H}}$), $\mathcal{X}$ ($\pi^{\mathcal{X}}(s) = a^{\mathcal{X}}$), or both. If it is $\mathcal{X}$, it would mean using all available sensors and actuators afforded to $\mathcal{X}$ in order to produce the desired outcome in the world. The outcome states of the world are then observed and fed back to the causal inferencing mechanism to determine if the predicted or intended outcome matches the perceived outcome, or whether the outcome was caused by the actor's action and not by another agent. $\mathcal{X}$'s beliefs will also be updated, including whether further control in the updated state of the world is possible. All these will impact SoA (cf. Sect. 3).

Further, consider for example the scenario wherein a supposed route was impassable due to a road traffic congestion or blockage caused by a typhoon or disaster, but the AI came up with an alternative route to the same desired destination, or to a new or unexpected but safer target destination. In other words, in situations that are unexpected, unanticipated, unforeseen or rare, it would be desirable for $\mathcal{X}$ to generate novel or innovative agentic opportunities. Let us assume $\pi^{\mathcal{X}}$ is no longer viable, e.g., it will only lead to an impassable path in the partially observable world, we now label as $\mathcal{W}$, and the originally intended (goal) destination, say $\mathcal{I}$, is no longer safe (Fig. 4d). $\mathcal{X}$ needs a new policy unknown to itself, even more to $\mathcal{H}$, and cannot be derived simply from what is perceivable only in $\mathcal{W}$. We propose a *Creator-Critic* learning in which $\mathcal{X}$ uses a Creator module to generate an extended version $\widetilde{\mathcal{W}}$ of the real world $\mathcal{W}$, which can provide a novel solution, say a path to a new intended state $\mathcal{I}'$. We assume $\mathcal{I}'$ can be characterized by $\mathcal{X}$ through some endogenous sources (e.g., forecasts from citizen sensors), but $\mathcal{X}$ has to learn the policy $\pi_{\widetilde{\mathcal{W}}}$ to reach $\mathcal{I}'$. $\mathcal{X}$ uses a Critic module to validate this policy. To this, we adapted the generative model-based actor-critic framework in [48, 49].

The Creator generates plausible alternative states of the world via $\widetilde{\mathcal{W}}$ that $\mathcal{X}$ (more so $\mathcal{H}$) may not have initially predicted or perceived as possible. The key here is that $\widetilde{\mathcal{W}}$ should not be fictitious enough not to be applicable to the real context $\mathcal{X}$ (and $\mathcal{H}$) is in. Selecting a suitable metric to measure the difference between the generated states and the new intended state $\mathcal{I}'$ is crucial. The reward can be designed as $\tilde{r}(s, a) = \mathcal{L}(s') - \mathcal{L}(\tilde{s}')$, where $\mathcal{L}$ is the measured distribution distance between the next real/generated ($s'/\tilde{s}'$) and intended ($\mathcal{I}'$) states. $\mathcal{L}$ can be formulated as a discriminator score that can be computed using a similarity metric, e.g., *Wassertein-1* or earth mover's distance used in [48]. The job of the Critic is to critique the actor $\pi_{\widetilde{\mathcal{W}}}(s)$ by training it to maximize $\tilde{r}(s, \pi_{\widetilde{\mathcal{W}}}(s)) + \mathcal{V}$ ($\widetilde{\mathcal{T}}(s, \pi_{\widetilde{\mathcal{W}}}(s), \tilde{s}')$), where $\mathcal{V}$ is a value function [48] and $\widetilde{\mathcal{T}}(s, \pi_{\widetilde{\mathcal{W}}}(s), \tilde{s}') = P(\tilde{s}'|\pi_{\widetilde{\mathcal{W}}}(s))$. The reward function being maximized here is different from the shared reward function $\mathcal{R}(\cdot; \theta)$ since the Critic is only concerned with how close to each other the generated and intended states are.

How then does the Creator-Critic learning account for SoA in $\mathcal{R}(\cdot; \theta)$? The answer lies on how the data for $\widetilde{\mathcal{W}}$ is generated. The transition function $\widetilde{\mathcal{T}}(\cdot)$ is derived from $\widetilde{\mathcal{W}}$, which would once again allow $\mathcal{X}$ to perform causative, interventional and coun-terfactual reasoning, i.e., given $\widetilde{\mathcal{T}}(\cdot)$ is equal to $P(\tilde{s}'|\pi_{\widetilde{\mathcal{W}}}(s))$, $P(\tilde{s}'|do(\pi_{\widetilde{\mathcal{W}}}(s)))$ and $P(\tilde{s}'_{do(\pi_{\widetilde{\mathcal{W}}}(s))}|(\tilde{s}')', (do(\pi_{\widetilde{\mathcal{W}}}(s))'))$, respectively. However, no new knowledge can be derived from using the original causal graph for $\mathcal{W}$. We imagine the Creator creating an aggregation of worlds, i.e., of causal graphs, which are knowledge from other human sources in various contexts: $CG_U = Agg(\{CG^i\})$ (e.g., see [50, 51] on combining causal networks). CG_U will allow $\mathcal{X}$ to infer other possible causal relations from other human sources who experienced other contexts that are plausibly applicable to $\mathcal{H}$'s (and $\mathcal{X}$'s) current situation. This will enhance the causal inferencing capabilities of $\mathcal{X}$, and pave the way for novel and innovative options to enhance $\mathcal{X}$'s beliefs and conditional plans, i.e., $(\tilde{b}, \tilde{\sigma}) = \triangle (b, \sigma)$, where $\tilde{b}$ and $\tilde{\sigma}$ are derived from the extended reality provided by CG_U. An optimal search for subgraphs in CG_U that are similar to $\mathcal{H}$'s causal graph must be done first, and with the found subgraphs as starting conditions, maximized transition probabilities can be computed. This would allow $\mathcal{X}$ to start with viable knowledge rather than start from scratch. Further, with each causal graph containing a reward value provided by $\mathcal{R}(\cdot; \theta)$, then the Creator, in effect, becomes SoA-cognizant.

An AI that can inspire new policies that are more useful in taking advantage of changing opportunities, and has a unique ability to adapt at will that which it sees as a useful model, will aid the human to behave optimally. If PT is supposed to shape user behavior toward specific goals, offering creative means for steering and influencing human choices and actions, then our framework clearly addresses this. More importantly, generating novel and innovative agentic opportunities increases SoA.

4.3 Computing for the Sense of Agency

This last aspect of our computational agenda brings us in full circle: $\mathcal{X}$ must recognize from behavioral phenotypes the dynamic contextual rise and fall of SoA in real-time. Traditional methods in psychological experiments (see [52]) use explicit measures through self-reports of one's own SoA over specific events. There are also implicit measures that use perceptual differences between self- and externally generated movements as measure of SoA. Both, however, have limitations: they require responses from subjects that interrupt their actions, and are less applicable when SoA dynamically changes. We hypothesize, however, that changes in SoA level may manifest as temporal changes in physiology (i.e., heart and respiratory rates), posture, gesture and vocal prosody. Here is the plausible connect: these signals have been used to effectively infer affective (emotion or mood) states, and the field of affective computing has tackled emotion recognition and emotion-based adaptive responses by an AI from such behavioral phenotypes using wearable and ambient sensors [53–55]. Evidence from cognitive neuroscience also shows that agency and affect constantly interact in our daily life in many ways [56, 57]. SoA can be modulated by affective factors, such as positive versus negative anticipation of the affective action outcome, high vs. low motivation to carry out an impending action, and acting in friendly vs. hostile environments [57, 58].

To model SoA, given a recognition function that outputs SoA as a positive state value, i.e., $\mathcal{F}_{SoA} : \varrho_{Ph} \times \varrho_{Po} \times \varrho_G \times \varrho_V \rightarrow \mathbb{Z}^+$, where the ϱ input parameters quantify the physiological, postural, gestural and vocal prosodic behavioral phenotypes, $\mathcal{X}$ uses this obtained knowledge of SoA level to update its beliefs and plans (cf. Sect. 4.1). Within CIRL, $\mathcal{X}$ can ask $\mathcal{H}$ to give an SoA estimate $l \in \mathbb{Z}^+$ to train $\mathcal{F}_{SoA}$, and $\mathcal{H}$ then cooperates with a self-report. The recognized SoA level shall be factored into the shared reward function's parameter θ, assuring that the reward is cognizant of the dynamic changes of SoA level. Once the AI has a good recognition and interpretation of SoA, $\mathcal{X}$ can further demonstrate empathy and trustworthiness by explaining how it senses and makes sense of the resulting SoA levels. It can then respond sensibly by persuading $\mathcal{H}$ on what it deems as optimal policies to help improve, and not deter, $\mathcal{H}$'s SoA.

5 From Formalisms to Practical Design

We want to bring down in this final discussion the computational underpinnings of our SoA-aware persuasive AI to an applicative perspective through an illustrative use case. We then summarize at the end the implications of our proposal in the design of PT.

A recent work by one of the authors [59] investigated the influence of affective persuasion on a driver's detour behavior, i.e., switching to an alternative expressway route. The objective was to persuade potential Tohoku expressway users to make a detour to the Joban expressway during a busy Japanese summer holiday period. In the field experiment, interventional materials, which include congestion forecast, suggestion to evade congestion, and negative affective prime were used (Fig. 5a). The last was employed to arouse intrinsic intent to make a detour. The results reported in the paper suggest that congestion forecast motivated detour intention, i.e., more participants were intended to take the Joban than the Tohoku expressway, or preferred to choose first the Joban expressway. Further, the emotional primes influenced detour intention, but with the degree of influence depending on prior experiences traveling to Tohoku, i.e., familiarity of the routes, and if little children are actually present in the car.

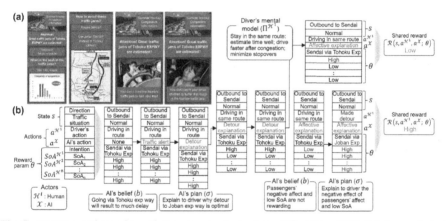

Fig. 5. (a) Interventions of an affect-persuasive technology (lifted from [59]). (b) A snapshot of how our notion of SoA-aware persuasive AI can be reflected on this PT.

We now reflect on how our AI may be realized on this PT (also depicted in Fig. 5b). First, $\mathcal{X}$ (our AI agent) perceives the world and builds its belief. Certainly, the car's navigational system and congestion forecasts from endogenous sources can be tools for $\mathcal{X}$ to build the states, actions, observations and transitions of its belief model. For example, $\mathcal{X}$'s belief would include driving towards the congested Tohoku expressway will result to getting delayed in traffic. With the belief that delay is imminent if $\mathcal{H}^1$ (the driver) stays in the same route (associative reasoning, $P(delay|same\_route)$), $\mathcal{X}$ estimates taking an alternative route (interventional, $P(no\_delay|do(detour\_Joban))$). $\mathcal{X}$ then acts by first explaining ($\mathcal{E}$) to $\mathcal{H}^1$ why proceeding in the same route will result to much delay and why a detour to Joban expressway is optimal. Here is an example that $\mathcal{H}^1$ has less computational ability than $\mathcal{X}$ ($\mathbb{A}^{\mathcal{H}^1} < \mathbb{A}^{\mathcal{X}}$) to foresee a traffic dilemma. $\mathcal{X}$

attempts to reconcile its beliefs and plans with $\mathcal{H}^1$'s through its explanations. But $\mathcal{H}^1$ may decide not to abide, and in the spirit of CIRL, $\mathcal{H}^1$ teaches $\mathcal{X}$ her mental model ($\Pi^{\mathcal{H}^1}$): based on her previous travels, she managed to do well as she drove faster at certain portions of the trip after the congestion, and took less stopovers than usual. $\mathcal{X}$ may then update its mental model based on $\mathcal{H}^1$'s input. This can also be a cue for $\mathcal{X}$ to confirm from $\mathcal{H}^1$ her SoA, which would seem high given her sense of control. However, $\mathcal{X}$ may have recognized the presence of other humans in the car, $\{\mathcal{H}^{i,i\neq1}\}$, and has inferred from their behavioral phenotypes ($\{\varrho_{(\cdot)}\}$) their SoA to be low (impairment or loss of control, hence diminished SoA, is generally associated with stress from adverse driving conditions like traffic congestion [60] and when a predictable negative valence outcome is realized [61]). Moreover, $\mathcal{X}$ may have recognized the presence of a child crying. $\mathcal{X}$ attempts to reconcile again, this time by explaining through negative affective appeals in favor of, say, the child passenger's SoA ($\Pi^{\mathcal{H}^1} + \mathcal{E} \to \widehat{\Pi}^{\mathcal{H}^2}$). $\mathcal{H}^1$ may then realize that a negative outcome is imminent unless she makes a detour, and therefore realizes she is not totally in control. Direct persuasion by $\mathcal{X}$ may now become more impactful amid $\mathcal{H}^1$'s diminished SoA (theory in Fig. 2). As we mentioned, most important to our interpretation is θ that should include a quantification of $SoA^{\{\mathcal{H}^i\}}$. Here, we see $\mathcal{H}^1$ and $\mathcal{X}$ to be both sensitive to $SoA^{\{\mathcal{H}^i\}} \in \theta$, and both jointly maximize $\mathcal{R}\left(s, a^{\mathcal{H}^1}, a^{\mathcal{X}}; \theta\right)$. We cannot illustrate in detail with this use case every element of our computational framework, but if we imagine, for example, a dire scenario in which $\mathcal{X}$ and $\mathcal{H}^1$ need to find a passable route while most roads are blocked, $\mathcal{X}$ may hypothesize an alternate, but applicable world $\widetilde{\mathcal{W}}$ and derive a viable policy $\pi_{\widetilde{\mathcal{W}}}$ (in Sect. 4.2).

From the above, what then should we reflect on in terms of what should be taken into account and what has to change in the way we think of PT if we want to design for the kind of technology we are proposing? In our framework, a PT must be afforded with suitable sensors, learning algorithms and actuators to autonomously perceive, build its adaptive models, and act in the world, respectively. This means that we need to start thinking of a PT that is an active participant capable of demonstrating possible changes. This active PT should be designed to interact in a collaborative fashion with the user, and with the primary goal of being beneficial to the user by sharing the user's desires and values. We should think of the PT providing the user with the faculty to give feedback and be allowed to question or challenge the decision-making processes of the PT. This would mean translating its machine-understandable thought processes to human-understandable explanations (e.g. [62]). Further, the PT should be privy to intrinsic human behavior that dynamically changes with changing complex contexts. This would require the PT appropriately asking the consenting user to provide labels of intrinsic behavior. For this to happen, the PT must build a relationship with the user founded in trust by making its decision-making processes transparent [45–47], and demonstrating empathic understanding of user behavior [53–55]. Lastly, this PT must be able to integrate heterogeneous knowledge from varied sources (e.g., massive data points streamed by physical sensors or public knowledge sourced by agency or citizen sensors) [63] to derive novel or innovative agentic opportunities.

6   Conclusion

It is only recent that the behavioral sciences, and even more recent the advanced techno-logical studies, have begun to understand the far-reaching influence of the SoA construct. We have argued in this paper that the understanding and manipulation of human SoA is essential for a persuasive AI to better adapt to user behavior.

We first presented evidence that shows SoA would matter in the design of PT. Second, we propound our theoretical framework that integrates cognitive, social and neuroscience theories on how SoA dynamically emergences or gets disrupted in complex situations. We then proposed a computational theory-of-mind framework for an SoA-aware per-suasive AI. To the best of our knowledge, no research has yet elucidated a cohesive alignment of theoretical and computational principles for an artificially intelligent PT that can sense and make sense of user behavior, and interact sensibly by being cognizant of and sensitive to the dynamic changes of human SoA.

References

1. Moore, J.W.: What is the sense of agency and why does it matter? Front. Psychol. **7**, 1272 (2016)
2. David, N., Obhi, S., Moore, J.W.: Sense of agency: examining awareness of the acting self. Front. Hum. Neurosci. **9**, 310 (2015)
3. Gallagher, S.: Philosophical conceptions of the self: implications for cognitive science. Trends Cogn. Sci. **4**, 14–21 (2000)
4. Pacherie, E.: The sense of control and the sense of agency. Psyche **13**(1), 1–30 (2007)
5. Gallagher, S.: Multiple aspects in the sense of agency. New Ideas Psychol. **30**(1), 15–31 (2012)
6. Haggard, P.: Sense of agency in the human brain. Nat. Rev. Neurosci. **18**, 196–207 (2017)
7. Legaspi, R., Toyoizumi, T.: A Bayesian psychophysics model of sense of agency. Nat. Commun. **10**, 4250 (2019)
8. Moore, J.W., Fletcher, P.C.: Sense of agency in health and disease: a review of cue integration approaches. Conscious Cogn. **21**(1), 59–68 (2012)
9. Welzel, C., Inglehart, R.F.: Values, agency, and well-being: a human development model. Soc. Indic. Res. **97**(1), 43–63 (2010)
10. Friston, K., Schwartenbeck, P., Fitzgerald, T., Moutoussis, M., Behrens, T., Dolan, R.J.: The anatomy of choice: active inference and agency. Front. Hum. Neurosci. **7**, 598 (2013)
11. Novak, J., Archer, J., Mateevitsi, V., Jones, S.: Communication, machines & human augmentics. Communication + 1 **5**, 8 (2016)
12. Limerick, H., Coyle, D., Moore, J.W.: The experience of agency in human-computer interactions: a review. Front. Hum. Neurosci. **8**, 643 (2014)
13. Asada, M., et al.: Cognitive developmental robotics: a survey. IEEE Trans. Auton. Mental Dev. **1**(1), 12–34 (2009)
14. Schillaci, G., Ritter, C.-N., Hafner, V.V., Lara, B.: Body representations for robot ego-noise modelling and prediction. Towards the development of a sense of agency in artificial agents. In: Proceedings of the 15th International Conference on Synthesis and Simulation of Living Systems (ALIFE 2016), pp. 390–397 (2016)
15. Legaspi, R., He, Z., Toyoizumi, T.: Synthetic agency: sense of agency in artificial intelligence. Curr. Opin. Behav. Sci. **29**, 84–90 (2019)

16. Olivieri, L.: Persuasive technologies and self-awareness: a philosophical-anthropological enquiry. Master's Thesis, University of Twente (2019)
17. Fogg, B.J.: Persuasive Technology: Using Computers to Change What We Think and Do. Morgan Kaufmann (2003)
18. Bogost, I.: Persuasive Games: The Expressive Power of Videogames. MIT Press (2007)
19. Fogg, B.J., Iizawa, D.: Online persuasion in facebook and mixi: a cross-cultural comparison. In: Oinas-Kukkonen, H., Hasle, P., Harjumaa, M., Segerståhl, K., Øhrstrøm, P. (eds.) PERSUASIVE 2008. LNCS, vol. 5033, pp. 35–46. Springer, Heidelberg (2008). https://doi.org/10.1007/978-3-540-68504-3_4
20. Munson, S.: Mindfulness, reflection, and persuasion in personal informatics. In: Proceedings of the SIGCHI Conference on Human Factors in Computing Systems (CHI 2012), pp. 1–4 (2012)
21. Nakajima, T., Lehdonvirta, V.: Designing motivation using persuasive ambient mirrors. Pers. Ubiquit. Comput. **17**, 107–126 (2013)
22. Adams, A.T., Costa, J., Jung, M.F., Choudhury, T.: Mindless computing: designing technologies to subtly influence behavior. In: Proceedings of the ACM International Conference on Pervasive and Ubiquitous Computing (UbiComp 2015), pp. 719–730 (2015)
23. Lee, U., et al.: Intelligent positive computing with mobile, wearable, and IoT devices: literature review and research directions. Ad Hoc Netw. **83**, 8–24 (2019)
24. Berberian, B., Sarrazin, J.-C., Le Blaye, P., Haggard, P.: Automation technology and sense of control: a window on human agency. PLoS One **7**(3), e34075 (2012)
25. Wen, W., Kuroki, Y., Asama, H.: The sense of agency in driving automation. Front. Psychol. **10**, 2691 (2019)
26. Dennett, D.C.: The Intentional Stance. The MIT Press, Cambridge (1987)
27. Złotowski, J., Proudfoot, D., Yogeeswaran, K., Bartneck, C.: Anthropomorphism: opportunities and challenges in human robot interaction. Int. J. Soc. Robot. **7**, 347–360 (2014)
28. Damen, T.G.E., Müller, B.C.N., van Baaren, R.B., Dijksterhuis, A.: Re-examining the agentic shift: the sense of agency influences the effectiveness of (self)persuasion. PLoS ONE **10**(6), e0128635 (2015)
29. Georgeff, M., Pell, B., Pollack, M., Tambe, M., Wooldridge, M.: The belief-desire-intention model of agency. In: Müller, J.P., Rao, A.S., Singh, M.P. (eds.) ATAL 1998. LNCS, vol. 1555, pp. 1–10. Springer, Heidelberg (1999). https://doi.org/10.1007/3-540-49057-4_1
30. Ajzen, I.: From intentions to actions: a theory of planned behavior. In: Kuhl, J., Beckmann, J. (eds.) Action Control. SSSSP, pp. 11–39. Springer, Heidelberg (1985). https://doi.org/10.1007/978-3-642-69746-3_2
31. Barlas, Z., Obhi, S.S.: Freedom, choice, and the sense of agency. Front. Hum. Neurosci. **7**, 514 (2013)
32. Caspar, E.A., Christensen, J.F., Cleeremans, A., Haggard, P.: Coercion changes the sense of agency in the human brain. Curr. Biol. **26**, 585–592 (2016)
33. Chambon, V., Sidarus, N., Haggard, P.: From action intentions to action effects: how does the sense of agency come about? Front. Hum. Neurosci. **8**, 320 (2014)
34. Frith, C.D., Blakemore, S.J., Wolpert, D.M.: Abnormalities in the awareness and control of action. Philos. Trans. R. Soc. Lond. B Biol. Sci. **355**, 1771–1788 (2000)
35. Wegner, D.M., Wheatley, T.: Apparent mental causation: sources of the experience of will. Am. Psychol. **54**, 480–492 (1999)
36. Gopnik, A., Meltzoff, A.N.: Learning, Development, and Conceptual Change. Words, Thoughts, and Theories. The MIT Press (1997)
37. Jara-Ettinger, J.: Theory of mind as inverse reinforcement learning. Curr. Opin. Behav. Sci. **29**, 105–110 (2019)
38. Pearl, J., Mackenzie, D.: The Book of Why: The New Science of Cause and Effect. Basic Books (2018)

39. Bareinboim, E., Pearl, J.: Causal inference and the data-fusion problem. Proc. Natl. Acad. Sci. USA (PNAS) **113**(27), 7345–7352 (2016)
40. Meganck, S., Leray, P., Manderick, B.: Learning causal Bayesian networks from observations and experiments: a decision theoretic approach. In: Torra, V., Narukawa, Y., Valls, A., Domingo-Ferrer, J. (eds.) Modeling Decisions for Artificial Intelligence, vol. 3885, pp. 58–69. Springer, Heidelberg (2006). https://doi.org/10.1007/11681960_8
41. Baker, C.L., Jara-Ettinger, J., Saxe, R., Tenenbaum, J.B.: Rational quantitative attribution of beliefs, desires and percepts in human mentalizing. Nat. Hum. Behav. **1**, 0064 (2017)
42. Velez-Ginorio, J., Siegel, M., Tenenbaum, J., Jara-Ettinger, J.: Interpreting actions by attributing compositional desires. Cogn. Sci. (2017)
43. Hadfield-Menell, D., Dragan, A., Abbeel, P., Russell, S.: Cooperative inverse reinforcement learning. In: Proceedings of the 30th Annual Conference on Neural Information Processing Systems (NIPS 2016), pp. 3916–3924 (2016)
44. Malik, D., Palaniappan, M., Fisac, J.F., Hadfield-Menell, D., Russell, S., Dragan, A.D.: An efficient, generalized Bellman update for cooperative inverse reinforcement learning. In: Proceedings of the 35th International Conference on Machine Learning (ICML), vol. 80, pp. 3391–3399 (2018)
45. Arrieta, A.B., Díaz-Rodríguez, N., Del Ser, J., Bennetot, A., Tabik, S., Barbado, A., et al.: Explainable artificial intelligence (XAI): concepts, taxonomies, opportunities and challenges toward responsible AI. Inf. Fusion **58**, 82–115 (2020)
46. Vilone, G., Longo, L.: Explainable artificial intelligence: a systematic review. arXiv:2006.00093 [cs.AI] (2020)
47. Chakraborti, T., Sreedharan, S., Kambhampati, S.: The emerging landscape of explainable AI planning and decision making. In: Proceedings of the 29th International Joint Conference on Artificial Intelligence (IJCAI 2020), Survey Track, pp. 4803–4811 (2020)
48. Huang, Z., Zhou, S., Heng, W.: Learning to paint with model-based deep reinforcement learning. In: Proceedings of the 2019 IEEE/CVF International Conference on Computer Vision (ICCV), pp. 8708–8717 (2019)
49. Dargazany, A.: Model-based actor-critic: GAN + DRL (actor-critic) => AGI. arXiv:2004.04574 [cs.AI] (2021)
50. Drudzel, M.J., Díez, F.J.: Combining knowledge from different sources in causal probabilistic models. J. Mach. Learn. Res. **4**, 295–316 (2003)
51. Feng, G., Zhang, J.-D., Liao, S.S.: A novel method for combining Bayesian networks, theoretical analysis, and its applications. Pattern Recogn. **47**(5), 2057–2069 (2014)
52. Tapal, A., Oren, E., Dar, R., Eitam, B.: The sense of agency scale: a measure of consciously perceived control over one's mind, body, and the immediate environment. Front. Psychol. **8**, 1552 (2017)
53. Tao, J., Tan, T.: Affective computing: a review. In: Tao, J., Tan, T., Picard, R.W. (eds.) ACII 2005. LNCS, vol. 3784, pp. 981–995. Springer, Heidelberg (2005). https://doi.org/10.1007/11573548_125
54. Legaspi, R., Fukui, K., Moriyama, K., Kurihara, S., Numao, M., Suarez, M.: Addressing the problems of data-centric physiology-affect relations modeling. In: Proceedings of the 15th Int Conference on Intelligent User Interfaces (IUI 2010). ACM, New York (2010)
55. Legaspi, R., Kurihara, S., Fukui, K., Moriyama, K., Numao, M.: An empathy learning problem for HSI: to be empathic, self-improving and ambient. In: Proceedings of the Conference on Human System Interactions (HSI), pp. 209–214 (2008)
56. Synofzik, M., Vosgerau, G., Voss, M.: The experience of agency: an interplay between prediction and postdiction. Front. Psychol. **4**, 127 (2013). https://doi.org/10.3389/fpsyg.2013.00127
57. Gentsch, A., Synofzik, M.: Affective coding: the emotional dimension of agency. Front. Hum. Neurosci. **8**, 608 (2014)

58. Christensen, J.F., Di Costa, S., Beck, B., Haggard, P.: I just lost it! Fear and anger reduce the sense of agency: a study using intentional binding. Exp. Brain Res. **237**, 1205–1212 (2019)

59. Xu, W., Kuriki, Y., Sato, T., Taya, M., Ono, C.: Does traffic information provided by smart-phones increase detour behavior? In: Gram-Hansen, S.B., Jonasen, T.S., Midden, C. (eds.) PERSUASIVE 2020. LNCS, vol. 12064, pp. 45–57. Springer, Cham (2020). https://doi.org/10.1007/978-3-030-45712-9_4

60. Hennessy, D.A., Wiesenthal, D.L.: The relationship between traffic congestion, driver stress and direct versus indirect coping behaviours. Ergonomics **40**, 348–361 (1997)

61. Yoshie, M., Haggard, P.: Effects of emotional valence on sense of agency require a predictive model. Nat. Sci. Rep. **7**, 8733 (2017)

62. Ehsan, P., Tambwekar, T., Chan, L., Harrison, B., Reidl, M.: Automated rationale generation: a technique for explainable AI and its effects on human perceptions. In: Proceedings of the 24th Int Conference on Intelligent User Interfaces (IUI 2019), pp. 263–274 (2019)

63. Legaspi, R., Maruyama, H.: Complexity-based thinking in systems intelligence for systems resilience. In: Proceedings of the 11th International Conference on Systems (ICONS), pp. 6–13 (2016)

Designing Effective Dialogue Content for a Virtual Coaching Team Using the Interaction Process Analysis and Interpersonal Circumplex Models

Gerwin Huizing[(✉)] , Randy Klaassen , and Dirk Heylen

University of Twente, Drienerlolaan 5, 7522 NB Enschede, The Netherlands
{g.h.huizing,r.klaassen,d.k.j.heylen}@utwente.nl

Abstract. Much of the research in the field of virtual coaching agents focuses on interactions between a single agent and the user of the application. Another approach could be to give each user a personal virtual coaching team. This makes it possible to present multiple perspectives, and to have coaches with different expertise debate with each other. This could make the content presented more engaging and the system more persuasive. However, currently guidelines and theory to base designs for content for virtual coaching teams on is scarce. In this paper we present a study in which we set out to design content for a virtual coaching team to talk about general health topics with older adults. We based the content for our study on our implementation of two different models from social psychology used to classify interactive behaviour: the Interaction Process Analysis (IPA) and Interpersonal Circumplex (IPC) models. After testing our implementation of the models with a pilot test, we conducted an online study with 242 older adult participants. We compared the content modelled using the IPA model to the content modelled using the IPC model. For the IPA modelled content compared to the IPC modelled content the virtual coaching team came across more positively, the quality of their coaching was perceived to be better, the interaction experience was rated as better, their ability to persuade was better, and their group cohesion (task and social cohesion) was perceived to be better. We conclude that the IPA model is preferred over the IPC model when designing health coaching content for virtual coaching teams, and discuss possible reasons why. Furthermore, we recommend designers of health coaching content to test other models to base content designs on, and to measure the impact of differently modelled content in both more and less sophisticated coaching systems.

Keywords: Dialogue content design · Virtual coaching team · Interaction Process Analysis · Interpersonal Circumplex · Multi-perspective persuasion · Group discussion

R. Ali et al. (Eds.): PERSUASIVE 2021, LNCS 12684, pp. 19–32, 2021.
https://doi.org/10.1007/978-3-030-79460-6_2

1 Introduction

1.1 Background

Research in the field of virtual agent coaching often focuses on an interaction between a single coach and the user of the application [1–3]. Though these systems giving users an interaction with a single coach can be beneficial, the potential benefits of talking to a coaching team of virtual agents have not been explored as much [4]. André, Rist and colleagues described a team of virtual characters in a presentation setting [5]. They discussed characters taking on different roles in a sales presentation with their differing personalities. Their preliminary findings from informal tests showed that different personalities could be recognized, and that the team was interesting to watch. Furthermore, previous work [6] on showed an increase in persuasion when using multiple virtual agents as compared to a single virtual agent in the context of movie recommendations.

Having multiple coaches enables the design of coaching content showing multiple perspectives on issues the user is dealing with in a natural way, as each perspective could be represented by a separate coach. Another benefit of the approach is that it makes it possible for the system to have the coaches debate each other on their perspectives, showing pros and cons of each approach. This makes the coaching and persuasion more transparent, and supports users in their thinking on how to solve their issues. Furthermore, using a virtual coaching team could make interactions more engaging, and make the coaches seem more humanlike, because designers would be able to control how the coaches interact with each other and make these interactions effective performances. For example, if the user is not proactive in the interaction, they could have the coaches discuss the issues the user is facing without their active participation. That way the user could be informed in an engaging and interactive way without the need for their input at all times. To make sure the interactions with the team are enjoyed and for the team to come across as a group of experts working together, it could also be important to make sure they are seen as a cohesive team. These things could all affect the user experience. For example, users could experience more enjoyment during the interaction [6], and it could increase their willingness to actively participate in coaching sessions [6]. This better user experience could potentially keep users engaged for a longer time. The improvement in engagement could lead to improving the adherence of users, because it gives the virtual coaching team more chances to build a relationship with the users [1], and users will be more willing to interact with the system [2]. Furthermore, both individual and group coaching have been shown to be effective in persuading people to attain their goals in the real world [7]. This group coaching was in a setting with one coach and multiple participants, but as we have argued the addition of more coaches might only make the coaching more effective. Adherence and persuasion are some of the key goals of many virtual coaching systems, as the designers usually want the system to help guide users through a gradual change process, which takes time and requires users to work with the advice given by the system.

However, there are multiple challenges when designing a system that uses multiple virtual coaches, such as the division of roles between coaches in the team, how to make each coach a distinct character, and which coach should cover what and how the coaches should interact with each other in the multi-party dialogue. These issues stem from the aforementioned lack of examples in literature in the field of virtual agent coaching to base the system on. For many systems designers can fall back on basing their design on interactions that take place in the real world. However, most interactions in the healthcare and coaching domains are not between multiple coaches or experts and a single patient or client. This makes it hard to find material of a group interaction in this domain to model interactions after.

1.2   The Models

Due to the aforementioned lack of examples to base the dialogues on, we decided to design the content for several coaching dialogues based on two psychological models of interaction. The first model we used was the Interaction Process Analysis (IPA) model [8] originally based on a method used to study interactions in small groups. It was originally used to classify, summarize, and analyse direct face-to-face interactions and data that came out of these interactions based on the interpretation and classification of behaviour by the observers with regards to what the function of the behaviour was by intent or effect. The observations were of discussion groups. Broadly speaking, the model consists of four categories of behaviour. These are the positive reactions, attempted answers, questions, and negative reactions. The positive reactions and negative reactions are focused on dealing with the social-emotional area of communication in the group. The attempted answers and questions are focused on dealing with the task-related area of communication in the group. We decided to use this model as it is well established, it originally came from a discussion group setting, it approaches behaviour from a functional perspective, and its categories of behaviour are clearly described.

The second model we used was the Interpersonal Circumplex (IPC) model [9] originally based on observations of interpersonal behaviour in psychotherapeutic sessions, which were both one-on-one sessions as well as group sessions. The author showed that the theory could also be applied in other practical settings (the psychiatric hospital, psychosomatic medicine, industrial management, and group therapy) [9]. The theory was concerned with what kind of personality traits people displayed during interactions, and how to classify their behaviour. This model also consists of four categories of behaviour. These are dominant-hostile, submissive-hostile, submissive-friendly, and dominant-friendly behaviours. Dominant and submissive behaviour are opposites. Dominant behaviour comes through in trying to take the lead and the control during interactions. Submissive behaviour is seen in more withdrawn, deferring behaviour in which people do not want the spotlight during interactions. Hostile and friendly behaviour are the other opposites of each other. Hostile behaviour is more self-centred and shows a negative disposition towards others in the interaction. Friendly behaviour is more focused on the people they are interacting with and show a more positive disposition towards these people. Mixing these two dimensions of behaviour gives us our four categories. For example, submissive-friendly behaviour can be seen in someone who shows appreciation, or tries to cooperate, whereas dominant-hostile behaviour can be seen in someone who is very frank and honest when giving their opinion, or who clearly takes care of themselves before others. We decided to use this model as it is well established, it has been effectively used in group therapy and other group settings, it takes a more inter-personal approach compared to the IPA model that is more focused on the function of behaviour, and its categories of behaviour are clearly described.

1.3 Our Approach

In our study, we set out to work on the design of dialogues with a virtual coaching team. The two psychological models of interaction we chose label how contributions to an interaction by different participants can relate to each other in terms of support or conflict and other dimensions. As dialogues with a virtual coaching team would contain discussions of the choices regarding approach a user has, as well as negotiation about what approach to take, we felt our content would need to reflect this by properly modelling conflicts. This is why these models were selected to base our content design on.

Both models are intended for the analysis of human behaviour. In our study, we tried to use the four categories of behaviours given in each of these models and how the behaviours were described, to design the dialogue content for each coach in our coaching team. We also used the same method to author the content of the possible responses of the participants. These responses were always limited to four options, so that each response could be modelled after one category of behaviour for the model used for a dialogue. As both models were originally used to classify behaviour, this meant that we had to work the opposite way of what the models were originally designed for. Instead of classifying existing behaviour, we made new content based on the classification descriptions and examples of behaviour from the work of the original authors.

1.4 Research Questions

Our goal is to design coaching content for a team of multiple coaches. The dialogue that we write must be persuasive, as this will help the virtual coaching team convince users to follow their advice. We also want to empower users to make the choice they feel is best for them, by having the coaching team present them with several ways to effectively approach their problem. Furthermore, we want the team to be perceived as humanlike and as giving good quality coaching, and for people to enjoy their interaction with the team. This has the goal of encouraging more long-term engagement with the coaching team [2, 6]. Part of this is good group cohesion between the coaches, to help them come across as different people working towards the same goal together, and to run a smooth interaction [10]. Group cohesion consists of task cohesion, which is the degree to which group members work together to achieve a common goal, and social cohesion, which is the degree of connectedness and unity between group members, and whether they get along with each other. The aforementioned factors are of importance for the virtual coaching team to guide users through slow changes over time [2, 6]. Considering these factors of importance, we wanted to evaluate the following research questions about the effect of the differently modelled coaching dialogue content:

1. Which model would make the virtual coaching team come across more positively in its dialogue content?

2. Which model would make the virtual coaching team be seen as giving higher quality of coaching, though the information they give is the same in its dialogue content?
3. Which model would participants rate as having a higher interaction experience in its dialogue content?
4. Which model would more successfully persuade participants with its dialogue content?
5. Which model would make the virtual coaching team be perceived as having more task cohesion in its dialogue content?
6. Which model would make the virtual coaching team be perceived as having more social cohesion in its dialogue content?

1.5 Structure of This Paper

In the rest of this paper we describe the setup of the study we did, its results, and discuss what these results might mean. In the Materials and methods section we describe how we developed our content, how we designed the look and feel of our system, how we tested our initial design in a pilot study, and what we did with the outcomes of that pilot study to improve the system. We also describe the questionnaires we used to gather data to answer our research questions, how we selected and attained our sample of participants, and the design and procedure of our study. In the Results section we describe the tests we performed on the data, and present our summarized findings. Finally, in the Discussion and conclusion section we discuss the results of our study and how they can be interpreted. We mention limitations of our study, as well as potential avenues for future studies on designing content for virtual coaching agents and teams.

2 Materials and Methods

2.1 Materials

Content. We compared two different forms of conflict presentation styles in a virtual coaching session. One form based on the IPA model [8], and one form based on the IPC model [9]. Each model consisted of four broad categories in which behaviours were classified. These categories had some descriptions of what typifies the stance or behaviour. We implemented each category in the behaviour of one of four coaches that were part of the dialogue and one of four user response options when the user could respond.

We wrote the content for six dialogues based on these models, with three dialogues for each model. For these three dialogues per model, the virtual coaching team had three general health goals to discuss with the participants (losing weight, stress management, and sleeping better). The topics were chosen as they were general health and well-being topics that most participants would be familiar with. We chose to look at three topics to ensure that the findings were not specific to just one topic, but applied more generally to health and well-being coaching. In all the dialogues, the coaching team was discussing the setting of a new behaviour goal for the participant with them to help them reach their general health goal. Their advice was the same for each model for a topic.

Each of the four categories in both models was implemented as part of the content for one specific coach out of the team of four coaches. That coach represented that category in the model with what they said. This was done for all four coaches. The same was done on the participants' side by giving participants the opportunity to give their own input at a few points during the dialogues using four possible response options and basing each option on one of the four categories of possible behaviours in that model.

Table 1 summarizes the models and how we implemented them in a few key words to give an understanding of the types of behaviour we modelled. Each bolded text under both models is the name of one of the four categories in that model for a certain stance or kind of behaviour. Below that, we listed the descriptors of these stances or behaviours. Finally, between quotes we give examples from the dialogues on one of the three topics (losing weight) for the IPA modelled content and IPC modelled content to show how each kind of stance or behaviour was implemented. Do note that the quotes in Table 1 are all by the coaches, and are not all followed up by one another within the actual dialogue. They merely serve as examples.

Each dialogue was a group discussion in which the team was trying to help the participant achieve one of the aforementioned predetermined general health goals. Each dialogue consisted of a dialogue tree containing several conflicts, of which some were inter-coach conflicts, and some were conflicts with the participant. It branched based on participant replies at certain points. How many of the conflicts each participant got to see depended on how negative and hostile their responses were. At least one conflict was always presented. This conflict was between the coaches about the advice they were giving as a team. Examples of the dialogue trees for the IPA model and the IPC model can be found in our online annex[1], and you can contact us for further details.

System. We designed a simple prototype interface in Powerpoint containing 2D coaches sitting at a table and clickable buttons to respond (see Fig. 1). We decided that the coaches would communicate using text balloons, and that the participants could respond by pressing one of the buttons with text on it presented to them in the interface. This was to reduce the impact of appearance of individual coaches and the rest of the interface on how the message was perceived. Furthermore, it was to make the system easy to interact with, as participants would interact with it based on basic instructions.

In the online pilot study we used the prototype to test the interface and the implementation of the models in the content with four participants from the older adult population. We had them go through all six dialogues, and conducted semi-structured interviews with them. For each dialogue we had the participants indicate for each coach which category of behaviour in the model they thought they represented after we briefly introduced them to the models after the dialogue. We then asked them for their feedback on the interaction experience. We asked them to elaborate on their answers. Based on the feedback the content was improved to better reflect the behaviour from the models, to make the meaning clearer, and to make the coaching team more likeable. The interface was deemed to be fine. Participants needed little explanation, and did not have common complaints. We implemented the improved setup on the Qualtrics platform[2] by importing the pictures of

---

[1] https://www.edu.nl/batfq.

[2] https://www.qualtrics.com.

Table 1. Summarizing the IPA model [8] and IPC model [9]

Interaction Process Analysis (IPA)	Interpersonal Circumplex (IPC)
Positive reactions (coach 1) Shows solidarity, shows tension release, or agrees "You have been working hard, and I think that you are doing awesome! If you keep up your workout, you will get where you want to be in no time."	**Dominant-hostile (coach 1)** Narcissistic, competitive, sadistic, or aggressive "Frankly speaking, you need to do a lot more workouts before you will be anywhere near your weight goal."
Attempted answers (coach 2) Gives suggestion, gives opinion, or gives orientation "I would argue you also need to pay more attention to your diet. You are currently taking in a bit too much sweet stuff. If we can reduce your sugar intake, the process would be even easier."	**Submissive-hostile (coach 2)** Rebellious, distrustful, self-effacing, or masochistic "I am not too sure that just keeping up the workouts will be enough. You will really need to do a bit more than that. For example, to improve your diet."
Questions (coach 3) Asks for suggestion, asks for opinion, or asks for orientation "So what would be the first steps to have them reduce their sugar intake?"	**Submissive-friendly (coach 3)** Docile, dependent, cooperative, or overconventional "Can we please be nice to our coachee? We are working towards the same goal together, aren't we? Let's all form one team together."
Negative reactions (coach 4) Shows antagonism, shows tension, or disagrees "Hey! That is not nice to say. We do just fine. Check that ego a bit."	**Dominant-friendly (coach 4)** Hypernormal, responsible, autocratic, or managerial "That is right. We are all here to help you. I think if you try to work out, and cut down on sweets, it should all go fine!"

the coaches around the table and their speech bubble and giving the participants several reply options through the Qualtrics answer options with the same text as the buttons had in the corresponding Powerpoint slide of the prototype.

Questionnaires. As mentioned, we were interested in how the content based on the models might differ in how the virtual coaching team came across, the perceived quality of their coaching, the interaction experience, their success at persuading, the perceived task cohesion, and the perceived social cohesion. We used questionnaires that measured these constructs. The items the questionnaires were rephrased to be about the coaching team as a whole. The questionnaires were presented in order. Within each questionnaire the items were presented in a random order, if possible. The full questionnaires can be found in our aforementioned online annex (see Footnote 1), and you can contact us for further details.

The first set of questionnaires that we used was the Godspeed Questionnaire Series [11]. These questionnaires measure five constructs regarding the way agents come across

Fig. 1. Prototype of the system showing the four coaches at a table, with the yellow coach speaking (see text balloon) and the user responses to what the yellow coach said being shown below in the blue text boxes

to participants: anthropomorphism, animacy, likeability, perceived intelligence, and perceived safety. We used all the questions in each questionnaire. The questionnaires in the Godspeed Questionnaire Series have often been used in the field of virtual agents, and are still being used in this field [12].

The next questionnaire we used was an adjusted version of the Coaching Behaviour Scale for Sport [13], or CBS-S. This questionnaire was used to measure the construct of perceived quality of coaching given by the coaching team. We had to exclude some scales and items from the questionnaire, as they were not applicable in our context. We did not use items on the scales of physical training and fitness, technical skills, competition strategies, personal rapport, and negative personal rapport. We also excluded a few items on the scales of mental preparation and goal settings. We added items on the perceived coaching ability of the coaching team under a "coaching quality" scale.

We made a selection that fit our context of items from an earlier study on estimating group cohesion [10] to measure the construct of group cohesion. We also rephrased the items to be statements participants could indicate their agreement with. We selected six items from the task cohesion category, and six items from the social cohesion category.

For the construct of persuasiveness, we used a questionnaire consisting of two self-developed items. In the first item we gave a statement to indicate agreement with. It was a statement saying that the participant would try out the recommended behaviour if they had the health goal in the dialogue. The second item asked them to explain their answer to the first item. Answering the second item was optional.

The questionnaire that we used to measure the construct of interaction experience contained six self-developed items about whether participants were satisfied with how the conversation went, if they would recommend using this coaching team, and if they would use it again. Participants could indicate their agreement with each item.

2.2 Sampling and Participants

We recruited our participants through the Prolific platform[3]. We selected people that were between 50–100 years of age, had normal or corrected-to-normal vision, and were fluent in the English language. This was of importance, as our target audience for this experiment was older adults. Furthermore, our system required a lot of reading in English. This required our participants to have normal levels of vision and a good comprehension of the English language. Using G*Power [14], we calculated a priori our sample size needed to be 199 participants or more to detect a small effect size ($d = .20$) or larger with an error probability of .05 and a power of .80. A total of 242 (81 men, 161 women, 0 other, 0 did not want to say) participants between 50–87 years of age ($M = 57.50$, $SD = 6.66$) were recruited. They were monetarily compensated for their participation in line with the amount that was recommended on the Prolific platform.

2.3 Design and Procedure

Design. We conducted a within-subject user study. We divided our participants into three groups. Each group had dialogues with the coaching team about one of the three different general health topics (losing weight, stress management, and sleeping better), and was presented with one dialogue based on the IPA model and one dialogue based on the IPC model. This allowed us to compare the two differently modelled kinds of content. The order in which the two dialogues were presented was counterbalanced.

Procedure. The user study was made available online. At the start of the study participants were presented with a page containing information that explained the goal of the study, the data that would be collected, the kind of tasks they needed to perform, and the possible risks that were involved by participating. If anything was unclear, or they had any issues, they could contact the main responsible researcher. The participant could accept to participate in the study by signing the informed consent form, or indicate on the form that they no longer wanted to participate, which would terminate their participation immediately. They could also close their browser at any time.

Once they signed the informed consent form, they were asked to fill out demographic information. Then they were presented with a scenario containing context information for the upcoming coaching dialogue, and instructions on how to interact with the coaches. Once the first dialogue and related questionnaires were finished, they moved on to the next dialogue. Afterwards, the same questionnaires were presented to them. Finally, they were debriefed and sent back to Prolific to register that they completed their participation in the study. A session averagely lasted an estimated 30 min.

3 Results

We conducted a series of paired sample T-tests on the scales and questionnaires that we used. As we made a substantial amount of comparisons, we used the stricter Benjamini–Hochberg procedure [15] to correct the p-values. Even though the participants were

---

[3] https://www.prolific.co.

divided into three groups, we merged the data of all 242 participants for each scale and questionnaire, which allowed us to analyse the performance of both models overall. The item for the persuasion questionnaire could only be evaluated for one of the three groups with the topic of losing weight, as an error was made in the question for the other two groups. For this item only the 82 participants in the group with the topic of losing weight were used in the analysis of the persuasion construct. The results of our analyses can be found in Table 2. The first column shows the name of the measurement scale. In the second column, the difference between the mean scores for the IPA model (IPA: M) dialogues and the mean scores for the IPC model (IPC: M) dialogues can be found with a 95% confidence interval (IPA: M – IPC: M). The Cohen's d in the third column was calculated using the difference between these mean scores. The fourth column shows the Benjamini–Hochberg procedure [15] corrected p-values.

Table 2. Results for the IPA model [8] and IPC model [9]

Variable name	IPA: M – IPC: M (95% CI)	Cohen's d	p corrected
Research question 1: Coaching team impressions			
Godspeed: Anthropomorphism	.28 (.17 to .39)	.29	p < .001
Godspeed: Animacy	.25 (.14 to .35)	.26	p < .001
Godspeed: Likeability	.75 (.61 to .89)	.76	p < .001
Godspeed:Perceived Intelligence	.49 (.38 to .61)	.53	p < .001
Godspeed: Perceived Safety	.48 (.37 to .60)	.49	p < .001
Research question 2: Quality of coaching			
Adjusted CBS-S: Mental preparation	.29 (.18 to .41)	.30	p < .001
Adjusted CBS-S:Goal setting	.45 (.33 to .57)	.46	p < .001
Adjusted CBS-S: Quality of coaching	.45 (.32 to .57)	.45	p < .001
Research question 3: Interaction experience			
Interaction experience	.87 (.67 to 1.06)	.52	p < .001
Research question 4: Persuasiveness			
Persuasion	.55 (.23 to .86)	.35	p = .001
Research question 5: Group cohesion (task)			
Group cohesion: task cohesion	.38 (.21 to .54)	.31	p < .001
Research question 6: Group cohesion (social)			
Group cohesion: social cohesion	.40 (.23 to .57)	.33	p < .001

4 Conclusion

4.1 Discussion

Our results show that the content we designed based on the IPA model outperformed the content based on the IPC model. With regards to how the coaching team came across, the IPA content especially made them come across as more likeable, intelligent, and safe to interact with compared to the IPC content (see Table 2, row 5–7, column 3). Their quality of coaching was especially appreciated for its goal setting and general coaching quality for the IPA content as compared to the IPC content (see Table 2, row 10–11, column 3), even though dialogues for both models had goal setting. Finally, the interaction experience was better for the IPA content as compared to the IPC content (see Table 2, row 13, column 3). All other measurements showed a significant preference by participants for IPA modelled content, but the differences were smaller.

The question is why the IPA modelled content performed better than the IPC modelled content. It could be because the IPA model describes behaviour that is more neutral in tone than the IPC model. This could be better suited for a virtual coaching team context, as a neutral stance can create a feeling of a safe environment where you can speak your mind [16]. Furthermore, people might have come into a health and wellbeing coaching dialogue with the expectation that their coaches would be supportive and neutral in tone. The more positive as well as negative stances in the IPC modelled content might have gone against these expectations, and negatively impacted the coaching experience, and perception of the coaching team. Furthermore, the emotional stances in the dialogues with IPC content may have made some participants anxious and uncomfortable during the dialogues. These factors could have impacted how persuasive the coaching team managed to be, favouring the dialogues based on IPA content over those based on IPC content. Furthermore, the more neutral tone in the IPA modelled content might have made the arguments of the coaching team feel more convincing.

Another possibility is that simply having two coaches that took a more negative stance in the IPC modelled content, as opposed to just one coach with a negative stance in the IPA modelled content, may have made the difference. The lower amount of hostile and negative coaches could explain the difference in how the coaching team came across better in the dialogues based on IPA content than the ones based on IPC content. These differences could also have had a negative impact on the interaction experience, leading to the preference for the dialogues based on the IPA content over the dialogues based on the IPC content. A coaching team with less negative voices could also come across as more cohesive, and more focused on the task at hand, which could explain why the IPA content was rated higher on group cohesion compared to the IPC content. One could also argue it is hard to appreciate the coaching abilities of a coaching team that has a more negative tone. This could distract from their coaching and make the person the coaching team is talking to feel less supported. This might explain why the coaching team using the IPA modelled content would be seen as giving better quality coaching compared to the using the IPC modelled content. The previous factors could also explain why the dialogues based on the IPA content turned out to be more persuasive than the dialogues based on the IPC content. It may also have been hard to persuade people when the coaching team sounded negative in the dialogues based on the IPC content compared to the dialogues based on the IPA content. Generally, people do not feel motivated when those telling them what to do are being negative.

Another alternative explanation for our findings could be that the differences in style and tone described in the previous paragraphs were not well liked by the targeted user group of older adults. Based on their experience with healthcare providers, our older adult participants might have had specific expectations of how a virtual coaching team would conduct itself [17]. They might have expected a neutral presentation of information, and avoidance of open conflict between the coaches as well as themselves during a coaching dialogue. If they did come in.with notions that open conflicts should not be part of a coaching conversation, and that a more neutral stance should be taken by professional coaches, the IPC modelled content might have conflicted more heavily with these notions than the IPA modelled content. This could explain some, or all of the higher ratings across our measurements for the IPA modelled content compared to the IPC modelled content.

4.2 Limitations

The first limitation is that the content used in this study was mostly written by the first author of this paper. Thus, the differences found may have been based on their ability to implement the categories in both models in the content for the coaching dialogues. We tried to control for this with the pilot test, as well as by having other researchers evaluate the dialogues. However, it is still possible that the writer of our content, the researchers checking the content, and the pilot study participants did not find all the issues with the implementation of both models in the coaching dialogue content. Another limitation of this study is that it did not contain many qualitative measures. This meant that we had less data on why one of the models outperformed the other in our measurements. The next limitation is that we conducted our entire study online through the Prolific platform. This means that we cannot conclusively say that our participants were all separate individuals, or that they met all our selection criteria. Though the researchers involved did their best to take out responses by participants that did not understand the text completely, some other problematic participants may have slipped through. The final limitation is that our focus was mostly on the content. This made our presentation itself rather simple. Whether our findings would hold for a more realistic virtual coaching team, or even a real-life coaching team is hard to say.

4.3 Future Work

The potential for virtual coaching teams has thus far been relatively unexplored. We focused on how to design content for systems using such virtual coaching teams. We found that IPA modelled content outperformed IPC modelled content on several key metrics. Thus, we can tentatively recommend other content designers for virtual coaching to take a look at the IPA model to base their coaching content and coach behaviour on. However, this is just a first step in exploring content design for virtual coaching teams. Future work should focus on further expanding the models used to base content design on. Furthermore, we recommend that these models are used to design dialogues for more sophisticated virtual coaching team systems to see whether they can still impact the key metrics that we measured here. More advanced representations of a virtual coaching team, or a more elaborate interface might have an effect on the impact the content has. A controlled study without user interaction might also be of interest in the future. The current study focused on the interactions with the user in a live setting, and tried to represent both models to the full extent in these interactions. However, this did make for more variables to account for when comparing the results for each model. A study in which, for example, video material of characters acting out a certain kind of behaviour from the models is evaluated could give other valuable insights. An alternative approach could be taken by looking at behaviour in human-human teams in other settings and looking at other related research, and attempt to adapt the behaviours to this domain. However, the domain is quite specific and so it is questionable whether simply adjusting this behaviour would match the setting of a virtual coaching team. Finally, in future studies of this nature we would recommend to check the expectations of a coaching team the participants have prior to their interactions. This could be done using a combination of questions about their expectations, and them rating how well coaching was done in footage of coaching interactions. There are still many questions to be answered about how to design virtual coaching teams and content for such teams, but the potential upside of answering these design questions could be enormous.

References

1. Bickmore, T., Gruber, A., Picard, R.: Establishing the computer-patient working alliance in automated health behavior change interventions. Patient Educ. Couns. **59**(1), 21–30 (2005)
2. Bickmore, T., Schulman, D., Yin, L.: Maintaining engagement in long-term interventions with relational agents. Appl. Artif. Intell. **24**(6), 648–666 (2010)
3. Gardiner, P.M., et al.: Engaging women with an embodied conversational agent to deliver mindfulness and lifestyle recommendations: a feasibility randomized control trial. Patient Educ. Couns. **100**(9), 1720–1729 (2017)
4. Huizing, G., Klaassen, R., Heylen, D.: Multi-perspective persuasion by a council of virtual coaches. In: Proceedings of the Eighth International Workshop on Behavior Change Support Systems, Aalborg, Denmark, 21 April. CEUR-WS.org (2020). http://CEUR-WS.org/Vol-2662/BCSS2020_paper2.pdf
5. André, E., Rist, T., van Mulken, S., Klesen, M., Baldes, S.: The Automated Design of Believable Dialogues for Animated Presentation Teams. Embodied Conversational Agents, Cambridge, MA, USA, pp. 220–255 (2001)
6. Kantharaju, R., Pease, D., De Franco, D., Pelachaud, C.: Is two better than one? Effects of multiple agents on user persuasion. In: Proceedings of the 18th International Conference on Intelligent Virtual Agents, CoRR abs/1904.05248 (2018)
7. Losch, S., Traut-Mattausch, E., Mühlberger, M.D., Jonas, E.: Comparing the effectiveness of individual coaching, self-coaching, and group training: How leadership makes the difference. Front. Psychol. **7**, 629 (2016). https://doi.org/10.3389/fpsyg.2016.00629
8. Bales, R.F.: Interaction Process Analysis: A Method for the Study of Small Groups, 1st edn. Addison-Wesley Press, Inc., Cambridge (1951)
9. Leary, T.: Interpersonal Diagnosis of Personality: A Functional Theory and Methodology for Personality Evaluation, 1st edn. Wipf and Stock Publishers, Eugene (2004)
10. Hung, H., Gatica-Perez, D.: Estimating cohesion in small groups using audio-visual nonverbal behavior. IEEE Trans. Multimed. **12**(6), 563–575 (2010)

11. Official Godspeed Questionnaire Series. http://www.bartneck.de/2008/03/11/the-godspeed-questionnaire-series/. Accessed 15 Feb 2021
12. Aneja, D., McDuff, D., Czerwinski, M.: Conversational error analysis in human-agent interaction. In: Proceedings of the 20th ACM International Conference on Intelligent Virtual Agents (IVA 2020), Article 3, pp. 1–8. Association for Computing Machinery, New York (2020). https://doi.org/10.1145/3383652.3423901
13. Côte, J., Yardley, J., Hay, J., Sedgwick, W., Baker, J.: An exploratory examination of the coaching behaviour scale for sport. Avante Res. Note **5**(2), 82–92 (1999)
14. Faul, F., Erdfelder, E., Lang, A.G., Buchner, A.: G*Power 3: a flexible statistical power analysis program for the social, behavioral, and biomedical sciences. Behav. Res. Methods **39**, 175–191 (2007)
15. Benjamini, Y., Hochberg, Y.: Controlling the false discovery rate: a practical and powerful approach to multiple testing. J. Roy. Stat. Soc.: Ser. B (Methodol.) **57**(1), 289–300 (1995)
16. Smith, C.L.: How coaching helps leadership resilience: the leadership perspective. Int. Coach. Psychol. Rev. **10**(1), 6–19 (2015)
17. Parekh, N., Gahagan, B., Ward, L., Ali, K.: 'They must help if the doctor gives them to you': a qualitative study of the older person's lived experience of medication-related problems. Age Ageing **48**(1), 147–151 (2019)

Towards Adaptive Robotic Tutors in Universities: A Field Study

Melissa Donnermann$^{(\boxtimes)}$, Philipp Schaper, and Birgit Lugrin

Human-Computer Interaction, University of Wuerzburg, Würzburg, Germany
melissa.donnermann@uni-wuerzburg.de

Abstract. Learning in university setting includes the challenging task of self-motivation of the learner. The use of social robots has been shown to support the learner in their social learning process. In this paper, we address the motivation of learners in terms of self-determination theory as a theoretical framework to address need satisfaction. To this end, we conducted a field study using an adaptive robotic tutor that supports learners in exam preparation using an online learning session. With the aim to not only benefit motivation, but also academic success, we draw from research in social robotics in education as well as from adaptive tutoring, to create an adequate learning scenario. Adaptation is realized by a simple content and learner model and resulted in a significantly higher perceived use of the tutoring compared to a control condition. Our results also showed descriptive benefits such as increased perceived tutor quality, need satisfaction and motivation resulting from the adaptive tutoring. Finally, we found significantly better exam performance with the robotic tutor in the adaptive or non-adaptive version relative to students not participating in the robotic tutoring.

Keywords: Human-robot interaction · Higher education · Adaptive tutoring · Technology supported learning

1 Introduction

Self-directed and lifelong learning is of great relevance in today's knowledge society. However, it requires maintaining a high level of motivation and attention, which is challenging for many learners. The requirement for self-directed learning is particularly high in adult education, especially at universities. In this context, the transfer of knowledge is often unidirectional and offers little space for interactivity and limited individual tutoring. Self-study is required, which is demanding for students, as it requires effective learning strategies for self-motivation and provides nearly no individual support or feedback on the learning process. This challenge has become more pronounced due to the COVID-19 pandemic, because most university courses switched to online lectures, which made individual and personal support by teachers even less available. Technology-supported education can be a useful approach to support this change to self-directed learning,

© Springer Nature Switzerland AG 2021
R. Ali et al. (Eds.): PERSUASIVE 2021, LNCS 12684, pp. 33–46, 2021.
https://doi.org/10.1007/978-3-030-79460-6_3

however it often has a crucial weakness: the social context of learning is missing. It is known that social interaction between teachers and students has a positive effect on many aspects of learning, such as academic achievement, intellectual skills and especially motivation [24–26].

Understanding and enhancing learners' motivation is critical to support them in their learning process. One established approach to address motivation in an educational context is self-determination theory [18]. The theory postulates a continuum for motivation, ranging from purely extrinsic to intrinsic motivation, with more self-determined and therefore autonomous motivation on the latter end. Influencing motivation is tied to the idea that motivation of humans is connected to the three psychological needs for autonomy, competence and relatedness. Satisfaction of these three needs is fundamental to increase and internalize motivation during learning [5]. Therefore, these basic needs should be considered when planning a learning scenario. The need of autonomy can be supported by providing choice, and decreased by a feeling of being controlled. The feeling of competence can be supported by optimal challenges and positive feedback [6] and should also be related to the degree of subjective knowledge. The feeling of relatedness is a third factor to increase motivation and is based on interpersonal contacts and might be related to the social connection to the tutor.

Social robots are an especially noteworthy group of pedagogical agents to address these psychological needs due to their physical presence and their ability to show social behavior. A robotic tutor can therefore combine the benefits of technology-enhanced learning, as well as some aspects of a physically present teacher or tutor, as well as integrate its own specific benefits such as less shame for the learner when making errors [8]. Therefore, they can act as persuasive technology with the aim to benefit the user's attitude and behavior while learning. To date, the use of social robots in higher education is rare. In our former work [8]) we have successfully integrated a robotic tutor into a university course in a tutoring scenario, and improved the learning success and experience for the students, demonstrating the applicability of social robots in this context. However, more individual support was desired by the participating students. Thus, we are expanding this line of research by implementing an adaptive version of a robotic tutor and test its benefits. To investigate the degree of persuasion of an adaptive robotic tutor on the learner's motivation we addressed need satisfaction and the perception of the robot.

2   Social Robots in Higher Education

Social robots are designed to interact with humans in a natural, interpersonal way [3] and support their users through social interaction. Because this social component enables the robot to show persuasive behavior and thus potentially influence the attitudes and behavior of the users, one of their main areas of application is education. To benefit learning, robots can take on different roles in respect to the learner: either as a passive tool or as an active part of the learning situation. In the latter case, the robot may either solely present the learning content to the user or it can more strongly shape the learning process as a learning assistant. In this role, the robot is used in combination with a screen, where it asks questions, gives feedback or explanations in addition to the visual representation of the learning material and supports learning through social interaction [2]. Social robots in the role of such a supportive tutor have knowledge authority but are closer to the students and interact in an informal way. This kind of learning assistant has been shown to benefit the learning performance more compared to a teaching authority [20].

Research on social robots in education has mainly focused on children, with promising results in terms of affective and cognitive benefits [2]. So far, there has been little attention on adult education. However, due to their ability to show persuasive behavior, social robots bear great potential to address the challenges of university teaching, and online lectures in particular, and therefore to improve the learning experience. Based on the need for self-motivation in the university context, it would be of great interest to test if the benefits of robotic tutoring in children, such as positive effects on motivation and learning success [20] can be transferred into adult learning. First indications from one-to-one tutoring can be drawn from a study by Pfeifer and Lugrin [15], in which adults learned HTML basics in a robot-supported learning environment. Results show that all participants improved their knowledge while females who learned with a female robot (and prototypical male learning material) benefited the most. Furthermore, Deublein et al. [7] set up a learning environment accompanied by a social robot in cooperation with the university's Center for Language Learning to teach Spanish as a second language. Results were promising as a robot who is trying to increase the learner's confidence and satisfaction tended to improve learning outcomes more. Rosenberg-Kima et al. [17] chose a different approach and focused on the potential of a social robot to support a collaborative group activity of university students, and compared it to a pen and paper, and a tablet condition. Albeit most survey items did not convey significant differences between the conditions, qualitative data revealed benefits of the robot such as objectivity, efficiency, improving time management and an overall positive perception of the robot. In our own former research, we conducted a field study on the use of robotic tutors in university teaching. The social robot acted as a tutor for exam preparation to an ongoing lecture. Qualitative interviews showed a high interest of the students and a positive evaluation of the offer. With regard to the promotion of motivation and attention, the participants attributed great potential to the robot and considered the tutoring useful. Quantitative data supported this benefit, as participants who took part in the robotic tutoring performed significantly better in the exam, relative to students who did not participate. However, participants wished for more individualization.

Adapting the robot's behavior to the user has already been shown to have positive effects on learning and the perception of the robot [12]. Adaptive intelligent tutoring systems aim to personalize instruction by adapting the system e.g. to the learner's knowledge level and learning styles based on their performance and actions in the learning environment. The aim is to provide the same benefits of one-to-one instruction [16]. Leyzberg, Spaulding and Scassellati [12] showed that personalized lessons of a robotic tutor helped adult users to solve puzzles significantly faster and are rated as more relevant compared to randomized lessons or no lessons at all. Schodde, Bergmann and Kopp [21] implemented a robotic tutor for language learning that adapts its next tutoring action based on the learner's knowledge state. An evaluation with adults showed that participants had a higher score of correct answers during the training in the adaptive condition, but no significant differences in a translation test after the intervention. In a further study, Leyzberg, Ramachandran and Scassellati [11] found similar results in an experiment with children: over five sessions participants either learned a second language with a robotic tutor that gave personalized or non-personalized lessons. Results showed that children who received personalized lessons based on their skills outperformed children who received non-personalized lessons. Adapting the robots behavior and the learning material to the learner bears great potential to address the psychological needs and thus to internalize motivation by introducing a flow-like state while learning if all basic psychological needs are met [4].

3   Contribution

Because of the great potential of social robots in higher education and the benefits of adaptive tutoring, we want to contribute to a better understanding on how to design and apply robotic tutors in universities by conducting a comprehensive field study. By implementing an adaptive tutoring system, we not only aim to provide an additional tutoring for students complementing online university teaching in a meaningful way, but also want to establish a technical system based on the self-determination theory. Based on the literature review and the results of related work in Sect. 2, we expect the following outcomes:

- H1: Exam performance is better with an adaptive robotic tutor than with a non-adaptive robotic tutor than without tutoring.
- H2: Perception of the robotic tutor is higher (in terms of tutor quality and perceived use) with the adaptive robotic tutor compared to a non-adaptive robotic tutor.
- H3: Competence, autonomy and relatedness are addressed to a higher degree with an adaptive robotic tutor relative to a non-adaptive robotic tutor.
- H4: Motivation is higher with an adaptive robotic tutor relative to a non-adaptive robotic tutor.

4   Learning Environment

To investigate the benefits of a robotic tutor's adaptive behavior on the learning process, a robot-supported online learning environment was implemented. The learning environment was set up as a voluntary individual tutoring accompanying a university course. Due to the COVID-19 pandemic and resulting need for online teaching, the experiment was designed as a Wizard of Oz experiment with a live video call between participants and the robot. The learning material, e.g. questions and answer options, is visually presented via screen-sharing of the experimenter. The robot, which acts as a supporting tutor using verbal and non-verbal behavior, is visible via the camera. The Nao[1] robot by Softbank Robotics was chosen as an interactive tutor in the learning environment. The learner is able to interact with the learning environment with the integrated chat of the video conferencing tool[2]. Each button has either a letter, a number or a combination of both, so the learner can refer to different topics or answer options and therefore navigate through the learning environment. The robot responds in a multimodal manner, using different communicative channels such as speech generated by a text-to-speech tool and gesture, thus scaffolding the social component of learning.

The learning environment starts with a short introduction by the robot. As there is no predefined structure, the learner is free to choose the topic he or she wants to practice. Once the learner chose a topic, the related question is displayed on the screen and verbalized by the robot. The participants is then able to select an answer option. Depending on the learner's answer, the robot gives adequate feedback: the robot praises in case of a correct answer, encourages the participant in case of an incorrect answer and gives explanations on the correct answer. We also provided the opportunity to repeat the robot's explanation. Figure 1 shows the setup of the learning environment. As it is set up as a Wizard of Oz experiment, the experimenter transfers the user's chat inputs to the HTML learning environment simultaneously to trigger robot behavior using touch input on a convertible notebook to not confuse the learner by mouse movements or clicking sounds.

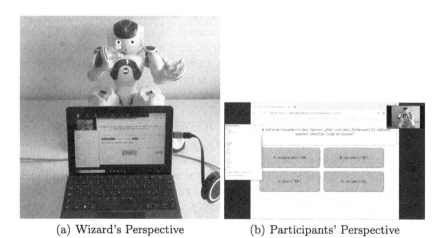

(a) Wizard's Perspective   (b) Participants' Perspective

Fig. 1. Experimental set-up

4.1   Learning Material

The learning materials are embedded in the curricula of the undergraduate course "Digital Media" at the University of Wuerzburg. The learning environment focuses on the web development sections of the lecture, which contain three main topics: basic coding in HTML, CSS and JavaScript. Each of these topics was divided into three subtopics with increasing difficulty, which contained between three and six exercises each. In total, the learning environment contains 35 exercises, including exercises to syntax, HTML elements, CSS selectors and JavaScript functions. Because there is no predefined sequence, the learner is able to choose exactly the topics he or she would like to recap. The structure of the learning environment is based on exercises without prior learning units, since it is intended to be a repetition of the lecture. The task types vary from single (15) (e.g. "Let's look at the loops below: Which for-loop counts up from 4 to 14 in steps of two?") or multiple choice (2) over cloze texts (10) and to assignment exercises (8).

4.2   Implementation of the Adaptive Robotic Tutor

We implemented two different versions of the robotic tutor: adaptive and non-adaptive. In sum, we set up the learning environment to respond to the learner's input using the robot's speech and non-verbal behaviors, additionally visual cues were given via the screen, such as highlighting the correct answer. The non-adaptive condition is limited to the functionality described above.

Adaptation in the other condition was realized in two ways: the robot's behavior as well as the HTML environment were adapted to the learner, based on a content model and a user model. The learning material is organized in a content model. For each exercise, the degree of difficulty, the required prior knowledge and connected exercises were defined, so each exercise is dependent on other exercises in multiple layers. As mentioned in Sect. 4.1, each of the three main topics contains three subtopics with three to six exercises each. The content model is organized along this structure in three layers: a superordinate topic layer, a subtopic layer and a layer for the single exercises. The exercises within a subtopic also build on each other, as they are in a predefined sequence. The subtopics are divided into three levels of difficulty (low, medium, high), which built on each other. In addition, the three main topics also partly build on each other, e.g. the basics of HTML are a requirement for the basic CSS exercises. Every subtopic (except HTML basics) has a certain required knowledge level. Which exercises are accessible to the learner depends on the current user model. First, the user model is defined by the user's prior knowledge, captured by self-assessment. At the beginning of the learning session, the learner was asked to assess his or her prior knowledge in the three main topics HTML, CSS and JavaScript by the question "how well did you understand the individual topics in the lecture?" with the options "poor", "average" and "well". Depending on which requirements are met, only exercises corresponding to the level of knowledge are displayed. By completing all exercises of a subtopic, the learner model is dynamically adapted, and the appropriate task from the content model are made available to the learner. By completing exercises, the user levels up independent of the correctness of the answers. It is possible to complete exercises multiple times, but only the first time adapts the user model. Users are not directly informed about leveling up, but may notice as more exercises are available. Furthermore, the robot adapts its behavior based on the learner's answers: if the answer is correct, this is briefly noted. If the answer is incorrect, the robot first explains which option is correct. In addition, it explains why the user's answer is wrong, depending on the chosen incorrect answer and thus gives hints on how to avoid such mistakes in the future (e.g. adaptive answer for the example exercise above: "Unfortunately that's wrong. Answer C would have been correct. Your answer is not correct, because the conditions for start and break are not correct, they are the wrong way round. var i = 4 is the start condition, where we start counting. $i \leq$ 14 is the abort condition, where we stop counting. In addition, the counting condition is not correct in your selected answer. According to the specification, we shall count in steps of two, but i++ counts in steps of one.") Therefore, the adaption of the robot's feedback to the user's answer is only done if the user chooses a wrong answer.

In the non-adaptive control condition, there is no content model and user model and every exercise is accessible from the beginning. There are no hints concerning the difficulty or requirements for an exercise. The feedback for a correct answer is equal to the adaptive condition. However, if the answer is incorrect, there is the same feedback independently from the chosen answer for each answer option (e.g. neutral answer for the example exercise above: "Unfortunately that's wrong. Answer C would have been correct. var = 4 is the start condition where we start counting. $i \leq$ 14 is the break condition where we stop counting, in this example up to and including 14. i + 2 states that we count plus two").

5   User Study

A field study was conducted to gain further insights about the effects of the adaptive robotic tutor. Because the university was closed for students during the first semester of 2020, the tutoring was designed as a private online learning session with the robot. Even though we might have shifted to a virtual agent instead of a social robot for the online setting, we decided to continue the use of a social robot, because our students already know the robot through previous studies. Furthermore, there are neither behavioral nor attitudinal differences comparing a telepresent robot to a virtual agent, which suggests that a telepresent robot is equally suitable in this context [14].

5.1   Participants

A total of N = 55 (53 female, 2 male) participants of the course "Digital Media" at the University of Wuerzburg took part in the study. Participation in the study was voluntary and participants received no further benefits. All participants stated that they intended to write the exam at the end of the semester. The mean age was M = 20.69 (SD = 1.61). Regarding prior knowledge of the robot, 30 participants already interacted with the robot before the study and 13 did not have any prior experience with the robot. The remaining participants had prior experience with the robot such as seeing it either in reality or on a screen, e.g. on the internet or television. All participants completed the study and answered all questions.

5.2   Questionnaires

The evaluation of the learning environment and the capacities of the robot as a tutor were measured by using the subscales Tutor Quality and Perceived Usefulness of the E-Learning Acceptance Measure [23]. Additionally we specifically asked in how far participants perceived the robot's feedback as appropriate on a scale from '1 – not appropriate at all' to '5 – very appropriate', and how they would rate the quality of the feedback on a scale from '1 – very poor' to '5 – very good'. To gaindeeper insights about a potentially different perception of the robot between the conditions, we used the Godspeed Questionnaire [1] with a total of 24 pairs of adjectives rated on a five-point polarity profile. To rate satisfaction of the three psychological needs we used a scale by Sheldon and Filak [22] with the subscales Autonomy, Relatedness and Competence containing three items each. Scales ranged from '1 – strongly disagree' to '5 – strongly agree'. Situational Motivation was measured using the Situational Motivation Scale [9], which consists of 16 items. Scales range from '1- corresponds not at all' to '7- corresponds exactly'. For deeper insights into learning experience we additionally used the subscale Interest/Enjoyment of the Intrinsic Motivation Inventory which is considered as indicator for intrinsic motivation [19] and contains 9 items on a seven-point Likert scale from '1 – not at all' to '7 – very true'. All items were translated into German and slightly adapted to the context if necessary. In the end, participants were asked about their prior experience with robots and demographic data such as age and gender. Participants were asked to rate their knowledge about the three topics HTML, CSS and JavaScript either '1 - poor', '2 - average' or '3 - good' before and after the learning environment. Approximately eight weeks after the study after the students received their grades for the exam, all participants were asked to anonymously provide their grades in order to find potential differences in the exam performance. Additionally they were asked in how far they perceived the learning environment retrospectively as useful for the exam.

5.3   Procedure

Participants registered online for a time slot and received an invitation with a link to participate in the study via a video conferencing tool. One participant attended a session at a time and participants were randomly assigned to one of the two conditions, resulting in n = 29 for the adaptive condition and n = 26 for the neutral condition. At the beginning of each session, the experimenter welcomed the participant and asked him or her to read and sign an online consent form. During that time, the video of the experimenter was not active. After participants accepted, the experimenter explained the procedure of the study. The experimenter then activated the camera and shared the browser window so that the robot and the HTML learning environment were visible to the participant. While the shared screen took most of the space of participants' screen, the robot was visible in a smaller window above or right, as this is a default setting of the video conferencing tool. Participants' audio and video was not active during the session unless they activated their microphone to talk to the experimenter. The experimenter started the learning session by pressing the start button. First, the robot welcomes the learner and explains the usage of the learning environment, especially the interaction with the learning environment, which is via the integrated chat of the video conferencing tool. At this point, the experimenter was neither visible nor hearable. The time to spend in the learning environment was limited to 40 min and was stopped by the experimenter after finishing the current exercise. The number of exercises completed was dependent on each student's individual learning pace. After the learning session, participants were asked to complete the online questionnaires described in Sect. 5.2 which took about ten to fifteen minutes.

6   Results

All analyses were conducted using SPSS 25 using an alpha of 0.05 if not noted otherwise. Group differences were calculated using T-Tests, and Mann-Whitney U tests if groups were smaller than 30. An overview of the descriptive data and statistical tests for H2, H3 and H4 is given in Table 1. Two participants had to be excluded from data analysis due to technical issues during the tutoring.

Hypothesis 1: Exam Performance. To test H1, we compared the exam results of all study participants (combining both experimental groups) which disclosed their exam grade (n = 37), to the performance of all other students of the exam who did not participate in the study (n = 112). Students were graded from 1 (best possible grade) to 5 (failed). Eighteen participants did not complete the second questionnaire that was asking for their grades in the exam. As shown in Fig. 2 performance was significantly better for the students which took part in the experiment (M = 2.23, SD = .84), relative to the rest of the class (M = 2.89, SD = 1.15) as indicated by a Welch's t-test $t(84.27) = 3.77$, $p < .001$, $d = 0.61$. Participants in the adaptive condition performed descriptively better in the exam relative to the control group, however this difference was not significant.

Hypothesis 2: Perceived Use and Tutor Quality. Concerning the perceived use of the robotic tutor as well as the tutor quality, we found that the subjective use of the tutoring after the exam was significantly higher in the adaptive condition compared to the control condition. The perceived use of the robotic tutor was

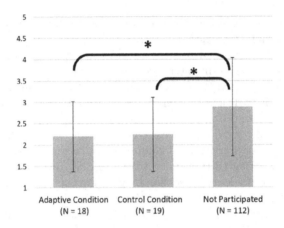

Fig. 2. Exam performance. Error bars represent SDs. * indicates significance at the $p < .05$ level.

practically as high as in the adaptive condition compared to the control condition and did not differ significantly. The perceived tutor quality in the adaptive condition was slightly higher relative to the control group but without a significant difference.

Hypothesis 3: Need Satisfaction. Regarding need satisfaction we found that: Need for relatedness was descriptively higher in the adaptive condition relative to the control group, however this difference was not significant. Need for autonomy was descriptively higher in the adaptive condition relative to the control group but without a significant difference. Need for competence was descriptively higher in the adaptive condition relative to the control group but did not differ significantly.

Hypothesis 4: Motivation. Situational intrinsic motivation as measured by the SIMS was descriptively higher in the adaptive condition relative to the control group, however this difference was not significant. Intrinsic motivation as measured by the Intrinsic Motivation Inventory was descriptively higher in the adaptive condition relative to the control group, however not significantly.

Additional Results. The need for autonomy across both conditions showed a significant positive correlation with the perceived used of the tutoring after the exam ($r = .45$, $p = .004$). The need for competence across both conditions showed a significant positive correlation with the subjective knowledge in CSS ($r = .42$, $p < .001$) and JavaScript ($r = .29$, $p = .033$) and was also positively but not significantly correlated with subjective knowledge in HTML ($r = .25$, $p = .077$). The need for relatedness across both conditions showed a significant positive correlation with perceived tutor quality ($r = .38$, $p = .005$).

Table 1. Mean values for subjective measures across both conditions including the range for each scale. Standard deviations in parentheses. U and p values show results for Mann-Whitney U tests with * indicating significance.

	n	Adaptive condition	n	Control condition	U	p
Perceived use after exam (1–7)	19	5.21(1.78)	19	4.16(1.50)	249	.046*
Tutor quality (1–7)	27	6.05(.72)	26	6.03(.65)	365.5	.796
Perceived use (1–7)	27	5.90(.78)	26	5.86(.62)	398	.723
Anthropomorphism (1–5)	27	2.69(.89)	26	2.63(.77)	347	.940
Animacy (1–5)	27	3.38(.62)	26	3.38(.53)	326	.655
Likeability (1–5)	27	4.60(.45)	26	4.48(.58)	377.5	.629
Perceived Intelligence (1–5)	27	4.40(.51)	26	4.36(.55)	360	.871
Perceived Safety (1–5)	27	3.01(.52)	26	3.01(.36)	347	.940
Need for relatedness (1–5)	27	4.07(.68)	26	3.95(.80)	367	.772
Need for autonomy (1–5)	27	4.46(.67)	26	4.35(.50)	399	.382
Need for competence (1–5)	27	3.27(.67)	26	3.14(.53)	415.5	.243
Situational intrinsic motivation (1–7)	27	5.73(.98)	26	5.49(.96)	412	.275
Intrinsic Motivation (1–7)	27	4.17(.67)	26	4.11(.70)	366	.789
Feedback appropriateness (1–5)	27	4.48(.51)	26	4.46(.65)	345	.903
Feedback quality (1–5)	27	4.15(.77)	26	4.19(.69)	342.5	.870

7 Discussion

Our results indicate that the robotic tutoring provided objective and subjective benefits for the participants. Foremost, we found significantly better exam performance of the participants relative to the rest of the course. Even though the manipulation did not result in significantly better exam performance relative to the control condition, the subjective use of the tutoring was significantly higher for the participants in the adaptive condition after the exam relative to the control condition. We consider this result especially noteworthy due to the relatively long time period between experiment and exam results (8 weeks). Even though self-selection in participation might have influenced this result, it demonstrates that opting for a session with the robotic tutor is beneficial. Ratings of the robotic tutor were high in general. Especially tutor quality with mean values above six on a scale from 1 to 7, and likability with mean values around 4.5 on a scale from 1 to 5 support the applicability of robotic tutors in higher education independently of the adaptation. The adaptive version of the robotic tutor was designed to better address the basic psychological needs of self-determination theory, namely relatedness, autonomy and competence. We found no significant effect of this manipulation, but the questionnaire data shows slightly higher need satisfaction for all three needs, this also holds true for situational intrinsic motivation as well as general intrinsic motivation. Based on the consistent differences, as well as the patterns of significant correlations of related constructs with need satisfaction in all three areas, we consider our implementation of adaptation as promising. In summary, the adaptive version of the robot was rated slightly better (even though not significantly) across all scales, which might indicate benefits of the adaptive tutoring on several levels that need further exploration.

The fact that there were no significant differences between the groups in the perceived quality of the feedback and in how far participants perceived the robot's feedback as appropriate may indicate that the adaptive elements are possibly too subtle to be sufficiently perceived. Furthermore, adaptation only occurred if mistakes were made. As indicated by the generally high ratings of the robot the control condition already offers high quality tutoring which makes it difficult to compare it to a slightly better version of the tutoring. Another possible reason for the lack of significant results could be the online setting. The physical presence of a robotic tutor appears to have a positive impact on learning outcomes compared to a virtual robot or no agent [10,13,14]. Albeit there are no differences comparing a telepresent robot to a virtual agent, most studies that compare a copresent robot with a telepresent robot found a preference towards the copresent robot [14]. Therefore, the robot may not be able to develop its full potential in an online setting.

8   Conclusion and Future Work

In this contribution, we explored whether a robotic tutor (with or without adaptation) can benefit learning in higher education in terms of motivation and academic success. To this end, we conducted a field study and integrated a robotic tutor into an existing university course, which both had to take place online due to the COVID pandemic situation, to demonstrate its applicability in an online setting. With significantly better exam results, the robotic tutoring appears to have a benefit in learning even at a university level. We further found indications that an adaptive version of the robotic tutor can be beneficial compared to a non-adaptive version in terms of perceived use of the training, but found no significant differences in the other survey items, albeit the adaptive condition was rated marginally better throughout.

In the future, the distinction of an adaptive version should be extended by implementing additional and clearer adaptive features to get more conclusive results. This adaptation should be tested in a long-term experiment, where the system keeps adapting to the user over several learning sessions, for example to strengthen the feeling of relatedness and elaborating the content and learner model. This would allow to replicate the pattern of results, ideally with a more pronounced and subsequently significant effect. Additionally long term motivation can be taken into account, as well as the internalization of motivation as suggested by self-determination theory, which should occur if the basic needs are addressed during the tutoring sessions. We therefore plan to continue this approach of integrating robotic tutors in adult learning and will improve our currently simple model of adaptation to better react to the individual learner. Because we do not expect a robot to develop its full potential in an online setting, we plan to continue our research in one-to-one presence tutoring.

References

1. Bartneck, C., Kulić, D., Croft, E., Zoghbi, S.: Measurement instruments for the anthropomorphism, animacy, likeability, perceived intelligence, and perceived safety of robots. Int. J. Soc. Robot. **1**(1), 71–81 (2009)
2. Belpaeme, T., Kennedy, J., Ramachandran, A., Scassellati, B., Tanaka, F.: Social robots for education: a review. Sci. Robot. **3**(21), eaat5954 (2018)
3. Breazeal, C., Dautenhahn, K., Kanda, T.: Social robotics. In: Siciliano, B., Khatib, O. (eds.) Springer Handbook of Robotics, pp. 1935–1972. Springer, Cham (2016). https://doi.org/10.1007/978-3-319-32552-1_72
4. Deci, E.L., Ryan, R.M.: The "what" and "why" of goal pursuits: human needs and the self-determination of behavior. Psychol. Inquiry **11**(4), 227–268 (2000)
5. Deci, E.L., Ryan, R.M., Williams, G.C.: Need satisfaction and the self-regulation of learning. Learn. Individ. Differences **8**(3), 165–183 (1996)
6. Deci, E.L., Vallerand, R.J., Pelletier, L.G., Ryan, R.M.: Motivation and education: the self-determination perspective. Educ. Psychol. **26**(3–4), 325–346 (1991)
7. Deublein, A., Pfeifer, A., Merbach, K., Bruckner, K., Mengelkamp, C., Lugrin, B.: Scaffolding of motivation in learning using a social robot. Comput. Educ. **100**(125), 182–190 (2018)
8. Donnermann, M., Schaper, P., Lugrin, B.: Integrating a social robot in higher education - a field study. In: 2020 29th IEEE International Conference on Robot and Human Interactive Communication (RO-MAN), pp. 573–579. IEEE (2020)
9. Guay, F., Vallerand, R.J., Blanchard, C.: On the assessment of situational intrinsic and extrinsic motivation: the situational motivation scale (sims). Motiv. Emot. **24**(3), 175–213 (2000)
10. Kennedy, J., Baxter, P., Belpaeme, T.: The robot who tried too hard: social behaviour of a robot tutor can negatively affect child learning. In: 2015 10th ACM/IEEE International Conference on Human-Robot Interaction (HRI), pp. 67–74. IEEE (2015)
11. Leyzberg, D., Ramachandran, A., Scassellati, B.: The effect of personalization in longer-term robot tutoring. ACM Trans. Hum.-Robot Interact. (THRI) **7**(3), 1–19 (2018)
12. Leyzberg, D., Spaulding, S., Scassellati, B.: Personalizing robot tutors to individuals' learning differences. In: 2014 9th ACM/IEEE International Conference on Human-Robot Interaction (HRI), pp. 423–430. IEEE (2014)
13. Leyzberg, D., Spaulding, S., Toneva, M., Scassellati, B.: The physical presence of a robot tutor increases cognitive learning gains. In: Proceedings of the Annual Meeting of the Cognitive Science Society, vol. 34 (2012)
14. Li, J.: The benefit of being physically present: a survey of experimental works comparing copresent robots, telepresent robots and virtual agents. Int. J. Hum.-Comput. Stud. **77**, 23–37 (2015)
15. Pfeifer, A., Lugrin, B.: Female robots as role-models? - the influence of robot gender and learning materials on learning success. In: Penstein Rosé, C., et al. (eds.) AIED 2018. LNCS (LNAI), vol. 10948, pp. 276–280. Springer, Cham (2018). https://doi.org/10.1007/978-3-319-93846-2_51
16. Phobun, P., Vicheanpanya, J.: Adaptive intelligent tutoring systems for e-learning systems. Proc.-Soc. Behav. Sci. **2**(2), 4064–4069 (2010)
17. Rosenberg-Kima, R., Koren, Y., Yachini, M., Gordon, G.: Human-robot-collaboration (hrc): Social robots as teaching assistants for training activities in small groups. In: 2019 14th ACM/IEEE International Conference on Human-Robot

Interaction (HRI), pp. 522–523, March 2019. https://doi.org/10.1109/HRI.2019.8673103

18. Ryan, R.M., Deci, E.L.: Self-determination Theory: Basic Psychological Needs in Motivation, Development, and Wellness. Guilford Publications (2017)

19. Ryan, R.M., Mims, V., Koestner, R.: Relation of reward contingency and interpersonal context to intrinsic motivation: a review and test using cognitive evaluation theory. J. Pers. Soc. Psychol. **45**(4), 736 (1983)

20. Saerbeck, M., Schut, T., Bartneck, C., Janse, M.D.: Expressive robots in education: varying the degree of social supportive behavior of a robotic tutor. In: Proceedings of the SIGCHI Conference on Human Factors in Computing Systems, pp. 1613–1622 (2010)

21. Schodde, T., Bergmann, K., Kopp, S.: Adaptive robot language tutoring based on bayesian knowledge tracing and predictive decision-making. In: Proceedings of the 2017 ACM/IEEE International Conference on Human-Robot Interaction, pp. 128–136 (2017)

22. Sheldon, K.M., Filak, V.: Manipulating autonomy, competence, and relatedness support in a game-learning context: new evidence that all three needs matter. Br. J. Soc. Psychol. **47**(2), 267–283 (2008)

23. Teo, T.: Development and validation of the e-learning acceptance measure (ELAM). Internet High. Educ. **13**(3), 148–152 (2010)

24. Tiberius, R.G., Billson, J.M.: The social context of teaching and learning. New Directions Teach. Learn. **1991**(45), 67–86 (1991)

25. Velez, J.J., Cano, J.: The relationship between teacher immediacy and student motivation. J. Agric. Educ. **49**(3), 76–86 (2008)

26. Witt, P.L., Wheeless, L.R., Allen, M.: A meta-analytical review of the relationship between teacher immediacy and student learning. Commun. Monogr. **71**(2), 184–207 (2004)

The Use of a Tablet to Increase Older Adults' Exercise Adherence

Sumit Mehra[✉], Jantine van den Helder, Ben J. A. Kröse, Raoul H. H. Engelbert,
Peter J. M. Weijs, and Bart Visser

Amsterdam University of Applied Sciences, Amsterdam, The Netherlands
s.mehra@hva.nl

Abstract. Sufficient physical activity can prolong the ability of older adults to live independently. Community-based exercise programs can be enhanced by regularly performing exercises at home. To support such a home-based exercise program, a blended intervention was developed that combined the use of a tablet application with a personal coach. The purpose of the current study was to explore to which extent tablet engagement predicted exercise adherence and physical activity. The results show that older adults (n = 133; M = 71 years of age) that participated 6 months in a randomized controlled trial, performed at average 12 home-based exercised per week and exercised on average 3 days per week, thereby meeting WHO guidelines. They used the tablet app on average 7 times per week. Multiple linear regressions revealed that the use of the app predicted the number of exercises that were performed and the number of exercise days. We conclude that engagement with a tablet can contribute to sustained exercise behavior.

Keywords: Older adults · Physical activity · Exercise · Persuasive technology · Tablet · Behavior change

1 Introduction

Ageing is associated with a decline in daily functioning and mobility [1, 2]. Physical activity can delay the onset and slow down the decline associated with ageing. Older adults that exercise on a regular basis, can prevent functional impairments and prolong the ability to live independently [3, 4]. Various community centers across the world offer senior citizens to exercise on a weekly basis in a group under guidance of an instructor [5–7]. Participating once a week in an exercise group, however, is not sufficient for achieving health benefits [8–10]. WHO guidelines prescribe a higher frequency, intensity and duration of physical activity [11]. Due to the limitations group-based programs face, meeting the guidelines is often not possible [12].

Over the past few years various eHealth or mHealth interventions have been developed to increase physical activity in older adults [13–19]. In order to enhance existing community-based exercise programs, a novel blended intervention, VITAMIN, was developed with end-users [20, 21]. The intervention consisted of a personalized home-based exercise program that was supported by a tablet, in combination with a personal

© Springer Nature Switzerland AG 2021
R. Ali et al. (Eds.): PERSUASIVE 2021, LNCS 12684, pp. 47–54, 2021.
https://doi.org/10.1007/978-3-030-79460-6_4

coach [22, 23]. The intervention distinguished itself by a) designed to complement existing community-based programs rather than a stand-alone intervention, b) specifically supports home-based exercises, c) uses blended technology as a mode of delivery and d) design that was theoretically based on behavior change techniques. Furthermore, to increase the efficacy of the exercise program, also nutrition counseling was included. A previously conducted randomized controlled trial (RCT) compared the blended home-based exercise program – with or without nutrition counseling – to a control group that only participated weekly in existing community-based exercise programs. The study showed that during the 6-month intervention period the majority (64.5%) of participants adhered to the recommendation to perform at least two times a week home-based exercises [24]. It remains unclear, however, how participants' engagement with the tablet contributed to exercise adherence. The aim of the present study was not to study the effectiveness of the intervention by comparing it to a control group, which was done in the recently published RCT study [24], but to explore to which extent the tablet engagement predicts exercise adherence in older adults by conducting a secondary analysis of the aggregated data of both RCT groups that received a tablet.

2   Methods

2.1   Study Design

A randomized clinical trial (RCT) was conducted to assess the effectiveness of the blended intervention in terms of health outcomes. It consisted of a 6-month intervention period. The protocol that describes the RCT in detail has previously been published [23]. The exercise program was supported by a client-server system that consisted of a front-end tablet application for end-users and a back-end web-based dashboard for coaches that guided the participants. The design of tablet application was based on behavior change techniques that are rooted in self-regulation [22]. The components of the app included an interactive module for goal setting, a library containing over 50 instructional videos of home-based exercises, a possibility to compose a personal training schedule, the ability to track progress and to receive feedback from a personal coach. A usability study demonstrated that the intended users were able to operate the app in an effective and efficient manner [21].

2.2   Measures

Home-Based Exercise Adherence. Participants compiled, with the help of an appointed coach, a personalized exercise program with exercises that varied in the duration, repetitions and difficulty level. Participants were recommended to perform at least two times a week the home-based exercises. During the 6-month intervention period, participants registered with the tablet when they completed their personalized home-based exercises. Based on log data the following frequencies were determined: a) how many days per week they performed exercises, for instance 4 out of 7 days, and b) the total number of exercises they completed per week. To preserve.

Tablet Engagement. Based on the log data the number of times the tablet app was opened per week was determined (app logins) during the 6-month intervention period.

Physical Activity Level. As an exploratory measure, at baseline and after 6 months the participants' physical activity in daily life was assessed by asking participants to keep track of all activities during a period of 3 days using a paper diary. For each participant a physical activity level (PAL) was determined by calculating the average metabolic equivalent of task (MET) per 24 h.

Motivation. At baseline and after 6 months the motivation to exercise was measured by the Behavioral Regulation in Exercise Questionnaire-2 (BREQ-2), a validated questionnaire containing 19 Likert items on a 5-point scale [25]. The BREQ-2 distinguishes five forms of motivation derived from the self-determination theory: amotivation 4 items), external regulation (4 items), introjected regulation (3 items), identified regulation (4 items) and intrinsic regulation (4 items).

Season. To account for possible seasonal effects, for each participant the offset to midsummer was calculated, by determining the number of days between the date the participant started the intervention and the median of the calendar year (day 183). The minimum score (0) represents midsummer, the maximum score (182) represents midwinter.

Other. Age, gender, recruitment strategy and assignment to RCT-arm was recorded for all participants (Table 1).

Table 1. Overview of the measures analyzed during the 6-month intervention period.

Start of intervention (baseline)	During intervention (0 to 6 months)	End of intervention (6 months)
Physical Activity Level (PAL)	Exercise adherence: • Number of performed exercises per week • Number of days exercises were performed per week	Physical Activity Level (PAL)
Motivation (BREQ-2)	Tablet engagement: • Number of times app has been used per week	Motivation (BREQ-2)
Participants & intervention characteristics: age, gender, recruitment strategy, RCT-group, season		

Data Analysis. Data of participants that were assigned to either group 2 (blended exercise program) or group 3 (blended exercise program with nutrition counseling) was aggregated, resulting in a dataset of all trial participants that received a tablet and coaching to support home-based exercises. For motivation de five BREQ-2 subscales were converted to a single score by using the relative autonomy index [26]. For the home-based exercise adherence and tablet engagement, after data cleansing an average score was calculated for the 6-month intervention period. These scores were treated as continuous data in further analyses. Furthermore, multivariate linear regressions were conducted to determine which included variables predict the home-based exercise adherence. The inclusion of variables as predictors, was based on subject-matter knowledge of the authors. The software package SPSS Statistics version 25 was used to perform the analysis (IBM Corp., 2018).

3   Results

3.1   Participants

At baseline 133 participants were randomly assigned to an intervention group. The average age was 71.48 (SD 6.39) years old and 92 of the 133 (69.2%) participants were female. In total 103 of the 133 (77.4%) participants completed the 6-month intervention.

3.2   Exercise Adherence and Tablet Engagement

During the 6-month intervention period, the average app logins per week was 6.72 (SD 4.81). They performed on average 12.53 (SD 11.34) home-based exercises per week and exercised on average 2.88 (SD 1.74) days per week.

3.3   Prediction of Exercise Adherence

Prediction of the Number of Exercises Performed Per Week. A multiple linear regression analysis was performed to predict the number of exercises performed per week, based on age, gender, motivation (baseline), physical activity level (baseline), RCT group, recruitment strategy, season and average app logins. A significant regression equation was found ($F_{8,115} = 10.26$, $P < 0.001$), with an R^2 of .42. Tablet logins, season and recruitment strategy were significant predictors for the number of performed exercises ($P < .0005$, $P = .018$, $P < .0005$, respectively). The number of performed exercises was equal to $-2.48 + 1.12$ (app logins) $+ 1.68$ (30*offset to midsummer) $+ 13.43$ (recruitment strategy), where recruitment through local community centers is coded as 0, and recruitment through postal mailing is coded as 1. The number of performed exercises increased by 1.12 for each app login, 1.68 for every 30 days the start of the intervention deviated from midsummer and participants recruited through postal mailing performed 13.43 more exercises than participants recruited through local community centers. Age, gender, motivation (baseline), physical activity level (baseline) and RCT group did not significantly predict the number of performed exercises ($P \geq .05$).

Prediction of the Number of Days Per Week Exercises Were Performed. A second multiple linear regression analysis was performed to predict the number of days per week exercises were performed, based on age, gender, motivation (baseline), physical activity level (baseline), RCT group, recruitment strategy, season and average app logins. A significant regression equation was found ($F_{8,115} = 8.81$, $P < 0.001$), with an R^2 of .38. Tablet logins, season and recruitment strategy were significant predictors for the for number of days per week exercises were performed ($P < .0005$, $P = 0.029$, $P = 0.007$, respectively). The number of days per week exercises were performed was equal to 1.74 + .20 (app logins) + .24 (30*offset to midsummer) + 1.18 (recruitment strategy), where recruitment through local community centers is coded as 0, and recruitment through postal mailing is coded as 1. The number of days per week exercises were performed increased by .20 for each app login, .24 for every 30 days the start of the intervention deviated from midsummer and participants recruited through postal mailing performed 1.18 more days per week exercises than participants recruited through local community centers. Age, gender, motivation (baseline), physical activity level (baseline) and RCT group did not significantly predict the number of days per week exercises were performed ($P \geq .05$).

4   Discussion

4.1 Principal Findings

The aim of the intervention was to support older adults in performing home-based exercises. In a process evaluation carried out earlier, participants indicated that they felt the tablet and coach were useful [27]. The results of the current study complement these findings. Data derived from the tablet shows that the participants performed on average approximately 13 home-based exercises per week, distributed over 3 days. Participants demonstrated substantive exercise behavior. Participants' engagement with the tablet appears to have contributed to this. The frequency of tablet use predicted the number of days and the number of exercises performed. This affirms the rationale of the intervention that technology can support exercise behavior in older adults.

Besides intervention characteristics, there were a number of other predictors found. A seasonal effect on exercise behavior was observed. Participants tended to perform more frequent home-based exercises in the winter, compared to the summer. The reason for this could be that older adults prefer outdoor activities, if the weather allows it, thereby limiting the intensity of a home-based exercise program. Physical activity was also predicted by age. Surprisingly, this effect was minute. The strongest predictor was the participants' physical activity at baseline. Existing habits appear to play a dominant role.

4.2 Limitations

Previously, a process evaluation was carried out by interviewing participants after they completed the intervention. The conclusions of that study were based on a small number of participants that had to reflect on their behavior over the past 6 months. In contrast, the current study uses log data of the tablet as a more objective and accurate estimations of exercise behavior of all participants. It does not rely on participants' recollection from memory. Nevertheless, also this data source is not impeccable. It cannot be ruled out that participants registered on the tablet that they completed exercises, whilst in reality they did not perform any exercises. The tablet data on exercise completion remains a self-report measure.

Tablet engagement was measured by tracking how often users opened the app. Based on the log data it was, however, not possible to observe how users interacted with the app. Consequently, no conclusions can be drawn which components within the app played a specific role. Furthermore, due to technical issues the number of app logins was not registered flawlessly. As a result, some datapoints on tablet engagement were unusable. To determine if this influenced the results, an alternative measure for tablet activity was used. Participants were asked with a questionnaire how often on average they used the app over the past 6 months. Analysis of this alternative measure was similar to the analysis based on app logins, indicating that use of the app logins was not problematic, despite the technical errors.

This post-hoc study combined data of two groups that participated in the randomized controlled trial; a group that received a tablet and coaching and a group that received tablet, coaching and nutrition advice. Although the two groups differed to which intervention component they were exposed, the analysis used in this study, did not reveal any association between group membership and exercise behavior or physical activity. This validated the choice of the authors to pool the data of both groups, instead of performing the described analysis for both groups separately.

4.3 Conclusions

The blended exercise intervention successfully increased the exercise frequency in older adults. Tablet engagement appears to have contributed to this. The frequency of app use predicted the number of exercises and the number of days exercises were performed. The findings suggest that the use of a tablet, in combination with coaching, is a promising strategy to stimulate exercise behavior of older adults. More research is needed how to incorporate general physical activity.

Please note, there is an extended version of this paper available with additional analysis [28].

References

1. Walston, J., et al.: Research agenda for frailty in older adults: toward a better understanding of physiology and etiology: summary from the American geriatrics society/national institute on aging research conference on frailty in older adults. J. Am. Geriatr. Soc. **54**(6), 991–1001 (2006). https://doi.org/10.1111/j.1532-5415.2006.00745.x
2. de Vries, N.M., et al.: Effects of physical exercise therapy on mobility, physical functioning, physical activity and quality of life in community-dwelling older adults with impaired mobility, physical disability and/or multi-morbidity: a meta-analysis. Ageing Res. Rev. **11**, 136–149 (2012). https://doi.org/10.1016/j.arr.2011.11.002

3. Fried, L.P., et al.: Frailty in older adults: evidence for a phenotype. J. Gerontol. Ser. A Biol. Sci. Med. Sci. **56**, M146–M157 (2001). https://doi.org/10.1093/gerona/56.3.M146
4. Warburton, D.E.R., Nicol, C.W., Bredin, S.S.D.: Health benefits of physical activity: the evidence. Can. Med. Assoc. J. **174**, 801–809 (2006). https://doi.org/10.1503/cmaj.051351
5. Taylor, A.H., Cable, N.T., Faulkner, G., Hillsdon, M., Narici, M., Van Der Bij, A.K.: Physical activity and older adults: a review of health benefits and the effectiveness of interventions. J. Sports Sci. **22**(8), 703–725 (2004). https://doi.org/10.1080/02640410410001712421
6. King, A.C.: Interventions to promote physical activity by older adults. J. Gerontol. Ser. A Biol. Sci. Med. Sci. **56**(Supplement 2), 36–46 (2001). https://doi.org/10.1093/gerona/56.suppl_2.36
7. King, A.C., Rejeski, W.J., Buchner, D.M.: Physical activity interventions targeting older adults: a critical review and recommendations. Am. J. Prev. Med. **15**(6), 316–333 (1998). https://doi.org/10.1016/S0749-3797(98)00085-3
8. Nelson, M.E., et al.: Physical activity and public health in older adults: recommendation from the American college of sports medicine and the American heart association. Med. Sci. Sports Exerc. **39**, 1435–1445 (2007). https://doi.org/10.1249/mss.0b013e3180616aa2
9. Chodzko-Zajko, W.J., et al.: Exercise and physical activity for older adults. Med. Sci. Sports Exerc. **41**(7), 1510–1530 (2009). https://doi.org/10.1249/MSS.0b013e3181a0c95c
10. Stiggelbout, M.: Once a week is not enough: effects of a widely implemented group based exercise programme for older adults; a randomised controlled trial. J. Epidemiol. Community Heal. **58**, 83–88 (2004). https://doi.org/10.1136/jech.58.2.83
11. World Health Organization: Global Recommendations on Physical Activity for Health (2010)
12. Schutzer, K.A.K.A., Graves, B.S.S.: Barriers and motivations to exercise in older adults. Prev. Med. (Baltim) **39**, 1056–1061 (2004). https://doi.org/10.1016/j.ypmed.2004.04.003
13. Muellmann, S., Forberger, S., Möllers, T., Bröring, E., Zeeb, H., Pischke, C.R.: Effectiveness of eHealth interventions for the promotion of physical activity in older adults: a systematic review. Prev. Med. (Baltim) **108**, 93–110 (2018). https://doi.org/10.1016/J.YPMED.2017.12.026
14. Müller, A.M., Khoo, S.: Non-face-to-face physical activity interventions in older adults: a systematic review. Int. J. Behav. Nutr. Phys. Act. **11**, 35 (2014). https://doi.org/10.1186/1479-5868-11-35
15. Yerrakalva, D., Yerrakalva, D., Hajna, S., Griffin, S.: Effects of mobile health app interventions on sedentary time, physical activity, and fitness in older adults: systematic review and meta-analysis. J. Med. Internet Res. **21**(11), e14343 (2019). https://doi.org/10.2196/14343
16. Kwan, R.Y.C., et al.: The effect of e-health interventions promoting physical activity in older people: A systematic review and meta-analysis. Eur. Rev. Aging Phys. Act. **17**, 1–17 (2020). https://doi.org/10.1186/s11556-020-00239-5
17. Stockwell, S., et al.: Digital behavior change interventions to promote physical activity and/or reduce sedentary behavior in older adults: a systematic review and meta-analysis, Exp. Gerontol. **120**, 68–87 (2019). https://doi.org/10.1016/j.exger.2019.02.020
18. Robbins, T.D., Lim Choi Keung, S.N., Arvanitis, T.N.: E-health for active ageing; a systematic review. Maturitas. **114**, 34–40 (2018). https://doi.org/10.1016/j.maturitas.2018.05.008
19. Elavsky, S., Knapova, L., Klocek, A., Smahel, D.: Mobile health interventions for physical activity, sedentary behavior, and sleep in adults aged 50 years and older: a systematic literature review. J. Aging Phys. Act. **27**, 565–593 (2019). https://doi.org/10.1123/japa.2017-0410
20. Mehra, S., et al.: Attitudes of older adults in a group-based exercise program toward a blended intervention; a focus-group study. Front. Psychol. **7**, 1827 (2016). https://doi.org/10.3389/fpsyg.2016.01827
21. Mehra, S., et al.: Supporting older adults in exercising with a tablet: a usability study. J. Med. Internet Res. **21**, e11598 (2019). https://doi.org/10.2196/11598

22. Mehra, S., et al.: Translating behavior change principles into a blended exercise intervention for older adults: design study. JMIR Res. Protoc. **7**, e117 (2018). https://doi.org/10.2196/res prot.9244

23. van den Helder, J., et al.: A digitally supported home-based exercise training program and dietary protein intervention for community dwelling older adults: protocol of the cluster randomised controlled VITAMIN trial. BMC Geriatr. **18**, 183 (2018). https://doi.org/10.1186/s12877-018-0863-7

24. Helder, J., et al.: Blended home-based exercise and dietary protein in community-dwelling older adults: a cluster randomized controlled trial. J. Cachexia Sarcopenia Muscle. **11**(6), 1590–1602 (2020). https://doi.org/10.1002/jcsm.12634. jcsm.12634

25. Markland, D., Tobin, V.: A modification to the behavioural regulation in exercise questionnaire to include an assessment of a motivation. J. Sport Exerc. Psychol. **26**, 191–196 (2004). https://doi.org/10.1123/jsep.26.2.191

26. Ryan, R.M., Connell, J.P.: Perceived locus of causality and internalization: examining reasons for acting in two domains. J. Pers. Soc. Psychol. **57**, 749–761 (1989). https://doi.org/10.1037/0022-3514.57.5.749

27. Mehra, S., van den Helder, J., Visser, B., Engelbert, R.H.H., Weijs, P.J.M., Kröse, B.J.A.: Evaluation of a blended physical activity intervention for older adults: mixed methods study. J. Med. Internet Res. **22**(7), e16380 (2020). https://doi.org/10.2196/16380

28. Mehra, S., Helder, J. van den, Kröse, B.J.A., Engelbert, R.H.H., Weijs, P.J.M., Visser, B.: Predicting Exercise Adherence and Physical Activity in Older Adults Based on Tablet Engagement: A Post-hoc Study. (2021). arXiv:2101.10140 [cs.HC]

Towards an Automatic Generation
of Persuasive Messages

Edson Lipa-Urbina[1], Nelly Condori-Fernandez[1,2,3(✉)], and Franci Suni-Lopez[1]

[1] Universidad Nacional de San Agustín de Arequipa, Arequipa, Peru
{elipau,ocondorif,fsunilo}@unsa.edu.pe
[2] Universidade da Coruña, A Coruña, Spain
n.condori.fernandez@udc.es
[3] VU University Amsterdam, Amsterdam, Netherlands
n.condori-fernandez@vu.nl

Abstract. In the last decades, the *Natural Language Generation* (NLG) methods have been improved to generate text automatically. However, based on the literature review, there are not works on generating text for persuading people. In this paper, we propose to use the SentiGAN framework to generate messages that are classified into levels of persuasiveness. And, we run an experiment using the Microtext dataset for the training phase. Our preliminary results show 0.78 of novelty on average, and 0.57 of diversity in the generated messages.

Keywords: Text generation · SentiGAN · Persuasive message

1 Introduction

The messages used to persuade a target audience in certain domains (e.g., marketing) have demonstrated to be very effective. However, the production of persuasive message requires a profound knowledge of receptor's characteristics as well as the involvement of a variety of stakeholders. For companies and organizations, this translates into time and money.

Automatic text comprehension and generation are very important in the areas of Natural Language Processing (NLP) and Natural Language Generation (NLG) respectively. In the literature, exist different methods for automatically generating text, which means that its operation does not require human intervention. Despite this growing interest in proposing techniques and models for the automatic text generation (e.g., [8,11,14]), there is not yet evidence on automatic message generation that can be used to persuade people. Currently there are some works that address the design of persuasive message for behavior change (e.g., [3]), and others focused on detection of persuasion in texts or conversations [6]. In this paper, we focus on the automatic generation of persuasive messages, through the application of SentiGAN [11], a short text generation framework based on Generative Adversarial Network (GAN). We consider that our work might contribute not only to reduce time, but also to enhance the novelty and

© Springer Nature Switzerland AG 2021
R. Ali et al. (Eds.): PERSUASIVE 2021, LNCS 12684, pp. 55–62, 2021.
https://doi.org/10.1007/978-3-030-79460-6_5

diversity of the generated persuasive messages in certain domains. To do this, we exploit the Microtext corpus [13] as a training dataset, which is a database that contains classified messages based on the Cialdini principles [2]. Moreover, we implement two metrics for measuring how novel and diverse are the messages generated by our approach. The paper is organized as follows: Sect. 2 discusses the related works on text generation. Then, we present our approach in Sect. 3. Our evaluation is reported in Sect. 4. And Sect. 5 contains the conclusions and future work.

2   Related Works on Text Generation

Unsupervised text generation is an important research area in natural language processing. The recurrent neural networks (RNN) are usually used for the processing and prediction of time series. In this context, we can see a sentence as a sequence of data (i.e., words), which is ordered according to the probability of the next word. Over the past decade, several approaches focused on using some varieties of RNN in text generation (e.g., [4,5,9–11]). However, RNN-based approaches have two main drawbacks when is used to generate texts. First, RNN-based models are always trained through the maximum likelihood approach, which lacks exposure bias [1]. Second, the loss function is not specified at the RNN output to ensure high sample quality. It means that these RNN-based approaches use the loss function to train the model at a word level, when the performance is generally evaluated at a sentence level.

Another related works are the models based on a generative adversarial network (GAN) with a strategic gradient of reinforcement learning such as [4,7,11,14]. For instance, SeqGAN was proposed by Yu et al. [14], which confronts the generator differentiation problem by directly updating the gradient policy. The impacts of these variations of GANs are not exceptionally diverse, and none of these strategies can produce samples with assorted qualities.

In contrast with our proposal, all these reviewed works focus only on the text generation, but not in the persuasiveness of the sentence. So, we propose to use the SentiGAN model [11] to generate messages classified in different levels of persuasiveness (i.e., using the six principles of Cialdini [2]). The SentiGan model was proposed by Key Wang and Xiaojun Wan [11] and it is based on SeqGAN [14], the authors used multiple generators and a discriminator with the goal of making each generator focus on generating texts with k types of sentiment (i.e., k sentiment tags).

3   The Persuasive Messages Generator

As shown in Fig. 1, the core of our generator is based on the SentiGAN framework [11], which includes K generators and one multi-class discriminator. Moreover, as we aim to generate persuasive messages, a database containing samples of sentences labeled accordingly to the Cialdini's persuasive principles is needed.

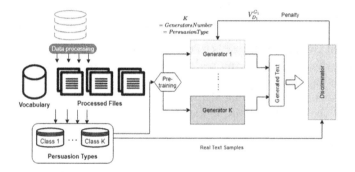

Fig. 1. The persuasive message generator based on SentiGAN [11].

In this paper, for illustrating the applicability of SentiGAN, we used an existing Microtext Corpus as our training dataset (More details about our training dataset can be found at Sect. 4.1).

Given that the GAN model generates and classifies sequences of n words, where n varies depending on the objective of the model. For instance, SentiGAN consider sequences of 15 words. As our database contain a huge number of samples that exceed this number, a processing of these samples with the least-lost of information is highly required. In our proposal, we start the **(1) data processing phase**, by using the rolling windows technique [15]. This technique tries to create window segments of length W from data y_i, $i = 1, ..., l$, where l is the length of the data. The data sequence is divided into $l - W + 1$ segments. For our generator, the window size was set arbitrarily at 17 words. Thanks to this segmentation, the size of the training data was increased as well.

Then we obtain a vocabulary, by ordering the words, contained in each persuasion type file, by their occurrence frequency. This vocabulary is used to encode all the messages to be used in the training phase.

The outcome of the data processing phase is the set of **processed files** classified by persuasion types.

Before starting the **(2) model training phase**, a pre-training on the generator and discriminator models is performed. This way, both models are able to understand the structure of a sentence (syntactic aspect, without considering the semantics). A benefit of the pre-training is the reduction of the training time because our generator is not trained from scratch.

In the following, we explain the model training, by introducing the structure and learning objectives of **the SentiGAN framework**, and explaining briefly its corresponding training algorithm.

This framework uses k generators $\left\{G_i\left(X|S;\theta_g^i\right)\right\}_{i=1}^{i=k}$ and a discriminator $D\left(X;\theta_d\right)$, where θ_g^i, θ_d are the parameters of the i-th generator and discriminator respectively. In order to initialize the generators input, we use the prior input noise z sampled from the P_z distribution (e.g., a normal distribution).

The SentiGAN framework aims to achieve two adverse learning objectives: i) The goal of the i-th generator G_i is to generate text with the i-th type of persuasion that can fool the discriminator. Specifically, it focuses on minimizing the penalty-based target, which was one of the main contributions in this model. ii) The goal of the discriminator is to distinguish between synthetic texts (texts generated by the generators) and real texts with k types of persuasion (samples from the training dataset).

We implemented the training algorithm such as specified in SentiGAN (More details about the algorithm can be found at [11]).

4   Experiment

In this section, we present the experimental evaluation carried out with the purpose of measuring the diversity and novelty of the generated persuasive messages.

4.1   Training Dataset

Due to the lack of datasets containing classified persuasive messages, in this experiment we have used only the Microtext corpus [13] for training our generator. This unique database contains a set of hostage negotiation dialogue transcripts, which are classified in 9 categories. 7 of out them are based on the Cialdini's principles (i.e., commitment and consistency, liking, authority, scarcity, reciprocity, social proof) [2] and the other two categories were: *No persuasion present* and *Other*. Originally there are 6 principles, but the authors of the corpus separated the principle of *Commitment and Consistency* into two different categories obtaining 7 types of persuasion. As part of our first analysis of the dataset, we divided it into files according to their classification to obtain the number of samples (messages) in each principle, which was not mentioned in [13]. Table 1 shows the overall description of Microtext corpus in terms of number of samples, percentage and one illustrative example for each category.

From this table, we observe that 88.4% of the available samples are classified as *no persuasion present*, whereas a 4.6% of samples are categorized as *Others* category to represent persuasive samples that do not fit into one of the above categories, and the 7% of the remaining samples fall into the last seven categories.

As GAN frameworks tend to have better results with large training datasets, in this experiment, we selected the three first categories that contain more samples (commitment, liking and consistency). Thus, we trained 3 different models, each one with a single generator. 500 samples were generated for each trained model. And the samples with less than two words were removed.

4.2   Variables and Metrics

In the following, we present our variables that were identified in this experiment:

- **Novelty:** This metric provides information about how different the generated sentences and the training corpus are. We define the novelty [12] of each generated sentence S_i as follows:

$$Novelty(S_i) = 1 - max\left\{\varphi(S_i, R_j)_{j=1}^{j=|C|}\right\} \tag{1}$$

Table 1. Overall description of the microtext corpus [13]

Category	# Samples	%	Example
No Persuasion	16672	88.4%	ya im smoking cigarettes and drinking coffee
Other	870	4.6%	the more you fight it the worse trouble there is
Commitment	614	3.3%	well give you a pack of cigarettes for one brownie
Liking	278	1.5%	okay well we appreciate you know we appreciate your trusting us we continue to trust you
Consistency	152	0.8%	<name> you told me the daughter is not going anyplace till you spoke to your wife now we let you talk to your wife all right
Authority	92	0.5%	theres right now theres a nurse over here and she says leave him sleep for the moment
Scarcity	79	0.4%	not the point either the point is ive set some demands and if theyre not met then the people are going to die
Reciprocity	54	0.3%	can you tell her im here on the phone with you will she understand that
Social Proof	46	0.2%	well i think if you talked to a lot of other people in this world that you would find that thats not the case

where C is the sentence set of the training corpus, φ is Jaccard similarity function, the result value is between 0 and 1, where 1 is totally novelty and 0 is totally equal to training dataset.

- **Diversity:** This metric is used to see if the generator can produce a variety of sentences. Given a collection of generated sentences S, we define the diversity [12] of sentences S_i as follows:

$$Diversity(S_i) = 1 - max\left\{\varphi(S_i, S_j)_{j=1}^{j=|S|, j\neq i}\right\} \qquad (2)$$

where φ is the Jaccard similarity function. We calculate the maximum Jaccard similarity between each sentence S_i and other sentences in the collection, the result value is between 0 and 1, where 1 is full diverse, and 0 is equal to generated dataset.

Regarding our independent variables, the type of GAN framework is identified as a variable that can influence on our results, and the SentiGAN model as our single treatment. This experiment is exploratory in nature and no specific hypotheses have been formulated.

4.3 Results

After applying both novelty and diversity metrics, our measurement results per category of persuasive message are shown in Table 2. Regarding novelty, we obtained an averaged score for the 3 models of 0.78. As the obtained values are close to 1 (maximum value), we can consider that our generated samples of texts have a good degree of novelty since there is a notable difference between the training data and the generated data. Regarding diversity, the results vary between 0.5 and 0.65, obtaining 0.65 in *Consistency*, which is the category with fewer training examples in contrast to the other two categories. However, we obtained the lowest diversity (0.5) for the Commitment category, which contains the large number of training examples. This may be due to the large amount of data that was used for pre-training, this data would be adding novelty to the models with fewer samples for training.

While we were dealing with samples of our generated persuasive text, some grammatical errors were noticed that are also present in the training data set. We also noticed that the context and domain of each sample is related to the base data set. Both observations highlight the importance of the quality and characteristics of the training database.

Table 2. Measurement results of the generating models per category

Category	Novelty	Diversity	Examples
Commitment	0.79	0.50	– no i need she helped her to the precinct
			– what <name> thats if you all right but its the same bullshit that theyd let at cops
			– i dont have the police taken care of a pack of it because of
Liking	0.78	0.56	– well i told you you could throw the gun in the plane lets face it you coulda
			– okay were gonna hear the glory to you later
			– your hanging in there with us because im sure that you understand our problem its got just
Consistency	0.77	0.65	– i dont think you can really see ya come out
			– [laughs] honey who called you
			– <ht02> have to do me a favor

5   Conclusions and Future Work

The aim of the present research was to examine the SentiGAN framework as an alternative solution to automatically generate messages that can be used to persuade a certain audience. We used an existing corpus of Microtext, whose data were previously processed and trained to generate 500 samples for each type of persuasion (commitment, liking, consistency), which were evaluated in terms of novelty and diversity.

The research has shown that our SentiGAN-based deployed generator can produce messages with an acceptable level of novelty. However, there is still a room to improve the diversity of our generated samples. Besides, through a non-systematic analysis, we observed some grammatical errors in our inherited microtext corpus generated messages. A natural progression of this work is to assess the intelligibility and the correct classification of persuasion. Thus, the most important limitation lies in the fact that our approach highly depends on the training dataset quality. Further work should be carried out to create new persuasive datasets that can be used by automatic generators in different domains.

Acknowledgments. This work has been supported by CONCYTEC - FONDECYT within the framework of the call E038-01 contract 014-2019. N. Condori Fernandez wish also to thank Datos 4.0 (TIN2016-78011-C4-1-R) funded by MINECO-AEI/FEDER-UE.

References

1. Bengio, S., Vinyals, O., Jaitly, N., Shazeer, N.: Scheduled sampling for sequence prediction with recurrent neural networks. In: Advances in Neural Information Processing Systems, pp. 1171–1179 (2015)
2. Cialdini, R.B., Cialdini, R.B.: Influence: The Psychology of Persuasion, vol. 55. Collins, New York (2007)
3. Ciocarlan, A., Masthoff, J., Oren, N.: Kindness is contagious: study into exploring engagement and adapting persuasive games for wellbeing. In: Proceedings of the 26th Conference on User Modeling, Adaptation and Personalization, pp. 311–319 (2018)
4. Guo, J., Lu, S., Cai, H., Zhang, W., Yu, Y., Wang, J.: Long text generation via adversarial training with leaked information. In: Thirty-Second AAAI Conference on Artificial Intelligence (2018)
5. Hoogi, A., Mishra, A., Gimenez, F., Dong, J., Rubin, D.: Natural language generation model for mammography reports simulation. IEEE J. Biomed. Health Inform. **24**(9), 2711–2717 (2020). https://doi.org/10.1109/jbhi.2020.2980118
6. Iyer, R.R., Sycara, K.: An unsupervised domain-independent framework for automated detection of persuasion tactics in text. arXiv preprint arXiv:1912.06745 (2019)
7. Lin, K., Li, D., He, X., Zhang, Z., Sun, M.T.: Adversarial ranking for language generation. In: Advances in Neural Information Processing Systems, pp. 3155–3165 (2017)
8. Mirza, M., Osindero, S.: Conditional generative adversarial nets. arXiv preprint arXiv:1411.1784 (2014)
9. Semeniuta, S., Severyn, A., Barth, E.: A hybrid convolutional variational autoencoder for text generation. In: Proceedings of the 2017 Conference on Empirical Methods in Natural Language Processing, pp. 627–637. Association for Computational Linguistics, Copenhagen, Denmark (September 2017). https://doi.org/10.18653/v1/D17-1066
10. Toshevska, M., Stojanovska, F., Zdravevski, E., Lameski, P., Gievska, S.: Explorations into deep learning text architectures for dense image captioning. In: Proceedings of the 2020 Federated Conference on Computer Science and Information Systems. IEEE (September 2020). https://doi.org/10.15439/2020f57

11. Wang, K., Wan, X.: Sentigan: generating sentimental texts via mixture adversarial networks. In: IJCAI, pp. 4446–4452 (2018)
12. Wang, K., Wan, X.: Automatic generation of sentimental texts via mixture adversarial networks. Artif. Intell. **275**, 540–558 (2019)
13. Young, J., Martell, C., Anand, P., Ortiz, P., Gilbert IV, H.T., et al.: A microtext corpus for persuasion detection in dialog. In: Workshops at the Twenty-Fifth AAAI Conference on Artificial Intelligence. Citeseer (2011)
14. Yu, L., Zhang, W., Wang, J., Yu, Y.: Seqgan: Sequence generative adversarial nets with policy gradient. In: Thirty-First AAAI Conference on Artificial Intelligence (2017)
15. Zivot, E., Wang, J.: Modeling Financial Time Series with S-PLUS® vol. 191. Springer Science & Business Media, Heidelberg (2007)

Persuasive Social Robot Using Reward Power over Repeated Instances of Persuasion

Mojgan Hashemian[1,2]([⊠]), Marta Couto[2], Samuel Mascarenhas[2], Ana Paiva[1,2], Pedro A. Santos[1,2], and Rui Prada[1,2]

[1] Instituto Superior Técnico, Lisbon, Portugal
{mojgan.hashemian,ana.s.paiva,pedro.santos,rui.prada}@tecnico.ulisboa.pt
[2] INESC-ID, Lisbon, Portugal
{marta.couto,samuel.mascarenhas}@gaips.inesc-id.pt

Abstract. This paper presents a user-study with Emys social robot that aims to persuade subjects to select a less-desirable choice. In this study, within a game scenario, Emys attempts to use its social power resources, specifically reward power, to persuade the user to select an alternative such that the user indicates less interest in it. This persuasion attempt is repeated over three times to investigate this effect within repeated persuasion instances. The study consists of three conditions: no/low/high reward. The results indicated that the higher reward does not necessarily lead to higher persuasion and the effect of social power does not decay over repeated persuasion instances.

Keywords: Persuasion · Social power · Social robot · HRI

1 Introduction

Recent advancement of technology has brought the opportunity to have robots in our everyday life. To make the interaction with such robots more natural and pleasant, a large number of researchers have been investigating different factors within Human-Robot Interaction (HRI).

Particularly, the coexistence of robots and humans provides different social situations similar to human-human interaction. For instance, the presence of social robots in daily life opens up the question if such social robots can be persuasive when conflict happens. Recently, researchers have shown an increased interest in robotic persuaders. To date, persuasive robots have been used within different applications, such as exercising [1], behavior change [2], recruiting participants [3], etc.

This work was funded by AMIGOS project (PTDC/EEISII/7174/2014), and partially supported by national funds through Fundação para a Ciência e a Tecnologia (FCT) with reference UID/50021/2021.

Previous studies have used different theories of social psychology to achieve persuasion. For instance, the Elaboration Likelihood Model (ELM) [4] in [1]. One other factor that influences the persuasion effect is social power [5]. Recent evidence suggests that social power endows persuasiveness to social robots, however, so far this effect is tested only within a single attempt [6]. It is not clear if the effect of social power on persuasion remains constant over repeated persuasion instances.

It has been reported that "at present, it may appear impossible to predict a priori how power affects persuasion." Specifically, the underlying processes between power and persuasion have not always been clear, contradicting findings have been reported. For instance, some theories assume a linear relationship between the two, while others assume a curvilinear profile. However, it has commonly been assumed that high power leads to high persuasion [5].

Based on the formalization presented in [7], we assume a direct linear relationship between social power level and the reward level. To be more specific, an increase in the level of rewards leads to higher social power. That being said, a higher valued reward leads to higher power and hence compliance. Hence, we expect that the increase in power leads to higher persuasion (H1 in Sect. 2.2). In addition, based on the model proposed in [7], considering fixed values of the parameters in each persuasion attempt, we expect that this effect remains constant over a series of repeated instances of persuasion (H2). In the next section, we discuss the design of a user-study we designed to investigate the aforementioned goal.

In sum, we aim to investigate the effect of different levels of social power on persuasion by designing a user-study with different values of reward. More importantly, this study aims to investigate the effect of social power on persuasion over a series of repeated persuasion instances.

2   Research Method

This section addresses the design we used to examine the research questions raised earlier. In general, social power stems from five different bases: reward, coercion, legitimate, referent, and expert [8]. Here, we focus only on one of the bases of power , i.e., the level of reward. To be more specific, as the power base, we selected "reward base". And as the factor of the model [7], we manipulate the value of the rewarding action (although it might have different values subjectively among different people).

2.1   Design

As mentioned earlier, we assume that the reward power has a direct linear relationship with the amount of promised reward [7]. Hence, considering a fixed value for other parameters, increasing the value of the reward increases the force of social power. Moreover, considering a proportional linear relationship between social power and persuasion, this increase in power leads to higher persuasion (to some extent before a reaction happens).

To answer the raised questions, we devised a mixed design study within a decision-making scenario, in which we manipulated the level of rewards a robot gives to participants. More specifically, we investigate the effect of repeated instances within subjects. In addition, we investigate the effect that different levels of exerted power may have between subjects. In particular, the study contains two reward values (levels) and a control condition with zero reward. In other words, in the control condition, social power is not activated. One third of the participants were assigned to each group randomly (high/low/no reward or HR/LR/0R respectively).

Specifically, in this design, the participant indicates his/her preference initially before the interaction, and later after a decision making process, the robot tries to persuade the user to change their mind and select another alternative. The participant is asked to select an option between the highest and the lowest preference. To persuade, the robot uses a reward social power strategy and the task is repeated to investigate the effect of social power on persuasion.

Thereby, we manipulated one independent variable which is the reward the participants receive. We also considered two dependent variables: 1) decisions or if the participants accepted/rejected the offer (objective measure), 2) how the participants perceive the robot (subjective measure).

2.2 Hypothesis

In this context, we expect to observe the following outcomes:

1. **H1.** Higher social power (of higher social reward) leads to higher persuasion.
2. **H2.** Over a repeated persuasions, the effect of power on persuasion does not decay, considering that the level of power is fixed.

2.3 Measure

Participants were requested to fill out a pre-questionnaire including demographics (Age, gender, Nationality, Occupation, Field of study). As we ran the experiment in English with mostly non-native English speakers, we asked the participants to rate their English proficiency on a 5-point Likert scale (1 Basic - Professional 5). Previous studies indicated different attitudes among people who interacted with robots earlier. Thus, we checked if the participants had already interacted with robots/Emys before this experiment.

Moreover, after finishing the task, we asked the participants to respond a post-questionnaire to have a better understanding of their perception. As the robot gave rewards to the participants, we measured the extent to which this endowed the robot Reward Social Power. Although we had recorded their decision makings, we asked them specifically if they changed at any iteration to make sure they understood the game, and to better understand why they made such decisions, we asked them to clearly state why they have accepted/rejected the offers. Finally, we use the Susceptibility to persuasion scale [9] to measure a relatively broad spectrum of factors leading to persuasion. We also applied the RoSAS questionnaire [10]. To further investigate the interaction of the participants within this task, we added a number of questions to the pre- and post-questionnaire (Table 1 in Appendix).

2.4   Participants

In this experiment, 90 people (39 females), aged between 18 and 79 years old (28.6 ± 16.9 and 1.6 S.E.), participated voluntarily in the response of receiving cinema tickets. The participants signed an informed consent form before participating, approved by the Ethical Committee of the University. Then we randomly assigned the subjects to the three conditions of the study and counterbalanced the data to have an equal number of females in each condition [30 people in LR (13 females), 30 people in HR (13 females), 30 people in 0R (13 females)].

3   Procedure

3.1   Task, Robot, and Environment

In the designed task, persuasion is operationalized within a fun game. The participants were asked to play a trivia game in three trials with different categories of questions. The game contains 6 categories ("Animals", "Arts", "Astronomy", "Geography", "Science", "Sport", "TV and Movie") and each category can be selected only once. Each category contains 5 questions and a correct answer to each question carries 1 point. The order of the questions in each category is the same for all participants to avoid the order effect on the responses.

To provide the incentive of the games, cinema tickets are given to the participants depending on the scores they collect. The higher the score, the more tickets they gain. Specifically, the participants could get more than one cinema ticket (up to three tickets) based on a predefined rule (the first 7 scores equal to a cinema ticket, each 8 more scores lead to another ticket). In this game, in each trial, the robot offers two of the mentioned categories and the participant selects one preferred category (without seeing the contents).

To have a better understanding of the user preferences, we ask them to define an ordering of the topics based on their interest or knowledge (after the pre-questionnaire and before starting the game). Based on this preference, the highest rated option will be offered against the lowest. We expect the participant to select his/her own highest ranked initially and then the robot tries to change his/her mind. The robot always offers an option which has not been selected by the participant.

In this task, we used the Emys robot mounted on a table in front of a touch-screen that is located between the subject and the robot (Figure 1 depicts the study setup). The study occurred in an isolated room. Each subject participated individually and during the game, the researcher stayed in the room to make sure no one cheats in the game (by searching the correct answers on the Internet). The robot mediated the game by introducing the procedure and the scoring rules. In this task, the robot was fully autonomous.

Fig. 1. Experiment Setup

4   Conclusion

In this paper, we present a user study performed to investigate the effect of different levels of social power (particularly reward social power) and repeated interactions on persuasion. We hypothesized that a higher level of social power would lead to higher persuasion, also having a fixed level of social power, this effect would not decay over time.

The result of this study did not verify the former neither subjectively nor objectively, and hence, we could not conclude if the increase in power leads to higher persuasion. This finding is similar to the results of the study reported in [11], in which the increase in ratings (that indirectly increased the level of reward) did not lead to any significant difference in decision-making of participants. Hence, we may conclude that persuasion does not have a linear relationship with the level of power exerted. This is also inline with recent research that indicated a nonlinear relationship between power and persuasion [12]. However, on the second and third trials, significantly higher persuasion was observed in the two reward conditions than 0R, meaning that the reward affects decision making (manipulation checked).

On the other hand, Ghazali et al. endorsed that exerting a strong persuasion attempt acts negatively and hence causes reactions and leads to low compliance [13]. Also, they indicated the reaction is associated with higher negative cognition and feeling of anger, which might be equivalent to a higher score of discomfort dimension of the RoSAS questionnaire. However, our results did not lead any significant differences in the score of discomfort for people who rejected more frequently compared to others (ANOVA: $F(2,89) = .411$, $p = .664$). In this case, although in HR condition the persuasion was stronger, reactance has not happened. In other words, the rejection was not due to the reaction felt.

Hence, our study verifies that power and persuasion do not have a linear relationship, however, further investigation is required to determine this nonlinear relationship. Moreover, further evidence is required to assess the reactance threshold. Apart from this, another potential reason for this insignificant finding might be the small difference between the scores in LR and HR conditions. Although we considered the higher reward to be more than half of the maximum potential achievable score (3 out of 5), participants might have valued this extra score differently than our expectations. A clear information about the state of their mind might be a clue to interpret the results.

Furthermore, the results lead to contradicting findings regarding the second hypothesis, i.e., repeated persuasion instances. Specifically, although we expected that the effect of power on persuasion remains unchanged over a repeated interaction, this hypothesis was verified only in two conditions, particularly in LR (low reward) and 0R (zero reward). In case of the latter (0R or the control condition), people tend to accept the suggestion to change decisions less frequently at the third trial. This might be very intuitive, as when they were not gaining any scores for changing, they trusted their own knowledge. Hence, using no power strategy, the robot did not have any persuasive power and people did not comply with the request.

However, unlike our expectation, in LR condition, using the same level of power, the robot gained higher persuasion at the end. Interestingly, this finding is inline with Ghazali et al. that the robot with mid-level of persuasion power was more successful than high-power or not robot. Regarding the robot perception, we did not find any significant differences in the scores of RoSAS questionnaire. One potential reason might be that in this study the difference between the dialogues in different conditions was minor and only one single strategy was used in the persuasion conditions. And additionally, the reward did not increase the likeability of the robot.

Taken together, these results suggest that using reward social power endows persuasiveness to social robots. And this effect is not fixed over repeated instances. The evidence from this study suggests that the increase in persuasion attempts by using reward social power does not lead to reaction, however, does not necessarily lead to higher compliance either. One limitation of this study is the use of the questionnaire only before and after the study. In other words, we do not have enough information about the user at each single trial. Hence, we could not measure the subjective measures (robot perception regarding persuasiveness or RoSAS).

Like any self-report measure, the primary questionnaire asking about the preference might not be a good measure of users' preferences. In fact, some people selected their less favorable choice initially and indicated in the open-ended question that they did not answer the question carefully. Hence, considering that there is a cheating incentive, we cannot make sure if they really selected their preferences carelessly or they decided to cheat. Moreover, the study is limited by the lack of information on reactance and a better measure is required.

A future study could assess the effect of different power levels to indicate the level threshold in which reactance happens. In other words, considerably more work will need to be done to determine the relationship between power level and persuasion regarding reactance.

In final words, these findings provide insights for future research that reward social power endows persuasiveness to robots. Further work needs to be done to establish whether other power bases are effective in persuasion.

5 Appendix

Table 1. Task Specific Questions

#	Pre-/post Q	Question
1	Pre-	In this specific game, if the robot promises you "a reward" in the game, to what extent do you think the robot will give the reward to you?
2	Post-	Consider this specific game, when the robot promised you "a reward" in the game, to what extent did you think the robot will give the reward to you?
3	Pre-	How much do you like trivia games and quizzes (In General)?
4	Pre-	How often do you go to the cinema?
6	Post-	How persuasive did you think EMYS was? (Not at all persuasive 1 - 5 Extremely persuasive) [Persuasion is an attempt to change somebody's opinion]
7	Post-	Emys was trying to change your mind
8	Post-	Emys could convince you to change categories
9	Post-	You felt compelled to change categories
10	Post-	Changing categories was a good idea

References

1. Winkle, K., Lemaignan, S., Caleb-Solly, P., Leonards, A., Turton, U., Bremner, P.: Effective persuasion strategies for socially assistive robots. In: 2019 14th ACM/IEEE International Conference on Human-Robot Interaction (HRI). IEEE, pp. 277–285 (2019)
2. Midden, C., Ham, J.: Using negative and positive social feedback from a robotic agent to save energy. In: Proceedings of the 4th International Conference on Persuasive Technology. ACM, p. 12 (2009)
3. Agnihotri, A., Knight, H.: Persuasive chairbots: a robot recruited experiment. In: 2019 14th ACM/IEEE International Conference on Human-Robot Interaction (HRI). IEEE, pp. 700–702 (2019)

4. Petty, R.E., Cacioppo, J.T.: The elaboration likelihood model of persuasion. In: Communication and Persuasion. Springer, New York, pp. 1–24 (1986) https://doi. org/10.1007/978-1-4612-4964-1_1
5. Briñol, P., Petty, R.E., Durso, G.R., Rucker, D.D.: Power and persuasion: processes by which perceived power can influence evaluative judgments. Rev. Gen. Psychol. **21**(3), 223 (2017)
6. Hashemian, M.: Persuasive social robots using social power dynamics. In: Proceedings of the 18th International Conference on Autonomous Agents and MultiAgent Systems. International Foundation for Autonomous Agents and Multiagent Systems, pp. 2408–2410 (2019)
7. Hashemian, M., Prada, R., Santos, P.A., Mascarenhas, S.: Enhancing social believability of virtual agents using social power dynamics. In: Proceedings of the 18th International Conference on Intelligent Virtual Agents, pp. 147–152 (2018)
8. French, J.R., Raven, B., Cartwright, D.: The bases of social power. Classics organ. theor. **7**, 311–320 (1959)
9. Modic, D., Anderson, R., Palomäki, J.: We will make you like our research: The development of a susceptibility-to-persuasion scale. PloS one **13**(3) (2018)
10. Carpinella, C.M., Wyman, A.B., Perez, M.A., Stroessner, S.J.: The robotic social attributes scale (rosas): development and validation. In: Proceedings of the 2017 ACM/IEEE International Conference on Human-robot Interaction. ACM, pp. 254–262 (2017)
11. Hashemian, M., Couto, M., Mascarenhas, S., Paiva, A., Santos, P.A., Prada, R.: Investigating reward/punishment strategies in the persuasiveness of social robots. In: Proceedings of the 29th IEEE International Conference on Robot and Human Interactive Communication (Ro-Man 2020), pp. 147–152 (2020)
12. Dubois, D., Rucker, D.D., Galinsky, A.D.: Dynamics of communicator and audience power: the persuasiveness of competence versus warmth. J. Consum. Res. **43**(1), 68–85 (2016)
13. Ghazali, A.S., Ham, J., Barakova, E.I., Markopoulos, P.: Effects of robot facial characteristics and gender in persuasive human-robot interaction. Front. Robot. AI **5**, 73 (2018)

Case Studies

Planning Habit: Daily Planning Prompts with Alexa

Andrea Cuadra$^{(\boxtimes)}$ ⓘ, Oluseye Bankole, and Michael Sobolev ⓘ

Cornell Tech, New York, NY 10044, USA
apc75@cornell.edu

Abstract. The widespread adoption of intelligent voice assistants (IVAs), like Amazon's Alexa or Google's Assistant, presents new opportunities for designers of persuasive technologies to explore how to support people's behavior change goals and habits with voice technology. In this work, we explore how to use *planning prompts*, a technique from behavior science to make specific and effective plans, with IVAs. We design and conduct usability testing ($N = 13$) on a voice app called *Planning Habit* that encourages users to formulate daily plans out loud. We identify strategies that make it possible to successfully adapt planning prompts to voice format. We then conduct a week-long online deployment ($N = 40$) of the voice app in the context of daily productivity. Overall, we find that traditional forms of planning prompts can be adapted to and enhanced by IVA technology.

1 Introduction

People encounter problems in translating their goals into action [16]—often termed the intention-behavior gap. *Planning prompts* is a technique that can help people make concrete and specific plans that they are more likely to follow-through on than larger, less achievable goals. Planning prompts have been demonstrated to be an effective, self-regulatory strategy in domains such as flu vaccination, voting, and insurance [39]. Research in behavior change and persuasive technology has began to explore the implementation of planning prompts for habit formation [33]. There is an opportunity to expand the use planning prompts to, now mainstream, IVAs.

IVAs have unique potential for persuasive design, because they can be used in an eyes- and hands-free manner and can be more intuitive to use for non-digital natives [35]. *We envision IVAs as a useful platform for transitioning planning prompts to voice format*, thereby expanding the opportunities for IVAs to support positive behavior change. However, the design of these interactions is complex [17], and thus requires careful attention and iteration. We present an exploratory study that examines how to adapt planning prompts from written to voice format (Fig. 1).

We are grateful for the support received from Deborah Estrin, Nicola Dell, and our voluntary participants. This work was supported by the National Science Foundation under Grant No. 1700832.

© Springer Nature Switzerland AG 2021
R. Ali et al. (Eds.): PERSUASIVE 2021, LNCS 12684, pp. 73–87, 2021.
https://doi.org/10.1007/978-3-030-79460-6_7

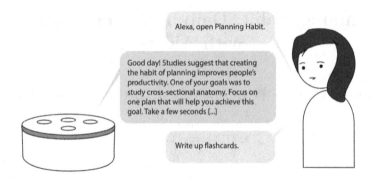

Fig. 1. Example interaction with *Planning Habit*, the Amazon Alexa skill, or voice app, created for this study. A user asks Alexa to open the *Planning Habit* skill. Alexa responds by stating the user's goal and instructing the participant to focus on one plan that will help her achieve that goal.

We make two contributions to research on persuasive technology and behavior change systems. First, we present finding from a research through design approach [49] for adapting planning prompts to IVA interactions. We design a voice app called *Planning Habit* that encourages users to formulate daily plans out loud. The design process surfaced common and generalizable challenges and allowed use to develop strategies to overcome these challenges. Second, we provide evidence for the use of IVAs to elicit spoken planning prompts from our quantitative and qualitative findings from a week-long feasibility study deployed via Amazon Mechanical Turk (mTurk), $N = 40$. These contributions are a unique result of the mixed methods employed: iterative design, in-the-wild deployment, and qualitative and quantitative analysis, and will be useful for researchers interested in designing IVA in behavior change systems and persuasive technologies.

2   Related Work

IVAs are voice-based software agents that can perform tasks upon request—they use natural language processing to derive intent from requests made by their users, and respond to those requests using speech and/or another modality (e.g., graphical output) [42]. We focused on the intersections of IVAs and behavior change which is currently nascent. We discuss existing work surrounding IVAs for behavior change and planning prompts research in context of persuasive and behavior change technology.

2.1   IVAs

Multiple lines of research recognize the potential of IVAs, and new research is emerging in many areas. One line of work focuses on technical advances, including distant speech recognition [21], human-sounding text-to-speech [24], and question answering, natural language inference, sentiment analysis, and document ranking [11,46]. Another line of work focuses on risks IVAs may introduce, including privacy concerns [8,22], vulnerabilities to attackers [8,28,48], inconsistent and incomplete answers to simple questions about mental health [27], and possible pitfalls that may occur in medical settings, such as misrecognition of medical names, or unexpected input [4]. A third line of research looks at IVAs at a more meta-level, characterizing current use and impact by analyzing usage logs [3], identifying trends from product reviews [30,36], or comparing different commercial IVAs [25,27,37]. Researchers have also examined the social role of IVAs [6,7,36], their conversational (or not) nature [2,9], their ability to help young children read and learn [45], and their promise as a tool to encourage self-disclosure [23,47].

Work at the intersections of IVAs and behavior change is more nascent. One example is "FitChat", which was developed by Wiratunga, et al. to encourage physical activity among older adults [44]. This study found that voice is a powerful mode of delivering effective digital behavior change interventions, which may increase adherence to physical activity regimes and provide motivation for trying new activities [44]. Sezgin et al. provide a scoping review of patient-facing, behavioral health interventions with voice assistant technologies that target self-management and healthy lifestyle behaviors [41]. However, this scoping review also includes many research papers using interactive voice response (IVR) systems [41], which are different from IVAs (we consider IVR systems to be the less-capable, usually telephone-based predecessors to IVAs). The study found that voice assistant technology was generally used to either: a) deliver education or counseling/skills, or b) monitor/track self-reported behaviors. It also found that research-adapted voice assistants, in contrast to standalone commercially available voice assistants, performed better regarding feasibility, usability, and preliminary efficacy, along with high user satisfaction, suggesting a role for voice assistants in behavioral health intervention research [41]. Our research explores a new perspective to the literature on IVAs and behavior change by examining how to adapt planning prompts, a behavior science technique, from written to voice format.

2.2   Planning Prompts

Planning prompts are a simple and effective behavioral technique to translate their goals into action [39]. Gollwitzer famously argued that simple plans can have a strong effect on goal achievement [16]. Planning prompts are subordinate to goals and specify "when, where and how" goals might be achieved while goals themselves specify "what" needs to be achieved [16]. Plans can be considered planning prompts if they contain specific details as described above. In a recent review, planning prompts were argued to be simple, inexpensive, and powerful nudges that help people do what they intend to get done [39]. Prior research has explored integrating implementation intentions into mobile devices by using contextual triggers and reinforcement was explored as a mechanism for habit formation [34,43]. In the context of digital well-being, the Socialize Android app [38] was developed with user-specified implementation intentions to replace undesired phone usage with other desired activities or goals. The process of generating action plans can be partly or completely automated, as exemplified by TaskGenies [20]. In the context of physical activity, DayActivizer [12] is a mobile app that tries to encourage physical activity by generating plans from contextual activity data. Contextual factors such as previous activity, location and time can help generate better plans for individuals [32]. A recent review of digital behavior change also highlighted the potential of implementation intentions for habit formation [33]. Because of the potential that IVAs may have to encourage behavior change, it is imperative that more research is conducted in this topic.

3   Design Process

In this work, we employ a research through design approach [13,18,49] to explore how the behavioral science technique of using planning prompts might be adapted from written to spoken format. Our design goal was to create a voice app or *skill* (Amazon's terminology for apps that run on their Alexa platform) that elicits spoken-out-loud planning prompts (see Fig. 1). We relied on evidence-based techniques from behavioral science paired with an iterative design process to make this technology engaging and persuasive. We now describe the three stages of our design process: our initial design, usability testing, and the final design.

3.1   Stage I: Initial Design

Our initial design is grounded in previous research on planning prompts for behavior change and habit formation [16,39] and persuasive and behavior change technologies [10,14]. Drawing on insights from this research, we formulated the following initial guidelines to ground our first prototype before evaluating it via user testing:

1. **Behavior science suggests that planning prompts will work aloud:** A *planning prompt's* purpose is to nudge people to think through how and when they will follow through with their plans [16,39]. Although the literature about planning prompts predominantly uses examples about written prompts [16,39], voice planning prompts may fulfill the same purpose. Thus, we formulated our first assumption—that planning prompts will also be effective at fulfilling the same purpose if they are spoken aloud.
2. **HCI research tells us users will need the voice app to allow them to interact with their plans:** Consolvo et al. in her guidelines for behavior change technology highlight the need for technology to be controllable [10]. In natural settings, people have the ability to revisit, revise, and "check-off" our plans, especially when written down. Thus, we planned for our digital skill to mimic those affordances by allowing users to interact with their plans.

We relied on these guidelines to inform our initial design. When a user opened the voice app, it asked the user whether or not she had completed the previous plan. If affirmative, the voice app gave the user the option to make a new plan. Otherwise, the user was given the opportunity to keep the previous plan.

Implementation. We built the voice app using Amazon Alexa, because of its popularity and robust developer ecosystem. We used Alexa Skills Kit (ASK), which is a compilation of open sourced Alexa application programming interfaces and tools to develop voice apps. We stored usage data in an external database.

3.2   Stage II: Usability Testing

Our initial research plan incorporated the Rapid Iterative Testing and Evaluation method (RITE method) [26] to ensure that our skill was easy to use. The RITE method is similar to traditional usability testing, but it advocates that changes to the user interface are made as soon as a problem is identified and a solution is clear [26]. We conducted usability tests (N = 13) with university students. At the beginning tests were performed in a lab setting (N = 10). Subsequently, usability testing was conducted in participant's apartments (N = 3).

For initial usability testing, participants were asked to create plans over a period of three simulated days, and then tell us about their experience using the skill. Each usability test lasted about 15 min. We spread out the usability tests over two weeks to allow for time to make design adjustments based on findings from these sessions. This testing exposed major challenges with the technology's transcription accuracy:

1. **The name of the skill was frequently misheard:** the name of the skill was originally "Planify." In usability tests, we found that Alexa did not recognize the invocation phrase, "open Plan-ify", when the participant did not have an American accent. Instead, it would frequently suggest opening other skills with the word "planet".
2. **The plans were incorrectly transcribed:** plans often had specific keywords that were misrecognized. For example, "*NSF proposal*" was transcribed to "NBA proposal," completely changing the meaning of the plan. This created confusion in two parts of our skill design: 1) when the IVA repeated the previous day's plan to the user, and 2) when the IVA confirmed the new plan.

We redesigned the skill to work around these challenges. We renamed the skill "Planning Habit," which was easier to consistently transcribe across accents. We also redesigned the skill so that it would not have to restate (nor understand) the plan after the participant said it, which was counter HCI guidelines surrounding giving visibility of the system's status and control [10, 29]. This was a deliberate effort needed to overcome limitations inherent to current language recognition technologies. The resulting interaction only had three steps: 1) request a plan, 2) listen to plan, and 3) end session by requesting the participant to check-in again the next day.

Once usability errors in the lab setting became rare, we conducted usability testing in participants' own homes to: 1) test that the Amazon Alexa skill we had developed worked over an extended period of time in participants' homes, and 2) test the back-end tracking of participants' daily interactions with *Planning Habit*. The data stored included the transcripts of the voice snippets of plans, the timestamps of each interaction, and the associated user identification (ID) number. This data helped us understand how each participant was interacting with the skills, and probe deeper when interviewing them about their experience later on. We recruited university student participants who already owned Amazon Alexa devices, were willing to install the skill, use it every day for at least a week, and participate in a 30-min interview at the end of the study. We did not offer compensation. We gave participants minimal instructions—to say, "Alexa, open Planning Habit," and then make a plan that would help them be more productive every day. For each interview two researchers were present, one asked questions and the other took notes. We asked participants to tell us about their experience, to describe the sorts of plans they made, how (if at all) the skill had affected them, what worked well, and what worked poorly. After each question, we dove deeper by asking for more details. For example, if a participant mentioned they stopped using the skill, we would ask why. For this part of the study, all participants used an Alexa smart speaker.

During the at-home testing phase, we saw glimpses of both how the Planning Habit tool might benefit participants along with further limitations of the tool. The benefits included:

- **Accountability.** One participant said that the skill affected him, because *"when [he] said [he] would do it, then [he] would."*
- **Help with prioritization.** Participants surfaced the skill's role in helping them prioritize, *"it's a good thing to put into your morning routine, if you can follow along with it it's a good way to plan your day better and think about what you have to prioritize."*
- **Ease of use.** Participants commented on the ease, *"it's easy to incite an Alexa, and easy to complete the [planning] task."*
- **Spoken format leading to more complete thoughts.** One participant said, *"it sounds weird when you say these things aloud, in that it feels like a more complete thought by being a complete sentence, as opposed to random tidbits of things."*

The limitations included:

- **Difficulty remembering the command and making effective plans.** Participants commented that it was difficult to remember the command to make the plans, and suggested that *"it would be useful to remind people of the command on every communication."*
- **Making effective plans.** Participants indicated that they did not have enough guidance about how to make their plans, or what sorts of plans to make. This need corresponds to previous research in behavioral science that highlights the need for training to use planning prompts effectively [33].

- **Error proneness.** Participants commented on the skill being *"very error prone."* Many of these errors had to do with Alexa abruptly quitting the skill for unknown reasons, or because the user paused to think mid-plan. Alexa comes configured to listen for at most eight seconds of silence, and Amazon does not give developers the ability to directly change that configuration. A participant stated, *"a couple of times I was still talking when it closed its listening period, and that made me think that 'huh, maybe Alexa is not listening to me right now.'"* Formulating planning prompts on the spot can require additional time to consider possible options, and make a decision about which one to pick.
- **Limited meaningfulness.** One participant indicated that he did not observe any meaningful improvement in how easy his life felt after having used the skill saying, *"I don't think it made my life any easier or anything of that nature."* Furthermore, many of the plans made, as judged by authors with behavior science expertise, were not likely to be effective. This suggests that participants were also not experiencing the benefits of getting closer to attaining a goal.

We explain how we addressed these issues in Sect. 3.3.

3.3 Stage III: Final Design

Based on the findings from the testing stage we restructured the skill to follow a structure that would provide more guidance and more motivation, and avoid transcription errors. We structured the conversation using the following components:

1. A **greeting** to create a personable start.
2. A **rationale** to increase motivation and understanding.
3. The **participant's goal** to establish grounding for making plans related to a goal the participant wants to attain, and thus to improve ability and motivation. We asked participants to type three work-related goals in an on-boarding questionnaire. We then personalized each participant's experience by copy-pasting their responses to the voice app's script.
4. A **planning tip** to improve ability to create effective plans.
5. **Thinking time** to allot extra time to formulate a plan.
6. A **goodbye tip** to improve ability to follow-through with their plans.

Additionally, we asked participants to include the daily command in their reminder, in order to reduce difficulty remembering the command. Each participant was instructed tell their Alexa device, "Alexa, set a daily reminder to open Planning Habit at [time in the morning]." We also added "thinking time", by playing background music for 14 seconds (with the option to ask for more when they expired) to give users extra time to think about their plans. By adding the music we were able to set clear expectations for the interaction, and avoid having Alexa quit before the user was ready to say their plan.

The final design had fewer steps than the original one, and included guidance after the plan is made. We selected a combination of different options for each component of the formula (i.e., greeting, rationale, participant's goal, planning tip, thinking time, and goodbye tip), and rotated them each day of the study.

4   Feasibility Study

We conducted a feasibility study on MTurk to explore the effects of Planning Habit with participants in more natural setting. To do so, we built on the work of Okeke et al., who previously used a similar approach deploying interventions to MTurk participants' existing devices [31]. Our goals were to understand what sorts of plans people would make, engagement with the voice app, and their opinions surrounding satisfaction, planning behavior improvement, and overall strengths and weaknesses of the voice app.

4.1   Method

We deployed the voice app for a period of one week with 40 mTurk participants. We asked participants to complete an on-boarding questionnaire, and instructed participants to install the skill and set daily reminders. Then, we asked participants to make a plan using the skill every day for six days. Last, we asked participants to fill out a post-completion questionnaire of the skill at the end of study. All study procedures were exempted from review by Cornell University's Institutional Review Board under Protocol 1902008577.

Participants and Procedure. A total of $N = 40$ participants (18F, 22M) passed all the checks we put in place. These checks included trick questions, submission of a screenshot of the daily reminder set on an Alexa device, a skill installation ID number, and back-end verification of usage logs. All participants indicated they interacted with Alexa (broadly, not specifically with *Planning Habit*) at least once a week, and most said they used it daily ($N = 25$). Most participants indicated they owned multiple Alexa devices ($N = 22$).

Participants were instructed to go to the Alexa skill store and install "Planning Habit". Then, they had to open the skill on their device, and enter the ID number that the app gave them into a questionnaire. Then, they were asked a series of demographic, and Alexa-usage questions. Next, they had to write three work-related goals (which were then incorporated into each participant's personalized voice app). Finally, participants were asked to set a reminder, and upload screenshot as evidence.

Participants were compensated $5 for completing the on-boarding questionnaire and installing the skill, and given a $10 bonus for interacting with the skill throughout the week and completing the final questionnaire. All $N = 40$ participants who successfully installed the skill and completed the on-boarding questionnaire received $5. Only 22 participants were eligible to receive full participation bonus of $10 at the end of the study. A few participants ($N = 2$) that demonstrated reasonable engagement, but did not fulfill all the requirements, received a reduced bonus of $5.

Measures and Evaluation. We evaluated the feasibility of adapting planning prompts from written to voice format by qualitatively analyzing usage data alongside responses from the post-completion subjective evaluations. For usage data, we measured the number of times each participant made a plan using *Planning Habit*, and searched for patterns or interesting insights in the plans they created. For subjective evaluation, we asked participants about their satisfaction with the voice app, self-perception of improvement in planning ability, and likeliness to continue using the skill or recommend to it to others.

4.2   Quantitative Findings

Most Participants Made at Least 3 Plans Throughout the Duration of the Study. Engagement results are based on the participants that successfully completed the on-boarding questionnaire and skill installation ($N = 40$). The metadata revealed that more than a third of the participants ($N = 14$) demonstrated 100% engagement, completing 6/6 plans.[1] Several participants ($N = 11$) made between 3 and 5 plans in total. A few participants ($N = 4$) made between 1 and 2 plans. The rest of the participants ($N = 11$) never made any plans.

For the rest of the sections, we report findings based on only the participants ($N = 22$) that interacted with the skill at least 3 days during the intervention, and completed the final questionnaire. We excluded responses from participants that did not complete more than 2 plans, as this level of usage does not constitute sufficient engagement with the skill to provide a genuine assessment. The discarded responses were extremely positive and vague. We ended up with a total of 129 plans for analysis after discarding plans from participants that did not sufficiently engage with the voice app.

Most Participants Were Somewhat or Extremely Satisfied with the Skill. Most (77%) reported that they were somewhat or extremely satisfied, some participants (18%) felt neutral, and a few (5%) reported dissatisfaction with the skill. Furthermore, when asked whether they would recommend the skill to others, most participants (59%) indicated they were at least somewhat likely to recommend to a close family member or friend. In addition, some participants (32%) said they would continue using the skill and only a few (14%) said they would not; the remaining participants (54%) were unsure.

Most Participants Indicated the Skill Helped Them Become Better Planners. Most participants (59%) indicated the skill helped them become better planners overall, suggesting that *Planning Habit* may be a feasible way to improve people's ability to make effective plans.

4.3   Qualitative Findings

We analyzed our qualitative data (the plans participants made throughout the deployment, and the open-ended questionnaire responses) by organizing the data

---

[1] There are 6 total plans, and not 7, because the first day of the week-long study was reserved for installation of the skill.

based on observed plan components, and comments surrounding satisfaction. The authors individually categorized the data, and met to discuss and reconcile differences.

1. Participants' Plans Incorporated the Tips for Effective Planning We Provided via Our Voice App. They did so by:

- **Indicating a location, a time, or a way of completing their plan.** For example, this plan mentions locations and a time, *"planet [sic] taking my kids to school and then going to the gym."*[2] The locations include school, and the gym. The time is relative, after taking the kids to school. Another participant made a plan to *"analyze at least five different distributions,"* in which the participant specified specific details (five different distributions) about a way to complete the plan. Per our categorization of the plans, 75% indicated a location, a time, or a way of completing their plan, 16% did not, and 9% were too ambiguous for us to categorize.
- **Participants made plans centered around their bigger goals.** A participant whose goal was to *"do more daily ed activities with [her] daughter"* made a plan to *"take [her] daughter to story time at [their] local library,"* a daily ed activity. We counted the number of plans that related to the participant's goals, and we found that 59% related to the goals, 11% did not relate to the goals, and 30% of plans were too ambiguous for us to determine whether they related to a goal or not.
- **Thinking about the things in the way of their goals, and how to overcome those obstacles.** On of the Planning Tips we provided said, "Take a moment to think about the things in the way of your goal. What's a single task that will help you overcome one of these?" One participated reacted to the tip to think about an obstacle by uttering the obstacle, *"[first] of all I don't have any money to renovate that trailer."* Another made a plan and provided an explanation of how his plan would help him overcome a scheduling obstacle, *"book a meeting for 4:30 so I can get out a little bit earlier today and go me[et] the client".* Our counts revealed that 19% of the plans mentioned an obstacle of some kind, 73% did not, and 8% were too ambiguous for us to categorize.

2. Participants Valued the Voice App's Guidance, but Wanted to Track Their Plans. Participants found the guidance from the skill to be valuable, and frequently mentioned that using the skill helped them think about their daily priorities and plan accordingly. Many responses echoed these sentiments, e.g., *"it was a good skill to get you to stop and think and plan out actions,"* or *"it was helpful to know what my priority was for the day."* However, participants

---

[2] In this plan, we may also observe the type of transcription inaccuracies that were surfaced earlier in the study—the word "plan" plus some other utterance was transcribed to "planet". In this part of the study, the transcriptions were available to us in the back-end, but not surfaced to the user via the voice app.

continued to express the need to track plan completion. Some participants indicated feeling limited by the lack of follow-through. For example, one participant said, *"I like the idea of starting the day with a plan but it almost feels like an empty gesture with no consequences or follow-up."* This constraint could potentially be solved if the skill was able to accurately transcribe people's plans and remind them what they said, but as described in Sect. 3.2, the inaccuracy of transcription hampered our ability to implement such tracking.

5   Discussion

We demonstrate the feasibility of adapting the behavioral technique of planning prompts from text to voice. Our planning prompt voice app proved to be easy-to-use and effective, which serves to validate the initial development work we did. Together, the incorporation of our tips in participants' plans, the relatively high levels of engagement with the voice app and satisfaction, and participants' perceived improvement in planning behavior, suggest that traditional forms of planning prompts can be adapted to and enhanced by IVA technology.

We encountered several challenges with the state-of-the-art of voice technologies that will be mitigated as the technology continues to improve. Many speech recognition milestones—such being able to recognize different voices, speech at different speeds, from different locations in a room—had to be achieved to let us interact with IVAs the way we do today [15]. There are many efforts to continue improving these technologies. For example, Mozilla's Common Voice dataset is part of an effort to bridge the digital speech divide, allowing people all over the world to contribute to it and to download the dataset to train speech-enabled applications [1]. Doing so will allow the technology to become better at recognizing more people's speech, a problem we encountered during our initial usability sessions, as described in Sect. 3.2. In addition, the state of speech recognition available to us limited the interactions we could build (e.g., checking-off plans). However, speech recognition technology is actively improving [19,40], meaning these challenges will eventually disappear. Currently, the technological constraints we encountered may hinder engagement, so it is important to continue considering features such as plan-tracking as the technology's ability to understand speech improves.

The promise of voice technology extends beyond speech recognition improvements. For example, understanding specific contexts for generating guidance can generate immense value. When guiding users to create effective planning prompts, it is important not to only transcribe the speech, but also understand the content in the plan (e.g., the plan's associated goal, when and where the plan is scheduled to happen, etc.), and to appropriately schedule the timing of the reminder. Using automation to understand the content in a plan could help generate personalized guidance to maximize a person's ability to create effective planning prompts. Furthermore, Cha et al. are generating research surrounding opportune moments for proactive interactions with IVAs, and identifying contextual factors, such as resource conflicts or user mobility, that may play an important role in interactions initiated by IVAs [5]. Such advancements could mean that we could design reminders to happen not just at a set time, but at opportune moments.

5.1 Limitations and Future Research

The exploratory nature of the study comes with its limitations. When we interacted with participants in person during our design process, we were able to understand nuances of the interactions in depth. Doing so allowed us to evolve the design of the voice app to the one we used for the feasibility study. However, during the feasibility study, we collected data automatically via questionnaires and usage logs, and did not have the opportunity to ask participants questions in real-time. By studying the voice app in a less-controlled setting, we were able to observe that many participants were highly engaged and found the voice app helpful. However, a hands-off deployment can introduce bias when subjectively classifying the plans participants made, because researchers cannot confirm their judgments with study participants. In our case, the inability to consult with participants during the feasibility study also added noise to our data, since we had to classify many plans as "other" due to ambiguity, or missing information. Finally, due to its exploratory nature, a long-term evaluation was outside of scope. Despite the limitations of this work, our design process and feasibility study allowed us to create a detailed picture of participants' experience using the our voice app, and generate valuable contributions.

6   Conclusion

This paper contributes a design exploration of implementing planning prompts, a concept for making effective plans from behavior science, using IVAs. We found that traditional forms of planning prompts can be adapted to and enhanced by IVA technology. We surfaced affordances and challenges specific to IVAs for this purpose. Finally, we validated the promise of our final design through an online feasibility study. Our contributions will be useful for improving the state-of-the-art of digital tools for planning, and provide insights for others interested in adapting insights and techniques from behavior science to interactions with IVAs.

References

1. Common voice by mozilla. https://voice.mozilla.org/en/datasets. Accessed 03 Mar 2020
2. Beneteau, E., Richards, O.K., Zhang, M., Kientz, J.A., Yip, J., Hiniker, A.: Communication breakdowns between families and alexa. In: Proceedings of the 2019 CHI Conference on Human Factors in Computing Systems, pp. 1–13 (2019)

3. Bentley, F., Luvogt, C., Silverman, M., Wirasinghe, R., White, B., Lottridge, D.: Understanding the long-term use of smart speaker assistants. In: Proceedings of the ACM on Interactive, Mobile, Wearable and Ubiquitous Technologies, vol. 2, no. 3, pp. 1–24 (2018)
4. Bickmore, T., Trinh, H., Asadi, R., Olafsson, S.: Safety first: conversational agents for health care. In: Moore, R.J., Szymanski, M.H., Arar, R., Ren, G.-J. (eds.) Studies in Conversational UX Design. HIS, pp. 33–57. Springer, Cham (2018). https://doi.org/10.1007/978-3-319-95579-7_3
5. Cha, N., et al.: Hello there! is now a good time to talk?: Opportune moments for proactive interactions with smart speakers
6. Cha, Y., Hong, Y., Jang, J., Yi, M.Y.: Jack-of-all-trades: A thematic analysis of conversational agents in multi-device collaboration contexts. In: Conference on Human Factors in Computing Systems - Proceedings, pp. 1–6 (2019)
7. Chin, H., Yi, M.Y.: Should an agent be ignoring it? A study of verbal abuse types and conversational agents' response styles. In: Conference on Human Factors in Computing Systems - Proceedings 1–6 (2019)
8. Chung, H., Iorga, M., Voas, J., Lee, S.: Alexa, can i trust you? Computer **50**(9), 100–104 (2017)
9. Clark, L., et al.: What makes a good conversation? Challenges in designing truly conversational agents. In: Conference on Human Factors in Computing Systems - Proceedings, pp. 1–12 (2019)
10. Consolvo, S., McDonald, D.W., Landay, J.A.: Theory-driven design strategies for technologies that support behavior change in everyday life. In: Proceedings of the SIGCHI Conference on Human Factors in Computing Systems (New York, NY, USA, 2009), CHI 2009, pp. 405–414. ACM, Boston (2009)
11. Devlin, J., Chang, M., Lee, K., Toutanova, K.: BERT: pre-training of deep bidirectional transformers for language understanding. CoRR abs/1810.04805 (2018)
12. Dogangün, A., Schwarz, M., Kloppenborg, K., Le, R.: An approach to improve physical activity by generating individual implementation intentions. In: Adjunct Publication of the 25th Conference on User Modeling, Adaptation and Personalization (New York, NY, USA, 2017), UMAP 2017, pp. 370–375 ACM (2017)
13. Easterday, M.W., Rees Lewis, D.G., Gerber, E.M.: The logic of design research. Learn.: Res. Practice **4**(2), 131–160 (2018)
14. Fogg, B.J.: Persuasive Technology: Using Computers to Change What We Think and Do. Ubiquity 2002, December 2002
15. Gold, B., Morgan, N., Ellis, D.: Speech and Audio Signal Processing: Processing and Perception of Speech and Music. Wiley, Hoboken (2011)
16. Gollwitzer, P.M.: Implementation intentions: strong effects of simple plans. Am. Psychol. **54**(7), 493–503 (1999)
17. Guzman, A.L.: Voices in and of the machine: source orientation toward mobile virtual assistants. Comput. Hum. Behav. **90**, 343–350 (2019)
18. Hiniker, A., Hong, S.R., Kohno, T., Kientz, J.A.: Mytime: designing and evaluating an intervention for smartphone non-use. In: Proceedings of the 2016 CHI Conference on Human Factors in Computing Systems (New York, NY, USA, 2016), CHI 2016, ACM, pp. 4746–4757 (2016)
19. Jia, Y., et al.: Leveraging weakly supervised data to improve end-to-end speech-to-text translation. In: ICASSP 2019–2019 IEEE International Conference on Acoustics, Speech and Signal Processing (ICASSP), IEEE, pp. 7180–7184 (2019)
20. Kokkalis, N., Köhn, T., Huebner, J., Lee, M., Schulze, F., Klemmer, S.R.: Taskgenies: automatically providing action plans helps people complete tasks. ACM Trans. Comput.-Hum. Interact. **20**(5), 27:1–27:25 (2013)

21. Kumatani, K., McDonough, J., Raj, B.: Microphone array processing for distant speech recognition: from close-talking microphones to far-field sensors. IEEE Sig. Process. Mag. **29**(6), 127–140 (2012)
22. Lau, J., Zimmerman, B., and Schaub, F.: Alexa, are you listening? Privacy perceptions, concerns and privacy-seeking behaviors with smart speakers. In: Proceedings of the ACM on Human-Computer Interaction 2, CSCW, pp. 1–31 (2018)
23. Lee, Y.-C., Yamashita, N., Huang, Y., Fu, W.: "i hear you, i feel you": encouraging deep self-disclosure through a chatbot. In: Proceedings of the 2020 CHI Conference on Human Factors in Computing Systems, pp. pp. 1–12 (2020)
24. Li, N., Liu, S., Liu, Y., Zhao, S., Liu, M., Zhou, M.: Close to human quality TTS with transformer. CoRR abs/1809.08895 (2018)
25. López, G., Quesada, L., Guerrero, L.A.: Alexa vs. siri vs. cortana vs. Google assistant: a comparison of speech-based natural user interfaces. In: Nunes, I. (eds.) International Conference on Applied Human Factors and Ergonomics, pp. 241–250. Springer, Heidelberg (2017). https://doi.org/10.1007/978-3-319-60366-7_23
26. Medlock, M.C., Wixon, D., Terrano, M., Romero, R., Fulton, B.: Using the rite method to improve products: a definition and a case study. Usability Professionals Association (2002)
27. Miner, A., Milstein, A., Schueller, S.: Smartphone-based conversational agents and responses to questions about mental health, interpersonal violence, and physical health. JAMA Intern. Med. **176**(5), 719–719 (2016)
28. Mitev, R., Miettinen, M., Sadeghi, A.-R.: Alexa lied to me: skill-based man-in-the-middle attacks on virtual assistants. In: Proceedings of the 2019 ACM Asia Conference on Computer and Communications Security, pp. 465–478 (2019)
29. Nielsen, J.: Ten usability heuristics (2005)
30. O'Brien, K., Liggett, A., Ramirez-Zohfeld, V., Sunkara, P., Lindquist, L.A.: Voice-controlled intelligent personal assistants to support aging in place. J. Am. Geriatr. Soc. **68**(1), 176–179 (2020)
31. Okeke, F., Sobolev, M., Dell, N., Estrin, D.: Good vibrations: can a digital nudge reduce digital overload? In: Proceedings of the 20th International Conference on Human-Computer Interaction with Mobile Devices and Services (New York, NY, USA, 2018), MobileHCI 2018, pp. 4:1–4:12. ACM, Barcelona, Spain
32. Paruthi, G., Raj, S., Colabianchi, N., Klasnja, P., Newman, M.W.: Finding the sweet spot(s): understanding context to support physical activity plans. In: Proceedings of ACM Interaction Mobile Wearable Ubiquitous Technology, vol. 2, no. 1, pp. 29:1–29:17 (2018)
33. Pinder, C., Vermeulen, J., Cowan, B.R., Beale, R.: Digital behaviour change interventions to break and form habits. ACM Trans. Comput.-Hum. Interact. **25**(3), , 15:1–15:66 (2018)
34. Pinder, C., Vermeulen, J., Wicaksono, A., Beale, R., Hendley, R.J.: If this, then habit: Exploring context-aware implementation intentions on smartphones. In: Proceedings of the 18th International Conference on Human-Computer Interaction with Mobile Devices and Services Adjunct (New York, NY, USA, 2016), MobileHCI 2016, pp. 690–697. ACM (2016)
35. Pradhan, A., Mehta, K., Findlater, L.: "Accessibility came by accident" use of voice-controlled intelligent personal assistants by people with disabilities. In: Proceedings of the 2018 CHI Conference on Human Factors in Computing Systems, pp. 1–13 (2018)
36. Purington, A., Taft, J.G., Sannon, S., Bazarova, N.N., Taylor, S.H.: "Alexa is my new bff" social roles, user satisfaction, and personification of the Amazon echo. In:

Proceedings of the 2017 CHI Conference Extended Abstracts on Human Factors in Computing Systems, pp. 2853–2859 (2017)

37. Reis, A., et al.: Using intelligent personal assistants to assist the elderlies an evaluation of Amazon Alexa, Google Assistant, Microsoft Cortana, and Apple Siri. In: 2018 2nd International Conference on Technology and Innovation in Sports, Health and Wellbeing (TISHW), pp. 1–5. IEEE (2018)

38. Roffarello, A.M., De Russis, L.: Towards detecting and mitigating smartphone habits. In: Adjunct Proceedings of the 2019 ACM International Joint Conference on Pervasive and Ubiquitous Computing and Proceedings of the 2019 ACM International Symposium on Wearable Computers (New York, NY, USA, 2019), UbiComp/ISWC 2019 Adjunct, pp. 149–152. ACM (2019)

39. Rogers, T., Milkman, K.L., John, L.K., Norton, M.I.: Beyond good intentions: prompting people to make plans improves follow-through on important tasks. Behav. Sci. Policy **1**(2), 33–41 (2015)

40. Sarı, L., Thomas, S., Hasegawa-Johnson, M.: Training spoken language understanding systems with non-parallel speech and text. In: ICASSP 2020–2020 IEEE International Conference on Acoustics, Speech and Signal Processing (ICASSP), pp. 8109–8113. IEEE (2020)

41. Sezgin, E., Militello, L., Huang, Y., Lin, S.: A scoping review of patient-facing, behavioral health interventions with voice assistant technology targeting self-management and healthy lifestyle behaviors. Behavioral Health Interventions with Voice Assistant Technology Targeting Self-management and Healthy Lifestyle Behaviors, 1 April 2019 (2019)

42. Shum, H.-Y., He, X.-D., Li, D.: From Eliza to XiaoIce: challenges and opportunities with social chatbots. Front. Inf. Technol. Electron. Eng. **19**(1), 10–26 (2018)

43. Wicaksono, A., Hendley, R.J., Beale, R.: Using reinforced implementation intentions to support habit formation. In: Extended Abstracts of the 2019 CHI Conference on Human Factors in Computing Systems (New York, NY, USA, 2019), CHI EA 2019, pp. LBW2518:1–LBW2518:6. ACM (2019)

44. Wiratunga, N., Wijekoon, A., Palihawadana, C., Cooper, K., Mendham, V.: Fitchat: conversational AI for active ageing

45. Xu, Y., Warschauer, M.: Young children's reading and learning with conversational agents. In: Conference on Human Factors in Computing Systems - Proceedings, pp. 1–8 (2019)

46. Yang, Z., Dai, Z., Yang, Y., Carbonell, J., Salakhutdinov, R.R., Le, Q.V.: Xlnet: generalized autoregressive pretraining for language understanding. In: Advances in Neural Information Processing Systems, pp. 5753–5763 (2019)

47. Yu, Q., Nguyen, T., Prakkamakul, S., Salehi, N.: I almost fell in love with a machine: speaking with computers Affects Self-disclosure. In: Conference on Human Factors in Computing Systems - Proceedings, pp. 1–6 (2019)

48. Zhou, M., Qin, Z., Lin, X., Hu, S., Wang, Q., Ren, K.: Hidden voice commands: attacks and defenses on the VCS of autonomous driving cars. IEEE Wirel. Commun. **26**(5), 128–133 (2019)

49. Zimmerman, J., Forlizzi, J., Evenson, S.: Research through design as a method for interaction design research in HCI. In: Proceedings of the SIGCHI Conference on Human Factors in Computing Systems, pp. 493–502 (2007)

Emotional Feedback to Mitigate Aggressive Driving: A Real-World Driving Study

Monique Dittrich[1]([✉]) and Nils Mathew[2]

[1] University of Würzburg, 97070 Würzburg, Germany
dittrich.monique@web.de

[2] Chemnitz University of Technology, 09111 Chemnitz, Germany

Abstract. Without doubt, aggressive driving is a serious hazard on our roads. The problem with common measures against aggressive driving (e.g., speeding cameras) is that they *force* drivers to change their behavior, which can make them feel even more aggressive and lead to reactance. As an alternative solution that *persuades* people to drive less aggressively, the *Driving Feedback Avatar* (DFA) was developed. The DFA is an in-car interface that provides visual feedback on a driver's behavior with a focus on aggressive driving. Summative feedback is represented by an avatar that gradually changes its emotional state depending on the behavior. Instant feedback is given in the form of a flashing light directly after the aggressive action occurred. The paper presents a driving study that investigated the effectiveness of the DFA in real traffic. In a within-subjects design, 32 participants completed a test drive with and without a prototype of the system while their driving behavior was logged. Based on the logs, nine behaviors that were considered indicators of aggressive driving were compared within both conditions. Although participants did not drive significantly less aggressively under the system's influence, it is remarkable that they generally showed less discrete aggressive driving behaviors (e.g., use of indicators) but—contrary to expectations—more continuous ones (e.g., speeding). The paper concludes with directions for future iterations of the DFA.

Keywords: Aggressive driving · Behavior change · Feedback · Avatar

1 Introduction

In 2019, 355,084 traffic accidents with personal injury were registered in Germany. Most of these accidents can be attributed to driving behaviors that are considered aggressive, such as inappropriate speed, insufficient distance, overtaking mistakes, or improper behavior towards pedestrians [1]. But not only the victims of aggressive driving have to face physical and mental consequences, also the aggressive driver himself suffers from his aggressive outbursts in the form of psychiatric distress and resulting heart-related diseases [2]. All in all, aggressive driving is a serious hazard on our roads—for the victim and the perpetrator. As these examples show, aggression behind the wheel can take many forms. In general, it can be differentiated between aggressive driving and hostile aggression, so called road rage. According to Shinar [3], aggressive driving is "a syndrome of

© Springer Nature Switzerland AG 2021
R. Ali et al. (Eds.): PERSUASIVE 2021, LNCS 12684, pp. 88–101, 2021.
https://doi.org/10.1007/978-3-030-79460-6_8

frustration-driven instrumental behaviors which are manifested in: (a) inconsiderateness towards or annoyance of other drivers (tailgating, flashing lights, and honking at other drivers), and (b) deliberate dangerous driving to save time at the expense of others (running red lights and stop signs, obstructing path of others, weaving)". In contrast, road rage refers to "hostile behaviors that are purposefully directed at other road users. These can be either driving behaviors (e.g., purposefully slowing a following vehicle or colliding with a lead vehicle) or non-driving behaviors (e.g., physically attacking someone)" [3]. The major differences between both definitions are the intention and the direction of the aggressive act. Instrumental aggression is intended to help the driver to move ahead by overcoming a frustrating obstacle. By this, he accepts that uninvolved or arbitrary others might be harmed. However, the aggression is not purposefully directed against them. In contrast, hostile aggression helps the driver to feel better, without the need to overcome the frustrating obstacle. In this case, the aggressive act is directed against a specific target, which may or may not be the source of frustration [3].

A common manifestation of aggressive driving is speeding. There are various measures against high-velocity driving, such as speeding cameras, speed limits, behavior-dependent insurance programs, or in-car speed assistants. What these interventions have in common is that they are based on coercion, deception, or material inducement, which contradicts the human need for freedom and might cause reactance [4]. Moreover, they have only short-term effects: near the surveillance of a speeding camera, people tend to drive even below the posted speed limit. As soon as the speeding camera has been passed, they start to exceed the speed limit again [5]. To cause a voluntary and stable change in behavior, the research objective was to mitigate aggressive driving using Persuasive Technology, i.e., "computerized software or information systems designed to reinforce, change or shape attitudes or behaviors or both without using coercion or deception" [6]. Before the persuasive system developed, the *Driving Feedback Avatar* (DFA), is introduced, scientific and commercial feedback systems for changing driving behavior are presented. Following, an on-road driving study is described that was conducted to investigate the effectiveness of the DFA. The paper concludes with the discussion of the study, focusing on its methodological limitations and future iterations of the DFA.

2   Related Work

As a model for the DFA, there are scientific and commercial in-car feedback systems that attempt to promote ecological driving. These systems recognize different behaviors that indicate ecological driving (e.g., acceleration, braking, gear shifting), summarize and score these behaviors, and provide the driver with feedback via the visual, acoustic, or haptic channels of the car. Dahlinger, Wortmann, Ryder, and Gahr [7], for instance, visualized a driver's fuel economy through a tree that was growing depending on fuel use (abstract feedback) and through a numerical score (concrete feedback). In a field experiment with 56 drivers, only the tree representation caused a significant reduction in fuel consumption. Meschtscherjakov, Wilfinger, Scherndl, and Tscheligi [8] examined the acceptance of five in-car systems for a more ecological driving style in an online survey with 57 respondents. Four systems were feedback-based: (i) the eco-accelerator pedal that exerts pressure against the driver's foot when wasteful acceleration is detected,

(ii) the eco-speedometer that changes its color depending on the fuel consumption, (iii) the eco-display that visualizes the fuel use through an animation of growing or vanishing leaves, and (iv) the eco-advisor that gives verbal hints for fuel-efficient driving. In addition, (v) a system that reduces fuel consumption by adjusting vehicle parameters automatically was evaluated. The eco-speedometer reached the highest acceptance ratings, followed by the automatic system. The eco-accelerator was the only solution that was rated negatively in terms of participants' intention to use the system and perceived usefulness. Adell, Varhelyi, and Hjalmdahl [9] equipped the personal vehicles of 22 participants with a feedback system that instantly gives an acoustic signal and a flashing red light when the speed limit is exceeded. In the field, the system reduced speeding violations, but participants rated the acoustic signal as annoying and irritating. Finally, *CarCoach* is an in-car interface that promotes prosocial driving [10]. The system monitors selected driving parameters (e.g., speed, brake position, steering angle, on-board system status), makes decisions about driving successes and mistakes, and gives a corresponding auditory and tactile feedback. The auditory feedback is either a negative warning (e.g., "please signal on") or a positive message ("thank you for signaling"), both given by a female audio voice. In addition, the steering wheel and the pedal vibrate. In a driving study with 18 participants, the effects of the feedback type (positive vs. negative) and the scheduling scheme (no feedback, continuous feedback, scheduled feedback) on the driving performance were tested. The results show that positive feedback increased performance when presented continuously, but not in the scheduled condition. Negative feedback decreased performance under both scheduling conditions.

While there are feedback systems that encourage ecological, slow, or social driving, no system is explicitly devoted to mitigate aggressive driving. Nevertheless, the applications presented demonstrate relevant design options, such as feedback modality (e.g., visual, acoustic, haptic), representation (abstract vs. concrete), or valence (positive vs. negative), that inspired the design of the DFA.

3   Driving Feedback Avatar

The DFA is an in-car interface that recognizes a driver's behavior and provides a corresponding visual feedback with a focus on aggressive driving. The main element is an avatar that is an abstraction of the Mercedes-Benz logo (Fig. 1). The avatar gradually changes its emotional state depending on the driver's behavior: if the driver behaves aggressively, the avatar gets angry (negative feedback). If no aggressive action occurs, the avatar becomes relaxed (positive feedback). Represented through the avatar's emotional state, the DFA gives the driver a summative feedback on his driving performance. In doing so, the avatar does not reflect the driver's emotion but expresses an intrinsic emotional state. In addition, the DFA gives an instant feedback in the form of an orange flashing light directly after the aggressive action occurred. The DFA was developed as part of a doctoral thesis, which is described in [11].

3.1   Avatar and Feedback Design

To express different emotional states, the avatar was animated in terms of color and motion. In total, nine states were modeled, ranging from angry to relaxed (Fig. 1). Their

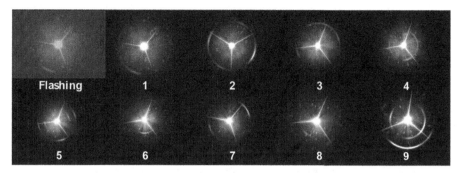

Fig. 1. Design of the avatar and its emotional states.

design was inspired by findings about color associations and the assignment of physiology in systems. For instance, anger is most likely associated with red, while the most common associations with relaxation are green and blue. There is also a positive correlation between the saturation of a color and the emotional arousal it evokes. Emotional arousal, in turn, correlates with the frequency of various physiological reactions (e.g., heart rate or respiration) [12]. While relaxation is a medium-arousal emotion, anger is a high-arousal emotion [13]. Consequently, for the anger-related states of the avatar (1 to 4) tones from the red color spectrum were used. The states associated with relaxation (6 to 9) were colored with tones of blue. The closer the states are to the poles, the higher their saturation so that the avatar appears grey in the neutral state (5). Moreover, the avatar shows pulsating movements that correspond to the arousal of the intended emotional state. The frequency is highest at the anger pole (1) and gradually decreases until it reaches the neutral state (5), where there is little movement. From the neutral state to the relaxation pole (9), the frequency increases again but remains below the frequency of the anger pole. In sum, the redder (or bluer) the avatar appears and the faster it moves, the more negative (or positive) the feedback is. The instant feedback is a visual alert, occurring directly after an aggressive action is recognized by the DFA (Fig. 1). For this, the system's display flashes two times per second by changing its color from black to orange [14].

To check how people perceive the colors and movements programmed into the avatar, four participants completed a free association task. In a randomized order, they were exposed to nine video sequences, each showing one of the emotional states of the avatar, and asked about their first impression. The emotional terms and expressions reported were grouped based on their semantical similarity. The negative states were mostly associated with negative terms and expressions such as "alarm, danger, emergency, attention," "blood, heartbeat, pulse," or "aggressive, rage, anger." The positive states were mainly described with positive words such as "cold, ice, water, fresh," "positive, enjoyable, friendly," or "calming, relaxing." The most common associations with the neutral state were "slow," "dead, stand by, nothing happens," and "neutral, normal." Overall, the emotional states that the participants inferred from the design of the avatar are in line with the authors' intention.

3.2 Feedback Algorithm

Feedback can change behavior in two ways: in the form of positive feedback that reinforces correct behavior or in the form of negative feedback that punishes incorrect behavior. Several studies have shown that the effectiveness of the approach depends on whether the behavior in question is associated with prevention or promotion. Behavior that is focused on prevention is understood as a necessity, as an obligation, or something that people have to change, while behavior focused on promotion is associated with a wish, a desire, or something that people want to change [15]. Individuals are more motivated and perform better after receiving negative feedback on prevention behavior and positive feedback on promotion behavior [16]. Most persuasive systems address behavior people should change but do not want to change, such as bad eating habits or wasteful energy consumption. In both examples, it was found out that negative feedback provided by a robot or a pet-like avatar, respectively, has a positive effect on behavior change, relative to positive feedback [17, 18]. It was assumed that also the mitigation of aggressive driving is prevention focused so that the DFA should mainly use negative feedback. The feedback algorithm of the DFA is a function of the number of recognized aggressive driving behaviors and their severity, which are multiplied and summed up to a score over the elapsed driving time. Every second no aggressive action is recognized, the score is improved by a small value. The score is constantly mapped on the emotional states of the avatar. If the upper (or lower) threshold of the current state is reached, the avatar changes to the next state. The DFA considers the following behaviors: (1) tailgating, (2) exceeding the speed limit, (3) not using the indicators before changing lanes, (4) using the indicators shortly before changing lanes, (5) verbally insulting other road users, (6) making insulting gestures towards other road users, (7) flashing headlights at a slower vehicle, (8) changing in one go from the right lane to the very left lane, (9) passing a single continuous center line. The behaviors were derived from a literature review on manifestations of aggressive driving [19–22]. The reviewed behaviors were filtered based on the following two criteria: (i) the possibility of being detected by the vehicle systems (e.g., cameras, radar, microphones, face or gesture recognition) and (ii) the likelihood of occurring on the highway. The severity of each behavior was determined in an online survey in which 1047 respondents were asked about the subjective valence of each behavior when it is observed in others [11]. Tailgating turned out to be the most severe behavior, followed by verbal insult and insulting gestures.

3.3 Persuasiveness

As an avatar-based feedback system, the DFA holds several principles that are supposed to persuade a driver to mitigate aggressive driving. Most common, Fogg [23] proposes the following seven persuasive principles: (i) reduction (narrowing complex activities to simple steps), (ii) tunneling (guiding through a sequence of actions), (iii) tailoring (relevant or personalized information), (iv) suggestion (advice about appropriate behavior), (v) self-monitoring (information on performance and progress), (vi) surveillance (others monitoring an individual's performance and progress), and (vii) conditioning (positive reinforcement). The DFA supports the driver in monitoring his performance and progress, which refers to Fogg's principle of self-monitoring. Moreover, it incorporates the principle of surveillance, since the driver is supposed to be monitored by the avatar. Finally, the DFA also uses some form of conditioning by punishing aggressive actions and reinforcing the absence of aggression. Accordingly, the DFA is supposed to have an inherently persuasive power, which leads to hypothesis H1: *the presence of the DFA reduces the frequency of aggressive driving behaviors, in particular, those that are fed back by the system.*

Beyond these persuasive features, the special thing about the DFA is its capability to express emotions, which can also have a persuasive effect that is rooted in the *Tamagotchi Effect* [24, 25]. According to the Tamagotchi Effect, the attribution of emotions to technology increases a user's emotional attachment to the system. If people feel attached to a system, this promotes their care-taking behavior towards it so that emotional attachment functions as a moderator in this relationship. In case of the DFA, the emotional design of the avatar is supposed to trigger a driver's emotional attachment to the system, which is supposed to moderate the effect of the DFA on behavior change. To check whether the design of the avatar actually contributes to the development of emotional attachment, hypothesis H2 is formulated: *people feel emotionally attached to the DFA.*

4   Method

To test the hypotheses, a driving study in real traffic, using a wizard-of-oz prototype of the DFA, was conducted. Since human subjects were involved, the study was approved and supervised by the Mercedes-Benz IRB. The internal IRB process reviews, for example, participants' fitness to drive, driver distraction caused by the study setup, or data protection regulations.

4.1   Wizard-of-Oz Setup

A wizard-of-oz is a prototypical system that is manually handled by a human operator to simulate the functionality of a system that does not yet exist [26]. The wizard of the DFA was built into a Mercedes-Benz E-class, which was equipped with a logging system to record the participants' driving behavior. The wizard consisted of (1) a tablet that displayed the avatar (avatar tablet), (2) a tablet with a graphical interface to operate the wizard (annotation tablet), (3) a tablet that was connected to the logging system and visualized participants' driving data in real time (monitoring tablet), and (4) a laptop running the DFA application (Fig. 2). The avatar tablet was fixed on top of the center console display so that it was clearly visible from the driver's seat and did not cover driving-relevant information as in the instrument cluster. The annotation tablet was held in hand by the experimenter, who was sitting behind the driver's seat and manually annotated the nine behaviors defined in Sect. 3.2 *Feedback Algorithm*. Discrete behavior, i.e., a single action at a time, was annotated by pressing a button, including activation of indicators, verbal insult, insulting gesture, flashing headlights, and lane change. Continuous behavior, i.e., a sequence of actions over a period of time, was opted in once started and opted out at the end, including tailgating and speeding. The annotation data was the input for the DFA application to calculate the aggressive driving score that determined the avatar's emotional state. Supporting the experimenter with the annotation task, the monitoring tablet was installed at the back of the driver's seat so that the experimenter was able to see it. The DFA application automatically created a CSV file including the annotation tags.

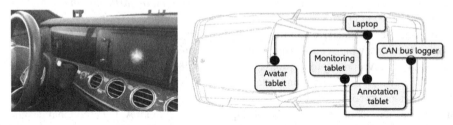

Fig. 2. Avatar tablet (left) and wizard-of-oz setup (right).

4.2 Procedure

The study included two test drives with the test vehicle driven by the participants. In a random order, they completed one drive with the wizard (system condition) and one drive without it, i.e., the avatar tablet was not installed (baseline condition). There was one week between the trials, with both trials taking place on the same weekday and time of day to keep situational conditions constant. The test route was a 50-km-long highway section in the area of Stuttgart, Germany. Participants were guided by the on-board navigation system. In both conditions, one of four experimenters (2 female, 2 male) accompanied the drive as inconspicuously as possible (e.g., no talking, no flashy clothes, seating outside the participants' field of view). Each participant completed both trials with the same experimenter. In both conditions, the experimenter annotated the relevant aggressive driving behaviors following an annotation guide. In a cover story, participants were told that the study is aimed at collecting naturalistic driving data for the development of future driving assistance systems and that the experimenter accompanies the drive to monitor the logging system installed for this purpose. Thus, it would be important to drive as naturally as possible. They were debriefed at the end of the second trial.

Before the first drive, participants were introduced to the vehicle and the route on a map. After each drive, they filled in a questionnaire about driver distraction and the naturalness of driving. In the system condition, they also answered a questionnaire about their emotional attachment to the DFA and were interviewed about the perceived functionality of the DFA by the experimenter.

4.3 Measures

The scope of the analysis was on the nine aggressive driving behaviors fed back by the DFA. The data were extracted from the records of the logging system. First, cases with a driving speed of less than 70 km/h were removed to filter out congestion phases. Second, cases representing a relevant behavior were determined. For the behaviors verbal insult and insulting gestures, no logs were available. The data were derived from the annotated data and merged with the logged data. Finally, all data were standardized to minutes per hour (for continuous behaviors) or counts per hour (for discrete behaviors), relative to the participants' individual driving time.

Participants' emotional attachment to the DFA was measured by adapting the *Mother-to-Infant Bonding Scale* (MIBS), which originally captures a mother's feelings towards her newborn [27]. The scale was used since no measure exists that focusses on the initial interaction between a user and a system and the emotionality of this interaction. The MIBS consists of three positive attributes (e.g., "protective") and five negative attributes (e.g., "aggressive") that are rated using the options 0 "not at all," 1 "a little," 2 "moderately," 3 "a lot," and 4 "very much". The MIBS score is the sum of all ratings with a maximum of 32 (negative items transcoded). Driver distraction was addressed through the *Driving Activity Load Index*, including the dimensions effort of attention, visual demand, auditory demand, temporal demand, interference, and situational stress [28]. The dimensions are assessed using a 22-level slider scale (1 "low" to 22 "high"). The naturalness of driving was operationalized by (i) the familiarity with the handling of the test vehicle (1 "very unfamiliar" to 7 "very familiar"), and (ii) the deviation from normal driving, including driving speed, following distance, use of indicators, timing of indicating, and verbal insult (e.g., 1 "I drove faster than usual" to 4 "I drove as usual" to 7 "I drove slower than usual").

4.4 Participants

Participants were recruited via the Mercedes-Benz user study pool, with the focus on people who regularly drove a car similar to the test vehicle in size, equipment, and performance. They received an expense allowance of 80 euro. In total, 32 participants (15 female, 16 male, 1 no answer) completed both trials. On average, they were 46.3 years old ($SD = 13.9$, min: 21, max: 67). Of the participants, 54.8 percent drove between 10,000 and 30,000 km in the last year by car ($<$10,000 km: 19.4%; $>$30,000 km: 25.8%). Eleven regularly drove a Mercedes-Benz E-class or C-class. Other cars driven were, for example, Opel Insignia, Volkswagen Passat, or Audi A5. Participants felt very familiar with the test vehicle under both conditions ($M_S = 6.44$, $SD_S = .80$; $M_B = 5.91$, $SD_B = 1.59$). Moreover, they indicated driving as usual in terms of speed ($M_S = 4.16$, $SD_S = .68$; $M_B = 4.00$, $SD_B = .67$), following distance ($M_S = 4.00$, $SD_S = .36$; $M_B = 4.03$, $SD_B = .31$), use of indicators ($M_S = 4.06$, $SD_S = .25$; $M_B = 4.03$, $SD_B = .18$), and timing of indicating ($M_S = 4.03$, $SD_S = .47$; $M_B = 4.03$, $SD_B = .31$). Compared to normal, they made less verbal insults in the study ($M_S = 4.69$, $SD_S = 1.18$, $t(31) = 3.31$, $p = .002$; $M_B = 4.97$, $SD_B = 1.28$, $t(31) = 4.27$, $p = .000$). Driver distraction was generally low, with the DFA having no impact ($M_S = 4.27$, $SD_S = 2.69$; $M_B = 4.45$, $SD_B = 2.74$; $t(27) = -.46$, $p = .650$).

5 Results

The data of three participants were excluded from the analysis, resulting in 29 valid datasets. In one case, no data was logged in the first trial due to technical problems. In the other cases, both trials were not comparable due to traffic obstructions.

5.1 Aggressive Driving

On average, a drive took 25 min ($SD = 4$) in the baseline condition and 26 min ($SD = 2$) in the system condition. The behavior "passing a single continuous center line" was never shown. The relative frequencies of the remaining eight behaviors were compared within both conditions using one-tailed paired sample t-tests to address H1, i.e., *the presence of the DFA reduces the frequency of aggressive driving behaviors, in particular, those that are fed back by the system*. When driving with the DFA, participants less often missed to use the indicators before changing lanes (34.9% decrease) or to signal the lane change earliest one second before the maneuver (10.6%); they flashed their headlights less frequently (21.8%); they less often changed lanes in one go (65.3%); and they expressed fewer verbal insults (37.1%), as shown in Table 1 and Fig. 3. However, only the decline of the behavior "changing lanes in one go" was statistically significant ($M_B = 1.18$, $SD_B = 2.32$; $M_S = .41$, $SD_S = .91$; $t(28) = 2.34$, $p = .013$) with a moderate effect (Cohen's $d = .44$) [29]. Contrary to expectations, some behaviors also increased under the influence of the DFA. In the system condition, participants exceeded the speed limit more often (18.6% increase; specified as driving at least 10 km/h faster than the posted speed limit); they tailgated more often (29.1%; specified as following the vehicle ahead with a distance less than half of the safe distance); and they made more insulting gestures (106.7%). Still, none of the comparisons was statistically significant when interpreting the two-tailed test. Overall, H1 has to be rejected since only one of eight behaviors showed a significant change in the assumed direction.

Table 1. Paired sample t-tests ([a]one-tailed, [b]two-tailed) of the behaviors within the conditions.

Behavior	Baseline		System		$t(28)$	p	Cohen's d
	M	SD	M	SD			
No indicator	1.49	1.54	.97	1.33	1.62[a]	.058	.44
Short indicator	29.47	25.99	26.36	20.35	.78[a]	.222	.14
Flashing headlights	.55	2.98	.43	1.90	.55[a]	.277	.10
Changing lanes in one go	1.18	2.32	.41	.91	2.34[a]	.013	.44
Verbal insult	.97	2.62	.61	1.50	.82[a]	.210	.15
Speeding	11.38	7.85	13.50	8.10	−1.33[b]	.196	.25
Tailgating	9.41	7.31	12.15	10.52	−1.82[b]	.080	.34
Insulting gestures	.15	.58	.31	1.92	−.58[b]	.568	.11

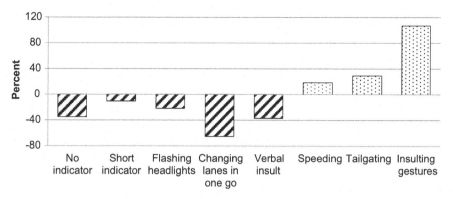

Fig. 3. Proportional difference of behaviors, relative to the baseline condition.

5.2 Emotional Attachment

Hypothesis H2 states that *people feel emotionally attached to the DFA*. The emotional attachment score can reach a value between 0 (no attachment) and 32 (high attachment). On average, participants have a score of 22.56 ($SD = 4.09$, *min*: 13, *max*: 29), which is significantly higher than the possible average score of 16 ($t(31) = 9.08, p = .000$). With an effect size of Cohen's $d = 1.60$, this is even a strong effect [29]. Since the emotional attachment is above average, H2 is accepted.

5.3 Perceived Functionality

In the interviews, participants name 13 different behaviors which they assume to be fed back by the system. Only three of these behaviors are actually considered by the system, including improper distance to a preceding vehicle (named by 17 participants), improper speed (9), and incorrect use of indicators (1). Of the participants, eight say that they did not notice the flashing instant feedback and ten say that they did not observe a change in the appearance of the avatar.

6 Discussion

When driving with the DFA, participants showed some behaviors generally less often (no/short indicator, verbal insult, flashing headlight, changing lanes in one go) and other behaviors—contrary to expectations—more frequently (speeding, tailgating, insulting gestures). Apart from the unintended changes, most of the comparisons did not reach statistical significance and had only small effects thus H1, i.e., *the presence of the DFA reduces the frequency of aggressive driving behaviors, in particular, those that are fed back by the system,* is rejected. With H2 it was hypothesized that *people feel emotionally attached to the DFA*. Since participants' emotional attachment was above average, H2 is accepted. Nevertheless, the assumed moderated effect of emotional attachment on the relationship between the DFA and aggressive driving was not tested because there was no direct effect of the DFA on aggressive driving. The following sections discuss the most important methodological and design decisions that could have influenced the outcome of the study.

6.1 Methodological Limitations

Behavior change is a challenge and there are many reasons *why* an intervention has not the desired effect. In consideration of the methodological setup of the present study, it should be taken into account that the participants knew that a logging system was monitoring their driving. Thus, the logging system inherently served as a persuasive system and could have interfered with the effect of the DFA. Likewise, the presence of the backseat experimenter could have affected the participants' driving. According to the *Passenger Effect*, people drive safer when accompanied by others [30]. Although this influence was supposed to be controlled by having accompaniment on both test drives and although participants stated that they drove as usual, (unconsciously) they could have driven more conservative. According to their own statements, they were more reserved to use verbal insults. Moreover, the analyzed aggressive driving behaviors are not a validated metric of the construct but a technology-driven composition of potentially relevant actions. The selected behaviors could have measured something other than aggressive driving or a different set of behaviors could be a better indicator of the construct. Finally, the effect sizes revealed should be put into context, because the small effects of the DFA— whether being in the right or wrong direction—might be trivial in a group of "normally" aggressive individuals, but meaningful for pathologically or criminally aggressive drivers [31].

6.2 Design Considerations

Based on the empirical findings, the last section discusses design considerations for future iterations of the DFA that provide an answer to the question of *how* the system could be more effective. First, although participants' emotional attachment to the DFA was above average, it might have been too low to moderate the effect of the system on aggressive driving. Future designs of the DFA should offer features that make the driver feel more attached to the system. Studies in Human-Computer-Interaction found out that one way to do so is to personalize technology [32] or to promote longer usage [33]. To personalize the DFA, the driver could create a customized avatar or give it a name. A smartphone application of the DFA could allow using the system outside the car and thus extend the context and time of use.

Second, no participant was able to identify all of the behaviors considered by the DFA, which suggests that the feedback logic was difficult to understand and learn. To overcome this lack of usability, the system should be more self-explanatory. For instance, the feedback could be enriched by icons or short textual instructions that direct the driver's attention to the relevant behavior, point out the gap between the current and the desired behavior, or provide information on how to correct the behavior [34]. Moreover, the individual behaviors considered by the system could be made explicit and the score could be represented as a concrete numerical value.

Third, although it was checked that people infer the right information from the colors and movements programmed into the avatar, it cannot be ruled out that the participants had an aesthetic preference for the angry state. In this case, the negative feedback (unconsciously) functioned as a positive feedback and reinforced aggressive driving. In future investigation of the DFA, also the aesthetic perception of the avatar's emotional states has to be checked. In addition, future designs could allow the driver to configure the appearance of the avatar based on his aesthetic preferences (or aversions) so that it works as a reward (or punishment).

Fourth, it is remarkable that—without being statistically significant—most of the behaviors that increased under the influence of the DFA are continuous in nature, while all of the decreasing behaviors are discrete actions. This discrete-continuous dichotomy suggests that the system had different effects on different types of behavior. A similar assumption was raised with the differentiation between prevention and promotion behavior, suggesting that negative feedback is more effective to improve prevention behavior, while positive feedback is better when it comes to promotion behavior [15, 16]. In conclusion, it might be assumed that different types of aggressive driving behaviors require different types of feedback to be effectively changed. Consequently, the DFA should vary its feedback depending on the behavior in question. Future research is needed to classify aggressive driving behaviors and to define corresponding feedback requirements.

Last, regardless of the type of behavior, it is a fundamental debate whether positive or negative feedback is the right approach in the context of behavior change. With the DFA, the focus was on negative feedback, i.e., aggressive driving was punished, but prosocial or rule-consistent behavior was not actively rewarded. Just as there are studies that support this design decision, there is a body of research that emphasizes the advantages of positive feedback, relative to negative feedback. For instance, negative feedback is more likely than positive feedback to cause reactance—especially when it is perceived as threat by being unfair or patronizing [4, 35, 36]—and positive feedback is more likely than negative feedback to improve future performance [37]. In the context of aggressive driving, it is still an open question what the more effective approach is.

7 Conclusion

The present work explored the use of an avatar-based feedback system to mitigate aggressive driving. Although there is no statistical evidence for the effectiveness of the system, it was shown that it is possible to make drivers feel emotionally attached to an in-car interface by implementing emotional cues into it, which provides interesting insights for the affective technology community. Moreover, this work proposes design considerations that should be taken into account when developing an avatar-based feedback system, such as the aesthetic preferences of its user or the issue of personalization. Future research and design activities are needed to improve the effectiveness of the system proposed and to test it under more valid conditions.

References

1. Statistisches Bundesamt: Fehlverhalten der Fahrzeugführer bei Unfällen mit Personenschaden. https://www.destatis.de/DE/Themen/Gesellschaft-Umwelt/Verkehrsunfaelle/Tabellen/fehlverhalten-fahrzeugfuehrer.html
2. Smart, R.G., Asbridge, M., Mann, R.E., Adlaf, E.M.: Psychiatric distress among road rage victims and perpetrators. Can. J. Psychiatry. **48**, 681–688 (2003)
3. Shinar, D.: Aggressive driving: the contribution of the drivers and the situation. Transp. Res. Part F Traffic Psychol. Behav. **1**(2), 137–160 (1998)

4. Brehm, J.W.: Theory of Psychological Reactance. Academic Press, New York (1966)
5. Mäkinen, T., et al.: Traffic enforcement in Europe: effects, measures, needs and future. Technical Research Centre of Finland, Espoo (2003)
6. Oinas-Kukkonen, H., Harjumaa, M.: Towards deeper understanding of persuasion in software and information systems. In: Proceedings of the ACHI 2008 International Conference on Advances in Computer-Human Interaction, pp. 200–205. ACM, New York (2008)
7. Dahlinger, A., Wortmann, F., Ryder, B., Gahr, B.: The impact of abstract vs. concrete feedback information on behavior – insights from a large eco-driving field experiment. In: Proceedings of the CHI 2018 Conference on Human Factors in Computing Systems, pp. 379–390. ACM, New York (2018)
8. Meschtscherjakov, A., Wilfinger, D., Scherndl, T., Tscheligi, M.: Acceptance of future persuasive in-car interfaces towards a more economic driving behaviour. In: Proceedings of the Automotive'UI 2009 Conference on Automotive User Interfaces and Interactive Vehicular, pp. 81–88. ACM, New York (2009)
9. Adell, E., Várhelyi, A., Hjälmdahl, M.: Auditory and haptic systems for in-car speed management – a comparative real life study. Transp. Res. Part F Traffic Psychol. Behav. 11(6), 445–458 (2008)
10. Arroyo, E., Sullivan, S., Selker, T.: CarCOACH: a polite and effective driving COACH. In: Extended Abstracts of the CHI 2006 Conference on Human Factors in Computing Systems, pp. 357–362. ACM, New York (2006)
11. Dittrich, M.: Persuasive Technology to mitigate aggressive driving - A human-centered design approach (2020)
12. Clarke, T., Costall, A.: The emotional connotations of color: a qualitative investigation. Color Res. Appl. 33, 406–410 (2008)
13. Peter, C., Herbon, A.: Emotion representation and physiology assignments in digital systems. Interact. Comput. 18, 139–170 (2006)
14. Chan, A.H.S., Ng, A.W.Y.: Perceptions of implied hazard for visual and auditory alerting signals. Saf. Sci. 47, 346–352 (2009)
15. Higgins, E.T.: Beyond pleasure and pain. Am. Psychol. 52, 1280–1300 (1997)
16. Van Dijk, D., Kluger, A.N.: Task type as a moderator of positive/negative feedback effects on motivation and performance: a regulatory focus perspective. J. Organ. Behav. 32, 1084–1105 (2011)
17. Byrne, S., et al.: When i eat so bad, my pet looks so sad. J. Child. Media 6, 83–99 (2012)
18. Ham, J., Midden, C.J.H.: A persuasive robot to stimulate energy conservation: the influence of positive and negative social feedback and task similarity on energy-consumption behavior. Int. J. Soc. Robot. 6(2), 163–171 (2013). https://doi.org/10.1007/s12369-013-0205-z
19. Dula, C.S., Ballard, M.E.: Development and evaluation of a measure of dangerous, aggressive, negative emotional, and risky driving. J. Appl. Soc. Psychol. 33, 263–282 (2003)
20. Özkan, T., Lajunen, T.: A new addition to DBQ: positive driver behaviours scale. Transp. Res. Part F Traffic Psychol. Behav. 8, 355–368 (2005)
21. Harris, P.B., et al.: The prosocial and aggressive driving inventory (PADI): a self-report measure of safe and unsafe driving behaviors. Accid. Anal. Prev. 72, 1–8 (2014)
22. Alonso, F., Esteban, C., Montoro, L., Serge, A.: Conceptualization of aggressive driving behaviors through a Perception of aggressive driving scale (PAD). Transp. Res. Part F Traffic Psychol. Behav. 60, 415–426 (2019)
23. Fogg, B.J.: Persuasive Technology: Using Computers to Change What We Think and Do. Morgan Kaufmann Publishers, Burlington (2003)
24. Frude, N., Jandrić, P.: The intimate machine – 30 years on. E-Learn. Digit. Media 12, 410–424 (2015)
25. Lawton, L.: Taken by the Tamagotchi: how a toy changed the perspective on mobile technology. J. Grad. Stud. J. Fac. Inf. 2, 1–9 (2017)

26. Martelaro, N., Ju, W.: WoZ Way: enabling real-time remote interaction prototyping & observation in on-road vehicles. In: Proceedings of the CSCW 2017 Conference on Computer Supported Cooperative Work and Social Computing, pp. 21–24. ACM, New York (2017)
27. Taylor, A., Atkins, R., Kumar, R., Adams, D., Glover, V.: A new mother-to-infant bonding scale: links with early maternal mood. Arch. Womens Ment. Health **8**, 45–51 (2005)
28. Pauzie, A.: A method to assess the driver mental workload: the driving activity load index (DALI). IET Intell. Transp. Syst. **2**, 315–322 (2009)
29. Cohen, J.: Statistical Power Analysis for the Behavioral Sciences. Lawrence Erlbaum Associates, New Jersey (1988)
30. Nakagawa, Y., Park, K., Ueda, H., Ono, H.: Being watched over by a conversation robot enhances safety in simulated driving. Soc. Des. Eng. Ser. **16**, 1–33 (2017)
31. Fröhlich, M., Pieter, A.: Cohen's effektstärken als mass der bewertung von praktischer relevanz - implikationen für die praxis. Schweizerische Zeitschrift für Sport. und Sport. **57**, 139–142 (2009)
32. Mugge, R., Schoormans, J.P.L., Schifferstein, H.N.J.: Emotional bonding with personalised products. J. Eng. Des. **20**, 467–476 (2009)
33. Hertlein, K.M., Twist, M.L.C.: Attachment to technology: the missing link. J. Couple Relat. Ther. **17**, 2–6 (2018)
34. Feng, J., Donmez, B.: Design of effective feedback: understanding driver, feedback, and their interaction. In: Proceedings of the International Driving Symposium 2013 on Human Factors in Driver Assessment, Training and Vehicle Design (2013)
35. Spiekermann, S., Pallas, F.: Technology paternalism - wider implications of ubiquitous computing. Poiesis und Prax. **4**, 6–18 (2006)
36. Uludag, O.: Fair and square: how does perceptions of fairness is associated to aggression? Procedia Soc. Behav. Sci. **143**, 504–508 (2014)
37. Kluger, A.N., DeNisi, A.: The effects of feedback interventions on performance: a historical review, a meta-analysis, and a preliminary feedback intervention theory. Psychol. Bull. **119**(2), 254–284 (1996)

Mobile Persuasive Application for Responsible Alcohol Use: Drivers for Use and Impact of Social Influence Strategies

Abdul-Hammid Olagunju[1], Marcella Ogenchuk[2], and Julita Vassileva[1（✉）]

[1] MADMUC Lab, University of Saskatchewan, Saskatoon, Canada
`aholagunju@usask.ca`, `jiv@cs.usask.ca`
[2] College of Nursing, University of Saskatchewan, Saskatoon, Canada
`marcella.ogenchuk@usask.ca`

Abstract. Alcohol use disorder is a public health concern. We developed a persuasive mobile application as an intervention to discourage irresponsible alcohol use, which implements a tool for measuring self-reported alcohol consumption, based on AUDIT (Alcohol Use Disorder Identification Test). We set out to find the drivers influencing user acceptance of the mobile application and to evaluate the advantages of adding two commonly used social influence persuasive strategies (comparison and competition) to the set of persuasive strategies that are commonly used in health-related mobile apps (self-monitoring, goal setting, feedback, reward, reminder, and simulation). The effectiveness of two versions of the app were compared in a 30-day long controlled study involving 42 volunteers. The control version of the app deployed the strategies listed above, and the experimental version used all the persuasive strategies in the control version and in addition, two social influence strategies – comparison and competition. The results showed that an aesthetically pleasing user interface and user experience and perceived usefulness are the main drivers of intention to use a mobile app as an intervention to reduce irresponsible drinking. In the control version group, there was no significant difference in the AUDIT scores before and after the intervention, while in the group using the social version there was a significant improvement (decrease in the AUDIT score) after using the application. The contribution of this work is that it establishes the usefulness of a persuasive app in reducing risky drinking behaviours. It also shows the benefit of deploying the social influence strategies comparison and competition, in conjunction with other persuasive strategies commonly used in health promoting persuasive apps. It also confirms previous findings regarding the importance of aesthetically pleasing user interface and useful functionality in the design of persuasive applications to increase user intention to adopt them.

Keywords: Alcohol use disorder · Persuasive mobile application · Social influence strategy

© Springer Nature Switzerland AG 2021
R. Ali et al. (Eds.): PERSUASIVE 2021, LNCS 12684, pp. 102–114, 2021.
https://doi.org/10.1007/978-3-030-79460-6_9

1 Introduction

Alcohol consumption has become part of many people's social life. People consume alcohol for different reasons, such as to relieve stress, elevate moods, or due to external influence from peers or the environment. However, excessive alcohol use comes with serious medical and societal risks. When alcohol use starts causing clinically significant pains and impairment, it is known as alcohol use disorder (AUD) [1]. The World Health Organization has linked over 200 health conditions to the harmful use of alcohol, including infectious diseases such as hepatitis, tuberculosis, HIV/AIDS etc. [2]. For young adults, the risks associated with the use of alcohol include poorer performance on attention, visuospatial, memory and other executive function tasks [3].

The increase in the adoption of smart phones has created a unique opportunity for researchers and health practitioners to offer preventive measures to irresponsible alcohol use. The user adoption of the technologies has been shown to rely on their perceived usefulness, ease of use, and specifically for mobile web apps - their perceived aesthetics. Previous research has found that computerized interventions known as Persuasive Technology (PT) are effective in motivating behaviour change [4]. PT is a combination of hardware and software that uses the computer to reinforce or change attitude or behaviours without the use of coercion or deception [5]. There are many persuasive strategies that are being commonly deployed in PT applications supporting health-related behaviour change, e.g. self-monitoring, tailoring, feedback, reward, reminder, simulation. The decision which strategies to deploy depends on the specifics of the targeted behaviour to be changed. Research has shown that social learning (observing the behaviours of others to motivate one's behaviour) is one of the leading factors of binge drinking [6] especially among young adults, which suggests that social influence strategies may hold a promise.

We developed a persuasive mobile application, called CHEERS!, as an intervention to discourage irresponsible alcohol use. It implements a tool for measuring self-reported alcohol consumption, based on AUDIT (Alcohol Use Disorder Identification Test). We evaluated the effectiveness of the persuasive app in reducing dangerous drinking behaviour in a 30-days long user study. We evaluated the effectiveness of two app versions: one with a "standard" set of persuasive strategies and the second - augmented two social influence strategies - competition and comparison. We also verified the factors that drive user acceptance [10] of a mobile app for behaviour change towards responsible use of alcohol. Hence, this paper aims to address the following questions:

i.   *How effective is a persuasive mobile app in changing user behaviour towards more responsible drinking habits?*
ii. *Would adding social learning strategies – competition and competition – make the persuasive app more effective?*
iii. *Do usefulness, ease of use and aesthetics affect user intention to use a persuasive mobile app that encourages responsible alcohol usage?*

2   Background

Behaviour change theories constructs and concepts that are interrelated and map the underlying factors responsible for behaviour change, such as personal, social, and environmental characteristics [7]. Examples of common behaviour change models are the Health Belief Model (HBM), the Theory of Reasoned Actions (TRA), the Transtheoretical Model (TTM), the Social-Ecological Model (SEM), and the Social Learning Theory (SLT). As alcohol use in young people is often due to social factors, the Social Learning Theory provides a suitable framework for our application. The SLT postulates that acquiring a new behaviour can result from directly experiencing the consequences of the behaviour or by observing other people. The social cognitive theory (SCT) which is an extension of SLT [8] holds that behaviour is determined by expectations and incentives. It explains behaviour as reciprocal determinism – the dynamics and interaction between personal factors, behavioural factors and environmental factors. This inter-relationship makes this model the most suitable for this study unlike other models that do not consider explicitly the dynamics between a person's attitude and the (social) environment.

Persuasive Systems Design is a comprehensive framework developed to aid in the design and evaluation of systems capable of influencing users' attitudes or behaviors. Oinas-Kukkonen and Harjumaa [11] presented how the concept of functional triad – a conceptual framework that illustrates the three roles technology play in persuasion, tool, medium and social actor – can be transformed into a software requirement for easy implementation, design and evaluation. They categorized the design qualities of persuasive systems into primary task supports – features that help users perform the most important tasks of the Behavioural change elements, dialogue support – features that encourage some forms of dialogue with the user, social support – allow users to interact with other users, and system credibility supports – features that improves the reputation of the system.

Excessive drinking can cause illness and distress to the drinker and his family. It was on this premise that the Alcohol Use Disorder Identification Test (AUDIT) was created by the World Health Organization (WHO), to screen for excessive drinking and specifically to assist specialists to distinguish people who would benefit from reducing or stopping drinking. WHO defined the AUDIT as a *"a list of 10-item screening questionnaire including 3 questions on the amount and frequency of drinking; 3 questions on alcohol dependence; and 4 on problems caused by alcohol"* [12]. The total score attainable is 40; people with score under 20 are more likely to change their behaviour, while those with score over 20 likely indicate alcohol dependency. Feedback from the AUDIT tool can raise awareness of one's drinking habits and risk; in combination with educational materials and advice on reducing drinking can provide a good basis for intervention.

The Technology Acceptance Model (TAM) [10] has been used to explain the users' adoption of information system in health, business, education and other domains. The theoretical model consists of constructs for interpreting the acceptance of a new system by users. It holds that the actual usage of a system is dependent on the intention to use (ITU) of the user. The model also recognizes perceived usefulness and perceived ease of use as some of the factors that influences ITU and external factors such as aesthetics and credibility, as shown in Fig. 1.

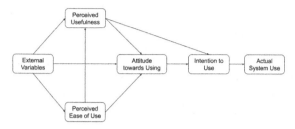

Fig. 1. Technology acceptance model Adapted from [10]

3 Methods

We designed and developed a mobile application, called "CHEERS", which has three functions: 1) implements the AUDIT tool to collect data from the user about their drinking habits, 2) provides educational resources regarding the impairment levels caused by different amounts of alcohol of different types, 3) persuades the user to engage in responsible drinking by deploying 6 persuasive strategies from the PSD model (self-monitoring, tailoring, feedback, reward, reminder, simulation), as well as two social influence strategies (competition and comparison). To answer the research questions defined in the Introduction, we carried out a field study.

The participants (n = 94) were recruited using social media, words or mouth and PAWS (University of Saskatchewan internal information management system), out of which 70 met the all the requirements: they completed the online prequalification form that was used to screen out participants below the age of 19 (Saskatchewan legal drinking age) and those that did not have a personal Android device. Fifty-five (55) participants downloaded the application, and 42 completed the study (answered the pre-qualification form, used the application daily for 30 days, and submitted the pre- and post-intervention questionnaires). The 42 participants were divided in to two groups: 22 participants (55%) were assigned to the control group and used the control version (CV) of the app and 20 (45%) in the social group and used the social version (SV) of the app. The study lasted for 30 days, and at the end of the study, participants were asked to answer the post-intervention questionnaire using the mobile app (the questionnaires were already included and deployed as part of the CHEERS app). All the participants gave consent to participate in the study, which was approved by the Behavioural Research Ethics Board of the University.

All the participants that downloaded the app to their phone completed a brief pre-app-usage questionnaire. The application encouraged participants to enter information about their drinking (*type of drink, volume of drink*); the time and app usage were recorded. The user self-recording the type, number and amount of drinks allowed the app to engage the user in self-monitoring their drinking, provided reward and a basis for comparison and competition. At the beginning of the study, each of the participants started with a performance score of 100. For every alcohol consumption recorded, the participant lost 10 points from their score. To regain their score, the participant had to restrain from alcohol for next 48 h (participants get a 5 point for every 24 h without an alcohol consumption recorded). On the completion of the 30 days of the study, participants were prompted to complete the post-app-usage questionnaire.

To evaluate the effect of social influence strategies, two versions of the application were implemented: a control version and a social version. The control version of the app implements the following persuasive strategies: self-monitoring, goal setting, feedback, reward, reminder, and simulation. The social version of the app contains the same strategies as the control version, and in addition, competition, and comparison (see Table 1). All participants could see their performance score as shown in Fig. 2. The participants using the social version could, in addition, monitor the average performance score of all participants in the study as shown in Fig. 2.

Table 1. Strategies implemented in the control and social version of CHEERS

Strategies	Control version	Social version
Self-monitoring	Yes	Yes
Tailoring	Yes	Yes
Feedback	Yes	Yes
Reward	Yes	Yes
Reminder	Yes	Yes
Simulation	Yes	Yes
Competition	No	Yes
Comparison	No	Yes

The CHEERS app also presented a visual cue for measuring a standard drink. This was shown in a soda can and the values for common alcohol beverages such as beer, light-beer, malt liquor, wine, fortified wines, and hard alcohol have been pre-loaded into that app. The participants could also add a custom drink, and the app would provide the measurement for the 1 standard drink inside a soda can help the user visualize the amount. This is illustrated in Fig. 3.

Other features built into the CHEERS app include: a collection of resources that educate participants about the health and societal risks of irresponsible alcohol use, the myths and facts of alcohol, a quiz with randomly generated questions, a game that simulates a social gathering that suggests different ways to decline alcohol when offered without losing face, and a logger that allow the participants to visualize the drinks logged over a period of time.

The AUDIT tool was used to measure the participants alcohol risk level before and after using the app and evaluate the effectiveness of the app as behaviour change intervention, i.e. to answer our research question (I). The AUDIT includes a total of 10 items, 3 items measure the alcohol frequency, 3 items measure alcohol dependence, and 4 items measure problems caused by alcohol. The answers provided for all the items were summed up to get the participant's AUDIT score.

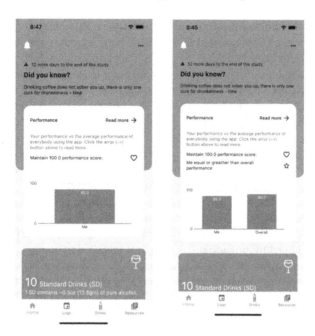

Fig. 2. Control Version (CV), left, and Social Version (SV), right or CHEERS app.

Fig. 3. CHEERS app showing list of common beverages (left) and what 1 standard drink of beer represents in a soda can (right)

To determine if there was any difference between the CV and the SV group resulting from the social strategy implemented in the SV and answer our research question (ii), we used a t-test to compare the AUDIT scores of the participants before and after using the app for the 2 versions of the app. A total of 24 participants' data were used in t-test analysis (12 for SV and 12 for CV) after removing the data for the participants that recorded 0 AUDIT score for both the pre- and post-app usage AUDIT questions.

To answer our research question (iii), we used the TAM standardized tool that was adapted to suit the context of this research. The TAM questionnaire consists of 10 items that measure the 'perceived usefulness', 'perceived ease of use', 'perceived aesthetics' and 'intention to use' of a specific technology. Each item is measured at a 7-point scale (1 = strongly disagree to 7 = strongly agree). The tool contains 3 items about participants perceived usefulness, 2 items about participants perceived ease of use, 4 items about participants perceived aesthetics and 1 item about intention to use. The participants answered these questions before and after using the app. The post-app usage questions were adapted to measure the participants intention to continue using the app after engaging with it for 30 days. To determine the relationship between the TAM constructs that drives the intention to use a mobile application that can help to reduce AUDIT score, like other TAM studies [13, 14], we dichotomized the TAM constructs (perceived usefulness, perceived ease of use, perceived aesthetics) along the median score of 5.9. All scores between 1–5.9 we categorized as disagree and scores between 6–7 were categorized as agree. Using the median as the cut off-points makes it easier to interpret the results and helps to differentiate between those who disagree or slightly agree and those who strongly agree with the items as reported from previous studies [13]. We used the Fisher's exact test to measure the relationship between the independent constructs (perceived ease of use, perceived usefulness and perceived aesthetics) and the outcome construct (intention to use), and we used Crammer's V to measure the strength of this relationships. All analyses were carried out using the SPSS statistical software.

4   Results and Discussion

This section presents the results from the study and discusses them considering the research questions defined in the introduction.

4.1   Evaluating the CHEERS App and the Effect of Social Influence Strategies

To evaluate the behaviour change effect of the application - question (i) - and to determine the difference (if any) between the CV and the SV group (RQ 2), we used a t-test to compare the AUDIT scores for both groups before and after using the app. The descriptive analysis is shown in Table 2, the summary of the dependent t-test - in Table 3.

This analysis shows a drop in the mean post-app AUDIT scores for both the CV and the SV. The mean score for the SV dropped from 14.08 to 11.83 and the mean score for the CV dropped from 13.58 to 13.00. The drop in AUDIT score means that the users' risk of Alcohol Use Disorder decreased by the end of the study. To find out if the effect is significant, we carried out a t-test. Table 3 shows the result of the t-test analysis carried out to determine if the difference in the means is significant.

Table 2. Summary of the AUDIT score for CV and SV before and after using the app.

Group	Pre-app usage		Post-app usage	
	Mean	Std. Dev.	Mean	Std. Dev.
Control	13.58	4.80	13.00	5.19
Social	14.08	4.38	11.83	2.89
Total	13.83	4.50	12.42	4.15

Table 3. Summary of T-Test analysis for the CV and SV. * represents p-value < 0.05

Group	T-value	P-value	Mean	Std Dev
CV	0.406	0.693	0.583	4.981
SV	2.215	0.049*	2.250	3.519

The t-test analysis of the AUDIT mean scores indicated that there was a marginally significant drop in the score for the SV, while the change in AUDIT scores for the CV was not significant. This implies that adding the two social strategies (competition and comparison) in the SV to the rest of the strategies deployed in the CV is essential in developing interventions that improve AUDIT scores. This answers our questions (i) and (ii).

This result supports findings from previous studies in other domains such as health [17], physical activities [18], education [19] and e-commerce [20] where social strategies have been used to promote behavior change. This result is important in health sciences, where any intervention that shows a decrease in the AUDIT score of a population is considered important, as this brings many other positive health effects. One needs to also consider the fact that the study was carried out during the summer of 2020, in during Covid-19 isolation measures and increased alcohol consumption [23].

4.2 User Acceptance of a Mobile Persuasive Ap for Responsible Alcohol Use

The descriptive statistics of the participants responses for the TAM tool are shown in Table 4.

The Fisher's Exact Test was used to determine the association between the TAM constructs and intention to use the app and the intention to continue using the app for pre-app usage and post-app usage respectively. Fisher's Exact test uses a crosstab table also known as contingency table to show the relationships between categorical variables. The Fisher's test is appropriate for a small sample size.

Figure 4 shows the relationship between ease of use and intention to use. The chart shows a positive association between ease of use and intention to use. The value of the Fisher's test also confirms this with high significant value of 0.015.

Table 4. Summary of TAM constructs for pre and post CHEERS app usage

Constructs	Pre-app app usage	Post-app app usage
	Mean/Std. Deviation	Mean/Std. Deviation
Ease of use	6.49/0.79	5.19/2.46
Usefulness	5.75/1.19	4.87/1.88
Aesthetics	6.43/0.79	5.15/2.25
Intention to use	6.125/1.20	5.05/2.05

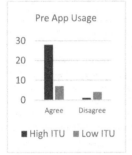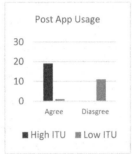

Fig. 4. Ease of use VS intention to use for pre (left) and post (right) app usage

Figure 5 illustrates the relationship between usefulness and intention to use. This chart shows that there is a positive relationship between usefulness and intention to use. Most of the participants that agree that the app is useful also agree to use the app. The value of the Fisher's test for this mapping is highly significant with a p-value of 0.001.

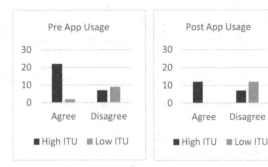

Fig. 5. Usefulness VS intention to use for pre (left) and post (right) app usage.

Figure 6 illustrates the relationship between aesthetics and intention to use. This relationship is also positive and shows that most of the participants that agree that the app is aesthetically appealing also agree to use the app. The Fisher's exact test for this aesthetics and ITU mapping is highly significant with a p-value of 0.001.

To determine the strength of this relations, we carried out Crammer's V test for symmetric measures to estimate the effect size. The result is shown in Table 5.

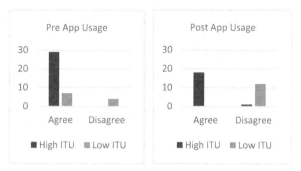

Fig. 6. Aesthetics VS Intention to use for Pre (left) and Post (right) App Usage.

Table 5. Effect size for the TAM construct. Small = 0.1, medium = 0.4, large = 0.5 for one degree of freedom [15]. * represents medium, ** represents large.

Constructs	df	Crammer's V	
		Pre-app usage	Post-app usage
Ease of use	1	0.444*	0.933**
Usefulness	1	0.526**	0.632**
Aesthetics	1	0.541**	0.935**

The result of our TAM shows that majority of the participants reported a high behavioral intention to use a mobile app to improve their AUDIT score with 72.5% reporting an average score of 6 or more (on a scale of 1 to 7) and 63.3% reported having high intention to continue using the app after the experimental 30 days period. The TAM constructs (ease of use, usefulness, and aesthetics) were significantly associated with intention to use and intention to continue using the CHEERS app.

We have been able to show, from the results presented in this study that people care about the user interface and user experience of a mobile application that helps to improve their AUDIT score and alcohol use behaviour, as aesthetics has the strongest effect on intention to use. The application must also be useful, i.e. the app must include features such as ability to monitor user's alcohol consumption and the effects of alcohol on the user; these are features that can help users to achieve their goal of improving their alcohol use behavior. The results of this study corroborate with findings in studies from other domains. For instance, Oyibo et al. [22] found the intention to use a mobile application to improve physical activities is significantly associated with usefulness and aesthetics.

Finally, the lower scores for intention to continue using the CHEERS app recorded for post-app usage, when compared to the score for the pre-app usage is due to the difference between users' perception and reality. The pre-app usage tool describes the app to the participants accompanied with a mockup of what the app would look like, the participants then created an image in their head of what the complete app should include. However, after using the app for 30 days, some of the expectations might not have been met and could have created a change in user perception. This is in line with previous studies that shows high attrition rates of 30–70% for longitudinal studies [16].

5   Summary, Conclusions, Limitations, and Future Work

This study investigated the receptiveness to using a mobile based PT as a means of improving *AUDIT Scores*. It also investigates the effectiveness of social strategies in promoting positive behavioral changes towards *responsible* alcohol use. We developed two versions of a cross-platform mobile application, a control version that implements the following strategies: self-monitoring, goal setting, feedback, reward, reminder, and simulation. The social version of the app implemented all the strategies in the control version, and in addition, the social strategies comparison and competition. Our results indicate that the intervention is likely effective over a 30-day use period as demonstrated by a decrease in AUDIT score. A decrease in the score indicates a substantial decrease in the number and frequency of alcohol consumption. Though difference was not significant for the group using the control version and it was marginally significant for the group using the social version, we believe that this is due to the small size of the two groups and a larger experiment will bring stronger results. Thus, our results indicate that the social strategies amplify the persuasive effect of the application, which answers our third research question. To the best of our knowledge, this is the first study to examine the use of *an app and* PT to *decrease* the alcohol risk level *using AUDIT scores*.

We used a quantitative approach to collect data about the drivers of user acceptance of the applications by adapting the TAM to suit the context of this research. The results demonstrated that good user interface and user experience (aesthetics), and the inclusion of features that help users achieve their goal (usefulness) were the strongest drivers.

We designed, developed, deployed a real-life mobile persuasive app for reducing alcohol risk scores, give insights to users into their alcohol consumption. The mobile application can serve as a tool to educate users [9] about alcohol usage and its risk, a measurement tool providing a visual cue about standard drink measurement and a reflection tool enabling the users to visualize their alcohol consumption over a period. This is the first work that explored the implementation of two social-influence strategies (comparison and competition) in the context of PT aiming to reduce alcohol risk and it can provide a starting point for future studies of the usefulness of other social strategies, such as collaboration. The significant results recorded in the evaluation of the social strategies and the participants willingness to continue using the app shows that social learning can be an effective tool in motivating *a decrease in risky alcohol use*. Future studies can explore and evaluate other strategies as well as improve on the ones highlighted in this study.

There are many limitations of this work, which suggest directions for future research. First, the ability of participants to report their behavior accurately and truthfully, while using a substance that is known to impair their cognitive ability and judgement, can be problematic. Given that, a field data collection approach that includes an ecological momentary assessment might be helpful in ensuring more accurate participant self-reporting. Second, our study did not consider explicitly other factors that may influence the effectiveness of the persuasive intervention, for example, previous experience with alcohol use. For example, personalization has been shown to play a role in amplifying the effect of persuasive strategies and it is definitely worth exploring in this context. Another limitation is that the participants were recruited online and did not belong to a specific group. Social strategies in persuasive apps are most effective if applied in a group of users who know each other or at least believe that the other users with whom they compare or compete are sharing some similarities with them. Future studies can explore settings where participants are members of a particular group, for example, in a high school or a university. The demographic spread of the participants is another limitation. The large majority (83%) of the participants that completed the study were with African ethnicity, so the results presented from this study may not generalize to another ethnicity, especially as research has shown that culture can have a moderating effect on the effectiveness of persuasive strategies [21]. Exploring the effectiveness of the persuasive app and specifically the social strategies on participants of different demographics (adolescents, young adults, adults, older adults, with different gender and culture) provide more directions for future research. One more limitation is the duration of the experiment. While 30-days is a comparatively long period since, generally, longitudinal studies are scarce in Persuasive Technologies research, it is unclear if the effect of reduced drinking behaviour (measured by the reduced AUDIT score of participants) would have persisted after the end of the experiment. Many of the participants expressed a wish to continue using the app, so it would be important to check the scores with and without using the app, post-intervention. Future work can look into the long-term effect of these strategies by conducting the study over several months and years because the longer that the participants decrease their AUDIT score, the higher the likelihood they will have positive health outcomes.

Acknowledgement. This research was funded by the Natural Sciences and Engineering Research Council of Canada (NSERC) Discovery Grant Program of the last author.

References

1. American Psychiatric Association: Diagnostic and statistical manual of mental disorders. 5th edn. (2013). https://doi.org/10.1176/appi.books.9780890425596
2. Scott-Sheldon, L.A.J., Carey, K.B., Cunningham, K., Johnson, B.T., Carey, M.P.: Alcohol use predicts sexual decision-making: a systematic review and meta-analysis of the experimental literature. AIDS Behav. **20**, 19–39 (2016)
3. Spear, L.P.: Effects of adolescent alcohol consumption on the brain and behaviour. Nat. Rev. Neurosci. **19**(4), 197–214 (2018)
4. Cunningham, J.A., Kypri, K., McCambridge, J.: The use of emerging technologies in alcohol treatment. Alcohol Res. Health. **33**(4), 320–326 (2010)
5. Fogg, B.J.: Persuasive computers: perspectives and research directions. www.captology.org. Accessed 02 Mar 2020

6. Durkin, K.F., Wolfe, T.W., Clark, G.A.: College students and binge drinking: an evaluation of social learning theory. Sociol. Spectrum **25**(3), 255–272 (2005)
7. Glanz, K., Bishop, D.B.: The role of behavioral science theory in development and implementation of public health interventions. Ann. Rev. Public Health **31**(1), 399–418 (2010)
8. Bandura, A.: Social cognitive theory. In: Handbook of Theories of Social Psychology, vol. 1, pp. 349–374. SAGE Publications Inc. (2012)
9. Widyasari, Y., Nugroho, L., Permanasari, A.: Persuasive technology for enhanced learning behavior in higher education. Int. J. Educ. Technol. High. Educ. **16**, 1–16 (2019)
10. Davis, F.D.: Perceived usefulness, perceived ease of use, and user acceptance of information technology. MIS Q.: Manage. Inf. **13**(3), 319–339 (1989)
11. Oinas-Kukkonen, H., Harjumaa, M.: Persuasive systems design: key issues, process model, and system features. Commun. Assoc. Inf. Syst. **24**, 28 (2009)
12. Alcohol Use Disorders Identification Test (AUDIT). https://pubs.niaaa.nih.gov/publications/audit.htm. Accessed 20 June 2020
13. McFadyen, T., et al.: The feasibility and acceptability of a web-based alcohol management intervention in community sports clubs: a cross-sectional study. JMIR Res. Protocols **6**(6), e123 (2017)
14. Yoong, S.L., et al.: Childcae service centers' preferences and intentions to use a web-based program to implement healthy eating and physical activity policies and practices:a cross-sectional study. J. Med. Internet Res. **17**, e108 (2015)
15. Cohen, J.: Statistical Power Analysis for the Behavioral Sciences. 2nd edn. Lawrence Erlbaum Associates (1988)
16. Gustavson, K., Von Soest, T., Karevold, E., Roysamb, E.: Attrition and generalizability in longitudinal studies: Findings from a 15-year population-based study and a Monte Carlo simulation study. BMC Public Health **12**(1), 918 (2012)
17. Orji, R., Oyibo, K., Lomotey, R.K., Orji, F.A.: Socially-driven persuasive health intervention design: competition, social comparison, and cooperation. Health Inf. J. **25**, 1451–1484 (2018)
18. Oyibo, K., Orji, R., Vassileva, J.: Developing culturally relevant design guidelines for encouraging physical activity: a social cognitive theory perspective. J. Healthc. Inf. Res. **2**(4), 319–352 (2018). https://doi.org/10.1007/s41666-018-0026-9
19. Orji, F.A., Vassileva, J., Greer, J.: Personalized persuasion for promoting students' engagement and learning (2018). Accessed 16 Sept 2020
20. Orji, R., Reisinger, M., Busch, M., Dijkstra, A.: Tailoring persuasive strategies in E-commerce. In: Proceedings of the Personalisation in Persuasive Technolgy Workshop, Persuasive Technology, Amsterdam, The Netherlands (2017)
21. Oyibo, K.: Designing culture-tailored persuasive technology to promote physical activity. https://harvest.usask.ca/handle/10388/12943. Accessed 14 Sept 2020
22. Oyibo, K., Adaji, I., Vassileva, J.: Mobile web design: the effect of education on the influence of classical and expressive aesthetics on perceived credibility. In: Marcus, A., Wang, W. (eds.) HCII 2019. LNCS, vol. 11584, pp. 66–79. Springer, Cham (2019). https://doi.org/10.1007/978-3-030-23541-3_6
23. Canadian Centre on Substance Use and Addiction: Covid-19 and Increased Alcohol Cosumption: NANOS Poll Summary Report (2020). https://www.ccsa.ca/covid-19-and-increased-alcohol-consumption-nanos-poll-summary-report

Improving Context-Aware Habit-Support Interventions Using Egocentric Visual Contexts

Mina Khan[1]([✉]), Glenn Fernandes[1], Akash Vaish[1], Mayank Manuja[1], Pattie Maes[1], and Agnis Stibe[2,3]

[1] MIT Media Lab, 75 Amherst Street, Cambridge, MA, USA
glennfer@mit.edu, pattie@media.mit.edu
[2] Metis Lab, EM Normandie Business School, Le Havre, France
agnis@transforms.me
[3] INTERACT Research Unit, University of Oulu, Oulu, Finland

Abstract. Habits are automatic actions in stable contexts and can help sustain behavior change. State-of-the-art context-aware habit-support interventions are, however, in predominantly non-visual contexts (time, geolocation, and physical activity), and not in egocentric visual contexts, e.g., eating, meeting people, etc. Using a survey, N = 51 participants, we identified the user-desired visual contexts and interventions mediums for habit support. Based on our survey, we created a wearable system, named PAL, with privacy-preserving on-device deep learning, to deliver real-world habit-support interventions in personalized visual contexts. In our 4-week study, N = 10 participants, interventions using PAL's personalized visual contexts led to >75% increase in habit formation, compared to <40% increase in habit formation using interventions in only non-visual contexts. The habits also persisted in the post-study evaluations 1 and 10 weeks later. Thus, PAL's interventions using personalized visual contexts improve real-world habit formation for sustainable behavior change.

Keywords: Persuasive technology · Wearable · Context-aware · Interventions · Habits · Personalized · Deep learning · Visual contexts

1 Introduction

Persuasive Technologies aim to support behavior change, but commonly used behavior change techniques like reminders induce dependency and behavior change does not persist after the users stop using the apps [31]. Habits are automatic actions in stable contexts [28] and can help sustain behavior change [17,40].

Triggers/contexts have been key for Persuasive Technologies [6] and context-aware technologies can provide interventions in automatically-detected contexts in our everyday lives. State-of-the-art context-aware habit-support interventions

© Springer Nature Switzerland AG 2021
R. Ali et al. (Eds.): PERSUASIVE 2021, LNCS 12684, pp. 115–131, 2021.
https://doi.org/10.1007/978-3-030-79460-6_10

are in contexts involving geolocation, physical motion, and time [29]. However, research shows that users want habit-support interventions in more contexts, e.g., indoor locations and specific objects [29]. Also, habit-formation research has used contexts like brushing teeth [13] and lunch [34], which are currently not automatically detected to deliver context-aware habit-support interventions.

Deep learning-based computer vision models can detect diverse visual contexts, e.g., objects, [37] to provide more information about the user's context. We explore if context-aware interventions using egocentric visual contexts, e.g., eating, brushing teeth, etc., can improve real-world habit-support interventions.

We conducted a user survey with 51 participants (Sect. 3) to identify the desired habit-support intervention contexts and mediums. Our survey showed that people want habit-support in five types of visual contexts (generic faces, objects, custom faces, custom activities, and custom indoor locations), but are wary of using wearable cameras because of privacy concerns. In addition, audio output was the most desired intervention medium for habit support.

In light of our survey, we created a wearable system, named PAL (Sect. 4), to deliver open-ear audio interventions in personalized visual contexts for habit support. Considering camera-related privacy concerns, we used on-device deep learning so that user data is not sent to the cloud/another device for model training or inference. We used deep learning models, tested in real-life settings, to recognize the five types of visual contexts highlighted in our survey.

We designed a 4-week habit-formation study (Sect. 5) with 10 participants to compare the efficacy of PAL's habit-support interventions using personalized visual contexts with interventions using non-visual contexts. Our results (Sect. 6) show more habit formation with interventions using visual contexts (>75% increase) than with interventions using only non-visual contexts, i.e., geolocation, physical activity, and time (<40% increase). The habits also persisted in the post-study surveys 1 and 10 weeks later. We discuss our findings in Sect. 7.

We make three contributions: i. a survey, $N = 51$ participants, identifying the user-desired visual contexts and intervention mediums for habit support; ii. a wearable system, named PAL, with privacy-preserving on-device deep learning, to deliver habit-support interventions in personalized visual contexts; iii. a 4-week study, $N = 10$ participants, with 1 and 10 week later post-study evaluations, showing almost double habit formation with PAL's interventions using personalized visual contexts than with interventions using only non-visual contexts.

2   Related Work

Contexts have always been key to behavior change and persuasive technologies. The Fogg Behavior Model [6] recommends triggers, which tie new behaviors to existing contexts/routines. The need for context-awareness and just-in-time interventions has also been highlighted for persuasive technologies [12, 35].

Our work leverages interdisciplinary insights from habit formation and deep learning to create a wearable system for just-in-time habit-support interventions using personalized visual context detection. Our related work falls into three categories: i. Context-based Habit-support Interventions, ii. Context-aware (Non-habit) Behavior Change Interventions, and iii. Wearable Visual Context Detection. To the best of our knowledge, there are no wearable systems for just-in-time habit-support interventions using personalized visual context detection.

2.1 Context-Based Habit-Support Interventions

Instead of time-based reminders, research suggests leveraging the context-based nature of habits to avoid forgetfulness, e.g., by tying medication reminders to existing routines [33]. Time-based reminders have been shown to have higher adherence but lower automaticity than event-based triggers (without reminders), e.g., after lunch [34]. Researchers have used 'plan reminders' to remind the users of their context-based habit goals [38,39], but these are not in automatically recognized contexts. Non-visual contexts, i.e., time, location, and physical activity, have been used for habit-support interventions [29] in automatically detected contexts, but there are no automatic context-aware habit-support interventions in personalized visual contexts.

2.2 Context-Aware (Non-habit) Behavior Change Interventions

Context-aware interventions, not focused on habit formation, have been investigated in context-aware behavior change systems [9], e.g., using location [26], computer usage [26], physiological signals [2,19,25], multimodal sensing (e.g., heart rate, movement, and computer usage [14]), and even locally-installed motion sensors for activity sensing [22]. Unlike the existing non-visual context detection techniques, wearable visual context detection can recognize faces, objects, activities, scenes, etc., in a mobile context. However, there are no wearable systems for just-in-time behavior change interventions using personalized visual contexts.

2.3 Wearable Visual Context Detection

Deep learning-based egocentric visual context recognition exists, e.g., for memory support [20,21] and visual assistance [1,27], and some systems even distort images for enhancing privacy [4]. There are also on-device deep learning systems for computer vision [18,24]. However, unlike PAL, there are no wearable systems with on-device deep learning for privacy-preserving detection of personalized visual contexts for context-aware habit or behavior change support.

3 Habit-Support Interventions Design

In order to identify the user preferences for habit-support interventions in visual contexts, we conducted a survey about the desired habit-support intervention contexts, intervention mediums, and context detection preferences: *"Think of a habit you would like to develop, i.e. what and when would you do. Q1. When*

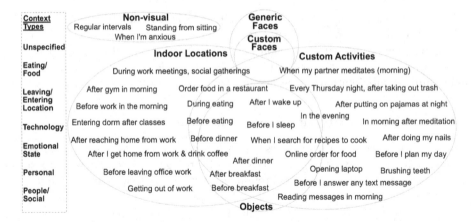

Fig. 1. Open-ended survey responses, N = 51 participants, for the desired habit-support intervention contexts, grouped by one non-visual and five possibly visual categories.

would you like interventions? (Intervention Contexts); Q2. How would you like the intervention? (Intervention Mediums); Q3. Would you like interventions in visual contexts? (no/maybe/yes); Q4. Would you like to use a camera? (no/maybe/yes); Q5. Why/why not?"

We recruited 51 participants ($\mu = 29$ yrs, $\sigma = 10.85$ yrs; 20 males, 30 females; 5 countries; 14 students, 24 professionals, 13 unknown), without any inclusion or exclusion criteria, using our social media and department emailing list.

We summarize the survey results and corresponding design decisions below.

3.1 Intervention Contexts

Only 4 of the 51 desired intervention contexts (Q1) were strictly non-visual, i.e., involving only time, geolocation, or emotional state, while the rest involved visual contexts. We categorized the visual contexts using a combination of 5 broad categories, i.e., generic faces, generic objects, custom faces, custom activities, and custom indoor locations (Fig. 1). We decided to detect the five types of visual contexts for habit-support interventions, and allow users to choose a combination of contexts for habit-support interventions since some contexts involved multiple contexts, e.g., "meditation in morning" involves time and visual contexts.

3.2 Intervention Mediums

We categorized the open-ended responses (Q2). Audio output was the most popular (45%), followed by text notifications (25%), ambient notes (14%), text or audio messages (8%), no reminders (4%), and unknown (4%). Since audio interventions were the most desired, we chose wearable open-ear audio output to privately, seamlessly, and unobtrusively deliver interventions anywhere.

3.3 Cameras and Privacy

Many participants indicated (N = No, M = Maybe, Y = Yes) that they wanted "Interventions in visual contexts" (Q3: 2N, 16M, 33Y) but due to "privacy concerns" (open-ended responses, Q5), did not want to use "Wearable cameras" (Q4: 23N, 15M, 13Y). Thus, we decided to use on-device deep learning for visual context detection so that user images are not sent to the cloud/another device and can be automatically deleted after on-device model training and/or inference. Also, any images saved for user labeling of custom faces, contexts, and indoor locations are deleted right after labeling.

4 PAL Implementation

We developed a wearable system, named PAL, for context-aware habit-support interventions in egocentric visual contexts. PAL has a wearable device, with on-device deep learning, for interventions in personalized visual contexts, and a mobile app for goal-setting, data labeling, and non-visual context detection.

4.1 Mobile App

The mobile app supports goal-setting and intervention context selection Fig. 2a and b), data labeling (Fig. 2c), and non-visual context detection.

We used implementation intentions [8] for goal-setting and intervention context selection. Implementation intentions are "if-then" action plans, e.g., if 'leaving home', then 'pick up fruits', and are commonly used for setting habit goals and interventions contexts [29,38,39]. We allow a combination of two contexts (using AND/OR) for habit-support interventions and include a 30-minute interval between interventions to avoid too many interventions.

The mobile app is connected to the wearable device over Bluetooth to configure the wearable device (e.g., turn off the camera, set intervention contexts, etc.), and for accessing the phone's non-visual context data, i.e., geolocation and physical activity, collected via Google's Places and Activity Transition APIs.

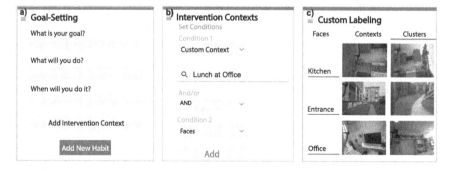

Fig. 2. Mobile app: (a) Goal-setting; (b) Context selection; (c) Custom labeling.

4.2   Wearable Device

PAL's wearable device has an on-body component connected to an on-ear component (Fig. 3). The on-ear component has a camera and speaker, and the on-body component has a microprocessor and a deep learning accelerator chip (Google Coral). There is also a button for taking custom training images.

We considered the on-ear placement suitable for not just open-ear audio output, but also the wearable camera. Cameras on non-face body parts are common, but due to their distance from the eyes, do not always capture the same scene as a user's eyes, especially when the user turns or tilts their head. Glasses are commonly used for on-face cameras but we decided to not use glasses frames as they are relatively bulky and pronounced on the face. Our on-ear camera captures ~70% of a person's visual context (1200 cm × 750 cm view ~1 m away).

On-device deep learning enables privacy-preserving context detection as the user images are not sent to the cloud/another device for training or processing. Also, it avoids time-consuming, power-hungry, and connectivity-dependent constant communication with the cloud/another device for real-time processing. The device consumes maximum 0.3A and our 2500 mAh battery lasts ~5 h.

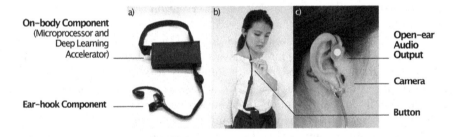

On-body Component
(Microprocessor and
Deep Learning
Accelerator)

Ear-hook Component

Open-ear
Audio
Output

Camera

Button

Fig. 3. (a) PAL's full wearable device with an on-device deep learning accelerator, (b) worn by a person, (c) with a close-up of the on-ear camera and audio output.

4.3   Context Detection Models

PAL has three types of models to recognize the aforementioned five types of visual contexts: i. Fully trained models for (generic) Object and Face Detection; ii. Low-shot custom-trainable models for Custom Face Recognition (1–2 training images) and Custom Context Recognition (for custom activities, ~10 training images); iii. Semi-supervised model, i.e., Custom Context Clustering (for indoor locations separated by geolocations). The model details are in Table 1.

We chose 90-item Common Objects in Context (COCO) [23] dataset for object detection as COCO includes several common objects like a book, cup, toothbrush, etc. We chose Weight Imprinting [30] for the Custom Context Recognition model because it adds new classes to the old ones, instead of replacing

Table 1. Models training and architecture details for visual context recognition.

Visual contexts	Models
Object Detection	MobileNet SSD v2 [11] trained on 90-item COCO [23]
Faces Detection	MobileNet SSD v2 [11] trained on Open Images v4 [16]
Custom Faces Recognition	FaceNet [32], 1–2 training images/face
Custom Context Recognition	Weight imprinting [30] (MobileNet v1 pre-trained on 1000-class ImageNet [3], ∼10 training images/context
Custom Context Clustering	Image Embedding (MobileNet v1 pre-trained on 1000-class ImageNet) clustered via Density-Based Spatial Clustering of Applications with Noise [5]

Table 2. In-the-wild evaluations, N = ∼1000 images, of visual context models. (We list F1-score, in addition to the accuracy, for models tested with imbalanced classes).

Visual contexts	Results
Object Detection	98.8% accuracy, F1-score = 0.79 (∼1000 instances)
Faces Detection	88.8% accuracy, F1-score = 0.9 (∼180 faces)
Custom Faces Recognition	86.9% accuracy (4 known faces, 120 instances)
Custom Context Recognition	87.2% accuracy (7 contexts, ∼350 images)
Custom Context Clustering	82% accuracy (19 indoor locations, ∼300 images)

the old classes, and thus, the users can incrementally add more custom contexts over time. Custom Context Recognition is intended for visually similar contexts, e.g., activities like brushing teeth, whereas Custom Context Clustering is for clustering different, yet connected, views of a context, e.g., indoor locations.

All models are trained and inferred on the wearable device. The user presses a button on the device to start and stop a custom training session (6 images per minute) and labels the images on the mobile app. We tested the models with ∼1000 in-the-wild images of 4 users for 2 days (1 image every 2 min). Each model had a ≥70% accuracy and ∼3 s inference time. The results are in Table 2.

5   Study Design

We designed a study to compare context-aware habit-support interventions using only non-visual contexts, i.e., time, physical activity, and location, [29] *(Group Control)* with those using personalized visual context detection *(Group PAL)*.

5.1   Participants

We recruited 10 participants via our department email list (N = 10; $\mu = 23$ yrs, $\sigma = 2.36$ yrs; 7 males, 3 females; all students). We randomly created 2 groups -

Group PAL (N = 5; $\mu = 23.2$ yrs, $\sigma = 2.39$ yrs; 3 males, 2 females), and Group Control (N = 5; $\mu = 22.8$ yrs, $\sigma = 2.59$ yrs; 4 males, 1 female). Both groups used PAL's system, but only Group PAL had access to visual contexts for interventions.

5.2   Measures

We used three measures: *i. Weekly Habit-Formation Questionnaire, ii. Weekly Experience Questionnaire*, and *iii. End-of-study Open-ended Interview*.

Weekly Habit-Formation Questionnaire: Behavior change is an intricate and long-term process, and instead of measuring behavior change, it is recommended to do "efficacy evaluations", which are "tailored to the specific behavior change interventions" [15]. Since our interventions were aimed at habit-formation, we used habit-formation as an "efficacy measure" [15]. We used the Self-Report Habit Index (SRHI) [36] and Self-Report Behavioural Automaticity Index (SRBAI) [7] as they are commonly used to quantify habit formation [29,34,39].

Weekly Experience Questionnaire and *End-of-study Open-ended Interview*: It is suggested that it is too limiting to treat behavior change as a binary variable [15], and that research must help better understand the behavior change process [10]. In order to evaluate the habit-formation experiences of each participant, we sent a Weekly Experience Questionnaire and conducted an end-of-study in-person interview. The Weekly Experience Questionnaire had 3 open-ended questions – "How was your behavior change experience?", "Did the system help or hinder you? How/why?", and "Is there anything else you'd like to add?".

5.3   Procedures

We conducted a 4-week study, with post-study evaluations 1 and 10 weeks later, to monitor if the habits persisted after the study.

Free-living behavior change evaluations are recommended [10] and we attempted to keep our study as "free-living" [10] as possible. The participants could use the system whenever they wanted to but did not have to. The participants also did not get any financial compensation or other incentives for study completion or habit execution. Similar to Pinder et al.'s habit-formation study with interventions in only non-visual contexts [29], we allowed participants to select personalized habit goals and intervention contexts. We did not collect user's sensor data, e.g., images and geolocation, for privacy reasons.

At the start of the study, we explained the habit-support system to the participants, guiding them about how they can set a target habit and custom intervention context, including training personalized visual contexts. For their target habit, each participant filled the Weekly Habit-Formation Questionnaire at the beginning of the study, at the end of every week for the 4-week study, and also 1 and 10 weeks after the study for post-study evaluations. At the end of every week during the study, the participants also filled the aforementioned

Table 3. Intervention contexts selected for habit-formation study: Group PAL (P1-P5) using visual contexts, and Group Control (P6-P10) using only non-visual contexts.

	Desired contexts	Chosen intervention context
P1	*"in room with partner"*	Custom Face[partner] AND Indoor Location[room]
P2	*"brushing teeth at night"*	Custom Context[Brushing Teeth] AND Time[8–9]
P3	*"phone/computer"*	Contexts = Object[Phone] OR Object[Computer]
P4	*"leaving lab in evening"*	Time[5–7] AND Indoor Location[lab exit]
P5	*"train station in morning"*	Context Cluster[train station] AND Time[9–11]
P6	*"dinner"*	Time[9–10] AND Location[home address]
P7	*"entering dorm room"*	Location[Dorm address]
P8	*"leaving home in morning"*	Time[8–10] AND Location = [home address]
P9	*"in evening at work"*	Time[5pm–7pm] AND Location = [office]
P10	*"in the morning"*	Time[10am–11am]

Weekly Experience Questionnaire. Finally, at the end of the 4-week study, we conducted an open-ended interview with the participants.

6 Results

Our 4-week study, plus post-study evaluations 1 and 10 weeks later, compared the efficacy of habit-support interventions using visual contexts with those using only non-visual contexts. We summarize the intervention contexts, quantitative habit formation, and qualitative experiences of our participants below.

6.1 Chosen Habit-Support Contexts

3 out of 5 participants (P6-8) in the control group could have used interventions in visual contexts. However, limited by only non-visual contexts, the participants chose an approximation, e.g., *Time[9–10] AND location[home]* for *"dinner"*. All Group PAL participants selected visual contexts and 4 out of 5 trained custom visual contexts, i.e., activities, faces, or indoor locations. The intervention contexts chosen and desired by each participant are in Table 3.

6.2 Quantitative Habit Formation

The 4-week increase in SRBAI was 77.1% (Group PAL) and 39.3% (Group Control), and the increase in SRHI was 75.7% (Group PAL) and 21.9% (Group Control). The average week-by-week change for the 4 weeks during the study was: {SRBAI = {Group PAL: [64%, 17%, −13%, 5.5%]; Control: [33%, 14%, −6%, −2.1%]}, and SRHI = {Group PAL: [59%, 21%, −7.9%, −1%]; Control: [26%, 2.3%, −7.3%, and 2.0%]}. Most of the changes in SRHI/SRBAI occurred in the first 2 weeks. Week 3 even had a decrease in SRHI/SRBAI since classes started in Week 3 and our participants, all of whom were students, mentioned getting 'busy'. SRHI/SRBAI remained relatively stable or in Week 4 and also in the post-study surveys 1 and 10 weeks later. The results are shown in Fig. 4.

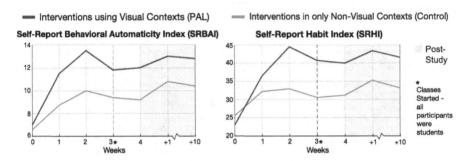

Fig. 4. Habit-formation results for study, N = 10, comparing interventions using visual contexts (Group PAL) with interventions in only non-visual contexts (Group Control).

6.3   Qualitative Responses

We noted the following 3 themes in our questionnaire and interview responses.

Intervention Contexts. Group PAL found interventions in the right contexts helpful (*P1: "reminders at the right time were helpful"*, *P3: "notifications while in front of my laptop to not mindlessly drift into work"*), especially when they were busy (*P4: "reminders especially as I got busy"*, *P2: "I did my habit even though I was busy!"*). The control group did not find the interventions in only non-visual contexts as helpful because they were not in the right moments (*P8: "reminders were not for the exact moments I wanted"*, *P6: "notifications at general times can be anxiety-inducing."*) – some ignored the notifications (*P9: "I did not notice the reminders because I was busy"*), while others used them as persistent, not just-in-time, reminders (*P10: "notification kept reminding me about focus(ing) on a healthy life"*).

System Usability. The participants did not have privacy or social acceptability problems with the camera. Some participants mentioned liking the camera (*P2: "liked the small and unnoticeable camera"*, *P3: "nice to be able to cover the camera with hair when needed"*), while others had minor complaints (*P5: "headphones and winter cap cover the camera"*) or suggestions (*P4: "a hardware switch to turn off the camera in restrooms"*). Moreover, three participants found the device 'heavy' and one of them even mentioned that (*"P4: I didn't wear the device for very long due to its bulkiness"*), whereas two participants complained about the limited battery life (*"P1: battery doesn't last full day"*). Lastly, four participants had minor issues due to mobile app crashes and battery drain.

Emotions and Self-perceptions. After the study, Group PAL participants, in general, indicated a firmer belief in their ability to change (*"P2: (I learned) I can take out time for activities I thought there wasn't time for"*, P5: *"being able to do what I had planned to do gave me the confidence to change"*, P3: *"As I practiced more, it became a part of my day"*), compared to the control group participants, two of whom were apprehensive even after they were able to change (*P5: "I was successful, I am happy but I am also worried that I'll be able to keep it going."*). Group PAL participants felt good (*P1: "I was successful...felt really good"*, *P4: "healthy lifestyle doesn't only keep you physically fit but also happy and confident"*), but the control group did not mention anything explicitly.

7 Discussion

We developed a wearable system for just-in-time habit-support interventions in personalized visual contexts, and used it to compare the efficacy of habit-support interventions using visual contexts with those using only non-visual contexts. We leveraged deep learning to extend real-world habit-support interventions to wearable egocentric visual contexts and our study shows that interventions using personalized egocentric visual contexts can support better real-world habit formation for behavior change than the existing habit-support interventions in only non-visual contexts, i.e., time, geolocation, and physical activity. We discuss the key findings, limitations, and recommendations of our study below.

7.1 Key Findings

We summarize our key findings for quantitative and qualitative results for interventions using visual contexts versus interventions in only non-visual contexts.

Quantitative Habit Formation. Our 4-week study with total 10 participants showed almost double habit formation with interventions using personalized wearable egocentric visual contexts than with interventions in only non-visual contexts. The habits also persisted in the post-study surveys 1 and 10 weeks later, showing sustainable habits without long-term dependence on app support.

Interventions in Visual Contexts. All Group PAL participants selected interventions in at least one visual context, and though we did not measure the context detection accuracy in our 4-week study due to privacy reasons, the participants mentioned receiving interventions in helpful contexts. Even though cameras usually have privacy concerns, Group PAL's participants did not mention any because their images were not sent to the cloud/another device for processing and all the images for custom labeling were also deleted right after the users labeled them. Overall, the participants found interventions using visual contexts timely and useful, even during the participants' busy days, and the camera was usable because of its small size and proper data privacy and control measures.

Interventions in only Non-visual Contexts. Some participants wanted contexts, e.g., "dinner", "leaving home", and "entering dorm room", which were not only perfectly recognizable using non-visual contexts, i.e., time, geolocation, and physical activity, and could have been better recognized by adding visual context detection. Thus, the participants did not receive interventions in their exact desired contexts an had to either remember to do their habits in their exact desired contexts or do the habits based on the non-visual context interventions.

Moreover, the participants were not always doing the same activity in only time or geolocation-based contexts, and doing the desired habits when they received the intervention meant that their actions were not in stable contexts, e.g., the participant could be having dinner or working at 9 pm. Habits form in stable contexts and unstable contexts may have hindered habit formation.

Finally, interventions in only non-visual contexts were disruptive and even anxiety-inducing because the exact activities the participants were doing in the non-visual contexts varied and it was not ideal to disrupt them. Thus, the participants ignored the interventions and even skipped habits when they were busy.

7.2   Limitations and Future Work

Our work has the following three limitations and directions for future work.

Device Usability and Functionality. Since our device was a lab-made prototype, it was relatively bulky and had to be recharged for day-long use. However, with industrial design and manufacturing as well as further advancements in on-device deep learning hardware and models, the wearable device could be made much smaller and also have a longer battery life. Also, further research into on-device deep learning models could open up new possibilities for visual context detection, including human-in-the-loop personalized visual context detection.

Study Size and Participants. Our study is an initial investigation into using visual context detection for habit-support interventions. We kept our study group small to evaluate the detailed experience of each user. Future iterations of our work may involve larger-scale studies with more participants, and also, potentially more diverse groups, e.g., people with specific behavior change needs.

Behavior Change Measurement. We did not measure actual behavior change using sensor data or self-report because of privacy reasons and because we did not want to put implicit pressure on the participants to change their behaviors, knowing that they were being monitored or had to self-report. Instead, we used habit formation as an efficacy measure since our system was designed for habit support [15]. In the future, visual context sensing can be extended to objectively track behavior change and even offer closed-loop behavior change interventions.

7.3   Recommendations and Implications

We have three main recommendations. First, consider including personalized visual contexts as users want interventions in personalized visual contexts. Second, use on-device deep learning to keep user data private. Third, use visual context detection to deliver habit-support interventions for better habit formation. PAL supports better real-world habit formation using egocentric visual contexts, and can also be further useful for privacy-preserving visual context tracking and for non-habit-support behavior change interventions in egocentric visual contexts.

8   Conclusion

Habit formation helps sustain behavior change [17,40]. We investigated if adding egocentric visual contexts to the existing non-visual mobile contexts can improve context-aware habit-support interventions in the real world. We conducted a user survey about the desired habit-support intervention contexts and mediums. Based on our survey, we created a wearable system, named PAL, to deliver habit-support interventions in personalized visual contexts, while preserving user privacy using on-device deep learning. Our study shows that using personalized visual contexts for context-aware habit-support interventions leads to more habit formation than interventions using only non-visual mobile contexts. The habits also persisted 10 weeks after the study. Thus, PAL's wearable interventions in egocentric visual contexts improve real-world context-aware habit-support interventions for better habit formation and sustainable behavior change.

Appendix: Model Evaluation Data

We share below additional details about the in-the-wild data collected for evaluating our machine learning models.

1. Overall: 13 locations (9 indoors - 4 eateries, 2 shops, 1 dorm, 1 house, 1 office; 4 outdoors - 1 shopping area, 1 roadside walkway, 1 train station, 1 residential area).
2. Object detection: 618 persons, 282 books, 48 TV screens, 45 laptops, 30 chairs, 25 bottles, 14 cars, 13 teddy bears, 8 keyboards, 7 microwaves, 7 cell phones, 6 potted plants, 5 couches, 4 bowls, 3 sandwiches, 3 trains, 2 clocks, 2 refrigerators, 2 sinks, 2 dining tables, 1 toilet, 1 umbrella, 1 bus, and 1 bicycle.
3. Custom activities: brushing teeth, making coffee, eating lunch, working in own office, working in an open office area, playing pool, playing foosball ($\sim$50 images each) (Fig. 5).

Fig. 5. Example images, N = ~1000, from in-the-wild evaluations of on-device models.

References

1. Bauer, Z., Dominguez, A., Cruz, E., Gomez-Donoso, F., Orts-Escolano, S., Cazorla, M.: Enhancing perception for the visually impaired with deep learning techniques and low-cost wearable sensors. Pattern Recogn. Lett. **137**, 27–36 (2019)
2. Costa, J., Adams, A.T., Jung, M.F., Guimbretière, F., Choudhury, T.: EmotionCheck: a wearable device to regulate anxiety through false heart rate feedback. GetMobile **21**(2), 22–25 (2017)
3. Deng, J., Dong, W., Socher, R., Li, L.J., Li, K., Fei-Fei, L.: ImageNet: a large-scale hierarchical image database. In: 2009 IEEE Conference on Computer Vision and Pattern Recognition, pp. 248–255. IEEE (2009)
4. Dimiccoli, M., Marín, J., Thomaz, E.: Mitigating bystander privacy concerns in egocentric activity recognition with deep learning and intentional image degradation. Proc. ACM Interact. Mob. Wearable Ubiquit. Technol. **1**(4), 1–18 (2018)
5. Ester, M., Kriegel, H.P., Sander, J., Xu, X., et al.: A density-based algorithm for discovering clusters in large spatial databases with noise. In: KDD, vol. 96, pp. 226–231 (1996)
6. Fogg, B.: A behavior model for persuasive design. In: Proceedings of the 4th International Conference on Persuasive Technology, Persuasive 2009, pp. 40:1–40:7. ACM, New York (2009). https://doi.org/10.1145/1541948.1541999
7. Gardner, B., Abraham, C., Lally, P., de Bruijn, G.J.: Towards parsimony in habit measurement: testing the convergent and predictive validity of an automaticity subscale of the self-report habit index. Int. J. Behav. Nutr. Phys. Act. **9**(1), 102 (2012)

8. Gollwitzer, P.M.: Implementation intentions: strong effects of simple plans. Am. Psychol. **54**(7), 493 (1999)

9. Hardeman, W., Houghton, J., Lane, K., Jones, A., Naughton, F.: A systematic review of just-in-time adaptive interventions (JITAIs) to promote physical activity. Int. J. Behav. Nutr. Phys. Act. **16**(1), 31 (2019)

10. Hekler, E.B., Klasnja, P., Froehlich, J.E., Buman, M.P.: Mind the theoretical gap: interpreting, using, and developing behavioral theory in HCI research. In: Proceedings of the SIGCHI Conference on Human Factors in Computing Systems, CHI 2013, pp. 3307–3316. ACM, New York (2013)

11. Howard, A.G., et al.: MobileNets: efficient convolutional neural networks for mobile vision applications, April 2017

12. IJsselsteijn, W., de Kort, Y., Midden, C., Eggen, B., van den Hoven, E.: Persuasive technology for human well-being: setting the scene. In: IJsselsteijn, W.A., de Kort, Y.A.W., Midden, C., Eggen, B., van den Hoven, E. (eds.) PERSUASIVE 2006. LNCS, vol. 3962, pp. 1–5. Springer, Heidelberg (2006). https://doi.org/10.1007/11755494_1

13. Judah, G., Gardner, B., Aunger, R.: Forming a flossing habit: an exploratory study of the psychological determinants of habit formation. Br. J. Health. Psychol. **18**(2), 338–353 (2013)

14. Kaur, H., Williams, A.C., McDuff, D., Czerwinski, M., Teevan, J., Iqbal, S.T.: Optimizing for happiness and productivity: modeling opportune moments for transitions and breaks at work. In: Proceedings of the 2020 CHI Conference on Human Factors in Computing Systems, pp. 1–15 (2020)

15. Klasnja, P., Consolvo, S., Pratt, W.: How to evaluate technologies for health behavior change in HCI research. In: Proceedings of the SIGCHI Conference on Human Factors in Computing Systems, CHI 2011, pp. 3063–3072. ACM, New York (2011)

16. Kuznetsova, A., et al.: The open images dataset v4: unified image classification, object detection, and visual relationship detection at scale. arXiv preprint arXiv:1811.00982 (2018)

17. Kwasnicka, D., Dombrowski, S.U., White, M., Sniehotta, F.: Theoretical explanations for maintenance of behaviour change: a systematic review of behaviour theories. Health Psychol. Rev. **10**(3), 277–296 (2016)

18. Lane, N.D., Bhattacharya, S., Mathur, A., Georgiev, P., Forlivesi, C., Kawsar, F.: Squeezing deep learning into mobile and embedded devices. IEEE Pervasive Comput. **16**(3), 82–88 (2017)

19. Lee, E., Lee, W., Cho, J.: Moonglow: wearable device which helps with cognitive behavioral therapy for panic disorder patients. In: Proceedings of the 2018 ACM International Joint Conference and 2018 International Symposium on Pervasive and Ubiquitous Computing and Wearable Computers, UbiComp 2018, pp. 126–129. ACM, New York (2018)

20. Lee, H., Upright, C., Eliuk, S., Kobsa, A.: Personalized object recognition for augmenting human memory. In: Proceedings of the 2016 ACM International Joint Conference on Pervasive and Ubiquitous Computing: Adjunct, pp. 1054–1061 (2016)

21. Lee, H., Upright, C., Eliuk, S., Kobsa, A.: Personalized visual recognition via wearables: a first step toward personal perception enhancement. In: Costa, A., Julian, V., Novais, P. (eds.) Personal Assistants: Emerging Computational Technologies. ISRL, vol. 132, pp. 95–112. Springer, Cham (2018). https://doi.org/10.1007/978-3-319-62530-0_6

22. Lee, J., Walker, E., Burleson, W., Kay, M., Buman, M., Hekler, E.B.: Self-experimentation for behavior change: design and formative evaluation of two

approaches. In: Proceedings of the 2017 CHI Conference on Human Factors in Computing Systems, pp. 6837–6849 (2017)

23. Lin, T.-Y., et al.: Microsoft COCO: common objects in context. In: Fleet, D., Pajdla, T., Schiele, B., Tuytelaars, T. (eds.) ECCV 2014. LNCS, vol. 8693, pp. 740–755. Springer, Cham (2014). https://doi.org/10.1007/978-3-319-10602-1_48

24. Mathur, A., Lane, N.D., Bhattacharya, S., Boran, A., Forlivesi, C., Kawsar, F.: Deepeye: resource efficient local execution of multiple deep vision models using wearable commodity hardware. In: Proceedings of the 15th Annual International Conference on Mobile Systems, Applications, and Services, pp. 68–81 (2017)

25. McEuen, A., Proffitt, J., Camba, J.D., Kwon, E.S.: &You: design of a sensor-based wearable device for use in cognitive behavioral therapy. In: Duffy, V.G., Lightner, N. (eds.) Advances in Human Factors and Ergonomics in Healthcare. AISC, vol. 482, pp. 251–260. Springer, Cham (2017). https://doi.org/10.1007/978-3-319-41652-6_24

26. Nahum-Shani, I., et al.: Just-in-Time adaptive interventions (JITAIs) in mobile health: key components and design principles for ongoing health behavior support. Ann. Behav. Med. **52**(6), 446–462 (2018)

27. Nishajith, A., Nivedha, J., Nair, S.S., Shaffi, J.M.: Smart cap-wearable visual guidance system for blind. In: 2018 International Conference on Inventive Research in Computing Applications (ICIRCA), pp. 275–278. IEEE (2018)

28. Pinder, C., Vermeulen, J., Cowan, B.R., Beale, R.: Digital behaviour change interventions to break and form habits. ACM Trans. Comput. Hum. Interact. **25**(3), 15:1–15:66 (2018)

29. Pinder, C., Vermeulen, J., Wicaksono, A., Beale, R., Hendley, R.J.: If this, then habit: exploring context-aware implementation intentions on smartphones. In: Proceedings of the 18th International Conference on Human-Computer Interaction with Mobile Devices and Services Adjunct, pp. 690–697. ACM, September 2016

30. Qi, H., Brown, M., Lowe, D.G.: Low-shot learning with imprinted weights. In: Proceedings of the IEEE Conference on Computer Vision and Pattern Recognition, pp. 5822–5830 (2018)

31. Renfree, I., Harrison, D., Marshall, P., Stawarz, K., Cox, A.: Don't kick the habit: the role of dependency in habit formation apps. In: Proceedings of the 2016 CHI Conference Extended Abstracts on Human Factors in Computing Systems, pp. 2932–2939 (2016)

32. Schroff, F., Kalenichenko, D., Philbin, J.: FaceNet: a unified embedding for face recognition and clustering. In: Proceedings of the IEEE Conference on Computer Vision and Pattern Recognition, pp. 815–823 (2015)

33. Stawarz, K., Cox, A.L., Blandford, A.: Don't forget your pill! designing effective medication reminder apps that support users' daily routines. In: Proceedings of the SIGCHI Conference on Human Factors in Computing Systems, pp. 2269–2278 (2014)

34. Stawarz, K., Cox, A.L., Blandford, A.: Beyond self-tracking and reminders: designing smartphone apps that support habit formation. In: Proceedings of the 33rd Annual ACM Conference on Human Factors in Computing Systems, CHI 2015, pp. 2653–2662. ACM, New York (2015)

35. Tikka, P., Oinas-Kukkonen, H.: RightOnTime: the role of timing and unobtrusiveness in behavior change support systems. In: Meschtscherjakov, A., De Ruyter, B., Fuchsberger, V., Murer, M., Tscheligi, M. (eds.) PERSUASIVE 2016. LNCS, vol. 9638, pp. 327–338. Springer, Cham (2016). https://doi.org/10.1007/978-3-319-31510-2_28

36. Verplanken, B., Orbell, S.: Reflections on past behavior: a self-report index of habit strength 1. J. Appl. Soc. Psychol. **33**(6), 1313–1330 (2003)
37. Voulodimos, A., Doulamis, N., Doulamis, A., Protopapadakis, E.: Deep learning for computer vision: a brief review. Comput. Intell. Neurosci. **2018** (2018)
38. Wicaksono, A., Hendley, R., Beale, R.: Investigating the impact of adding plan reminders on implementation intentions to support behaviour change. Interact. Comput. **31**(2), 177–191 (2019)
39. Wicaksono, A., Hendley, R.J., Beale, R.: Using reinforced implementation intentions to support habit formation. In: Extended Abstracts of the 2019 CHI Conference on Human Factors in Computing Systems, pp. 1–6 (2019)
40. Wood, W., Neal, D.T.: Healthy through habit: interventions for initiating & maintaining health behavior change. Behav. Sci. Policy **2**(1), 71–83 (2016)

Emotions and User Experience

Disparate Impact Diminishes Consumer Trust Even for Advantaged Users

Tim Draws[1,2(✉)] , Zoltán Szlávik[1,3] , Benjamin Timmermans[1,4] ,
Nava Tintarev[5] , Kush R. Varshney[6] , and Michael Hind[6]

[1] IBM Center for Advanced Studies Benelux, Amsterdam, The Netherlands
[2] Delft University of Technology, Delft, The Netherlands
t.a.draws@tudelft.nl
[3] myTomorrows, Amsterdam, The Netherlands
zoltan.szlavik@mytomorrows.com
[4] IBM Research, Amsterdam, The Netherlands
b.timmermans@nl.ibm.com
[5] Maastricht University, Maastricht, The Netherlands
n.tintarev@maastrichtuniversity.nl
[6] IBM Research, Yorktown Heights, NY, USA
{krvarshn,hindm}@us.ibm.com

Abstract. Systems aiming to aid consumers in their decision-making
(e.g., by implementing persuasive techniques) are more likely to be effective when consumers trust them. However, recent research has demonstrated that the machine learning algorithms that often underlie such
technology can act unfairly towards specific groups (e.g., by making more
favorable predictions for men than for women). An undesired disparate
impact resulting from this kind of algorithmic unfairness could diminish
consumer trust and thereby undermine the purpose of the system. We
studied this effect by conducting a between-subjects user study investigating how (gender-related) disparate impact affected consumer trust in
an app designed to improve consumers' financial decision-making. Our
results show that disparate impact decreased consumers' trust in the
system and made them less likely to use it. Moreover, we find that trust
was affected to the same degree across consumer groups (i.e., advantaged
and disadvantaged users) despite both of these consumer groups recognizing their respective levels of personal benefit. Our findings highlight
the importance of fairness in consumer-oriented artificial intelligence systems.

Keywords: Disparate impact · Algorithmic fairness · Consumer trust

1 Introduction

Applications that seek to advise or nudge consumers into better decision-making
(e.g., concerning personal health or finance) can only be effective when consumers trust their guidance. Trustworthiness is an essential aspect in the design

T. Draws, Z. Szlávik and B. Timmermans—Current affiliation.

© Springer Nature Switzerland AG 2021
R. Ali et al. (Eds.): PERSUASIVE 2021, LNCS 12684, pp. 135–149, 2021.
https://doi.org/10.1007/978-3-030-79460-6_11

of such *persuasive technology* (PT); i.e., technology aiming to change attitudes or behaviors without using coercion or deception [26,28,41]; because consumers are unlikely to use (or be persuaded by) systems that they do not trust [23,35]. Recent research has identified several factors that affect consumer trust in this context; including consumers' emotional states [1] as well as the system's reliability [26] and transparency [35]. Moreover, it has been argued that trust also depends on *moral expectations* that consumers have towards the technology they use [26,35]. Consumer trust could increasingly depend on such moral expectations as more systems implement machine learning algorithms (e.g., in personal health [33,35] or finance [20] applications) that make them harder to scrutinize.

A specific moral expectation that acts as a requirement for trust in this context may be *fairness* [39]. When nudges and advice are tailored to the individual consumer using machine learning, consumers may expect that the system acts fairly towards different consumer groups (e.g., concerning race or gender). Nudging or advising such that the degree of positive impact that the system has on consumers' lives *varies* with group membership could constitute an undesired *disparate impact*. For example, a *robo-advisor* (i.e., PT designed to improve consumers' financial situation [20]) could have a disparate impact by systematically recommending "safer", lower-risk investments to female consumers compared to male consumers, yielding them lower returns. Such disparate impact would violate the moral expectation of fairness and thereby undermine consumer trust.

Employing machine learning in consumer-oriented applications often holds the promise of increasing their usefulness to the individual consumer [33,46] but also bears a greater vulnerability for disparate impact. Recent research has demonstrated that machine learning algorithms may unfairly discriminate based on group membership [2,6,27]. Such discrimination is referred to as *algorithmic unfairness* if a pre-defined notion of fairness is violated [27,42] and can easily lead to an undesired disparate impact [6,13]. For example, outcomes in advice from robo-advisors may differ between groups, given that financial advice has historically been gender-biased to the disadvantage of female consumers [5,24] and algorithmic unfairness often results from disparities in the historical data that is used to train the algorithm [27]. Although several methods have been developed to mitigate algorithmic unfairness [7], in many cases it is currently not possible to do so to a satisfactory degree [8].

Disparate impact is thus a realistic issue that could undermine the efficacy of consumer-oriented artificial intelligence (AI) systems. It has been argued that fairness plays a key role in fostering trust in AI [4,34,37,39,40]. However, to the best of our knowledge, no previous work has *studied* the influence of undesired disparate impact (i.e., as a result of algorithmic unfairness) on consumer trust. It is further unclear whether unfairly advantaged consumers are affected to the same degree as disadvantaged consumers in this context. That is, the influence of disparate impact on consumer trust may depend on *perceived personal benefit* (i.e., advantaged users trusting the system's advice despite disparate impact as long as they personally benefit) or not (i.e., advantaged users losing trust in lockstep with disadvantaged users despite a perceived personal benefit). We study the effect of disparate impact on consumer trust at the use case of gender bias in robo-advisors by investigating the following research questions:

- **RQ1.** Does an apparent disparate impact of a robo-advisor affect the degree of trust that consumers place in it?
- **RQ2.** Does disparate impact affect the trust of unfairly advantaged consumers to a different degree than that of unfairly disadvantaged consumers?

To answer these questions, we conducted a between-subjects user study where we exposed participants to varying degrees of disparate impact of a robo-advisor (i.e., advantaging male users; see Sect. 3). Our results show that disparate impact negatively affected consumer's trust in the robo-advisor and decreased their willingness to use it (see Sect. 4). Furthermore, we find that, despite both groups recognizing their respective personal (dis)advantage, *both* the disadvantaged group (women) as well as the advantaged group (men) experienced the same decrease in trust when learned about a disparate impact of the robo-advisor. Our findings underline the importance of ensuring algorithmic fairness in consumer-oriented (AI) systems when aiming to maintain consumer trust.

2 Background and Related Work

We study the effect of disparate impact on consumer trust at the use case of gender bias in robo-advisors. Our reasons for choosing the financial domain here are threefold. First, algorithmic decision-making is already widespread in consumer-oriented financial applications (e.g., in robo-advisors) [20]. Second, algorithmic decision-making in such systems is highly impactful: it directly affects consumers' financial situations and thereby their life quality. Third, (human) financial advice has traditionally been gender-biased, underestimating and disadvantaging female consumers [5,24]. Historical data on financial advice thus contain these biases. If the algorithms that underlie robo-advisors are trained using these data, robo-advisors may have according disparate impact.

Trust in AI Systems. Consumers do not use systems that they do not trust [23]. That is why trust is an important aspect in the interaction between consumer-oriented AI systems (e.g., those implementing PT) and consumers [1,26,35,41]. Recent research has linked trust in such systems to the reliability [26] and transparency [35] of the system at hand as well as consumers' emotional states [1] and moral expectations [26,35]. Such moral expectations may gain in importance as systems increasingly rely on machine learning algorithms [20,30,33,35,46]. Moreover, whereas in some cases consumers fall prey to *automation bias* (i.e., a tendency to prefer automated over human decisions) [10], in other cases, they experience what has been referred to as *algorithm aversion*: a tendency to prefer human over algorithmic advice [11,29,32]. Research has shown that algorithm aversion can be the result of witnessing how an algorithm errs [12]. Especially in cases where a machine learning algorithm acted *unfairly*, leading to an undesired disparate impact (i.e., violating consumers' moral expectations and reflecting erroneous decision-making), consumer trust could thus be diminished.

Measuring and Mitigating Algorithmic Unfairness. Research has demonstrated that machine learning algorithms can make biased (unfair) predictions to the disadvantage of specific groups [2,6,27,43]. For instance, AI systems may discriminate between white and black defendants in predicting their likelihood of re-offending [2] and between male and female consumers in predicting their creditworthiness [43]. Several methods have been proposed to measure and mitigate biases in algorithmic decision-making [7,15,21,22,27,47]. Despite these efforts, the measurement and mitigation of algorithmic bias remain challenging [8,27].

Disparate Impact and Trust. Algorithmic fairness has been identified as a core building block of trustworthy AI systems [4,34,37,39,40], yet few studies directly investigate the relationship between algorithmic fairness (or disparate impact) and consumer trust. Participants in one study reported that learning about algorithmic unfairness induced negative feelings and that it might cause them to lose trust in a company or product [45]. Consumers have further expressed general concerns about disparate impact of AI on a societal level [3] and are more likely to judge decisions as less fair and trustworthy if they are made by an algorithm as opposed to a human [19]. However, it has also been shown that the degree to which people are concerned about disparate impact depends on their personal biases [31,36]. What remains unclear is to what extent disparate impact (as a result of algorithmic unfairness) affects consumer trust and, if so, who (i.e., unfairly advantaged and disadvantaged consumers) are affected in particular.

3   Method

To investigate the two research questions identified in Sect. 1, we conducted a between-subjects user study. The setting of this study was a fictional scenario in which a bank offers a robo-advisor – called the *AI Advisor* – to its customers. We aimed to perform a granular analysis of the effect of disparate impact on consumer trust by exposing participants to different degrees of disparate impact supposedly caused by the *AI Advisor* and measuring their attitudes towards this system. Specifically, we analyzed whether the different degrees of disparate impact affected participant's *trust* (i.e., whether they believed that the AI Advisor would make correct predictions and therefore benefit its users). To differentiate between this general notion of trust and related attitudes, we also measured *willingness to use* and *perceived personal benefit* concerning the *AI Advisor*.

3.1   Operationalization

Dependent Variables. Our experiment involved measuring participants' attitudes towards the *AI advisor*; specifically *trust, willingness to use, perceived personal benefit*. Each variable was measured twice: once after participants saw general user statistics (Step 1; see Sect. 3.3) and once after participants saw gender-specific user statistics on the *AI advisor* (Step 2). We computed difference scores from these two measurements that reflected how seeing the gender-specific statistics affected participant's attitudes as compared to their baseline attitudes.

- *Change in Trust (Continuous).* Participants rated their trust by responding to the item "In general, the AI advisor can be trusted to make correct recommendations" on a 7-point Likert scale. We coded all responses on an ordinal scale ranging from -3 (strongly disagree) to 3 (strongly agree) and subtracted the second measurement from the first to compute the *change in trust*. Values could thus range from -6 to 6.
- *Change in Willingness to Use (Categorical).* Participants could respond to the item "I would personally use the AI Advisor" with either "yes" or "no". We recorded whether their answer had changed (i.e., "yes" to "no" or vice versa) or stayed the same in the second measurement. This variable thus encompassed three categories.
- *Change in Perceived Personal Benefit (Continuous).* Participants rated their perceived personal benefit by responding to the item "I would personally benefit from using the AI advisor" on a 7-point Likert scale. To compute the *change in perceived personal benefit*, we again subtracted the second measurement from the first. Values could thus range from -6 to 6.

Independent Variable. Our experiment varied depending on the condition that a participant was placed in (see Sect. 3.3):

- *Condition.* During the experiment, we showed participants a table with user statistics of bank customers that use the *AI advisor*. These statistics, supposedly showing the average change in bank account balance for users and non-users of the *AI Advisor*, split by gender, differed depending on the condition a participant had been placed in. Each participant saw only one of four conditions: the *control* condition (in which the statistics were balanced across genders, reflecting an absence of disparate impact) or one of three experimental conditions – which we call *little bias*, *strong bias*, and *extreme bias* – that reflected varying degrees of disparate impact in favor of male consumers. Specifically, these different degrees of disparate impact represented scenarios in which female users of the *AI advisor* were disadvantaged but still benefited from using the *AI advisor* (little bias), did not benefit from the *AI advisor* (strong bias), or would in fact benefit from *not* using the *AI advisor* (extreme bias). Table 1 shows the numbers that were shown in the second statistics table in each of the conditions.

Individual Differences and Descriptive Statistics. We took two additional measurements to enable more fine-grained analyses and describe our sample:

- *Gender.* Participants could state which gender they identified with by picking from the options "male", "female", and "other/not specified".
- *Age.* Participants could write their age in an open text field.

3.2 Hypotheses

Based on the research questions **RQ1** and **RQ2** introduced in Sect. 1, the related work from Sect. 2, and the experimental setup described in this section, we formulated several hypotheses. We expected that disparate impact will decrease

Table 1. Fictional gender-specific statistics shown to participants during the second step of the study across. Only the top left two cells (concerning users of the *AI Advisor*) differed across conditions, reflecting varying degrees of disparate impact.

	Using AI Advisor	Not Using AI Advisor		Using AI Advisor	Not Using AI Advisor
Male	20%	10%	Male	25%	10%
Female	20%	10%	Female	15%	10%
All	20%	10%	All	20%	10%
	Control condition			*Little bias* condition	

	Using AI Advisor	Not Using AI Advisor		Using AI Advisor	Not Using AI Advisor
Male	30%	10%	Male	35%	10%
Female	10%	10%	Female	5%	10%
All	20%	10%	All	20%	10%
	Strong bias condition			*Extreme bias* condition	

consumer trust (H1a) and that consumers will be less likely to use the *AI Advisor* (H1b) if it has disparate impact (i.e., the stronger the disparate impact, the lower consumer trust and willingness to use the *AI Advisor*). We predicted that disparate impact would affect the perceived personal benefit of male consumers differently compared to female consumers (i.e., following what the displayed statistics suggest; H2a). Accordingly, we further expected that the decrease in trust described in H1a would be moderated by gender (H2b). That is, we predicted that the trust of advantaged consumers (i.e., men) would be affected differently compared to disadvantaged consumers (i.e., women).

- **H1a.** Consumers who are exposed to statistics that reveal a disparate impact of a robo-advisor in favor of male users will *trust this system less* to give correct recommendations compared to consumers who are exposed to balanced statistics.
- **H1b.** Consumers who are exposed to statistics that reveal a disparate impact of a robo-advisor in favor of male users will be *less likely to use this system* compared to consumers who are exposed to balanced statistics.
- **H2a.** The effect of statistics suggesting a disparate impact of a robo-advisor in favor of men on *perceived personal benefit* is moderated by gender.
- **H2b.** The effect of statistics suggesting a disparate impact of a robo-advisor in favor of men on *consumer trust* is moderated by gender.

3.3   Procedure

We set up our user study by creating a task on the online study platform *Figure Eight*.[1] Before commencing with the experiment, participants were shown a short introduction and asked to state their gender and age. The experiment consisted of two steps. Whereas Step 1 was the same for all participants, Step 2 differed depending on which one of four conditions a participant had been assigned to.

Step 1. We introduced participants to a fictional scenario in which they could activate a robo-advisor – called the *AI advisor* – in their banking app:

> *"Imagine your bank offers a digital assistant called the 'AI advisor'. If you activate the AI advisor in your banking app, it will monitor your financial situation and give you relevant recommendations that may improve your financial situation. For example, it may suggest saving strategies or recommend investments."*

Additionally, to promote the idea that the AI Advisor is generally reliable, participants were given an idea of whether people benefit from using the *AI Advisor*:

> *"Overall statistics suggest that people benefit from using the AI advisor. The bank account balance of bank customers who use the AI advisor increases by an average of 20% every year, whereas the balance of customers who don't use the AI advisor increases by an average of only 10% per year."*

Below was a table displaying the mentioned statistics. We then measured trust, willingness to use, and perceived personal benefit concerning the *AI Advisor*.

Step 2. Participants were led to a new page for the second step of the experiment. Here we added some additional information on the AI advisor:

> *"Next to general statistics on all bank customers, we can also look at how the AI advisor performs for subgroups of bank customers. Below you can see the change in bank account balance for men and women in particular."*

Below this text was a table similar to the table in Step 1, but with two added rows that showed the average change in bank account balance per year for men and women in particular (see Table 1). Whereas the statistics for all bank customers overall, as well as for men and women *not* using the *AI advisor* was the same in all conditions, the statistics for men and women *using* the *AI advisor* varied depending on the condition they were assigned to (see Sect. 3.1). Each Table 1 shows the displayed statistics for male and female users per condition. We then again measured trust, willingness to use, and perceived personal benefit.

---

[1] Since conducting this study in June 2019, *Figure Eight* has been renamed to *Appen*. More information can be found at https://appen.com.

3.4   Statistical Analyses

Testing H1a and H2b. To test whether there is an effect of disparate impact on consumer trust (H1a) that is moderated by gender (H2b), we conducted a classical ANOVA with *condition* and *gender* as between-subjects factors and *change in trust* as the dependent variable. A significant main effect of *condition* on *change in trust* in this analysis would suggest that *change in trust* differed between conditions (H1a). In this case, we would perform posthoc analyses to investigate the differences between the conditions in more detail. A significant interaction effect between *condition* and *gender* would suggest that the conditions had a different effect for the disadvantaged group (i.e. female participants) compared to the advantaged group (i.e., male participants; H2b).

We further conducted a Bayesian ANOVA according to the protocol proposed by van den Bergh et al. [38]. Bayesian hypothesis tests involve the computation of the *Bayes factor*, a quantitative comparison of the predictive power of two competing statistical models [44]. The Bayes factor weighs the evidence provided by the data and thus allows for direct model comparison. Practically, comparing different models (i.e., including or excluding an interaction effect of *condition* and *gender*) this way allowed for a richer interpretation of our results. We performed the Bayesian ANOVA using the software JASP [16] with default settings. We computed *Bayes Factors* (BFs) by comparing the models of interest to a *null model*[2] and interpreted them according to the guidelines proposed by Lee and Wagenmakers [18], who adopted them from Jeffreys [17].

Testing H1b. We tested whether disparate impact affected participants' willingness to use the *AI Advisor* by conducting a chi-squared test between *condition* and *change in willingness to use*. A significant result in this analysis would suggest that the number of participants' who changed their willingness to use the *AI Advisor* differed across conditions.

Testing H2a. We conducted another ANOVA with *condition* and *gender* as between-subjects factors and *change in perceived personal benefit* as dependent variable to test whether *gender* acted as a moderator here. A significant interaction effect in this analysis would indicate that this was the case.

Significance Threshold and Correction for Multiple Testing. In all classical analyses we conducted, we aimed for a type 1 error probability of no more than 0.05. However, by conducting our planned analyses we automatically tested a total of seven hypotheses: three in each ANOVA (i.e., two main effects and one interaction) and one in the chi-squared test. This meant that the probability of committing a type 1 error rose considerably [9]. Therefore, we adjusted our significance threshold by applying a Bonferroni correction, where the desired type 1 error rate is divided by the number of hypotheses that are tested [25]. In our main analyses we thus handled a significance threshold of $\frac{0.05}{7} = 0.007$ and only regarded results as statistically significant if their *p*-value fell below this adjusted threshold. The same procedure was applied for posthoc analyses

---

[2] The *null model* in this procedure consisted of only an intercept.

comparing each of the four conditions with each other as this meant conducting $\binom{4}{2} = 6$ hypothesis tests (i.e., adjusting the threshold to $\frac{0.05}{6} = 0.008$).

3.5 Participants

We recruited 567 participants via the *Figure Eight* pool of contributors (554) and direct contacts (13). Seventy-three participants were excluded from the study because they either filled at least one of the obligatory text fields with less than 10 characters, took less than 60 s to complete the task, or took more than 10 min to complete the task. Furthermore, we did not analyze data of five participants who stated "other/not specified" as their gender because our study involved a disparate impact between male and female consumers.

After exclusion, 489 participants remained. Of those, 238 (49%) were male and 251 (51%) were female; with a mean age of 41.9 (sd = 13.1). Participants recruited by Figure Eight received $0.10 as payment for participation. Random allocation to the four conditions resulted in 124, 121, 121, and 122 participants in the *control, little bias, strong bias,* and *extreme bias* conditions, respectively.

4 Results

H1a: Disparate Impact Decreased Consumer Trust. As hypothesized, *change in trust* differed across conditions ($F = 6.906$, $p < 0.001$; see the left-hand panel of Fig. 1). The results from the Bayesian ANOVA confirm this result, showing strong evidence for a main effect of condition ($BF_{10} = 70.02$, see Table 2). To test for differences between the individual conditions, we conducted posthoc analyses (i.e., Mann-Whitney U tests). Only the difference between the *control* and *extreme bias* conditions was significant ($W = 9368$, $p < 0.001$). This suggests that participants lost trust due to disparate impact, but also that the unfairness needed to be comparatively extreme for this effect to occur.

Table 2. Bayesian ANOVA with *change in trust* as dependent variable.

Models	P(M)	P(M|Data)	BF_M	BF_{10}	Error %
Null model	0.200	8.209e−4	0.003	1.000	
Condition	0.200	0.057	0.244	70.024	0.001
Gender	0.200	0.004	0.018	5.413	1.533e−6
Condition + gender	0.200	0.735	11.116	895.772	1.638
Condition + gender + condition * gender	0.200	0.202	1.012	245.894	1.978

H1b: Disparate Impact Decreased Willingness to Use. In accordance with disparate impact negatively affecting trust (H1a), it decreased participants'

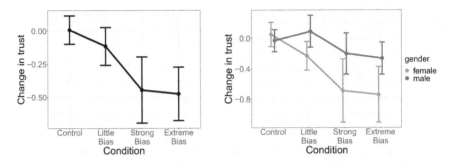

Fig. 1. *Change in trust* across conditions for all participants (left-hand panel) and split by gender (right-hand panel). The error bars represent 95% confidence intervals.

Table 3. *Change in willingness to use* across conditions. The labels −, =, and + reflect changes from "yes" to "no", no change, "no" to "yes", respectively.

Change	Condition			
	Control	Little Bias	Strong Bias	Extreme Bias
−	1	9	23	16
=	121	111	97	105
+	2	1	1	1
Total	124	121	121	122

willingness to use the *AI Advisor* (see Table 3). The increasing proportion of participants who changed their attitude from "yes" to "no" as conditions reflected stronger disparate impact was statistically significant ($\chi^2 = 25.06$, $p < 0.001$).

H2a: Gender Moderated the Effect of Disparate Impact on Perceived Personal Benefit. As expected, the results from the second ANOVA show a significant interaction effect of *condition* and *gender* on *change in perceived personal benefit* ($F = 8.525$, $p < 0.001$). This means that male participants' perceived personal benefit was affected differently compared to that of female participants. More specifically, Fig. 2 shows that whereas men's perceived personal benefit did not change due to seeing the gender-specific user statistics across conditions, female participants perceived increasingly lower levels of personal benefit as disparate impact (to their disadvantage) became more severe.

H2b: Male Consumers Experienced the Same Decrease in Trust as Female Consumers. In contrast to what we hypothesized, we do not find a significant interaction effect of *condition* and *gender* on *change in trust* ($F = 2.094$, $p = 0.096$; see the right-hand panel of Fig. 1). We can therefore not conclude that the conditions had a different effect on male participant's *change in trust* compared to that of female participants. The Bayesian ANOVA confirms this result: the model containing just two main effects for condition and gender explain the data best (BF$_{10} = 895.77$; see Table 2) and roughly four times better than the model that includes the interaction effect ($BF_{10} = 245.89$). This suggests that unfairly advantaged and disadvantaged participants (i.e., men and women, respectively) experienced the same decrease in trust due to algorithmic unfairness despite diverging levels of perceived personal benefit (H2a).

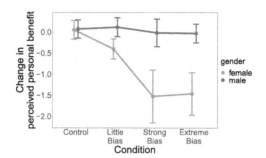

Fig. 2. *Change in perceived personal benefit* across conditions and split by gender. The error bars represent 95% confidence intervals.

5 Discussion

In this paper, we presented a between-subjects user study that aimed to investigate the influence of algorithmically-driven disparate impact on consumer trust at the use case of gender-bias in robo-advisors. Our results suggest that disparate impact – at least when it is extreme – decreases trust and makes consumers less likely to use such systems. We further find that, although disadvantaged and advantaged users recognize their respective levels of personal benefit in scenarios of disparate impact, both experience equally decreasing levels of trust when they learn about a disparate impact caused by the system at hand. Our work contributes to a growing body of literature that highlights the importance of ensuring fairness and avoiding disparate impact of consumer-oriented AI systems.

5.1 Implications

Our findings have implications for consumers as well as industry. Consumers should be aware that machine-learning-based applications can be biased. If disparate impact is an important factor for consumer trust, consumers need to think critically when using such systems. One potential way forward for consumers would be to demand from companies to publish independently carried out research into the (algorithmic) fairness and impact of their products.

Publishers of consumer-oriented AI systems need to establish algorithmic fairness in their products and avoid disparate impact to serve consumers effectively. Our findings show that failing to do so may lead to a decrease in consumers' trust and willingness to use such systems.

5.2   Limitations and Future Work

Our study is subject to at least five important limitations. First, we studied the effect of disparate impact on consumer trust at a specific use case: a binary gender bias in robo-advisors. This makes our results difficult to generalize because many other forms of bias (including those based on race, religion, or sexual orientation) as well as other AI systems (e.g., for recommendations of medical treatment, tourist attractions, or movies) exist. It is easy to imagine how consumer trust could be affected differently when, for example, disparate impact concerns small minorities, multitudes of gender identities (or another consumer characteristic), a chosen group membership such as consumers' profession, or a system that is less impactful on consumers' personal lives than a robo-advisor. On a related note, we here positioned women in the disadvantage and men in the advantage (i.e., the setting that corresponds to biases in human financial advice) but it is not certain if we were to obtain the same results if the (dis-)advantage was distributed the other way round. Future work could explore these different scenarios to help generalize and better understand the relationship between the effect of disparate impact on consumer trust.

Second, our finding that advantaged and disadvantaged users experienced the same decrease in trust appears to go counter to previous research suggesting that people make stronger fairness judgments when they are personally affected [14]. However, it is not clear from our results to what degree advantaged users (i.e., men) felt personally affected; e.g., because they have women in their lives who they deeply care about. The role of personal relevance in the effect of disparate impact on consumer trust thus remains to be clarified by future research.

Third, our results show a decreasing trend in consumer trust as conditions become more extreme, but show a statistically significant difference only between the control and extreme bias conditions. Future work could examine these differences (also across domains) in more detail to establish the relationship between *the level of* disparate impact and consumer trust (e.g., to determine what lies within and beyond an "acceptable margin" of disparate impact).

Fourth, we studied fairness related to group membership (i.e., gender), which might elicit a different (moral) evaluation than fairness on the individual level. Our results show that trust can decrease despite perceived personal benefit. However, this effect might have been caused by a sense of loyalty towards the disadvantaged group. An interesting direction for future work is to study whether similar patterns emerge when disparate impact concerns individuals; e.g., when advantaged and disadvantaged subjects are randomly chosen.

6   Conclusion

We presented a user study investigating the effect of algorithmically-driven disparate impact (i.e., when algorithm outcomes adversely affect one group of consumers compared to another) on consumer trust. Specifically, we studied the effect of *gender-bias* in an application that aimed to persuade consumers' to make better financial decisions. We found that disparate impact decreased participants' trust and willingness to use the application. Furthermore, our results show that the trust of unfairly advantaged participants was just as affected as that of disadvantaged participants. These findings imply that disparate impact (i.e., as a result of algorithmic unfairness) can undermine trust in consumer-oriented AI systems and should therefore be avoided or mitigated when aiming to create trustworthy technology.

Acknowledgements. This research has been supported by the *Think Forward Initiative* (a partnership between ING Bank, Deloitte, Dell Technologies, Amazon Web Services, IBM, and the Center for Economic Policy Research – CEPR). The views and opinions expressed in this paper are solely those of the authors and do not necessarily reflect the official policy or position of the Think Forward Initiative or any of its partners.

References

1. Ahmad, W.N.W., Ali, N.M.: A study on persuasive technologies: the relationship between user emotions, trust and persuasion. Int. J. Interact. Multimed. Artif. Intell. **5**(1), 57–61 (2018). https://doi.org/10.9781/ijimai.2018.02.010
2. Angwin, J., Larson, J., Mattu, S., Kirchner, L.: Machine bias: there's software used across the country to predict future criminals and it's biased against blacks. ProPublica (2019). https://www.propublica.org/article/machine-bias-risk-assessments-in-criminal-sentencing
3. Araujo, T., Helberger, N., Kruikemeier, S., de Vreese, C.H.: In AI we trust? Perceptions about automated decision-making by artificial intelligence. AI Soc. **35**(3), 611–623 (2020). https://doi.org/10.1007/s00146-019-00931-w
4. Arnold, M., et al.: FactSheets: increasing trust in AI services through supplier's declarations of conformity. IBM J. Res. Dev. **63**(4–5) (2019). https://doi.org/10.1147/JRD.2019.2942288
5. Baeckström, Y., Silvester, J., Pownall, R.A.: Millionaire investors: financial advisors, attribution theory and gender differences. Eur. J. Financ. **24**(15), 1333–1349 (2018). https://doi.org/10.1080/1351847X.2018.1438301
6. Barocas, S., Selbst, A.D.: Big data's disparate impact. Calif. Law Rev. **104**(671), 671–732 (2016)
7. Bellamy, R.K., et al.: AI fairness 360: an extensible toolkit for detecting and mitigating algorithmic bias. IBM J. Res. Dev. **63**(4–5) (2019). https://doi.org/10.1147/JRD.2019.2942287
8. Corbett-Davies, S., Goel, S.: The Measure and Mismeasure of Fairness: A Critical Review of Fair Machine Learning. arXiv Preprint arXiv:1808.00023 (2018)
9. Cramer, A.O.J., et al.: Hidden multiplicity in exploratory multiway ANOVA: prevalence and remedies. Psychon. Bull. Rev. **23**(2), 640–647 (2015). https://doi.org/10.3758/s13423-015-0913-5
10. Cummings, M.L.: Automation bias in intelligent time critical decision support systems. Collect. In: AIAA 1st Intelligent Systems Technical Conference, Technical Paper, vol. 2, pp. 557–562 (2004). https://doi.org/10.2514/6.2004-6313
11. Diab, D.L., Pui, S.Y., Yankelevich, M., Highhouse, S.: Lay perceptions of selection decision aids in US and non-US samples. Int. J. Sel. Assess. **19**(2), 209–216 (2011). https://doi.org/10.1111/j.1468-2389.2011.00548.x
12. Dietvorst, B.J., Simmons, J.P., Massey, C.: Algorithm aversion: people erroneously avoid algorithms after seeing them err. J. Exp. Psychol. Gen. **144**(1), 114–126 (2015). https://doi.org/10.1037/xge0000033

13. Feldman, M., Friedler, S.A., Moeller, J., Scheidegger, C., Venkatasubramanian, S.: Certifying and removing disparate impact. In: Proceedings of the 21th ACM SIGKDD International Conference on Knowledge Discovery and Data Mining, pp. 259–268 (2015)
14. Ham, J., van den Bos, K.: Not fair for me! the influence of personal relevance on social justice inferences. J. Exp. Soc. Psychol. **44**(3), 699–705 (2008). https://doi.org/10.1016/j.jesp.2007.04.009
15. Hardt, M., Price, E., Srebro, N.: Equality of opportunity in supervised learning. In: Advances Neural Information Processing Systems, pp. 3323–3331 (2016)
16. JASP Team: JASP (Version 0.14) (2020)
17. Jeffreys, H.: Theory of Probability. Oxford University Press, Oxford (1939)
18. Lee, M.D., Wagenmakers, E.J.: Bayesian Cognitive Modeling: A Practical Course. Cambridge University Press, Cambridge (2014). https://doi.org/10.1017/CBO9781139087759
19. Lee, M.K.: Understanding perception of algorithmic decisions: fairness, trust, and emotion in response to algorithmic management. Big Data Soc. **5**(1), 1–16 (2018). https://doi.org/10.1177/2053951718756684
20. Lieber, R.: Financial Advice for People Who Aren't Rich, April 2014. https://www.nytimes.com/2014/04/12/your-money/start-ups-offer-financial-advice-to-people-who-arent-rich.html
21. Mary, J.J., Calauzènes, C., Karoui, N.E.: Fairness-aware learning for continuous attributes and treatments. In: ICML 97, pp. 4382–4391 (2019). http://proceedings.mlr.press/v97/mary19a.html
22. Mehrabi, N., Morstatter, F., Saxena, N., Lerman, K., Galstyan, A.: A Survey on Bias and Fairness in Machine Learning. arXiv Preprint arXiv:1908.09635 (2019)
23. Muir, B.M., Moray, N.: Trust in automation. Part II. Experimental studies of trust and human intervention in a process control simulation. Ergonomics **39**(3), 429–460 (1996)
24. Mullainathan, S., Noeth, M., Schoar, A.: The market for financial advice: an audit study. SSRN Electron. J. (2012). https://doi.org/10.2139/ssrn.1572334
25. Napierala, M.A.: What Is the Bonferroni correction? (2012). http://www.aaos.org/news/aaosnow/apr12/research7.asp
26. Nickel, P., Spahn, A.: Trust, discourse ethics, and persuasive technology. In: Persuasive Technology: Design for Health and Safety, 7th International Conference Persuasive Technology 2012, pp. 37–40. Linköping University Electronic Press (2012)
27. Ntoutsi, E., et al.: Bias in data-driven artificial intelligence systems—an introductory survey. Wiley Interdiscip. Rev. Data Min. Knowl. Discov. **10**(3), 1–14 (2020). https://doi.org/10.1002/widm.1356
28. Oinas-Kukkonen, H., Harjumaa, M.: Towards deeper understanding of persuasion in software and information systems. In: Proceedings of 1st International Conference on Advanced Computer Interaction, ACHI 2008 (2008). https://doi.org/10.1109/ACHI.2008.31
29. Önkal, D., Goodwin, P., Thomson, M., Gönül, S., Pollock, A.: The relative influence of advice from human experts and statistical methods on forecast adjustments. J. Behav. Decis. Mak. **22**(4), 390–409 (2009). https://doi.org/10.1002/bdm.637
30. Orji, R., Moffatt, K.: Persuasive technology for health and wellness: State-of-the-art and emerging trends. Health Inform. J. **24**(1), 66–91 (2018). https://doi.org/10.1177/1460458216650979
31. Otterbacher, J., Checco, A., Demartini, G., Clough, P.: Investigating user perception of gender bias in image search: the role of sexism. In: 41st International ACM

SIGIR Conference on Research and Development in Information Retrieval, SIGIR 2018, pp. 933–936 (2018). https://doi.org/10.1145/3209978.3210094

32. Promberger, M., Baron, J.: Do patients trust computers? J. Behav. Decis. Mak. **19**(5), 455–468 (2006). https://doi.org/10.1002/bdm.542

33. Purpura, S., Schwanda, V., Williams, K., Stubler, W., Sengers, P.: Fit4Life: the design of a persuasive technology promoting healthy behavior and ideal weight. In: Proceedings of SIGCHI Conference on Human Factors in Computing Systems, pp. 423–432 (2011)

34. Rossi, F.: Building trust in artificial intelligence. J. Int. Aff. **72**(1), 127–133 (2019)

35. Sattarov, F., Nagel, S.: Building trust in persuasive gerontechnology: user-centric and institution-centric approaches. Gerontechnology **18**(1), 1–14 (2019). https://doi.org/10.4017/gt.2019.18.1.001.00

36. Smith, J., Sonboli, N., Fiesler, C., Burke, R.: Exploring user opinions of fairness in recommender systems. In: CHI 2020 Workshop Human-Centered Approaches to Fair Responsible AI (2020). http://arxiv.org/abs/2003.06461

37. Toreini, E., Aitken, M., Coopamootoo, K., Elliott, K., Zelaya, C.G., van Moorsel, A.: The relationship between trust in AI and trustworthy machine learning technologies. In: Proceedings of 2020 Conference on Fairness, Accountability, and Transparency, FAT* 2020, pp. 272–283 (2020). https://doi.org/10.1145/3351095.3372834

38. Van Den Bergh, D., et al.: A tutorial on conducting and interpreting a Bayesian ANOVA in JASP. Annee Psychol. **120**(1), 73–96 (2020). https://doi.org/10.3917/anpsy1.201.0073

39. Varshney, K.R.: Trustworthy machine learning and artificial intelligence. XRDS Crossroads ACM Mag. Students **25**(3) (2019). https://doi.org/10.1145/3313109

40. Varshney, K.R.: On mismatched detection and safe, trustworthy machine learning. In: 2020 54th Annual Conference on Information Sciences and Systems, CISS 2020 (2020). https://doi.org/10.1109/CISS48834.2020.1570627767

41. Verbeek, P.P.: Persuasive technology and moral responsibility toward an ethical framework for persuasive technologies. Persuasive **6**, 1–15 (2006)

42. Verma, S., Rubin, J.: Fairness definitions explained. In: Proceedings of International Workshop on Software Fairness, FairWare 2018, pp. 1–7. Association for Computing Machinery, New York (2018). https://doi.org/10.1145/3194770.3194776

43. Vigdor, N.: Apple card investigated after gender discrimination complaints. New York Times (2019)

44. Wagenmakers, E.-J., et al.: Bayesian inference for psychology. Part I: Theoretical advantages and practical ramifications. Psychon. Bull. Rev. **25**(1), 35–57 (2017). https://doi.org/10.3758/s13423-017-1343-3

45. Woodruff, A., Fox, S.E., Rousso-Schindler, S., Warshaw, J.: A qualitative exploration of perceptions of algorithmic fairness. In: Proceedings of the Conference on Human Factors in Computing Systems, vol. 2018-April, pp. 1–14 (2018). https://doi.org/10.1145/3173574.3174230

46. Yang, Q., Banovic, N., Zimmerman, J.: Mapping machine learning advances from HCI research to reveal starting places for design innovation. In: Proceedings of the Conference on Human Factors in Computing Systems, vol. 2018-April, pp. 1–11 (2018). https://doi.org/10.1145/3173574.3173704

47. Zafar, M.B., Valera, I., Rodriguez, M.G., Gummadi, K.P.: Fairness beyond disparate treatment & disparate impact: learning classification without disparate mistreatment. In: 26th International World Wide Web Conference on WWW 2017, pp. 1171–1180 (2017). https://doi.org/10.1145/3038912.3052660

Towards Better Rating Scale Design: An Experimental Analysis of the Influence of User Preference and Visual Cues on User Response

Maliha Mahbub[⊠], Najia Manjur, and Julita Vassileva

Department of Computer Science, University of Saskatchewan,
Saskatoon, SK S7N 5C9, Canada
{mam789,nam907}@mail.usask.ca, jiv@cs.usask.ca

Abstract. With the rise of dependency of online shopping and service providers, consumer ratings and reviews help users decide between good and bad options. Prior studies have already shown that the layout and visual cues provided with a rating scale can affect the users' responses. This paper aims to explore: 1) users' reaction to certain visual cues in rating scales, and 2) users' preference in rating scale designs and how it influences the rating scores. A survey ($n = 187$) was conducted to collect user ratings of popular products with six different rating scale designs, using two types of visual icons (stars and emojis) and colour-schemes (using a warm-cool and a traffic-light metaphors). Statistical analysis from the survey shows that users prefer the scale with most visually informative design (traffic-light metaphor colours with emoji icons). It also shows that users tend to give their true ratings on scales they like most, rather than the scale design they are most familiar with. Based on these results, it can be concluded that user involvement is desirable in selecting the rating scale designs, and that visual cues with cognitive metaphors can ensure more accurate (truthful) rating scores from users. Our approach has novelty because we elicited the users' own opinion on what their accurate or "true" rating is rather than only relying on analysing the data received from the rating scores. Our work can offer insights for online rating scales designs to improve the rating decision quality of users and help online business platforms provide more credible ratings to their customers.

Keywords: Rating scale designs · True rating · Visual metaphor · Frequent pattern mining · User decision quality

1 Introduction

Word of Mouth or WOM has been a powerful driving force for sales and business since ages. WOM is an informal communication between private parties about the evaluation of goods and services based on their experience [3]. Online WOM

© Springer Nature Switzerland AG 2021
R. Ali et al. (Eds.): PERSUASIVE 2021, LNCS 12684, pp. 150–163, 2021.
https://doi.org/10.1007/978-3-030-79460-6_12

has a particularly strong hold on consumers' decision making [4]. For online marketplaces such as Airbnb, Uber, eBay, user ratings and reviews are used to build trust between consumers [7] and this trust is the foundation of their business. The user rating and review is therefore not an option anymore, it is an expectation for the users [7]; how users rate products has a huge economic impact on e-business. Although the economic effect of online user review is paramount [5,6], research shows that users can be affected by rating bias, which can hamper the review quality and effectiveness [12]. Users give different ratings of the same item when they are using different types of rating scales, and such biased ratings distort the rating score averages (and the reputations) of products [1]. Users often have certain preferences for rating scale designs as well [22], and depending on whether they like or dislike a give type of scale they may not give their truthful rating, i.e. the scale itself may bias the ratings they give. However, in most e-commerce sites, the user experience designers (UX designers) are guided by utilitarian or aesthetic considerations and are not aware of the subtle influence their choices may have on the resulting ratings by users. The effect of different rating scales and their design features (granularity, labelling, colour) and the users interpretation of them has been evaluated and analysed in many studies [11,17]. Each of them has suggested that these visual cues can trigger different reactions in users, which in turn can assist users to understand their rating process better and ease their effort of making rating decisions [18]. Our work offers a novel user-centric approach to address the problem, by asking the users making users aware of their inconsistent ratings given to the same items using 5-level scales with different type and colour and asking them to choose their true ratings among the ratings they have given for a product. We also asked users to select their preferred scale design and incorporated their own preferred rating scale designs and their true ratings in data analysis. We also investigated the effect of each visual feature, or lack thereof in the rating scale designs on the users' rating decisions. The study leads us to create guidelines to help UX designers in selecting certain visual cues in rating scales and including options for users to choose their preferred rating scales, to help them give their true (unbiased) ratings. By improving users' rating process this work contributes to improving the information available about online goods and services and helping them build deserved reputation.

2 Related Work

2.1 Rating Scales Design Impact

The impact of different rating scale design on user's rating behaviour has been an ongoing topic for research and investigation. The work by Chen et al. [1] suggested that the consumer feedback has improved sales at Amazon.com. The effects of design parameters of rating scales on the interaction of users with websites have been investigated in [2], which proved the presence of psychometric properties of scales. F. Cena and F. Vernero proposed a rating scale model by categorizing the features of rating scales presented on other works [8]. The body of work by F. Cena et al. in [9] provide new empirical information about the impact of rating scales on user ratings and proposed using linear functions to map ratings from one scale to another. The experiment conducted by Gena et al. [10], shows that the rating scales have their own "personality" while investigating how a recommender system can properly deal with values coming from heterogeneous rating scales. The user survey described in [22] presents the costs and benefit analysis associated with different rating scales and a qualitative evidence of users preferring certain rating scale design over others.

2.2   Users' Preference of Rating Scale

The survey results from [22] revealed a lot about users rating scale preferences, such as 5-star being the most popular scale design and their dislikes regarding sliders or more granular scales. The survey by Maharani et al. on [18] concludes that users prefer rating scales which have clear separation identifying low and high ends and 5-star rating scales as well. The work by Christoph et al. [13] investigates the role of different design aspects of rating scales that result in high user enjoyment and participation and that improves the overall rating performance. Using different rating scale icons such as smileys, star, heart, buttons or grids have been investigated and analysed in [14], which shows that heart and star icons received lower ratings compared to smileys and grid design had negative impacts on the ratings. The role of different rating scale designs such as thumbs up, star or sliders in reducing rating biases have been analysed in [16], where users have preferred using star ratings over sliders.

2.3   Use of Colour Cues for Rating Scale

The impact of colour on rating scales has been included and analysed in many studies [23]. It has been observed that using different colours to separate the different ends of a rating scale can help users in rating process [17,18]. The effect of using blue and red as positive and negative hues [25] for rating scales has been investigated by [17] and [18]. Another popular colour scheme, the traffic-light metaphor, where red is used as negative end and green as positive, has been applied in [26] to analyse the emotional response of users while rating. However, the actual role of using a scale that users prefer using and the role of visual cues in helping users to give true rating scores has not been investigated yet.

Our work differs from previous works as we propose a user study that takes input from the users themselves about the accuracy of the rating scores that they have given, i.e. which of the scores given by them reflects their true opinion (we call this "the user's true rating"). We investigated whether users prefer using a specific colour scheme and a rating scale that uses emoticons as visual cues and if they give their true ratings using their preferred scales. Our work also attempted to find how the overall rating scores were affected by the visual cues provided with the rating scales.

3   Methodology

In this section, we present our research hypotheses, user study design, the statistical and data mining tools used to validate our proposed hypotheses, research context and the demographics of participants.

3.1   Research Hypotheses

Users' preference for certain design cues/aspects of rating scales is a major factor in users' rating decisions [18]. Users' rating preference behaviour has been utilized to improve recommender system filtering in [24]. In this paper, we attempt to answer the following research question:

Do users provide true ratings on rating scale designs they prefer and if so, are preferred rating scales those that have more visually informative cues?

We answer this question by testing three hypotheses. We derive our first hypothesis from principle of nonredundancy [20], which states that the respondents tend to assign meanings to visual cues in rating scales to give adequate responses. In other words, the more visual cues a rating scale provides, the better the users can decide on their rating scores. We derive the second hypothesis based on the analysis in [14], which shows that users' preference in response formats have significant effect on survey outcomes. We hypothesize that users will give their true ratings when they use rating scales they prefer. The work in [17] shows that using numeric labelling on two ends of a response scale tends to push the responses towards the high (positive) end of scale. This is the basis of our third hypothesis which states that users tend to react more positively towards more visually informative scales.

H1: *Users prefer rating scale which provides visual cues that assist users in their rating process, than the ones they mostly use on the internet.*

H2: *Users give their true ratings on rating scale designs they prefer.*

H3: *Using user-preferred rating scales with more visual cues creates a positive bias in the ratings given by users.*

3.2   Rating Scale Designs for the User Study

We selected two separate factors for six rating scale designs: use of graphical icons and use of colour metaphors. Two separate icons: Star and Emoji and two colour schemes: traffic-light (red-yellow-green) and warm-cool (red-yellow-blue) have been used in the survey. For a neutral tone, an option of all-yellow colour scheme was used. The rating scale designs and their varying visual cues are shown in Fig. 1.

We selected two graphical icons (star and emoji) as rating scale points based on the rating scale model implemented in the work by F. Cena and F. Vernero in "A Study on User Preferential Choices about Rating Scales" [8]. In their model, the authors divided the rating scales into three categories: Human, Neutral and Technical scales. We used human emoji icon to represent human scale and star icon to represent neutral scale. We excluded the third category "Technical Scale",

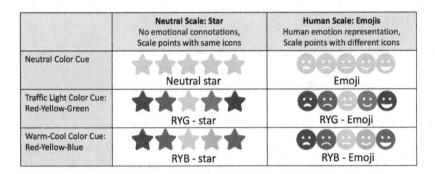

	Neutral Scale: Star No emotional connotations, Scale points with same icons	Human Scale: Emojis Human emotion representation, Scale points with different icons
Neutral Color Cue	Neutral star	Emoji
Traffic Light Color Cue: Red-Yellow-Green	RYG - star	RYG - Emoji
Warm-Cool Color Cue: Red-Yellow-Blue	RYB - star	RYB - Emoji

Fig. 1. The six rating scales and the visual cues used on them for the user study.

because they use no icons/image for scale points. Also, there have been many studies which provided strong evidence about technical scales such as slider or point system are not preferred or liked by the users [8,18,22].

In our experiment, we wanted to see if colours which themselves have certain emotional triggers can influence users' rating compared to neutral/monochromatic scales. We included two colour metaphors: Traffic-light metaphor in RYG-star and RYG-Emoji scale, and warm-cool metaphor RYB-star and RYB-Emoji Scale. Both colour cues have been previously used on rating scales to analyze their effects [25,26].

3.3   User Study Interface Design

Design Tools. The user study interface is developed using "React". React is an open source, declarative, front end JavaScript library used for building interactive user interfaces. The interface is deployed and managed on Heroku: a container-based cloud Platform as a Service (PaaS).

User Survey Process. The survey was conducted from May 2020 to August 2020. Participants for this study were mainly collected from the students of the University of Saskatchewan recruited on the PAWS announcement board (PAWS is the university's information system) and on the researchers' personal Facebook and LinkedIn pages. A total of 203 completed responses were received, out of which 187 were considered, removing duplicate and incomplete responses. The demographic of users participating in the survey are shown in table.

The user survey used 21 products divided into 7 categories to be rated by the users. The 7 product categories were: email, internet browser, photo editing app, social networking sites, toothpaste, fast food chain and soft drinks. We included 3 popular brands of products for each type. For example, in the email category, we included Gmail, Yahoo! mail and Outlook and so on.

The user rating scores and rating scale information are collected in three consecutive phases as following:

Table 1. Demographic of all participants

Total participants = 187	
Gender	Male = 79, 57.7% Female = 108, 42.2%
Age	16–24 (98, 52.4%) 24–35 (67, 35.8%) 36–45 (13, 6.9%) 46–55 (9, 4.81%))

Phase 1: **Select Products and Rate Them with Each of the Six Scales.**
The users were shown the products and asked to select the ones they have used,
as shown in section A of the Fig. 2. Then the users were asked to rate each of the
selected items one by one in random order, using each rating scales, as shown in
section B of Fig. 2.

Phase 2: **Select Preferred and the Most Common Rating Scales.** Next,
the users were shown the six rating scale designs which they have used and asked
to select one of the scales as their preferred scale over other scale designs. Then
they were asked to select the rating scale they have mostly seen around the
internet.

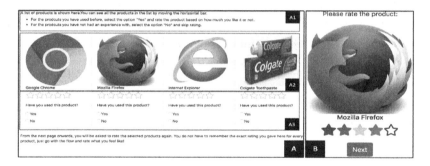

Fig. 2. User survey: users are asked to select products to rate (A). Users are asked to
rate selected products with the rating scales (B).

Phase 3: **Select The Most True Rating Score Among All Given Ratings.** Next, the users were shown each products they have rated and all the
ratings they gave for it using the different scales. The different scales were not
displayed, only the actual numeric value corresponding to each rating that they
had given was shown in a list, as shown in Fig. 3. The users were asked to select
the rating score that they think is best suited for the product. This was used as
the "true" rating (ground truth) for each user and each product they had rated.

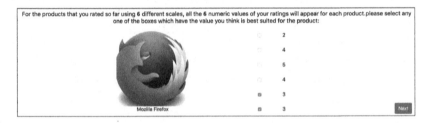

Fig. 3. The user selected 3 out of 5 as the best suited rating for Mozilla Firefox and user gave 3/5 using Emoji and RYB-Star scales.

4   Empirical and Statistical Evaluations

For evaluating the proposed hypotheses, two analytical tools were employed: data mining using Apriori algorithm and descriptive statistical analysis using median and interquartile range (IQR) analysis. Inferential statistical analysis (Kruskal-Wallis test and Wilcoxon signed -rank test) were also used to validate the significance of our findings.

Data Preparation: For our analysis, we collected the scales on which the users gave their true ratings in phase 3 of the survey and put them together with the preferred scale and the most common scale selected by users. For example in Fig. 3, the user selected 3 out of 5 as their true rating for the Mozilla firefox browser. This rating is given by the user on the Emoji and RYB-star rating scales so for this particular user, these two scales were stored as "chosen-scales", i.e. the scales where the user gives their true ratings. This is done for all the products a user have rated. Therefore, "chosen-scales" is the set of all the scales on which users have given their true ratings for each products. From the "chosen scale" set of each user, we derived three most frequently chosen scales by each user to see how many users have used their selected preferred rating scale to give the true rating for a product.

Frequent Set Mining and Association Rule Learning Using Apriori: The next step was to derive the most frequently used rating scale designs by the users to give their true ratings. We used Apriori - an algorithm for frequent item set mining and association rule learning over relational databases. Then we used a simple statistical data handler tool to find the percentage of preferred scale and most common scale in the frequent set of scales for each user. The Apriori algorithm finds frequent item sets from a given dataset by comparing item's frequency (support) with a threshold called minimum support e.g. check if support $\geq$ minimum_support [15]. For finding strong pattern from the selected frequent pattern, Apriori uses conditional probability compared with a confidence metric e.g. it checks if probability $\geq$ minimum_confidence to generate association rules. Afterwards, for finding interesting pattern within the strong pattern sets, the mining process uses correlation analysis. We have utilized *Lift* analysis to find the interesting patterns of our user reviewed dataset. We have applied Apriori on "chosen scale" data of each user dataset to find a set of the 3 most frequently appearing rating scale designs in the chosen scale set for each user. For our dataset, the selected thresholds are: support $\geq$ 0.9, confidence $\geq$ 0.8 and lift $\geq$ 0.8. Since we targeted to select only 3 most frequently chosen scales for each user, the threshold values were chosen to fit the target itemset generation in Apriori.

Table 1 shows a small portion of the data set (4 out of 187) processed by Apriori algorithm. Each row shows the rating scales where users have given their true ratings, according to Apriori algorithm. In the column Frequently Associated Itemset, the algorithm presents the rating scales which were most frequently used by individual users to give true ratings for all products. For example, in the first row of the Table 1, RYG-star, RYB-Star and RYG-Emoji were the most frequently used rating scale for a user to give the true ratings and the subsequent support, confidence and lift value (which all satisfy their minimum thresholds) for this set of scales are also shown in the rest of the columns. For each user, the frequent item set can have maximum 3 rating scale deigns which satisfies the minimum threshold decided by the Apriori algorithm. We have verified our frequently chosen rating scales in the same way for each of the 187 users as well.

Table 2. The association rule set for few users using Apriori

Frequently associated itemset	Support	Confidence	Lift
(RYG-star, RYB-star, RYG-Emoji)	0.86667	1.0	1.0
(RYG-Emoji, RYB-Emoji, Emoji)	0.97766	0.9	1.0
(RYG-star, Neutral-star, RYG-Emoji)	0.9	0.8	1.0
(RYG-Emoji, RYB-star, Neutral-star)	1.0	0.8	1.0

Preferred Scale vs Common Scale: For the data analysis, we have three columns now: preferred scale, most common scale and frequently chosen scales, as shown in Fig. 4. A small part of the user data is shown in Fig. 4 where the values in each row represent each user's information regarding rating scales. The preferred_Scale and most_Seen_Scale are both selected directly by the user in phase 2 of user study. The frequently_chosen_Scales column in Fig. 4 is the set of most frequently used rating scales by a user to give their true ratings and this rating scale set has been derived by applying the Apriori data mining algorithm.

Using a statistical data handler tool on this data, we calculated the percentage of rows where the values in the preferred_Scale column and the most_Seen_Scale column are present in the values in the column for frequently_chosen_Scales. For example, in the first row of the table in Fig. 4, if the preferred_Scale of a user is RYG-Emoji, and RYG-Emoji is also one of the frequently_Chosen_Scales, than that user has definitely used his/her preferred scale to give their true ratings for all products. The same kind of data analysis was performed for the most_Seen_Scale as well.

User_id	frequently_chosen_Scales	preferred_Scale	most_Seen_Scale
1kjhdbs	RYB-Emoji/ RYG-star/ RYG-Emoji	RYG-Emoji	Neutral-star
1kjr45fy	RYG-Emoji/Emoji/RYG-star	RYG-star	Neutral-star
1kjrd53t	Neutral-star/Emoji/RYG-emoji	Neutral-star	Neutral-star
1kjd42ri	Neutral-star/RYG-star/RYG-Emoji	RYG-Emoji	Neutral-star
1kjli58s	RYB-Emoji/ RYG-star/Neutral-star	RYG-star	Neutral-star

Fig. 4. The data about each user's ratings scales usage, preference, and familiarity.

Figure 5 shows how often each scale was selected by users as their preferred and as the most seen scale of all 6 scales. The most preferred scale was the RYG-Emoji scale and the most commonly seen scale was the Neutral scale.

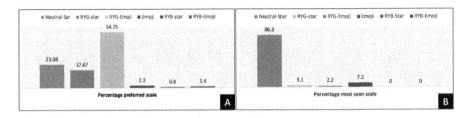

Fig. 5. Frequency of choosing scales as most preferred (A) and most seen (B).

Rating Score Analysis Using Median and IQR. Median is a statistical measure for the central tendency of the data, since it shows what the 'average' participant thinks, or their 'likeliest' response [19]. The IQR is a measure spread/dispersion of the responses (how strongly respondents agree with each other). A higher IQR indicates that users have divided/inconsistent opinions about the products while using that scale. Since our data is ordinal, the median and IQR measures are considered better fits for statistically describing the dataset [21]. Figure 6 represents the median of all six scales for the most popular 7 products (those selected and rated by more than 80% of users). Figure 7, shows the IQR of the ratings provided on each scale for the most popular the products by the user.

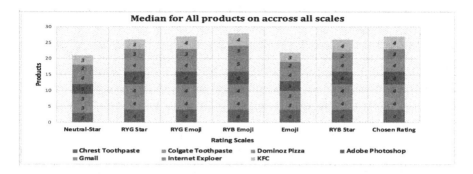

Fig. 6. Median for most popular products on each scale and median of rating value chosen by the user for each product. The highest value is 4 and lowest value is 1.

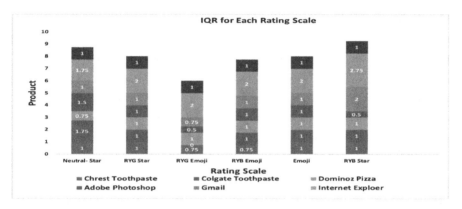

Fig. 7. IQR for popular products on each scale and IQR of rating value chosen by the user for each product. The highest value is 2 and lowest value is 0.5.

5   Results and Discussion

The frequent data mining and statistical tools delivered empirical evaluations for our proposed hypotheses, which are discussed in this section.

H1: Figure 5 shows that most users (54.75%) have chosen RYG-Emoji as their preferred scale design and 86.5% users selected the Neutral-Star as their most commonly seen rating scale design. It can also be noted that only 2.2% have selected the RYG-Emoji as commonly seen scale deign. This shows that users prefer a rating scale design that is different from the one they are most familiar with. The RYG-Emoji scale has both emoticons and a traffic-light colour scheme, which provide visual clues that likely reduce the cognitive load during the decision making process involved in giving a rating. To further support the findings, we performed Kruskal-Wallis test (a non-parametric version of the one-way ANOVA), which rejected the null hypothesis ($p = 4e^{-5}$) and confirmed that there is significant difference between the ratings provided on preferred scale design and most common scale design selected by the users. This validates the first hypothesis H1.

H2: By using Apriori algorithm, the most frequent sets of rating scale designs that users choose to give their true ratings for each product were derived. The preferred scale design and most common scale design of each user were compared to the set of most frequent true rating scales by using a statistical data handler tool. This analysis computes the percentage of users whose preferred rating scale is also present in the frequent true rating scales set. The results of the analysis, shown in Table 2, demonstrate that the majority (87.64%) of the users have used their preferred scale to give their true ratings to each products. This supports our second hypothesis that users give their true ratings using a rating scale design of their own preference. We validated this hypothesis using the users' own input about what their "true" rating was rather than only relying on analysis of the data received from the rating scores.

Table 3. The results showing users giving their true ratings in preferred vs most common rating scales

The percentage of users using preferred scale for giving their true rating	**87.64%**
The percentage of users using most common scale for giving their true rating	**41.33%**
The percentage of users using both scales for giving their true rating	**27.22%**
The percentage of users using neither scales for giving their true rating	**8.6%**

H3: From Fig. 6 it is evident that the medians for the RYG-Emoji and RYB-Emoji scales are higher than the medians of Neutral-star and Emoji scales. This reveals the tendency of users to give more positive ratings using the scales with more visual clues. The same trend can be even observed when we consider the median of the chosen ratings given by each user on each scale. On the other hand, the IQR of the ratings on RYG-Emoji scale is way lower than the Neutral-star scale, as shown in Fig. 7, which indicates that the ratings using visually informative scales are more consistent throughout the dataset than the scales with minimal visual cues. The confirmation of the first hypothesis, showed that the RYG-Emoji is the most preferred scale of users and Neutral-star is the most common scale design. This strongly supports our third hypothesis that providing meaningful visual cues is what users prefer when rating and it influences the users' rating decisions, resulting in them giving higher ratings. In order to further validate the significance of the results, we used Wilcoxon signed-rank test, a non-parametric paired test for the ratings on each scale for each of the 21 products. The results showed statistically significant differences ($p \leq 0.05$) for most of them, except for the Neutral-Star and Emoji scales and RYG-Emoji and RYB-Emoji scale for some products (where $p \geq 0.05$). This signifies the influence of a meaningful colour-scheme and icons on users' rating behaviour. In order to understand the general trend of ratings on each scale, we calculated the correlation between ratings given in each scale. Table 3 shows the that the ratings in Neutral-star scale are most strongly correlated to Emoji scale and most weakly correlated with RYG-Emoji. The ratings on RYG-Emoji, are most strongly correlated with RYB-Emoji and weakly correlated with Neutral-Star (Table 4).

Table 4. The correlation for each rating scale design

	Neutral-star	RYG-star	RYG-Emoji	RYB-Emoji	Emoji	RYB-star
Neutral-star	1.000000	0.606736	0.472941	0.481561	0.690765	0.294523
RYG-Star	0.606736	1.000000	0.461832	0.459968	0.546434	0.591077
RYG-Emoji	0.472941	0.461832	1.000000	0.695702	0.642572	0.447337
RYB-Emoji	0.481561	0.459968	0.695702	1.000000	0.670855	0.458534
Emoji	0.690765	0.546434	0.642572	0.670855	1.000000	0.500641
RYB-star	0.294523	0.591077	0.447337	0.458534	0.500641	1.000000

6   Limitations and Future Work

Our research lacks the qualitative evidence from users about the underlying reasons of certain rating scale deign preferences. For example, most likely the users' age and gender have influenced how they perceive the visual cues of rating scales since majority users of the study are young and female. Also, the sample size is comparatively small which can be a shortcoming when considering the rating scale design as a persuasive tool. In our future work, we wish to investigate if our findings hold with participants of different age groups and genders and personality. We also aim to diversify the items being rated in the current study to get a holistic view of how the preferred rating scale and visual heuristics used by users work for every type of online services.

7   Conclusion

We proposed three hypotheses and conducted a user study to investigate the effect of rating scale designs using visual cues on user preferences and their rating behaviours. The main contributions of this paper are as follows: First, our experiment showed that visually informative scales are preferred by most users over a neutral scale (yellow stars). Second, we presented empirical evidence about users' preference of rating scale designs and its impact on getting true ratings from users. Third, our statistical analysis illustrated that users tend to provide more positive and consistent ratings using more visually rich scales. We theorized that using a rating scale with meaningful visual icons and colour schemes can influence users to give positive ratings which they consider to be best-suited for a product. Our results provide substantial support to the theory and can be used as a persuasive tool for online rating systems or product sales sites. By including users' own preference of rating scale design in the rating process can persuade users to give more truthful and positive rating scores. The implications from the study show that rating scales can persuade users into giving positive ratings which can be used to promote a comparatively new product or service to deal with the cold start problem of recommender systems.

References

1. Chen, P.-Y., Wu, S.-Y., Yoon, J.: The impact of online recommendations and consumer feedback on sales. In: ICIS 2004 Proceedings, p. 58. AIS Electronic Library (2004)
2. Van Den Broek, E.: Design parameters of rating scales for Web sites. ACM Comput. Rev. **14**, 4-es (2014)
3. Singh, J.: Consumer complaint intentions and behavior: definitional and taxonomical issues. J. Mark. **52**(1), 93–107 (1988)
4. Zhang, K.Z., Zhao, S.J., Cheung, C.M., Lee, M.K.: Examining the influence of online reviews on consumers' decision-making: a heuristic-systematic model. Decis. Supp. Syst. **67**, 78–89 (2014)
5. Askalidis, G., Malthouse, E.C.: The value of online customer reviews. In: Association for Computing Machinery, RecSys 2016, vol. 10, pp. 155–158. ACM, Boston (2016). https://doi.org/10.1145/2959100.2959181
6. Chevalier, J.A., Mayzlin, D.: The effect of word of mouth on sales. Online book reviews (No. w10148). National Bureau of Economic Research (2003)
7. Askalidis, G., Su, J.K., Malthouse, E.C.: Understanding and overcoming biases in online review systems. Decis. Supp. Syst. **97**, 23–30 (2017)
8. Cena, F., Vernero, F.: A study on user preferential choices about rating scales. Int. J. Technol. Human Interact. (IJTHI) **11**(1), 33–54 (2015)
9. Cena, F., Gena, C., Grillo, P., Kuflik, T., Vernero, F., Wecker, A.J.: How scales influence user rating behaviour in recommender systems. Behav. Inf. Technol. **36**(10), 985–1004 (2007)
10. Gena, C., Brogi, R., Cena, F., Vernero, F.: The impact of rating scales on user's rating behavior. In: Konstan, J.A., Conejo, R., Marzo, J.L., Oliver, N. (eds.) UMAP 2011. LNCS, vol. 6787, pp. 123–134. Springer, Heidelberg (2011). https://doi.org/10.1007/978-3-642-22362-4_11
11. Moors, G., Kieruj, N.D., Vermunt, J.K.: The effect of labeling and numbering of response scales on the likelihood of response bias. Sociol. Methodol. **44**(1), 369–399 (2014)
12. De Langhe, B., Fernbach, P.M., Lichtenstein, D.R.: Navigating by the stars: investigating the actual and perceived validity of online user ratings. J. Consum. Res. **42**(6), 817–833 (2016). https://doi.org/10.1093/jcr/ucv047
13. Riedl, C., Blohm, I., Leimeister, J.M., Krcmar, H.: The effect of rating scales on decision quality and user attitudes in online innovation communities. Int. J. Electron. Commer. **17**(3), 7–36 (2013)
14. Toepoel, V., Vermeeren, B., Metin, B.: Smileys, stars, hearts, buttons, tiles or grids: influence of response format on substantive response, questionnaire experience and response time. Bull. Sociol. Methodol./Bulletin de Méthodologie Sociologique **142**(1), 57–74 (2019)
15. Han, J., Pei, J., Kamber, M.: Data Mining: Concepts and Techniques. Elsevier, New York (2011)

16. Adomavicius, G., Bockstedt, J., Curley, S., Zhang, J.: Reducing recommender systems biases: an investigation of rating display designs. Forthcoming, MIS Q. 19–18 (2019)
17. Tourangeau, R., Couper, M.P., Conrad, F.: Color, labels, and interpretive heuristics for response scales. Public Opin. Q. **71**(1), 99–110 (2007)
18. Maharani, W., Widyantoro, D.H., Khodra, M.L.: Discovering users' perceptions on rating visualizations. In: Proceedings of the 2nd International Conference in HCI and UX, pp. 31–38. ACM, Indonesia (2016). https://doi.org/10.1145/2898459.2898464
19. Kostoulas, A.: https://achilleaskostoulas.com/2014/02/23/how-to-interpret-ordinal-data/. Accessed 24 Oct 2020
20. Grice, P.: Studies in the Way of Words. Harvard University Press, Harvard (1989)
21. ResearchGate. https://www.researchgate.net/post/. Accessed 4 Nov 2020
22. Sparling, E.I., Sen, S.: Rating: how difficult is it? In: Proceedings of the Fifth ACM Conference on Recommender Systems, pp. 149–156. ACM, USA (2011)
23. Cheng, F.F., Wu, C.S., Yen, D.C.: The effect of online store atmosphere on consumer's emotional responses-an experimental study of music and colour. Behav. Inf. Technol. **28**(4), 323–334 (2009)
24. Ayub, M., et al.: Modeling user rating preference behavior to improve the performance of the collaborative filtering based recommender systems. PloS ONE **14**(8), e0220129 (2019)
25. Labrecque, L.I., Milne, G.R.: Exciting red and competent blue: the importance of color in marketing. J. Acad. Mark. Sci. **40**(5), 711–727 (2012). https://doi.org/10.1007/s11747-010-0245-y
26. Bonaretti, D., Bartosiak, M. L., Piccoli, G.: Cognitive anchoring of color cues on online review ratings. In: Twenty-third Americas Conference on Information Systems, Boston (2017)

Investigating User Perceptions of Persuasive Design Elements that Influence Perceived Credibility

Felix N. Koranteng[1]([✉]), Jaap Ham[1], and Isaac Wiafe[2]

[1] Eindhoven University of Technology, Eindhoven, The Netherlands
j.r.c.ham@tue.nl
[2] Department of Computer Science, University of Ghana, Legon-Accra, Ghana
iwiafe@ug.edu.gh

Abstract. Given the prevalent use of technology for human activities, the deter-minants of user perceptions of the credibility of technological systems must be understood. This study investigated how user perceptions of persuasive elements that are incorporated in Academic Social Networking Sites (ASNSs) influence the Perceived Credibility of these sites. Specifically, the effects of Personalization, Reduction, Tailoring, Self-Monitoring, Rehearsal, Simulation and Tunneling on Perceived Credibility are examined. An online survey was adopted to examine the research model. Partial Least Square techniques were used to assess the signifi-cance of the determinants on Perceived Credibility. Results indicate that Tailoring positively influences Perceived Credibility whereas Personalization has a negative significant effect. Implications for theoretical insights into Perceived Credibility and its determinants and design implication are discussed.

Keywords: Perceived Credibility · Persuasive design · Tailoring · Academic Social Networking Sites

1 Introduction

In today's world, people depend on technology. Technological advancements, particu-larly those relating to computing have pervaded almost all human activities and con-sequently, the credibility of these technologies is of major concern to users. Users use technology when they perceive it as credible [1]. Indeed, existing research has shown that user acceptance and use of technology are closely associated with their perceptions and beliefs about that technology [2]. Similarly, users' continuance intentions to use a technology are dependent on their perceptions of the technology's credibility [3].

As the number of technology users continues to grow and technology use continues to impact more domains of human existence (e.g., politics, sales), strategies that aim at increasing the credibility of technological systems become more important. In the current research, we argue that persuasive strategies could be a key solution to improving credibility. Specifically, we measure users' perceptions of persuasive strategies that are integrated into Academic Social Networking Sites (ASNSs) to support their tasks and

© Springer Nature Switzerland AG 2021
R. Ali et al. (Eds.): PERSUASIVE 2021, LNCS 12684, pp. 164–177, 2021.
https://doi.org/10.1007/978-3-030-79460-6_13

how these strategies influence their perception of ASNSs credibility. Persuasive strategies can be integrated into technological systems design to simulate specified user reactions [4]. Studies showed that persuasive strategies are capable of changing users' attitudes and behaviors towards the desired one [e.g., 5, 6]. Accordingly, there is a need to investigate the relationship between the implementation of these persuasive strategies into a system and the user's perceptions of the credibility of this system.

1.1 Background

Credibility is the believability of technology [7], and is derived from users' evaluation of technology qualities [8]. It is a derivative of the cognitive process that guides users to determine the trustworthiness and perceived quality of a technology (e.g., website) [9, 10]. Fogg and Tseng [11] argued that next to perceived expertise, perceived trustworthiness is a key component of credibility. In other words, for a technology to be perceived as credible, users must perceive it to be high in trustworthiness and expertise. Perceived trustworthiness is the degree to which users believe that technology has good intentions and will intentionally cause harm to them [11]. Moreover, perceived expertise is the degree to which a user perceives that a technology (as depicted by its attributes) as competent, experienced and knowledgeable [11]. Thus, some scholars believe that credible technologies are associated with positive user attitudes [12]. Consequently, several earlier studies have investigated the determinants of credibility [1, 13].

More specifically, some studies identified factors such as visual effects, aesthetics and usability as determinants of Perceived Credibility [e.g., 1, 14, 18]. Alsudani and Casey [15] demonstrated that aesthetics have a significant effect on web credibility whereas David and Glore [16] confirmed that user judgment of system credibility is determined by aesthetic factors. Recently, Oyibo, Adaji, Orji, and Vassileva [17] suggested that both expressive and classical aesthetics drive the Perceived Credibility of mobile websites. Other studies also posited that usability features play a key role in determining credibility [18]. Huang and Benyoucef [19] found that e-government websites that users perceived to have high usability were also perceived to be highly credible. Whereas Oyibo and Vassileva [20], and Oyibo and Vassileva [13] confirmed that aesthetics and usability influence perceived credibility, this effect was moderated by personality traits and culture respectively. It has also been argued that the features (characteristics) of a technology (e.g., website features) can influence perceptions of credibility [21] and according to the PSD framework features that support users' primary tasks are crucial in influencing user behavior [4].

The PSD framework outlines the guidelines for the design, development and evaluation of persuasive systems. It suggests that system design features can be optimized such that they influence users' behavior. Hence, the framework categorizes persuasive design principles into four categories. These are; Primary Task Support, Dialogue Support, Perceived Social Support and Perceived Credibility. The Primary Task Support principle defines the features that support users as they perform their core activities. The Dialogue Support principle states the features that make the system interactive to keep users active. The Perceived Social Support principle leverages social influence strategies to motivate users to perform their tasks. The Perceived Credibility principle explains the features that promote trust and belief in the system.

Among these principles, Lehto, Oinas-Kukkonen and Drozd [22] considered Primary Task Support as the most important system design principle. This is because Primary Task Support makes it easier for users to perform their tasks [4]. In essence, Primary Task Support improves user experience [23] and promotes trustworthiness [24].

Recent research showed that Primary Task Support is a determinant of Perceived Credibility [25]. Therefore, integrating Primary Task Support strategies in system design influences Perceived Credibility. Yet, the study failed to specify which Primary Task Support strategies are effective for promoting Perceived Credibility. The PSD framework outlines seven strategies (i.e., Personalization, Reduction, Tailoring, Self-Monitoring, Rehearsal, Simulation and Tunneling) under the Primary Task Support principle. The specific effects of these Primary Task Support strategies in determining user perceptions of system credibility are not clear: Some studies have suggested that certain Primary Task Support strategies enforce credibility perceptions. For instance, Briggs and De Angeli [26] opined that personalization can affect trust in online environments. Harjumaa, Segerståhl and Oinas-Kukkonen [27] have also suggested that tailoring could predict Perceived Credibility. Nonetheless, these suggestions lack empirical backing. Moreover, to the best of our knowledge, no study has investigated how Primary Task Support strategies affect Perceived Credibility. Given that primary task support strategies are crucial to promoting positive user perceptions [4], it is important to understand which primary task support features affect Perceived Credibility.

Therefore, the current study examines the influence of the Primary Task Support strategies outlined by Oinas-Kukkonen and Harjumaa [4] on the Perceived Credibility of Academic Social Networking Sites (ASNSs). ASNSs are online social spaces that support academics to articulate their network [28]. Examples of ASNSs include ResearchGate, Academic.edu and Mendeley. It is expected that the outcome of this study will guide designers to select appropriate strategies as they seek to design systems that are perceived to be credible. The next section describes the current study.

1.2 Current Study

The present study investigated whether the Primary Task Support strategies defined by Oinas-Kukkonen and Harjumaa [4] influence users' perceptions of credibility. The study further evaluated which of the Primary Task Support strategies is most relevant in determining users' perception of system credibility within ASNSs. As stated earlier, this study extends the findings of Koranteng et al., [25] by addressing its limitations. Specifically, it explores how the various primary task support features impact credibility.

Therefore, we hypothesized a positive significant relationship between the Primary Task Support strategies and Perceived Credibility and predicted that;

H1: Personalization has a positive significant influence on Perceived Credibility.
H2: Reduction has a positive significant influence on Perceived Credibility.
H3: Rehearsal has a positive significant influence on Perceived Credibility.
H4: Self-Monitoring has a positive significant influence on Perceived Credibility.
H5: Simulation has a positive significant influence on Perceived Credibility.
H6: Tailoring has a positive significant influence on Perceived Credibility.
H7: Tunneling has a positive significant influence on Perceived Credibility.

These hypotheses are graphically represented in Fig. 1. To test the hypotheses, we examined the significance of the path coefficients for each of these relationships. The procedures and techniques adopted to examine these relationships are detailed in the Results sections.

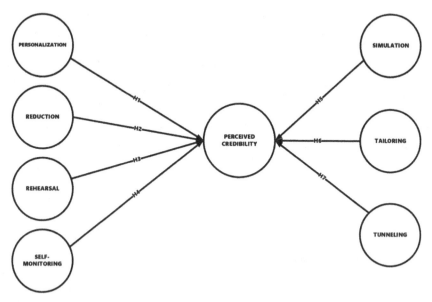

Fig. 1. Hypothesized model

2 Method

This study sampled participants from the Computer Science department of the University of Ghana, members of the British Computer Society Conference on Human-Computer Interaction (BCS-HCI), Judgment and Decision Making (JDM) mailing lists, and other professional bodies. Participation was voluntary and participants were selected using a combination of convenience and snowball sampling. The data collection lasted for two weeks. One hundred and thirty-six (131) valid responses were analyzed. All 131 participants indicated that they use ASNSs (including ResearchGate, Academia.edu, Mendeley, Google Scholar and LinkedIn) for various activities such as research, socialize, collaboration, academic visibility, accessing grants and provision of help to others. The descriptive analysis of the participants' demographics indicated that 79% were male, 20% were female, while 1% choose not to indicate their gender. The respondents' ages ranged from 18–25 years (30%), 26–35 years (38%), 35–45 years (21%), 45–55 years (10%), 56–65 years (1%). Also, majority (52%) of the respondents were master's degree holders, 31% were bachelor's degree holders, 13% had PhD degree and the remaining (4%) had other degrees (such as diploma and post-graduate diploma). Further, 40% of the respondents were students, 31% were faculty/researchers and the remaining 29%

categorized their occupations as university staff, government official, entrepreneur and computer professional.

2.1 Materials

To assess the relationships between a participant's perceptions of Primary Task Support strategies and Perceived Credibility, participants were tasked to complete the questionnaire. The questionnaire was in English and created using Google Forms (available at https://drive.google.com/file/d/13523mqdjnEaUWRr6KeMXJe3s0TPBP b9v/view?usp=sharing). It contained questions assessing (i) Personalization, (ii) Reduction, (iii) Rehearsal, (iv) Self-Monitoring, (v) Simulation, (vi) Tailoring (vii) Tunneling and (viii) Perceived Credibility. All questions could be answered on a seven-point Likert scale ranging from "Strongly Disagree" (1) to "Strongly Agree" (7). The questions in the questionnaire were generated based on Oinas-Kukkonen and Harjumaa's [4] conceptualization of the Primary Task Support strategies. The questionnaire also inquired about participants' demographics (e.g., age, gender, educational background and occupations) and ASNSs usage patterns.

2.2 Procedure

An email invitation was sent to participants to partake in the academic survey. After accepting the invitation, participants were asked to click a link to access the questionnaire. In the questionnaire, participants were asked to indicate if they use and their purposes for using ASNSs. Next, participants' opinions on the aforementioned Primary Task Support strategies were requested. Then, they were asked to report their demographic information. Finally, participants were thanked for their participation and could contact the researchers via email to receive further information about the study. No participant was given any gift, money or remuneration for participating.

3 Results

3.1 The Measurement Model

SmartPLS 3.2.8 software and Partial Least Square Structural Equation Modelling (PLS-SEM) techniques were adopted to analyze the proposed relationships. PLS-SEM was chosen because it provides techniques that are effective for analyzing measurement models [29]. Also, PLS-SEM is most suitable for studies that seek to predict the effect of one construct on another [29]. The constructs and their question items were examined for internal consistency, convergent validity, discriminant validity and common method bias as proposed by Wong [30]. Internal consistency was analyzed using Cronbach's Alpha (CA) and Composite Reliability (CR). These were all greater than 0.7. Convergent validity was evaluated with Average Variance Extracted (AVE) and it was greater than 0.5. To check common method bias, Variance Inflation Factor (VIF) was adopted and all the values were lesser than 3. The summary of the measurement model analysis is presented in Table 1. Also, non-response bias test was performed by comparing the analysis of 65 initial responses with the total (131) responses. The analysis revealed no significant differences between the results. This eliminated any doubt of non-response bias.

Table 1. Measurement model analysis

	CA	CR	AVE	VIF
Perceived credibility	0.921	0.950	0.864	
Personalization	0.911	0.923	0.750	1.55
Reduction	0.909	0.936	0.786	2.03
Rehearsal	0.878	0.922	0.798	2.12
Self-monitoring	0.853	0.910	0.771	1.99
Simulation	0.922	0.950	0.865	1.82
Tailoring	0.886	0.922	0.747	2.51
Tunneling	0.906	0.941	0.842	2.52

NB: CA: Cronbach's Alpha; CR: Composite Reliability; AVE: Average Variance Extracted; VIF: Variance Inflation Factor

Table 2. Discriminant Validity using Heterotrait-Monotrait Ratio

	Perceived credibility	Personalization	Reduction	Rehearsal	Self-monitoring	Simulation	Tailoring
Personalization	0.085						
Reduction	0.532	0.261					
Rehearsal	0.414	0.381	0.514				
Self-monitoring	0.368	0.441	0.681	0.568			
Simulation	0.303	0.331	0.404	0.625	0.496		
Tailoring	0.637	0.492	0.676	0.695	0.625	0.516	
Tunneling	0.483	0.126	0.596	0.700	0.615	0.660	0.627

Also, discriminant validity was measured with Heterotrait-Monotrait Ratio (HTMT). From the analysis, discriminant validity was determined since none of the correlations between the constructs loaded higher than 0.85 (see Table 2). This is particularly an important result since some researchers [31] believe that some of the Primary Task Support strategies (e.g., Personalization and Tailoring) are closely related and may be difficult to for users to distinguish them.

3.2 The Structural Model

The PLS-SEM bootstrap technique (5000 samples) was used to estimate the significance of path coefficients (β). A relationship was considered significant if the p-value (p) is greater than 0.05. In total, seven (7) determinants: Personalization (H1), Reduction (H2), Rehearsal (H3), Self-monitoring (H4), Simulation (H5), Tailoring (H6) and Tunneling (H7) were hypothesized to positively influence Perceived Credibility. Out of these, Tailoring was the only established determinant of Perceived Credibility ($\beta = 0.519, p < 0.000$). Contrary to our hypothesis, Personalization had a negative significant effect on Perceived Credibility ($\beta = -0.196, p < 0.048$). Also, Reduction ($\beta = 0.205, p > 0.05$), Rehearsal ($\beta = 0.011, p > 0.05$), Self-Monitoring ($\beta = -0.044, p > 0.05$), Simulation ($\beta = -0.013, p > 0.05$) and Tunneling ($\beta = 0.090, p > 0.05$) did not have any significant influence on Perceived Credibility. These determinants, however, explained 40.5% of the variance in Perceived Credibility (see Fig. 2).

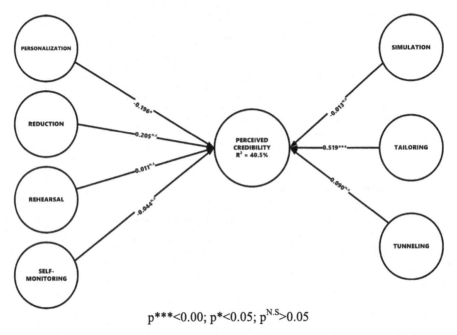

p***<0.00; p*<0.05; p^{N.S}>0.05

Fig. 2. The structural model

Further, the responses were categorized into subgroups and analyzed. For brevity, the subgroups that showed significant differences are discussed. First, two groups based on Frequency of Use were analyzed (see Fig. 2). This analysis showed significant differences between Frequent Users and Non-Frequent Users. For Frequent Users, Rehearsal had a significant positive influence on Perceived Credibility ($\beta = 0.320, p < 0.05$). All the other proposed determinants; Personalization ($\beta = -0.422, p > 0.05$), Reduction ($\beta = 0.032, p > 0.05$), Self-Monitoring ($\beta = 0.159, p > 0.05$), Simulation ($\beta = -0.106, p > 0.05$), Tailoring ($\beta = 0.220, p > 0.05$) and Tunneling ($\beta = 0.078, p > 0.05$) did not significantly influence Perceived Credibility. On the other hand, the analysis of Non-Frequent User group found Reduction ($\beta = 0.480, p < 0.02$) and Tailoring ($\beta = 0.582, p < 0.005$) as determinants of Perceived Credibility. Personalization ($\beta = -0.121, p > 0.05$), Rehearsal ($\beta = -0.133, p > 0.05$), Self-Monitoring ($\beta = -0.247, p > 0.05$),

Simulation ($\beta = 0.006, p > 0.05$) and Tunneling ($\beta = 0.061, p > 0.05$) were not found as determinants of Perceived Credibility. These results are presented in Fig. 3.

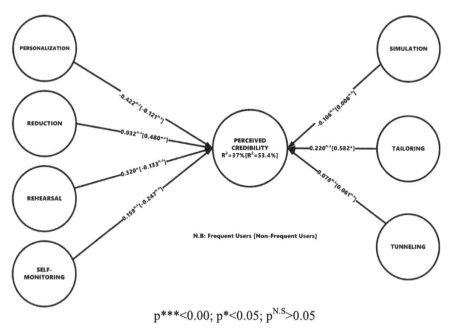

p***<0.00; p*<0.05; p$^{N.S.}$>0.05

Fig. 3. The structural model (frequency of use)

Second, the responses were analyzed based on respondents' occupation. Specifically, the responses were grouped under Students, Faculty/Researchers and Others. The Others category comprised university staff, entrepreneurs, public servants, computing professionals and government officials. For Faculty/Researchers group, only Reduction ($\beta = 0.411, p < 0.03$) was validated as a determinant of Perceived Credibility. The influence of the other proposed determinants of Perceived Credibility; Personlization ($\beta = -0.237, p > 0.05$), Rehearsal ($\beta = -0.079, p > 0.05$), Self-Monitoring ($\beta = 0.057, p > 0.05$), Simulation ($\beta = 0.169, p > 0.05$), Tailoring ($\beta = 0.151, p > 0.05$) and Tunneling ($\beta = 0.330, p > 0.05$) were non-significant. With regard to Students' subgroup, the results indicated that Tailoring ($\beta = 0.797, p < 0.01$) is the only determinant of Perceived Credibility. Personalization ($\beta = -0.147, p > 0.05$), Reduction ($\beta = 0.112, p > 0.05$), Rehearsal ($\beta = -0.016, p > 0.05$), Self-Monitoring ($\beta = 0.008, p > 0.05$), Simulation ($\beta = -0.194, p > 0.05$) and Tunneling ($\beta = -0.084, p > 0.05$) were not validated as determinants of Perceived Credibility. Additionally, the analysis of the Others subgroup revealed that none of the proposed determinants had a significant effect on Perceived Credibility (Fig. 4).

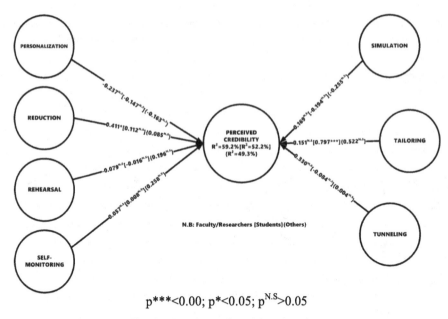

$$p*** < 0.00; p* < 0.05; p^{N.S.} > 0.05$$

Fig. 4. The structural model (occupation)

4 Discussion

As technology use continues to penetrate various human activities, the credibility of technological systems remains an issue of concern. Although some studies have examined some determinants of credibility, there is a need to explore other factors that influence credibility. In this light, this study investigated how strategies incorporated into technologies to support users' tasks (i.e., persuasive design features) influence their perceptions of credibility. Specifically, this paper examined how the Primary Task Support strategies proposed by Oinas-Kukkonen and Harjumaa [4] determine users' perceptions of the credibility of ASNSs. In line with this, PLS-SEM techniques were adopted to analyze the direct effect of Personalization, Reduction, Rehearsal, Self-Monitoring, Simulation, Tailoring and Tunneling on Perceived Credibility. These determinants accounted for 40.5% of the variance in Perceived Credibility.

Results showed that only one hypothesis (H6: Tailoring positively influences Perceived Credibility) was supported. That is, confirming the suggestion by Harjumaa, Segerståhl and Oinas-Kukkonen [27], results provided empirical evidence that Tailoring was a determinant of Perceived Credibility.

This indicates that the more users perceive that a technology is tailored to suit them, the more they perceive the technology to be credible. In the case of ASNSs, users perceived that the content produced by the ASNSs that they use was tailored to fit their needs. In line with this finding, earlier research showed that messages that are consistent with an individual's objectives are evaluated more favorably than inconsistent messages [32]. Similarly, based on basic information-processing mechanisms, matching information to an individual's characteristics may be more effective in influencing many psychological perspectives [33]. It can be argued that because the content produced for users on ASNSs is based on users' characteristics (e.g., their domain of research), users' perceptions of credibility were influenced. Likewise, many ASNSs use algorithms to adapt user's home feed based on their recent searches and other activities. This makes users perceive that the ASNSs offer content that is relevant to their needs, making users perceive ASNSs as credible. However, it was surprising that Tailoring was a significant determinant of Perceived Credibility for Non-Frequent Users but insignificant for Frequent Users. Perhaps, this may be because of how frequent ASNSs users are presented with new information. That is, although the content users interact with may be tailored to fit their objectives, Non-Frequent Users may see much newer information as and when they visit their ASNSs whereas Frequent Users may have to interact with repeated information. It is therefore important that ASNSs developers provide improved algorithms to increase the frequency of content updates, particularly for frequent users. In contrast to our hypothesis (i.e., H1), results showed that Personalization had a negative significant influence on Perceived Credibility. This finding suggests that when users are able (to a larger extent) to change the characteristics of a technology such that the technology fits their personality, then they will perceive the technology as less credible. Similarly, because users perceived ASNSs to allow personalization, they perceived ASNSs as not credible. This contradicts earlier studies that suggested that Personalization increases perceptions of credibility [26]. An explanation for this finding might be that Personalization is based on user data (e.g., gender, usage patterns and cultural orientation) which may lead to privacy concerns. This may raise privacy concerns, particularly in this online environment. Indeed, some studies have argued that monitoring is perceived as invasive and intrusive [34] and this may affect users' trust [35]. Therefore, users may perceive these technologies as less credible. At the same time, our results provided no evidence that for any particular subgroup a significant relationship existed between Personalization and Perceived Credibility. Perhaps, this is because many ASNSs are still exploring personalization techniques for different user groups. Therefore, future studies could explore the relationship between Personalization and Perceived Credibility among different user group contexts.

Next, Reduction did not have a significant influence on Perceived Credibility: Users did not perceive that when a technology breaks up complex tasks into more easy subtasks, then that technology is credible. An explanation could be that users of a technology have different purposes for using the technology: When technology is designed to have multiple functions, user perceptions that the technology supports their core tasks may be unclear [36]. For instance, the purposes for using ASNSs can be diverse and may include collaboration, academic visibility and socialization. It is possible that existing ASNSs cannot support all user activities, resulting in diverse user perceptions. It, therefore, becomes important that researchers segregate the purposes of technology usage to draw a valid relationship between the task users perform and users' perceptions. For instance, the core function of ASNSs is to facilitate research processes [37]. In line with this, an analysis of responses from Faculty/Researchers indicated that Reduction has a positive significant Influence on Perceived Credibility.

Also, the results from the general model indicated that Rehearsal does not determine Perceived Credibility. This relationship was confirmed for the Non-Frequent Users' group but it was present in the Frequent Users' group. This suggests that unlike the Non-Frequent Users group, Frequent Users of ASNSs, perceived that they are able to practice their activities and this affects their perception of ASNSs credibility. Indeed, ASNSs allow users to rehearse their tasks. For instance, sites such as ResearchGate aAcademia.edu allow users to search for articles and read answers to questions without logging onto the site. However, these functionalities are not readily visible and may be missed by Non-Frequent Users. Perhaps, this accounts for why Rehearsal was a non-significant determinant of Perceived Credibility for the group.

Moreover, Simulation was found to be a non-determinant of Perceived Credibility. Thus, although some studies have argued that Simulation increases persuasiveness [4], they do not influence perceptions of credibility. This might be because Simulation is not easily observed on many ASNSs. For example, neither Academia.edu nor ResearchGate indicates the after-effects of using the sites. Therefore, users may not be preview to the existence of the strategy on ASNSs. Thereby, Simulation cannot determine users' perceptions of ASNSs credibility.

The study also found that Self-Monitoring is not a determining factor of Perceived Credibility. This was similar in all the multigroup analysis cases. That is, users' perception that technologies provide ways for them to monitor and assess their performance, do not inform their credibility perceptions. Ideally, users' confidence in ASNSs was expected to increase since ASNSs advise users based on performance monitoring. Perhaps, performance monitoring on ASNSs is less relevant to users and would prefer other methods for providing advice.

Similarly, Tunneling did not have any significant effect on Perceived Credibility. The result suggests that users' perceptions of the extent to which ASNSs guide their performance of tasks do not inform their perceptions of the credibility of ASNSs. This is surprising because tunneling is known to improve user experience and helps them to achieve their target behavior [38]. ASNSs employ wizards to guide users through a predetermined sequence of actions or events. Whereas Guides such as wizards are meant to reduce users' cognitive burdens associated with task performance, they also reduce the user's choice of freedom [38]. Such coercion may negatively affect their experience and perceptions. That is to conclude that the effect of tunneling as a persuasive strategy needs further investigations.

As indicated earlier, this study is an extension of an earlier study with findings that deepen our understanding of how perceptions of Primary Task Support strategies affect users' perception of credibility. It has demonstrated that not all Primary Task Support strategies influence users' perceptions of credibility. Rather, Tailoring is the only significant predictor of Perceived Credibility. Therefore, for technology to be designed to be credible, it must be tailored to suit the users.

The study also revealed the Personalization reduces perceptions of credibility. That is, although some studies have highlighted that personalization increases persuasiveness [4], our findings suggest that higher perceptions of personalization rather decrease perceived credibility. In this light, developers who seek to design for perceived credibility must reduce the extent to which their designs are personalized.

Furthermore, the findings suggest that Reduction, Rehearsal, Simulation, Tunneling and self-Monitoring are not determinants of Perceived Credibility. Hence, these strategies may have little influence when designing technologies that prioritize credibility. However, designers may have to consider different user groups before incorporating these strategies to improve perceptions of credibility. For instance, Reduction plays a significant role in determining credibility among faculty and researchers whilst rehearsal may have a higher impact on frequent users of a technology. Nonetheless, these findings are measurements of user perceptions of Primary Task Support strategies and how they relate to Perceived Credibility. Therefore, future research may investigate the relationship between manipulation of these Primary Task Support strategies and perceived credibility or compliance and other behaviors that relate to credibility.

The study makes two main contributions. First, we extend the literature that discusses Perceived Credibility and its determinants. Unlike, previous studies, this study provides an alternative determinant of Perceived Credibility by specifying which Primary Task Support strategy improves perceptions of credibility. Next, in contrast to suggestions from some scholars [e.g., 31] that users view Personalization and Tailoring are closely related and may not separate, the validity of items used to measure these strategies in our study suggest that they are distinct and even produce different effects. These contributions are highly relevant because to the best of our knowledge this is one of the first studies in the domain of the persuasive systems that measure the direct effects of Primary Task Support strategies on Perceived Credibility.

5 Conclusion

The findings presented in this research are highly beneficial as they guide designers who seek to design technologies that are deemed as credible. Specifically, it broadens our understanding of which Primary Task Support strategies influence Perceived Credibility. The findings direct designers to focus on the Tailoring strategies when they seek to design technologies that are perceived to be credible. However, the findings discourage the incorporation of Personalization into technologies that prioritizes credibility.

Moreover, the findings also provide relevant revelations for researchers in the domain of persuasive technologies. That is, given the belief that the Personalization and Tailoring strategies are inseparable and must be combined, our study provides evidence that these strategies are distinct. Researchers can however base on this study and analyze the effects of Personalization and Tailoring strategies separately.

Finally, though this study was conducted in the domain of ASNSs, the findings inform the design of other technologies. Certainly, as Perceived Credibility remains a key factor that affects users' continuance intentions to use technology, the findings discussed in the study guide developers to build technologies that are perceived as credible.

References

1. Robins, D., Holmes, J.: Aesthetics and credibility in web site design. Inf. Process. Manag. **44**(1), 386–399 (2008)

2. Wiafe, I., Koranteng, F.N., Tettey, T., Kastriku, F.A., Abdulai, J.-D.: Factors that affect acceptance and use of information systems within the maritime industry in developing countries. J. Syst. Inf. Technol. (2019). https://doi.org/10.1108/JSIT-06-2018-0091
3. Adaji, I., Vassileva, J.: Perceived effectiveness, credibility and continuance intention in e-commerce: a study of Amazon. In: de Vries, P.W., Oinas-Kukkonen, H., Siemons, L., Beerlage-de Jong, N., van Gemert-Pijnen, L. (eds.) PERSUASIVE 2017. LNCS, vol. 10171, pp. 293–306. Springer, Cham (2017). https://doi.org/10.1007/978-3-319-55134-0_23
4. Oinas-Kukkonen, H., Harjumaa, M.: Persuasive systems design: key issues, process model, and system features. Commun. Assoc. Inf. Syst. 24(1), 28 (2009)
5. Wiafe, I., Abdulai, J.-D., Katsriku, F., Kumi, J.A., Koranteng, F.N., Boakye-Sekyerehene, P.: Controlling driver over-speeding with a persuasive and intelligent road marking system. Adv. Transp. Stud. 50(L-APRIL 2020), 19–30 (2020)
6. Ham, J., Cuijpers, R.H., Cabibihan, J.-J.: Combining robotic persuasive strategies: the persuasive power of a storytelling robot that uses gazing and gestures. Int. J. Soc. Robot. 7(4), 479–487 (2015)
7. Tseng, S., Fogg, B.J.: Credibility and computing technology. Commun. ACM 42(5), 39–44 (1999)
8. Solomon, M.R., White, K., Dahl, D.W., Zaichkowsky, J.L., Polegato, R.: Consumer Behavior: Buying, Having, and Being. Pearson, Boston (2017)
9. Alrubaian, M., Al-Qurishi, M., Alamri, A., Al-Rakhami, M., Hassan, M.M., Fortino, G.: Credibility in online social networks: a survey. IEEE Access 7, 2828–2855 (2018)
10. Oyibo, K., Adaji, I., Vassileva, J.: Mobile web design: the effect of education on the influence of classical and expressive aesthetics on perceived credibility. In: Marcus, A., Wang, W. (eds.) HCII 2019. LNCS, vol. 11584, pp. 66–79. Springer, Cham (2019). https://doi.org/10.1007/978-3-030-23541-3_6
11. Fogg, B.J., Tseng, H. : The elements of computer credibility. In: Proceedings of the SIGCHI conference on Human Factors in Computing Systems, pp. 80–87 (1999)
12. Kubiszewski, I., Noordewier, T., Costanza, R.: Perceived credibility of internet encyclopedias. Comput. Educ. 56(3), 659–667 (2011)
13. Oyibo, K., Vassileva, J. : The interplay of aesthetics, usability and credibility in mobile websites and the moderation by culture. In: Proceedings of the 15th Brazilian Symposium on Human Factors in Computing Systems, pp. 1–10 (2016)
14. Tractinsky, N., Katz, A.S., Ikar, D.: What is beautiful is usable. Interact. Comput. 13(2), 127–145 (2000)
15. Alsudani, F., Casey, M. C.: The effect of aesthetics on web credibility. In: Proceedings of the 23rd British HCI Group Annual Conference on People and Computers: Celebrating People and Technology, pp. 512–519 (2009)
16. David, A., Glore, P.: The impact of design and aesthetics on usability, credibility, and learning in an online environment. Online J. Distance Learn. Adm. 13(4), 43–50 (2010)
17. Oyibo, K., Adaji, I., Orji, R., Vassileva, J.: What drives the perceived credibility of mobile websites: classical or expressive aesthetics? In: Kurosu, M. (ed.) HCI 2018. LNCS, vol. 10902, pp. 576–594. Springer, Cham (2018). https://doi.org/10.1007/978-3-319-91244-8_45
18. Youngblood, N.E., Mackiewicz, J.: A usability analysis of municipal government website home pages in Alabama. Gov. Inf. Q. 29(4), 582–588 (2012)
19. Huang, Z., Benyoucef, M.: Usability and credibility of e-government websites. Gov. Inf. Q. 31(4), 584–595 (2014)
20. Oyibo, K., Vassileva, J.: The interplay of aesthetics, usability and credibility in mobile website design and the effect of gender. SBC J. Interact. Syst. 8(2), 4–19 (2017)
21. Flanagin, A.J., Metzger, M.J.: The role of site features, user attributes, and information verification behaviors on the perceived credibility of web-based information. New Media Soc. 9(2), 319–342 (2007)

22. Lehto, T., Oinas-Kukkonen, H., Drozd, F.: Factors affecting perceived persuasiveness of a behavior change support system. In: Proceedings of the International Conference on Information Systems (ICIS), pp. 1–15 (2012)

23. Shevchuk, N., Degirmenci, K., Oinas-Kukkonen, H.: Adoption of gamified persuasive systems to encourage sustainable behaviors: Interplay between perceived persuasiveness and cognitive absorption. In: International Conference on Information Systems, pp. 1–17 (2019)

24. Beldad, A.D., Hegner, S.M.: Expanding the technology acceptance model with the inclusion of trust, social influence, and health valuation to determine the predictors of German users' willingness to continue using a fitness app: a structural equation modeling approach. Int. J. Hum.-Comput. Interact. **34**(9), 882–893 (2018)

25. Koranteng, F.N., Ham, J., Wiafe, I.: The role of usability, aesthetics, usefulness and primary task support in predicting the perceived credibility of systems (Manuscript Submitted for Publication) (2020). Manuscript Submitted for Publication

26. Briggs, P.S., De Angeli, A.: Does personalisation affect trust in online advice? (2003)

27. Harjumaa, M., Segerståhl, K., Oinas-Kukkonen, H.: Understanding persuasive software functionality in practice: a field trial of polar FT60. In: Proceedings of the 4th International Conference on Persuasive Technology, pp. 1–9 (2009)

28. Koranteng, F.N., Wiafe, I.: Factors that promote knowledge sharing on academic social networking sites: an empirical study. Educ. Inf. Technol. **24**(2), 1211–1236 (2018). https://doi.org/10.1007/s10639-018-9825-0

29. Hair Jr., J.F., Hult, G.T.M., Ringle, C., Sarstedt, M.: A Primer on Partial Least Squares Structural Equation Modeling (PLS-SEM). Sage Publications (2016)

30. Wong, K.K.-K.: Partial least squares structural equation modeling (PLS-SEM) techniques using SmartPLS. Mark. Bull. **24**(1), 1–32 (2013)

31. Oyebode, O., Orji, R.: Deconstructing persuasive strategies in mental health apps based on user reviews using natural language processing. In: CEUR International Workshop on Behavior Change Support Systems, p. 2662 (2020)

32. Cesario, J., Grant, H., Higgins, E.T.: Regulatory fit and persuasion: transfer from feeling right. J. Pers. Soc. Psychol. **86**(3), 388 (2004)

33. Dijkstra, A.: The psychology of tailoring-ingredients in computer-tailored persuasion. Soc. Pers. Psychol. Compass **2**(2), 765–784 (2008)

34. Sewell, G., Barker, J.R., Nyberg, D.: Working under intensive surveillance: when does measuring everything that moves become intolerable? Hum. Relat. **65**(2), 189–215 (2012)

35. Weston, M.: Wearable surveillance–a step too far? Strateg. HR Rev. **14**(6), 214–219 (2015)

36. Hong, S.-J., Tam, K.Y.: Understanding the adoption of multipurpose information appliances: the case of mobile data services. Inf. Syst. Res. **17**(2), 162–179 (2006)

37. Wiafe, I., Koranteng, F.N., Owusu, E., Ekpezu, A.O., Gyamfi, S.A.: Persuasive social features that promote knowledge sharing among tertiary students on social networking sites: an empirical study. J. Comput. Assist. Learn. **36**, 636–645 (2020). https://doi.org/10.1111/jcal.12433

38. Calefato, C., Vernero, F., Montanari, R.: Wikipedia as an example of positive technology: how to promote knowledge sharing and collaboration with a persuasive tutorial. In: 2009 2nd Conference on Human System Interactions, pp. 510–516 (2009)

Exploring the Impact of Persuasive Features on Customer Satisfaction Levels of E-Commerce Websites Based on the Kano Model

Muna M. Alhammad[1] , Isaac Wiafe[2(✉)] , and Stephen R. Gulliver[3]

[1] King Saud University, Riyadh 11451, Saudi Arabia
malhammad@ksu.edu.sa
[2] Department of Computer Science, University of Ghana, Accra, Ghana
iwiafe@ug.edu.gh
[3] University of Reading, Reading RG6 6UD, UK
s.r.gulliver@henley.ac.uk

Abstract. This study investigated user needs and expectations in relation to the 28 persuasive features of the Persuasive Systems Design model. It adopted the Kano's model of customer needs and expectations to examine perceive user satisfaction or dissatisfaction levels of the various system features on e-commerce websites. The findings provide guidelines for designing e-commerce platforms and websites that seek to employ persuasive strategies to enhance user experience. It was observed that persuasive system features do not consistently affect user satisfaction and dissatisfaction levels. Features relating to dialogue support had the highest influence on user satisfaction levels; followed respectively by credibility support and primary task support. Social support features do not have a high influence on user satisfaction. No persuasive system feature emerged as a "must-be" feature.

Keywords: Persuasive system features · User satisfaction · Interactive e-commerce design · Kano model

1 Introduction

Research has demonstrated that although usability plays a key role in the success of e-commerce websites, it is not the main factor for success [1]. A successful e-commerce website needs to attract users, emphasize credibility to stimulate trust, enhance customer interactions, present products and services in an inspirational and attractive manner, and persuade customers (via application of persuasive features) to purchase from the website [2]. It must ultimately result in an experience that produces 'customer satisfaction'. As the argument on which factors are more relevant on e-commerce websites and its related ethical considerations continue to progress [3, 4], this study focuses its investigation on persuasive features that influences user satisfaction on e-commerce websites. Although persuasive features play a major role in e-commerce platforms [5], they have not been adequately explored [6]. In particular, the ability to select effective persuasive features to enhance persuasive experience remains unsolved.

© Springer Nature Switzerland AG 2021
R. Ali et al. (Eds.): PERSUASIVE 2021, LNCS 12684, pp. 178–192, 2021.
https://doi.org/10.1007/978-3-030-79460-6_14

Persuasive features trigger activities that promote continuous interactions on websites [7] and motivate consumers to use services or buy products from e-commerce websites [8, 9]. It has been argued that e-commerce websites need to exhibit persuasive functionalities in addition to providing information on product and services [2]. Although influence strategies have always been part of commercial activities and thus the need to incorporate them on e-commerce websites is not novel, the introduction of persuasive technologies, and behavior change support systems, presents an opportunity to e-commerce designers to enrich e-commerce websites. Persuasive systems design is the use of technological artefacts and features to influence user cognition to a predetermined one [10, 11]. Existing research has demonstrated that persuasive systems have been effective in areas such as health, education, environmental issues, and energy conservation; yet studies that focus on the use of persuasive features in e-commerce is lacking. In particular, the contextual value of specific types of persuasive features has not been adequately explored. Limited studies have examined or evaluated the persuasive power of website features and components in e-commerce [12]. However, this is vital, considering that e-commerce websites must influence customers in addition to providing brochures and catalogues of products and services. E-commerce website users may perceive satisfaction based on their interactions and experiences of the websites they use. Studies have shown that user satisfaction and persuasion are strongly correlated [13]. Accordingly, it is imperative to investigate persuasive features that promote customer satisfaction on e-commerce websites [14].

This study, therefore, seeks to examine how different persuasive features of e-commerce websites influence customers' satisfaction levels. Specifically, the perception of users concerning the 28 persuasive system features, proposed by Oinas-Kukkonen and Harjumaa [15], was assessed using Kano's model [16] to determine how customers classify them in terms of relevance. The findings of this study provide relevant information for further investigations on methods for selecting the most effective persuasive features: an issue which is challenging to persuasive systems designers.

2 Related Literature

2.1 Customer Satisfaction

It is almost impossible to initiate and establish long-term relationships with customers if their needs and expectations are not fully understood or met [17]. A good understanding of customers' needs and expectation is a necessary step to fulfil their satisfaction [18]. In interactive e-commerce websites, customer satisfaction is relevant [19] and thus several organizations use customer satisfaction ratings as a key indicator of performance [20]. Customer satisfaction is the assessment of the perceived difference between prior expectations and the actual performance of the product or service [21], and is an indicator of positive fulfilment of customer needs. Some researchers argue that customer needs and satisfaction are the ultimate objectives of every organization [22]. Accordingly, the need to meet their expectations cannot be overemphasized, particularly considering that these needs evolve over time [16]. In contemporary interactive e-commerce websites, customer satisfaction is considered as a key ingredient of success [19]. Thus, several theories, models, and frameworks have been proposed to extend knowledge and provide guidelines on how customer satisfaction can be achieved. Perhaps one of the most dominant theories applied in customer satisfaction research is Herzberg's motivation-hygiene theory (i.e. the two-factor theory) [23]. The theory distinguishes concepts of satisfaction and dissatisfaction as two distinct constructs. This notion is contrary to arguments made by Zhan and Dran [8] that considers satisfaction as distinct values of one dimension. Herzberg [24] argued that motivation and hygiene factors play an essential role in customer satisfaction. Even though these factors continue to remain relevant in contemporary investigations of customer satisfaction research, treating satisfaction and dissatisfaction as mutually exclusive constructs is problematic.

Due to the limitation of Herzberg's motivation-hygiene theory, some studies adopt SERVQUAL [25] for investigating satisfaction. SERVQUAL is a multi-item scale for measuring five main dimensions (i.e., Tangibles, Reliability, Responsiveness, Assurance and Empathy) of customer needs and perceptions on quality performance. SERVQUAL seeks to measure service quality, nonetheless, it has been adopted for accessing customer satisfaction in several studies: with the assumption that there is a relationship between service quality and customer satisfaction [26]. However, its use for measuring customer satisfaction is contentious, since arguments on the relationship between service quality and customer satisfaction are diverging [27–29]. It has been argued that the relationship between service quality and customer satisfaction is non-linear [16]. So, SERVQUAL is not suitable for assessing customer satisfaction, although it is useful for measuring service quality. The Kano's model [16] on the other hand addresses the limitations of SERVQUAL. The model categorizes service quality features based on their effects on customer satisfaction that support a business's strategic and tactical decisions [30]. This is a key step as it measures customers' perception of service quality features and categories them based on their influences on customer satisfaction. In this study, the Kano's model is used to measure customer satisfaction since it provides the relevant variables needed for the study.

2.2 Kano's Model of Customer Satisfaction

The Kano model distinguishes between four forms of customer expectations for product and service quality. This includes i) must-be features, ii) one-dimensional features, iii) attractive features and iv) indifferent features. The model has been applied in many fields, including service quality assessment [19], user experience assessment [8], and compensation systems [31]. It argues that for businesses to excel, the first three forms must be met. However, although the presence of "must-be" features is not noticeable by customers, their absence or non-performance leads to total dissatisfaction. One-dimensional features (i.e. performance or linear quality) are specific needs that are noticeable by customers when present. Hence, the presence of one-dimensional features is always noted, and the absence of one-dimensional features leads to customers dissatisfaction. Attractive or excitement features are attributes that are not expected by customers, yet their presence will delight them and inspire loyalty. Attractive features increase satisfaction levels, but their absence does not affect dissatisfaction. This is because attractive features seek to address hidden and unarticulated needs and it is mostly a challenge to identify them. Indifferent features do not influence customer satisfaction or dissatisfaction level and thus, they do not have an impact on customer satisfaction. The model provides a logical extension of Herzberg's motivation-hygiene theory [24] where Must-be features are similar to hygiene features, Attractive features maps to motivational features and One-dimensional features maps to bivalent features.

The KANO model: facilitates the identification of quality expectations and time transition of these quality factors [8]; is versatile, and has been adapted for a range of different purposes [32]; puts customer satisfaction first in design features of products and services; and has been successfully applied to assess attributes of website quality [8]. As such the KANO model is appropriate for assessing persuasive system features, i.e. to categorize features based on the influence of features on customer satisfaction, in order to provide a better understanding of customer requirement priority, and address the nature of changing quality features.

2.3   Persuasive Systems Features and E-Commerce Websites

Persuasion is a communication process involving an individual (persuader) sending a message to a recipient (persuadee), intending to influence the recipient's attitude and/or behavior; whilst leaving the recipient with the power of decision. Although this activity is not new, advancement in computer technology has enhanced its ease of application. Increasingly, systems and technologies are designed with the sole intention of altering cognition. Accordingly, new theories and frameworks [10, 14, 26, 27] have been proposed to facilitate the use of technological artefacts for influencing target user behavior. The Persuasive Systems Design model [15] is arguably the most used framework for designing and evaluating persuasive systems and has been used to assess persuasive experiences in several domains including enterprise resource management systems [36], alcohol and smoking management systems [37], and knowledge sharing among academics [38]. The Persuasive Systems Design model highlights seven postulates for analyzing and designing persuasive systems. It further argues that there are twenty-eight (28) persuasive features that can be categorized into four main areas: primary tasks (Reduction, Tunneling, Tailoring, Personalization, Self-Monitoring, Simulations, Rehearsal); dialogue support (Praise, Rewards, Reminders, Suggestion, Similarity, Liking, Social Role); Credibility support (Trustworthiness, Expertise, Surface credibility, Real-world feel, Authority, Third-party endorsements, Verifiability) and Social support (Social Learning, Social Comparison, Normative Influence, Social facilitation, Cooperation, Competition, Recognition (see [15] for a more detailed definition of each feature). These features have been used in a range of different domains to encourage certain target behavior. Some studies have argued that they influence users' purchase intentions [39] by providing good navigational usability, eliminate trust and security doubts, and promote smooth transactions.

3   Research Approach

An exploratory study was designed to investigate user preferences of persuasive features, i.e., how each persuasive feature influences user satisfaction levels with regard to e-commerce. A questionnaire was used to identify and classify customer perception into four categories as suggested by Kano et al. [16]. The functional or dysfunctional form of each of the 28 persuasive features was measured. As suggested by Xu et al. [40], the functional form was specified as 'how would you feel if this particular feature is presented in a product/service'. The dysfunctional form was specified as 'how would you feel if this particular feature is not presented in the product/service'. It is expected that Kano's model will classify persuasive features based on their impact on user satisfaction. Based on responses to the functional and dysfunctional forms of each question, customers' requirements for each feature were classified into different categories using the Kano Evaluation (see Table 2). The frequency distribution for each feature determined Kano's category classification [19]: with the highest response frequency being the dominant class. However, in situations where the dominant class is absent or sensitive to change in frequency, two additional measures are used to determine it (i.e. category strength and total strength) [41]. The quality response is measured by calculating the Satisfaction Coefficient (*CoS*) and the Dissatisfaction Coefficient (*CoD*) - as shown respectively in Eqs. 1 and 2; where A is Attractive, O is One-dimensional, M is Must-be and I is Indifferent (Table 1).

$$CoS = \frac{(A + O)}{A + O + M + I} \tag{1}$$

and

$$CoD = \left(\frac{(M + O)}{A + O + M + I}\right) \times (-1) \tag{2}$$

Table 1. Kano's evaluation framework

Customer requirements			Dysfunctional (negative) question				
			1		2	3	4	5
Functional (positive) question	1	Q			A	A	A	O
	2	R			I	I	I	M
	3	R			I	I	I	M
	4	R			I	I	I	M
	5	R			R	R	R	Q

A: Attractive, O: One-dimensional, M:Must-be, I: Indifferent, R: Reversal, Q: Questionable
1:I like it, 2:I expect it, 3:I'm neutral, 4:I can tolerate it, 5:I dislike it

Two independent samples were used for evaluating the same set of persuasive features in relation to physical and digital products. The separation of the product sought to reduce the length of the questionnaire and multiple evaluations. A pre-test was conducted using 6 participants and their recommendations were considered in the final version of the questionnaire. The CVSCALE was used and the pre-test results showed high internal reliability, with Cronbach's α values above the 0.7.

The questionnaire (see https://www.dropbox.com/s/dthnyjnviagpn0u/Questionaire. pdf?dl=0) was administered online using 'SmartSurvey.com'. The survey link was sent through different media channels, including Facebook, Twitter, LinkedIn, Emails and Amazon Mechanical Turk. A total of 500 links were sent. Amazon Mechanical Turk was used to target a diverse range of responses. All in all, 250 responses were obtained indicating a 50% response rate. A non-response bias analysis was conducted using the first 50 responses, and the findings indicated that non-responses did not affect the findings. Out of the 250 responses, 45 were excluded because 32 had no online shopping experience, and although the remaining 13 had shopped online before they have never browsed online shopping websites. The latter demonstrated a conflict in their responses and thus were excluded from the study.

4 Results

4.1 Respondents' Characteristics

A larger proportion of respondents were those who buy physical products. This was almost three-quarters (76.5%) of the respondents (see Table 2). Out of the total of 157 respondents who buy physical products often, 56% were females and 44% were males. Forty-nine per cent (49%) of respondents who buy physical product were between 25–34 years. Most respondents were either students (38.8%) or in full-time employment (36.3%). With respect to age, majority of respondents (49.8%) were between 25–34 years, and the remainder were 18–24 (23.9%), 35–54 (20.5%) and 5.8% for those over 55 years old. In terms of the highest qualification, 44.4% of the respondents hold a bachelor's degree, 35.1% have master's degree and 13.2% have a doctoral degree or equivalent. The least educational qualification was high school degrees (5.4%). The distribution of those who tend to buy digital products is similar to those who buy physical products except for gender, where male tend to buy digital products while female tend to buy more physical products. All respondents had experienced online shopping and bought an item online within the past six months. Respondents were from a range of different nationality including the UK, USA, Saudi Arabia, India and Pakistan. See Table 2 for details of respondents' characteristics.

4.2 Kano's Categorization of Persuasive Features

The Kano's categories for the 28 persuasive features were generated and the extent of satisfaction and dissatisfaction were also calculated (see Table 3). Variations in satisfaction and dissatisfaction levels were observed among the various persuasive features. Features relating to primary task support (PT) (i.e., reduction, tunneling, tailoring, personalization, self-monitoring, simulation and rehearsal) recorded coefficient of satisfaction (CoS) values ranging from 0.30–0.45. Thus, they impact customer satisfaction between 30–45%, whereas their absence may result in customers dissatisfaction (CoD) between 8 and 64% - see Table 3. The presence of personalization features in e-commerce websites was observed to increase customer satisfaction by 31%, however, its absence does not significantly affect customer dissatisfaction (8%). Tunneling and rehearsal increase customer's satisfaction (i.e., by 39% and 36% respectively) and their absence also impacts dissatisfaction levels (i.e., 47% and 46% respectively). Out of the seven primary task support features, one persuasive feature (i.e., self-monitoring) was found to be of significant importance since it had total strength value above 60%. Thus, it is classified as a "one-dimensional" feature (see Table 3). This indicates that the presence of self-monitoring increases customer satisfaction by 45% and affect dissatisfaction by 64%.

Dialogue support (DS) features (i.e., praise, rewards, reminders, suggestion, similarity, liking and social role) was observed to impact customer satisfaction levels between 23% and 63%; whilst their absence impacts dissatisfaction between 13% and 46% - see Table 3. Reward significantly impacts satisfaction because it recorded 65.9% for total strength value and was classified as being "attractive", i.e., presence of reward significantly improves customers satisfaction by 63%, yet its absence will not result in customers dissatisfaction (i.e. 23%). Liking had a total strength value of 58.5%, while customers extents of satisfaction and dissatisfaction were 45% and 46% respectively.

Table 2. Samples and total sample overview

		Physical	Digital	Total sample
Age	18–24	22.3%	29.2%	23.9%
	25–34	49%	52%	49.8%
	35–54	22.3%	14.6%	20.5%
	55+	6.4%	4.2%	5.8%
Gender	Male	44%	58.3%	47.3%
	Female	56%	41.7%	52.7%
Level of education	High school	5.7%	4.2%	5.4%
	Bachelor's degree	42.7%	50%	44.4%
	Master's degree	36.3%	31.2%	35.1%
	Doctoral degree	12.7%	14.6%	13.2%
	Other	2.5%	0%	1.9%
Current occupation	Employed	49.7	49.9	49.7
	unemployed	4.5%	0%	3.4%
	Homemaker	4.5%	6.2%	4.9%
	Retired	1.9%	2%	1.9%
	Student	38.8%	41.7%	39.5%
	Other	0.6%	0%	0.5%
Mean shopping experience in 6 months?		7 times	8 times	8 times
Browsing frequency	Rarely	7.6%	6.3%	7.3%
	Sometimes	27.4%	20.8%	25.8%
	Often	49.7%	47.9%	49.3%
	Always	15.3%	25%	17.6%

Table 3. Results of Kano's model analysis

	Motivation	Category based on frequency	Category strength	Total strength	Category based on strength	CoS	CoD
Primary task support	Reduction	I	27.8	44.9	I	0.37	−0.32
	Tunnelling	I	12.7	53.7	I	0.39	−0.47
	Tailoring	I	34.6	42.9	I	0.30	−0.28
	Personalisation	I	30.7	24.9	I	0.31	−0.08
	Self-Monitoring	O	8.3	65.9	O	0.45	−0.64
	Simulations	I	40.5	38.0	I	0.31	−0.22
	Rehearsal	I	16.1	53.7	I	0.32	−0.46
			24.39	**46.29**		**0.35**	**−0.35**
Dialogue support	Praise	I	52.7	25.4	I	0.23	−0.13
	Rewards	A	13.7	65.9	A	0.63	−0.23
	Reminders	I	40.0	36.1	I	0.26	−0.30
	Suggestion	I	36.6	39.5	I	0.33	−0.28
	Similarity	I	13.2	55.6	I	0.43	−0.43
	Liking	I	8.8	58.5	I	0.45	−0.46
	Social Role	I	38.5	38.0	I	0.33	−0.22
			29.07	**45.57**		**0.38**	**−0.29**
Credibility support	Trustworthiness	O	17.1	71.7	O	0.52	−0.66
	Expertise	O	9.3	68.8	O	0.43	−0.66
	Surface credibility	I	38.0	30.7	I	0.22	−0.28
	Real-world feel	O	12.2	69.3	O	0.49	−0.64
	Authority	I	31.2	45.4	I	0.30	−0.34
	3rd party endorsement	I	25.9	48.3	I	0.31	−0.37
	Verifiability	I	20.0	49.8	I	0.28	−0.46
			21.96	**54.86**		**0.36**	**−0.49**
Social support	Social Learning	I	50.2	26.8	I	0.24	−0.14
	Social Comparison	I	43.4	33.7	I	0.26	−0.22
	Normative Influence	I	48.8	29.8	I	0.24	−0.22
	Social facilitation	I	49.8	31.7	I	0.22	−0.24
	Cooperation	I	42.9	37.6	I	0.25	−0.29
	Competition	I	62.9	20.5	I	0.13	−0.14
	Recognition	I	34.1	40.0	I	0.35	−0.23
			47.44	**31.44**		**0.24**	**−0.21**

Credibility Support (CS) features (i.e., trustworthiness, expertise, surface credibility, real-world feel, authority, third-party endorsement and verifiability) were observed to impact customers satisfaction between 22% and 52%, and dissatisfaction between 28 and 66% - see Table 3. Trustworthiness, real-world feel, and expertise had total strength values of 71.7%, 69.3% and 68.8% respectively. These features fell into the category of "one-dimensional". Hence, their presence in e-commerce websites may increase customer's satisfaction by 52%, 49%, and 43% respectively and their omission will negatively impact it by 66%, 64%, and 66%.

Social support (SS) features (i.e., social learning, social comparison, normative influence, social facilitation, cooperation, competition and recognition) affects satisfaction levels between 13% and 35%, and dissatisfaction levels between 14% and 29% - see Table 3. This indicates a relatively weak form of influence on customer's satisfaction and dissatisfaction. All social support feature was observed to be in the "indifferent" category.

5   Discussion and Implications

Although some existing studies have investigated the relationship and impact of persuasion or persuasive systems features on e-commerce websites, none have investigated the phenomenon using the Kano model. Yet, the Kano model provides considerable insight on how customers/users of e-commerce websites evaluate their satisfaction levels. The findings and observations made from this study present several implications on persuasive system design features and e-commerce website designs in particular.

5.1   Primary Task Support Features

Persuasive system features such as primary task support are expected to facilitate user performance in accomplishing their objectives. Almost all primary task support features were indifferent to users of e-commerce platforms (except self-monitoring). This demonstrates that current e-commerce users do not pay much attention to activities that enhance their primary task. It is worth noting that the omission of primary task support as a persuasive feature is not the same as the omission of the primary task itself. That is, without primary task support, users are still be capable of perform all relevant activities on the websites, yet persuasive features, e.g. "one-click" purchase recommendations, the provision of virtual fitting rooms, and "wish-list", are expected to enhance the primary shopping experience. The classification of most primary task support features as indifferent is further supported by the argument that features, such as personalization, recommendation, and tailoring, do not play much of a role in how users perceive e-commerce websites [12]. Mostly, e-commerce website users prefer to enter their personal data at checkout rather than making use of personalization services provided by the sites.

This finding, however, contradicts much existing knowledge that argues that the provision of features that seek to support users to locate their desired products with ease is paramount in e-commerce websites. According to Chu et al. [12] users who have no specific product in mind find primary task support features more useful since, as such features make it easier to locate items. Also, first-time users expect websites to provide them with guides as to how they register or checkout during product purchase. It has also been argued that personalization eases information processing and thus creates positive emotional states in users [42]. Others [43] have argued that personalization is the epitome of persuasion on e-commerce websites. Additionally, even though tailored content is provided to support product selection, users consider such content as ordinary product categorization and do not believe that the tailored content meets their needs; a claim has also been validated by [12]. Other studies have demonstrated that the provision of search tools and clear layout of information are not paramount on e-commerce websites when compared to education, medicine and financial websites [8].

Self-monitoring emerged as a "one-dimensional" feature. Self-monitoring features provide e-commerce users with the tendency to monitor and adjust their activities or purchase behavior to ensure that it is appropriate based on how it is perceived by others. Findings from this study conform to studies that argue that the ability of users to monitor one's self is imperative in mobile shopping [44]. Self-monitoring plays a moderating role in website use [45] and thus it impacts e-commerce customer satisfaction levels. As a one-dimensional feature, it measures performance on a linear scale and thus it is noticeable by customers when present. Accordingly, it is recommended that designers of e-commerce website must ensure that they provide system support that facilitates users to monitor their actions.

5.2 Dialogue Support

The provision of advance Dialogue support features has become rampant in recent e-commerce platforms. For instance, features including ExpertClerk [46] have been designed to support customers on e-commerce platforms to imitate sales clerks. Others have advocated for the provision of search and choice support [47], yet findings from this study suggest that dialogue support features do not play a key role in e-commerce platform customer satisfaction. Six out of the seven persuasive dialogue support features (Praise, Reminders, Suggestion, Similarity, Liking and Social Role) were observed to be "Indifferent". The exception was Rewards, which was classified as an "Attractive". It is intriguing to note that most dialogue support features were perceived as indifferent in other studies [14], which also demonstrated that dialogue support features were the most dominant e-commerce platform system features. Considering that majority of the respondents were regular users of e-commerce websites, the findings corroborate with studies that claim that dialogue support is significant to new customers when compared to existing customer [48]. Dialogue support features facilitate buyer persuasion [49]. Accordingly, it can be inferred from this study that although the provision of dialogue support features on e-commerce platforms facilitates persuasion, users of these platforms do not perceive it as a contributor to their satisfaction levels. For instance, persuasive features such as reminders become helpful when used to notify shoppers of important issues but not when used as tools of product promotion.

Rewards emerged as the only attractive system feature. These findings agree with existing studies [49–51], which confirms that buyers consider rewards as a key factor to customer satisfaction level. Considering that rewards on e-commerce platforms provide direct and observable benefits to users, it is not surprising that users perceive it as an attractive feature. It is therefore suggested that designers of e-commerce websites must ensure that they involve features that reward users. As explained earlier, attractive features increase satisfaction levels. Considering that persuasive system designs intend to make a user perform a predetermined activity, it is vital that they include attractive features. It is however emphasized that rewards feature on e-commerce websites must target all category of users, this will facilitate regular visits to these websites.

5.3 Credibility Support

Credibility support features had the highest total strength (54.86%). Besides, it was observed to be the only category of features that recorded three features to be one-dimensional (i.e. Trustworthiness, Expertise and Real-world feel). This demonstrates that credibility plays a crucial role in customer satisfaction levels. System credibility has been demonstrated to be vital, as it contributes to users intention to use a system [38]. Perhaps, it can be considered to be the most important feature in persuasive systems design. With respect to e-commerce platforms, website credibility is essential to both users and customers.

The emergence of Trustworthiness, Expertise and Real-world feel as one-dimensional features show that customers and users of e-commerce websites always look out for these features as a measure of satisfaction and are dissatisfied when absent. It has been confirmed that the use of enhanced methods to improve credibility yields favorable customer responses on e-commerce platforms [52]. Some studies [14] have explained that Trustworthiness and Expertise are among the most used system features on e-commerce websites.

Surface credibility, Authority, Third Party Endorsement and Verifiability were all observed to be indifferent. Surface credibility relates to the appearance of the website, and this result suggests that e-commerce users do not consider the aesthetics features of the website as a key ingredient of their satisfaction levels. These findings support arguments by [53], that stipulates that surface credibility has less influence on regular application users. More importantly, further investigations need to be conducted to ascertain why credibility features including Authority, Third Party Endorsement and Verifiability were observed to be indifferent features.

5.4 Social Support

Although Social support features have been identified to promote e-commerce platforms [54], users perceive these features as indifferent. All social support features were observed to be indifferent and they also recorded the lowest total strength (i.e. 31.44%). Thus, they have no impact on user satisfaction levels. Particularly, Competition was observed to be perceived as the feature with the least impact on user satisfaction. It recorded the lowest total strength value of 20.5. Yet, others [38] have explained that perceive social support promotes user's intention to continuous use.

Studies have argued that social supports in virtual environments mostly seek to address user problems through the direct and indirect provision of information, experience, and advice [55]. Therefore, although such a feature may enhance trust among customers and users of e-commerce platforms [56], it has no impact on how these users perceive satisfaction. It is important to note that Social support features are the least utilized system features on e-commerce websites [14].

However, considering that shopping is a social event [57], it is surprising to observe that social support is not perceived to influence e-commerce website user satisfaction. Thus, there is a need for further studies to investigate this phenomenon to understand the drivers of such findings.

6   Conclusions and Future Work

This study explored user perceptions of persuasive features on e-commerce websites that influence their satisfaction or dissatisfaction levels using the Kano model. According to the Kano model, user satisfaction evolves, and although there are possibilities that perceptions of system features that influence user satisfaction levels on e-commerce websites may change, current findings indicate that no persuasive feature is perceived to be a "must-be" feature. This observation confirms that persuasive features are perceived as add-ons and is not perceived by customers as critical to the ecommerce experience. They enhance overall system qualities, create engagement and support decision-making processes. In this sense, they complement e-commerce design and support user appeal in a competitive environment. Hence, this study serves as a guide to understanding user preferences and contributes to the development of practical guidelines for designing persuasive e-commerce websites.

Three credibility support features (trustworthiness, Expertise and Real-world feel) were observed to be perceived by customers to impact satisfaction. That is, their presence is noticed by users and their absence results in dissatisfaction. Rewards emerged as the only system feature that users perceive to be attractive. All social support features were observed to be perceived by users as indifferent. Future work needs to investigate the causal effects of these findings. In addition, further investigations may be conducted on the impact of within-group cultural differences which might reveal differences on users' preferences of persuasive feature that impacts their satisfaction and dissatisfaction levels.

References

1. Schaffer, E.: Beyond usability designing for persuasion, emotion, and trust (PET designTM). Hum. Factors (2008)
2. Winn, W., Beck, K.: The persuasive power of design elements on an e-commerce web site. Tech. Commun. **49**(1), 17–35 (2002)
3. Abdullah, L., Ramli, R., Bakodah, H.O., Othman, M.: Developing a causal relationship among factors of e-commerce: a decision making approach. J. King Saud Univ. Inf. Sci. (2019)
4. Nisar, T.M., Prabhakar, G.: What factors determine e-satisfaction and consumer spending in e-commerce retailing? J. Retail. Consum. Serv. **39**, 135–144 (2017)
5. Kaptein, M., Parvinen, P.: Advancing e-commerce personalization: process framework and case study. Int. J. Electron. Commer. **19**(3), 7–33 (2015)
6. Wiafe, I., Nakata, K.: Bibliographic analysis of persuasive systems: techniques, methods and domains of application, pp. 2–5 (2012). http://www.ep.liu.se/ecp_article/index.en.aspx?issue=068;article=016
7. Wiafe, I., Koranteng, F.N., Owusu, E., Ekpezu, A.O., Gyamfi, S.A.: Persuasive social features that promote knowledge sharing among tertiary students on social networking sites: an empirical study. J. Comput. Assist. Learn. **36**(5), 636–645 (2020). https://doi.org/10.1111/jcal.12433
8. Zhang, P., Von Dran, G.M.: User expectations and rankings of quality factors in different Web site domains. Int. J. Electron. Commer. **6**(2), 9–33 (2001). https://doi.org/10.1080/10864415.2001.11044237
9. Kaptein, M., Duplinsky, S.: Combining multiple influence strategies to increase consumer compliance. Int. J. Internet Mark. Advert. **8**(1), 32–53 (2013)

10. Fogg, B., Microsystems, S., Fogg, B.: Persuasive computers: perspectives and research directions. In: SIGCHI Conference on Human Factors in Computing, vol. 98, no. April, pp. 225–232 (1998). https://doi.org/10.1145/274644.274677

11. Torning, K., Hall, C., Oinas-kukkonen, H.: Persuasive System Design: State of the Art and Future Directions (2009)

12. Chu, H.-L., Deng, Y.-S., Chuang, M.-C.: Persuasive web design in e-Commerce. In: Nah, F.-H. (ed.) HCIB 2014. LNCS, vol. 8527, pp. 482–491. Springer, Cham (2014). https://doi.org/10.1007/978-3-319-07293-7_47

13. Nanou, T., Lekakos, G., Fouskas, K.: The effects of recommendations' presentation on persuasion and satisfaction in a movie recommender system. Multimed. Syst. 16(4–5), 219–230 (2010)

14. Alhammad, M.M., Gulliver, S.R.: Online persuasion for e-commerce websites. In: Proceedings of the 28th International BCS Human Computer Interaction Conference (HCI 2014), vol. 28, pp. 264–269 (2014)

15. Oinas-Kukkonen, H., Harjumaa, M.: Persuasive systems design: key issues, process model, and system features. Commun. Assoc. Inf. Syst. 24(1), 28 (2009)

16. Kano, N., Seraku, N., Takahashi, N., Tsuji, S.: Attractive quality and must-be quality. J. Japanese Soc. Qual. Control 14(2), 39–48 (1984)

17. Buttle, F.: Customer relationship management: Concepts and technology. Sydney a Butterworth-Heinemann, vol. 1 (2009)

18. Shen, X.-X., Tan, K.C., Xie, M.: An integrated approach to innovative product development using Kano's model and QFD. Eur. J. Innov. Manag. 3(2), 91–99 (2000)

19. Zhao, M., Dholakia, R.R.: A multi-attribute model of web site interactivity and customer satisfaction. Manag. Serv. Qual. An Int. J. (2009)

20. Van Der Wiele, T., Boselie, P., Hesselink, M.: Empirical evidence for the relationship between customer satisfaction and business performance. Manag. Serv. Qual. Int. J. (2002)

21. Tse, D.K., Nicosia, F.M., Wilton, P.C.: Consumer satisfaction as a process. Psychol. Mark. 7(3), 177–193 (1990)

22. Hanan, M., Karp, P.: Customer Satisfaction How to Maximize, Measure, and Market Your Company's ultimate Product. American Management Association, Amacom (1989)

23. Herzberg, F., Mausner, B., Anyderman, B.: Motivation to Work. Wiley, New York (1959)

24. Herzberg, F.I.: Work and the Nature of Man (1966)

25. Parasuraman, A., Zeithaml, V., Berry, L.: SERVQUAL: a multiple-item scale for measuring consumer perceptions of service quality. Retail. Crit. Concepts 64(1), 140 (2002)

26. Zhang, P., von Dran, G.: Expectations and rankings of Web site quality features: results of two studies on user perceptions. In: Proceedings of the 34th Annual Hawaii International Conference on System Sciences, p. 10 (2001)

27. Tu, Y.-H., Hung, K.-M.: The influences of system quality and service quality to consumer satisfaction and loyalty in on-line game industry. In: *PICMET*. Technology Management for Global Economic Growth 2010, 1–5 (2010)

28. Kassim, N., Abdullah, N.A.: The effect of perceived service quality dimensions on customer satisfaction, trust, and loyalty in e-commerce settings. Asia pacific J. Mark. Logist. (2010)

29. Orel, F.D., Kara, A.: Supermarket self-checkout service quality, customer satisfaction, and loyalty: empirical evidence from an emerging market. J. Retail. Consum. Serv. 21(2), 118–129 (2014)

30. Baki, B., Basfirinci, C.S., AR, I.M., Cilingir, Z.: An application of integrating SERVQUAL and Kano's model into QFD for logistics services. Asia Pacific J. Mark. Logist. (2009)

31. Vaez Shahrestani, H., Shahin, A., Teimouri, H., Shaemi Barzoki, A.: Revising the Kano model for designing an employee compensation system: developing one-dimensional attributes. TQM J. 32(1), 78–91 (2019). https://doi.org/10.1108/TQM-05-2019-0153

32. Shahin, A., Pourhamidi, M., Antony, J., Park, S.H.: Typology of Kano models: a critical review of literature and proposition of a revised model. Int. J. Qual. Reliab. Manag. **30**(3), 341–358 (2013). https://doi.org/10.1108/02656711311299863
33. Wiafe, I., Nakata, K., Moran, S., Gulliver, S.R.S.R.: Considering user attitude and behaviour in persuasive systems design: the 3D-RAB model. In: 19th European Conference on Information Systems ECIS 2011 (2011). http://aisel.aisnet.org/ecis2011/186
34. Wiafe, I., Nakata, K., Gulliver, S.: Categorizing users in behavior change support systems based on cognitive dissonance. Pers. Ubiquit. Comput. **18**(7), 1677–1687 (2014). https://doi.org/10.1007/s00779-014-0782-3
35. Fogg, B.: Persuasive computers: perspectives and research directions. In: SIGCHI conference on Human Factors in Computing, vol. 98, no. April, pp. 225–232 (1998). https://doi.org/10.1145/274644.274677
36. Dabi, J., Wiafe, I., Stibe, A., Abdulai, J.-D.: Can an enterprise system persuade? The role of perceived effectiveness and social influence. In: Ham, J., Karapanos, E., Morita, P.P., Burns, C.M. (eds.) PERSUASIVE 2018. LNCS, vol. 10809, pp. 45–55. Springer, Cham (2018). https://doi.org/10.1007/978-3-319-78978-1_4
37. Lehto, T.T., Oinas-Kukkonen, H., Drozd, F.: Factors affecting perceived persuasiveness of a behavior change support system. In: Proceedings of International Conference Information Systems, no. February 2016, pp. 1–15 (2012)
38. Wiafe, I., Koranteng, F.N., Katsriku, F.A., Gyamera, G.O.: Assessing the impact of persuasive features on user's intention to continuous use: the case of academic social networking sites. Behav. Inf. Technol. , 1–19 (2020). https://doi.org/10.1080/0144929X.2020.1832146
39. Kaptein, M.: Adaptive persuasive messages in an e-commerce setting: the use of persuasion profiles. In: 19th European Conference Information Systems ECIS 2011 (2011)
40. Xu, Q., Jiao, R.J., Yang, X., Helander, M., Khalid, H.M., Opperud, A.: An analytical Kano model for customer need analysis. Des. Stud. **30**(1), 87–110 (2009)
41. Lee, M.C., Newcomb, J.F.: Applying the Kano methodology to meet customer requirements: NASA's microgravity science program. Qual. Manag. J. **4**(3), 95–106 (1997)
42. Saari, T., Ravaja, N., Laarni, J., Turpeinen, M., Kallinen, K.: Psychologically targeted persuasive advertising and product information in e-commerce. ACM Int. Conf. Proceeding Ser. **60**, 245–254 (2004). https://doi.org/10.1145/1052220.1052252
43. Pappas, I.O., Kourouthanassis, P.E., Giannakos, M.N., Chrissikopoulos, V.: Sense and sensibility in personalized e-commerce: how emotions rebalance the purchase intentions of persuaded customers. Psychol. Mark. **34**(10), 972–986 (2017). https://doi.org/10.1002/mar.21036
44. Celik, H., Kocaman, R.: Roles of self-monitoring, fashion involvement and technology readiness in an individual's propensity to use mobile shopping. J. Syst. Inf. Technol. **19**(3–4), 166–182 (2017). https://doi.org/10.1108/JSIT-01-2017-0008
45. Lin, C.S.: Exploring the personality trait of self-monitoring on technology usage of web portals. Cyberpsychol. Behav. **11**(2), 235–238 (2008). https://doi.org/10.1089/cpb.2007.0021
46. Shimazu, H.: ExpertClerk: a conversational case-based reasoning tool fordeveloping salesclerk agents in E-Commerce webshops. Artif. Intell. Rev. **18**(3–4), 223–244 (2002)
47. Sproule, S., Archer, N.: A buyer behaviour framework for the development and design of software agents in e-commerce. Internet Res (2000)
48. Adaji, I., Vassileva, J.: Tailoring persuasive strategies in E-commerce. CEUR Workshop Proc. **1833**, 57–63 (2017)
49. Abdul Hamid, N.A., Cheun, C.H., Abdullah, N.H., Ahmad, M.F., Ngadiman, Y.: Does persuasive E-commerce website influence users' acceptance and online buying behaviour? The findings of the largest E-commerce website in Malaysia. In: Baghdadi, Y., Harfouche, A. (eds.) ICT for a Better Life and a Better World. LNISO, vol. 30, pp. 263–279. Springer, Cham (2019). https://doi.org/10.1007/978-3-030-10737-6_17

50. Wang, C., Fu, W., Jin, J., Shang, Q., Luo, X., Zhang, X.: Differential effects of monetary and social rewards on product online rating decisions in E-Commerce in China. Front. Psychol. 11(July), 1–15 (2020). https://doi.org/10.3389/fpsyg.2020.01440

51. Keh, H.T., Lee, Y.H.: Do reward programs build loyalty for services? The moderating effect of satisfaction on type and timing of rewards. J. Retail. 82(2), 127–136 (2006). https://doi.org/10.1016/j.jretai.2006.02.004

52. Liew, T.W., Tan, S.-M., Ismail, H.: Exploring the effects of a non-interactive talking avatar on social presence, credibility, trust, and patronage intention in an e-commerce website. HCIS 7(1), 1–21 (2017). https://doi.org/10.1186/s13673-017-0123-4

53. Harjumaa, M., Oinas-kukkonen, H.: Understanding persuasive software functionality in practice : a field trial of polar FT60. Methodology 38, 1–9 (2009). https://doi.org/10.1145/154 1948.1541952

54. Adaji, I., Vassileva, J.: Perceived effectiveness, credibility and continuance intention in e-commerce: a study of Amazon. In: International Conference on Persuasive Technology, pp. 293–306 (2017)

55. Romaniuk, J.: The various words of mouth: moving beyond the 'road-to-damascus' conversion. J. Advert. Res. 52(1), 12–14 (2012)

56. Molinillo, S., Anaya-Sanchez, R., Liebana-Cabanillas, F.: Analyzing the effect of social support and community factors on customer engagement and its impact on loyalty behaviors toward social commerce websites. Comput. Human Behav. 108, 105980 (2020)

57. Zhang, H., Lu, Y., Gupta, S., Zhao, L.: What motivates customers to participate in social commerce? The impact of technological environments and virtual customer experiences. Inf. Manag. 51(8), 1017–1030 (2014). https://doi.org/10.1016/j.im.2014.07.005

The Role of Emotional Expression in Behavior Change Coaching by a Social Robot

Matouš Jelínek[1]([⊠]) and Kerstin Fischer[2] [iD]

[1] University of Southern Denmark Kolding, Kolding, Denmark
[2] University of Southern Denmark Sonderborg, Sønderborg, Denmark
kerstin@sdu.dk

Abstract. This experimental study evaluates the suitability of a social robot for inducing behavior change, where the robot serves as a behavior change coach. Using a simulation of the social robot Haru developed by the Honda Research Institute, this study measured the effect of the robot's emotional expressions and behaviors on behavior change and the perceived quality of the session.

The method for behavior change employed is the 'Tiny Habits' approach developed by (Fogg 2019), which assumes that behavior can be changed if a) the behavior to be changed is broken down into a tiny habit, b) this habit is anchored in the person's everyday life, and c) every success is celebrated. Based on these principles, a scripted dialogue was created to coach participants in a session in which they chose a behavior they wanted to change themselves.

The experiment proceeded with altogether 30 participants. In the experimental condition, the dialogue between participant and the robot simulator was interspersed with emotional expression and behaviors such as dancing, bowing and vocalizing. The control condition utilized the same setup with the robot simulator and provided participants with the same guidance, but without emotional expression.

Our results reveal a positive effect of emotional behavior on most of the measured variables. Compared to the baseline, the participants in the emotional condition had a higher motivation to change their behavior, felt more confident in applying the behavior change method, confirmed that they would think differently about behavior change and rated the quality of the lesson higher.

Keywords: Behavior change · Tiny Habit method · Persuasive technology

1 Introduction

In this paper, we want to find out whether a simulated robot can function as a persuasive technology that effectively supports people in their attempt to acquire a new habit and to what extent emotional expression by the robot facilitates the retention of the habit.

© Springer Nature Switzerland AG 2021
R. Ali et al. (Eds.): PERSUASIVE 2021, LNCS 12684, pp. 193–199, 2021.
https://doi.org/10.1007/978-3-030-79460-6_15

1.1 Behavior Change – Tiny Habits Method

Individual habitual behavior is a frequently repeated, learned behavior with a high degree of automaticity (Orbell and Verplanken 2010). It is also stably cued in context such that there is a link between a certain context and certain response (Gardner, 2015). The Tiny Habit method by BJ Fogg (2019) used for our behavior change coaching experiment, builds on these principles. The core of the model consists of three elements: a) the tiny habit itself, b) an anchor moment, and c) a celebration.

According to Fogg (2019), people often fail to change their behavior because they overestimate the level of their motivation and willingness to change; while a high aspiration or a final goal is essential, it is difficult to reach the final aspiration without regularly repeating it – which, according to his experience, is often too demanding. Fogg's response to this potential issue is to break down the habit into a simplified version of the aspiration (e.g. the aspiration to run every day can be broken down into taking on running shoes). Individuals who would like to acquire a new behavior should create a habit which they can perform every day, does not take longer than 30 s, and only requires little effort.

The second pillar of the Tiny Habit method, the anchoring, helps to firmly incorporate the tiny habit into everyday life. Another routine, already firm in an individual's daily routines, is employed to anchor the new tiny habit.

The third element is the celebration. By intentionally creating positive emotions, participants are rewarding the completion of their small steps and thus strengthening the position of tiny habits in the individuals' everyday life.

This potential effect of emotional experience on behavior change and habit retention was suggested also by Bargh and Morsella (2009). Moreover, in interactive storytelling, the display of emotional expression has been found to be important element for memory retention, and of the quality of the storytelling itself (Bavelas et al. 2002).

The current paper explores to what extent a one-time coaching session with the Tiny Habits method using a simulated social robot may lead to behavior change and what role emotional displays play in the retention of the new habit.

1.2 Robots as a Persuasive Technology

Previous work on robots as persuasive technologies is sparse, and none of the studies addressing persuasion target habit formation and longterm behavior change. For instance, Andrist et al. (2013) and (2015) investigate the effects of different speaking styles and find that robots that use persuasive speaking styles are more persuasive than robots that don't. Similarly, Fischer, Niebuhr et al. (2020) show that robots' speech characteristics influence the degree to which people follow their advice. Winkle et al. (2019) studied the effects of certain persuasive messages and document several effects. Ham et al. (2015) detect interaction effects on robot persuasiveness between robot speech and accompanying gestures, and Fischer, Langedijk et al. (2020) show that the effectiveness of persuasive messages by robots is influenced by mutual gaze. These studies confirm that robots that use persuasive signals may actually serve as persuasive technologies.

Previous work on emotional expression in robots has mostly focused on identifying the emotions expressed given the special robot morphologies and limited modalities for emotional expression (Fischer, Jung et al. 2019). Jung (2017) argues that emotional expression is socially required in social interactions. However, in Fogg's 'Tiny Habit' behavior change method, emotional expression plays a specific role, namely it is taken to reinforce habit formation. This particular role of emotional expression has not previously addressed in human-robot interaction research.

2   Case Study: Emotional Expression in Behavior Change Coaching

Our study aims to explore the effects of emotional expression in behavior change coaching by a social robot, focusing on the perceived quality of the lesson. Furthermore, we analyze the effects of the method on retention and motivation to change behavior by means of a questionnaire administered at least 10 days after the session.

2.1   Method

To measure the effect of emotional expression on the quality of the lesson and residual willingness to change behavior, two experimental conditions – experimental, i.e. emotional, and control – were created. In both conditions, we used the same script, presenting the Tiny Habit coaching session by the simulation of a social robot Haru from the Honda Research Institute in Tokyo. In both scenarios, the robot uses the same synthesized voice; however, in the experimental condition, the robot uses emotional expression, whereas in control condition 2 it does not. In both conditions, the robot behavior was controlled by a wizard operator (cf. Riek 2012).

2.2   Experimental Setup

The script that presents participants with the Tiny Habit method was created and divided into five sections. The core of the script, consisting of 66 utterances, explains the basics of the Tiny Habit method and is used to guide participants through the session. Furthermore, 82 additional utterances were created to give the robot operator the possibility to react to the most common questions, help participants to return to the core of the script and move forward in the session. These utterances were created based on extensive pilot testing and used in order to ensure a smooth interaction; however, on average only 3–4 of these specific utterances were used in each interaction, so that the interactions remain largely comparable.

In the experimental condition, the robot's behavior is enriched with emotional expression by means of behaviors other than speech, such as dancing, smiling, bowing or vocalizing, which were used 34 times per interaction, thus prolonging the average time to complete the core of the session from 15 to 17 min. In all other respects, the robot's behavior was identical across conditions.

The script itself was divided into five sections, reflecting the overall structure of the method as outlined by BJ Fogg (2019):

a)   In the short introduction, Haru presented the purpose of the session, introduced itself and explained the structure of the session.
b)   Participants were guided to define their aspirations.

c) Participants were explained the importance of making their aspirations tiny and helped to create a simplified version of their future habit.
d) The Tiny Habit formula was presented: After I *anchor moment, I will *tiny habit, and celebrate.
e) At the end, participants learned about the importance of celebrating their success and were given the chance to present their tiny habit.

The whole script was created in such a way that the robot was able to react to participants' most common questions – in addition, further clarifications of the concepts were prepared and used if needed (Fig. 1).

Fig. 1. Experimental setup of the behavior coaching session

Procedure: Participants, who volunteered to participate in the experiment, were seated in front of a screen with the robot simulation and presented with a paper that introduced them to the Tiny Habit method, expected length of the session and the fact they would be rewarded with chocolate. Part of this pre-session period was also an introduction to the Haru simulator in front of them. The script started with a question: "Hi, what is your name?" In case the participant did not reply, this was followed by the utterance "You can talk to me!", followed by the rest of the script. Participants were given a questionnaire at the end of their session; another one was sent to them after 10–14 days.

Materials: As stated above, the Haru robot was run as a simulator on a 27-inch LCD with a loudspeaker hidden behind the screen. The simulator itself runs on a laptop equipped with a Gazebo simulator environment. The whole setup was made in such a way that the robot could be teleoperated, using the Wizard-of-Oz method (Baxter et al. 2016). The operator was present in the same room, but out of the direct line of sight of the participant. The same wizard controlled the robot through all 30 interactions.

Participants: A total of 30 people with a mean age of 28.4, all residents of Southern Denmark, participated in the experiment. The 18 women and 12 men were distributed equally between the two conditions. Before the session, 39% of the participants had only seen a robot on TV, 28% had seen one or a few robots in reality, 23% had played or worked with one and 10% stated that they regularly work with robots. Most of the participants were international students while 23% were of Danish nationality.

Questionnaire: Every participant received a questionnaire after finishing the session. The first part of this questionnaire (q1–q5) focused on demographics such as age, nationality, line of study, and robot experience. In the second part of the questionnaire (q6–q7), participants rated their motivation to change their behavior before and after the session. The next two blocks of questions (q8–q14) focused on the course content, quality of the session and the learning outcomes. To measure the retention of the method, another questionnaire focusing on the progress with participant's behavior change was sent at least 10 days after the session.

2.3   Results

Questionnaire data from the experimental condition with emotional behaviors (C1) and control condition (C2) were compared, using a paired student t-test. Figure 2 presents the questionnaire results concerning the evaluation of the session. Participants interacting with the robot that uses emotional behaviors were significantly more willing to think differently about the behavior change (p = 0.0394), and we identified a positive statistical trend in their rating of the overall quality of the session (p = 0.0680).

		Experimental condition		Control condition		
		Mean	stdv	Mean	stdv	p
q7b	Motivation difference	1.40	-0.27	1.20	-0.36	0.2708
q8	Overall quality	4.33	0.49	3.93	0.88	0.0680
q9	Understanding concepts	4.40	0.63	4.40	0.63	0.5000
q10	In-depth	2.40	1.24	2.47	1.41	0.4458
q11	Was logical	4.47	0.52	4.40	0.74	0.3881
q12	Confident applying	4.47	0.52	4.20	1.08	0.1982
q13	Course tought you	2.67	0.90	2.53	1.36	0.3767
q14	Think differently	4.00	0.85	3.20	1.47	0.0394

Fig. 2. Statistical analysis of the data in C1 and C2 from the post-session questionnaire

Furthermore, t-test comparisons of the other questions revealed statistical tendencies towards more favorable ratings of the robot that used emotional behaviors.

Another statistical trend was identified in the post-experimental questionnaire focusing on participants' retention of the new habit. Those who had interacted with the robot in the experimental condition were more likely to maintain the habit they created during the session (p = 0.04). All the participants from the experimental condition carried out their new habit at least once, while the majority (66%) practiced their behavior at least twice (Fig. 3).

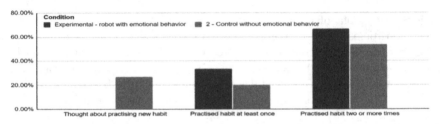

Fig. 3. Habit retention from post-questionnaire send at least 10 days after the initial session.

3 Discussion

The study shows that the robot's emotional behaviors have a significant effect on how participants think about behavior change. Furthermore, the results reveal positive effects on the perceived quality of the lesson and retention of the new habit. However, our findings, possibly influenced by the small number of participants, did not reveal any significant effects on other measured categories, such as the difference between motivation before and after the session or on understanding the concepts presented.

To evaluate the effects of Haru's emotional behaviors more precisely, the effect of particular behaviors used during the session should be measured. After the sessions, some of the participants mentioned that they disliked some particular behaviors, which may have influenced the results. Also, the effect of non-human behaviors used in the experimental condition (such as the visualization of a lotus flower, question mark or fireworks) could be evaluated independently in the future. Therefore, we are now conducting another study, measuring the effects of the habitual retention in another condition, which uses the same script but presents the contents as a website.

4 Conclusion

To conclude, there is a significant effect of emotional behavior on the perceived quality of the lesson and on the retention of the habit practiced. Therefore, a long-term effect can be expected. We can thus conclude that emotional expression has a positive effect on the quality of human-robot interactions in general and on behavior change coaching in particular. In addition, we can conclude that robots may be effective persuasive technologies, and that the Tiny Habits method is a suitable approach for robot-human behavior change coaching.

References

Andrist, S., Spannan, E., Mutlu, B.: Rhetorical robots: making robots more effective speakers using linguistic cues of expertise. In: 2013 8th ACM/IEEE International Conference on Human-Robot Interaction (HRI), pp. 341–348. IEEE (2013)

Andrist, S., Ziadee, M., Boukaram, H., Mutlu, B., Sakr, M.: Effects of culture on the credibility of robot speech: a comparison between English and Arabic. In: Proceedings of the Tenth Annual ACM/IEEE International Conference on Human-Robot Interaction, pp. 157–164 (2015)

Bargh, J.A., Morsella, E.: Unconscious behavioral guidance systems. In: Agnew, C.R., Carlston, D.E., Graziano, W.G., Kelly, J.R. (eds.) Then a Miracle Occurs: Focusing on Behavior in Social Psychological Theory and Research, pp. 89–118. Oxford University Press (2010)

Bavelas, J.B., Coates, L., Johnson, T.: Listeners as co-narrators. J. Pers. Soc. Psychol. **79**(6), 941–952 (2000)

Bavelas, J.B., Coates, L., Johnson, T.: Listener responses as a collaborative process: the role of gaze. J. Commun. **52**, 566–580 (2002). https://doi.org/10.1111/j.1460-2466.2002.tb02562.x

Fischer, K., Niebuhr, O., Jensen, L.C., Bodenhagen, L.: Speech melody matters – how robots can profit from using charismatic speech. ACM Trans. Hum.-Robot Interact. **9**(1), 1–21 (2020)

Fischer, K., Langedijk, R.M., Nissen, L.D., Ramirez, E.R., Palinko, O.: Gaze-speech coordination influences the persuasiveness of human-robot dialog in the wild. In: Wagner, A.R., et al. (eds.) ICSR 2020. LNCS (LNAI), vol. 12483, pp. 157–169. Springer, Cham (2020). https://doi.org/10.1007/978-3-030-62056-1_14

Fischer, K., Jung, M., Jensen, L.C., aus der Wieschen, M.: Emotion expression in HRI–when and why. In: 14th ACM/IEEE International Conference on Human-Robot Interaction (HRI), pp. 29–38. IEEE (2019)

Fogg, B.J.: Tiny Habits: The Small Changes That Change Everything. Virgin Books (2019)

Gardner, B.: A review and analysis of the use of "habit" in understanding, predicting and influencing health-related behaviour. Health Psychol. Rev. **9**(3), 277–295 (2015)

Ham, J., Cuijpers, R.H., Cabibihan, J.J.: Combining robotic persuasive strategies: the persuasive power of a storytelling robot that uses gazing and gestures. Int. J. Soc. Robot. **7**(4), 479–487 (2015)

Jung, M.F.: Affective grounding in human-robot interaction. In: 12th ACM/IEEE International Conference on Human-Robot Interaction (HRI), pp. 263–273. IEEE (2017)

Orbell, S., Verplanken, B.: The automatic component of habit in health behavior: habit as cue-contingent automaticity. Health Psychol. **29**(4), 374–383 (2010)

Riek, L.D.: Wizard of oz studies in HRI: a systematic review and new reporting guidelines. J. Hum.-Robot Interact. **1**(1), 119–136 (2012)

Winkle, K., et al.: Effective persuasion strategies for socially assistive robots. In: 14th ACM/IEEE International Conference on Human-Robot Interaction (HRI), pp. 277–285. IEEE (2019)

Exploring the Impact of Color on User Ratings: A Personality and Culture-Based Approach

Najia Manjur[✉], Maliha Mahbub, and Julita Vassileva

MADMUC Lab, University of Saskatchewan, Saskatoon, Canada
{nam907,mam789,jiv}@usask.ca

Abstract. Prior research have shown that, different features (such as, color, neutral point, granularity etc.) of rating scales have significant roles to play in shaping consumers' rating behavior. While investigating the impact of color, researchers have revealed significant conflicting patterns of bias in users' rating behavior, which indicate the inefficiency of the one-size-fits-all approach taken by them to investigate bias. In this paper, we address this gap by taking a personality and culture-based approach to explore the diversity in users' responses in relation to the influence of the color of rating scales. We designed an online survey by adopting five different rating scales and collected 176 participants' responses on a demographic and a personality assessment questionnaire and their ratings on different products. Our study shows that the use of colors in rating scales influences the responses of participants who are extrovert and from collectivist culture and provides the direction of score adjustment due to the bias. Taking the key findings into consideration, we also offer possible design guidelines to avoid potential rating bias.

Keywords: Rating behavior · Bias · Personality · Culture

1 Introduction

User-generated feedback has become an integral and influential part of different domains in online platforms that provides insights on consumers overall satisfaction and experience with a product or a service. However, users' ratings do not always represent the genuine feedback of their experience with products. They can be subject to bias evoked by different features of rating scales [2,5]. While rating bias caused by different scale features is widely explored by researchers, earlier research works investigating the bias originating from the use of color have some contradictory patterns. These contradictions mean that individuals respond differently to the presence of colors in the design of the scales. Since personality and culture are viewed as the consistent representatives of a person's individuality [13,17], a personality and culture-based approach to investigate rating bias can provide more insights on this. Besides, variance in the labels

© Springer Nature Switzerland AG 2021
R. Ali et al. (Eds.): PERSUASIVE 2021, LNCS 12684, pp. 200–206, 2021.
https://doi.org/10.1007/978-3-030-79460-6_16

associated with colors of the rating scales may have distorted the sole impact of colors, since the presence of labels alone can also exert influence on user response. In this paper, we attempt to answer the research question: *Do consumers with different personality traits and culture utilize the same color-based rating scale differently for the same product?* To this aim, we conducted a study with 176 participants and analyzed the pattern in user response in coloured scales. Taking insights from the study, we also suggested some design guidelines to avoid bias.

2   Related Work

Previous research works addressing the issue of bias induced by color-based scales have revealed some contradictory patterns of bias in users' rating behavior. In [16], the authors found that, using a scale with two endpoints shaded with different hues of two different colors can manipulate the users to perceive the subjective distance of the endpoints of the scale as longer than usual. As a consequence, users adjusted their score towards the higher end of the scale. On the other hand, [3] claimed that scales designed with contrasting color schemes can enhance the positive valence at the higher endpoint and vice versa at the lower endpoint, which can persuade the users to adjust their score towards the central area of the scale. The contradiction highlighted the limitation of not taking users' individuality into consideration. To address this issue, we took a personality and culture-based approach to investigate users' rating behavior since they are two very stable representatives of a user's individuality [13,17].

We leveraged the Big Five Model to categorize users into their personality traits, since it is currently one of the most comprehensive and widely employed models in psychology to predict personality types [9]. The five broad dimensional traits are: openness to experience (represents the appreciation for new experiences), conscientiousness (refers how individuals control and regulate their impulses), extraversion (refers to one's fondness for social engagement), agreeableness (refers to the tendency to maintain social harmony with others), and neuroticism (represents individuals who are prone to negative emotions) [11]. To categorize participants into their personality traits, we adopted the Big Five Inventory (BFI-44) where participants assess themselves by answering 44 questions using 5-point Likert scale [9].

Personality traits are correlated with their preference for colors [18]. For example, emotionally stable (low neuroticism) individuals prefer dark green. On the other hand, antagonistic (low agreeableness) people prefer dark blue. Every color carries an emotional property [1]. But because of being preferred by an individual, the color may play the role of a cognitive enhancer. However, users' susceptibility to such cognitive impact may vary according to their personality. For example, the magnitude of the impact could be higher for extroverts as they are more assertive and lower for raters with high conscientiousness because they are more cautious. Hence, the general approach taken by the existing works might not work.

To categorize users according to their culture, we adopted the individualism-collectivism dimension of Hofstede's framework. We decided to adopt this dimension since it best captures the variance in the global population [10]. Collectivists tend to make decisions driven by the goal of community benefit whereas individualists make their decisions focusing more on their personal goal [8]. According to [6], a country with a high individualism score will show an inclination towards the individualistic culture, whereas, a country with a low score will show an inclination towards the collectivist culture. The classification of the countries with respect to their culture is obtained from [6].

In terms of design variations, collectivists and individualists have very different choices of aesthetic preferences. Collectivists prefer interfaces which are colorful and visually appealing, whereas individualists do not exhibit any such preference [12,15]. These preferences may enhance the positive emotional valence which can influence the numerical interpretation of the scale. Therefore, the interpretation of color-based scales will vary in different cultures.

3 Methodology

To answer the research question, we conducted a user study that was designed to elicit participants' biased responses to different color-coded scales and map their rating behavior to their personality and culture.

3.1 Experimental Design

To collect the users' true ratings, we adopted the most widely used yellow star-based scale [4]. To represent the scales that may induce bias, we adopted star and emoji scales with endpoints shaded with two different sets of contrasting colors: red-yellow-green and red-yellow-blue combinations. We chose these two sets of color since they are the closest representations of color-based scales most commonly seen in different online platforms and the existing research works [3,16]. Each scale adopted in this study had a 5-points granularity but no labels. The study has four parts:

1. Completing the demographic survey on age, gender and home country.
2. Completing the Big Five personality assessment questionnaire.
3. Selecting and rating products using the yellow star-based scale (Fig. 1(a)).
4. Rating the products again using color-based scales (Fig. 1(b)).

3.2 Participants

The study was approved by the ethics board of the University of Saskatchewan. Initially, a total of 192 subjects' responses were collected. After assessing the reliability of their Big Five responses, the final database included the complete responses of 176 participants. The participants included 64 men, 110 women and majority (56.8%) of them aged between 21 to 30 years. The participants were from different countries including Bangladesh, Canada, China, etc.

Fig. 1. (a) Yellow star-based scale (b) color-based scales (c)an example of rating collection window (Color figure online)

4 Data Analysis and Results

We categorized the final dataset using two within-subject factors: personality and culture. First, we investigated the existence of bias in the rating behavior of each personality and cultural group using the Wilcoxon signed rank test [14]. Next, for each group that exhibited biased behavior, we applied Apriori algorithm [7] to identify the score that is being subject to bias and the direction of score adjustment resulting from the bias.

4.1 Personality-Based Rating Behavior Analysis

The analysis revealed that the ratings provided by *extroverts* in red-yellow-green star scale ($Z = -4.092$, $p = 0.000$) are statistically significantly different from their ratings in the baseline (yellow star) scale, with a small effect size ($r = 0.20$). Moreover, a statistically significant difference was also found between the ratings in red-yellow-blue star and the baseline scale ($Z = -4.242$, $p = 0.000$), with a small effect size ($r = 0.20$). However, no statistically significant difference was found in the rating behavior of any other group of personality trait. The rules generated from the Apriori algorithm reveal the direction of score adjustment resulting from the bias of *extroverts* (Table 1). For each of the five scales, rating scores were categorized in three distinct forms of representations of a low, a neutral and a high score as {1,2},{3} and {4,5} respectively, preceded by a rating scale X, where X={Y.Star, RYG.Star,RYB.Star, RYG.Emoji, RYB.Emoji}. The rules shown in bold font state that *extroverts* changed their genuine neutral score in color-based star scales and provided higher scores instead. However, the influence of the colored star scales did not influence *extroverts* who intended to give low or high scores. There was no difference in the rating behavior of *extroverts* using emoji scales from that using the baseline scale. Lastly, no significant difference was found in the rating behavior of any other group of personality traits.

Table 1. Five notable association rules for extroverts.

LHS	RHS	Support	Confidence	Lift
{Y.Star = {4,5}, RYG.Emoji = {4,5}, RYB.Emoji = {4,5}}	{RYB.Star = {4,5}}	0.30	0.98	1.69
{Y.Star = {1,2}, RYG.Star = {1,2}, RYB.Emoji = {1,2}}	{RYG.Emoji = {1,2}}	0.10	0.92	4.53
{Y.Star = {3}, RYG.Star = {4,5}}	**{RYB.Star = {4,5}}**	0.15	0.90	1.55
{Y.Star = {3}, RYB.Star = {4,5}}	**{RYG.Star = {4,5}}**	0.15	0.84	1.43
{Y.Star = {3}, RYG.Emoji = {3}}	{RYB.Emoji = {3}}	0.14	0.82	2.44

4.2   Culture-Based Rating Behavior Analysis

The analysis revealed a significant impact of the color-based scales on *collectivists*. The ratings provided by *collectivists* using red-yellow-green star scale are statistically significantly different from their corresponding ratings in the baseline ($Z = -3.824$, $p = 0.000$) with a small effect size (r = 0.15). The ratings assigned by them in red-yellow-blue star scale are also statistically significantly different from the yellow star ($Z = -4.186$, $p = 0.000$), having a small effect size r = 0.15. Furthermore, there is a significant difference between the baseline and red-yellow-green emoji scales ($Z = -2.016$, $p = 0.044$), effect size r = 0.09 and also between the yellow star and red-yellow-blue emoji scales ($Z = -2.369$, $p = 0.018$) with a small effect size (r = 0.10). There is no significant difference in the rating behavior of the individualists across the color-based scales. The rules generated from the Apriori algorithm reveal the direction of score adjustment resulting from the bias of *collectivists* (Table 2). The highlighted rules state that, while using a color-based star or emoji scale, *collectivists* adjusted their genuine neutral score towards higher scores. However, in cases of an originally given low or high score, color-coded scales had no influence on the ratings.

Table 2. Six notable association rules for collectivists.

LHS	RHS	Support	Confidence	Lift
{Y.Star = {4,5}, RYG.Emoji = {4,5}, RYB.Emoji = {4,5}}	{RYB.Star = {4,5}}	0.42	0.99	1.72
{Y.Star = {1,2}, RYG.Star = {1,2}, RYG.Emoji = {1,2}}	{RYB.Star = {1,2}}	0.11	0.94	5.30
{Y.Star = {3}, RYB.Star = {4,5}}	**{RYG.Star = {4,5}}**	0.07	0.83	1.44
{Y.Star = {3}, RYG.Emoji = {4,5}}	**{RYB.Emoji = {4,5}}**	0.06	0.82	1.47
{Y.Star = {3}, RYG.Emoji = {4,5}}	**{RYB.Star = {4,5}}**	0.06	0.79	1.38
{Y.Star = {3}, RYG.Star = {4,5}, RYB.Emoji = {4,5}}	**{RYG.Emoji = {4,5}}**	0.05	0.79	1.45

5   Discussion

The overall evaluation concludes that color-based star scales have a small but significant effect on the rating behavior of extroverts, since the scales would change their genuine neutral score to a high score in star scales under the influence of color. Extroverts are usually more assertive and enthusiastic, therefore, they were more susceptible to the influence of color. Because of their familiarity with star-based scales, participants might have been more spontaneous while providing feedback. Hence, the familiarity was probably the reason why the bias was only significant in star scales. No other possible rating bias was confirmed, possibly because prior findings on users' color preference in a general context might not necessarily reflect their preference in the context of UI.

Collectivists' preference for colorful and visually appealing decision-making interface influenced their rating decisions and hence they provided biased scores in scales with contrasting color schemes. Similar to extroverts, the colors have a small but significant effect on the rating behavior of collectivists, and the change was only evident from a neutral to a high score. On the other hand, the same features did not exert any influence on individualists. This is probably because of the lack of preference in individualists for a colorful interface.

In summary, consumers with different personality traits and culture will utilize similar color-based scale differently for the same product. Only extroverts and collectivists exhibit biased rating behavior. As a consequence of the bias, the neutral scores are pushed towards the high endpoints of the colored scales.

6   Design Recommendations

The results of this study suggest that using color in the design of rating scales can bias slightly positively the ratings of extrovert users and those from collectivist culture. Designers need to be aware of this, since it can be a way of manipulating user ratings. We recommend that to obtain truthful ratings, ratings systems need to be adapted to the culture and personality of users. Alternatively, the use of color and emoji in rating schemes should be avoided.

7   Conclusion

We investigated whether the presence of colors in rating scales can impact users' responses differently depending on their personality and culture. To this aim, we designed a user study integrated with the Big Five survey, a demographic survey and a rating collection process. The analysis shed light on the existence of bias in extroverts and collectivists in the presence of color-based scales. It also showed that the bias manipulated them to adjust their true neutral scores towards a higher score. In summary, we demonstrate that the color of a scale can solely be responsible for instigating bias in users' ratings. The limitation of this study lies in the small sample size of respondents. A follow-up study can be conducted in the future with a larger group of participants. Moreover, the effectiveness of the proposed design implications can also be investigated.

References

1. The emotional value of color (2009). http://www.tek-unique.com/the-emotional-value-of-color/. Accessed 20 May 2020
2. Adomavicius, G., Bockstedt, J., Curley, S., Zhang, J.: Reducing recommender systems biases: an investigation of rating display designs. Forthcoming, MIS Q. 19–18 (2019)
3. Bonaretti, D., Bartosiak, M.L., Piccoli, G.: Cognitive anchoring of color cues on online review ratings. In: 23rd Americas Conference on Information Systems, AMCIS 2017, Boston, MA, USA, 10–12 August 2017. Association for Information Systems (2017). http://aisel.aisnet.org/amcis2017/HumanCI/Presentations/2
4. Cena, F., Gena, C., Grillo, P., Kuflik, T., Vernero, F., Wecker, A.J.: How scales influence user rating behaviour in recommender systems. Behav. Inf. Technol. **36**(10), 985–1004 (2017)
5. Cosley, D., Lam, S.K., Albert, I., Konstan, J.A., Riedl, J.: Is seeing believing? How recommender system interfaces affect users' opinions. In: Proceedings of the SIGCHI Conference on Human Factors in Computing Systems, pp. 585–592 (2003)
6. Geert Hofstede: Hofstede insights. https://www.hofstede-insights.com/country-comparison/. Accessed 19 July 2020
7. Han, J., Pei, J., Kamber, M.: Data Mining: Concepts and Techniques. Elsevier, Amsterdam (2011)
8. Hook, J.N., Worthington Jr., E.L., Utsey, S.O.: Collectivism, forgiveness, and social harmony. Couns. Psychol. **37**(6), 821–847 (2009)
9. John, O.P., Srivastava, S., et al.: The big five trait taxonomy: history, measurement, and theoretical perspectives. Handbook Pers. Theory Res. **2**(1999), 102–138 (1999)
10. Laroche, M., Kalamas, M., Cleveland, M.: "i" versus "we": how individualists and collectivists use information sources to formulate their service expectations. Int. Mark. Rev. **22**(3), 279–308 (2005)
11. McCrae, R.R., John, O.P.: An introduction to the five-factor model and its applications. J. Pers. **60**(2), 175–215 (1992)
12. Oyibo, K., Ali, Y.S., Vassileva, J.: An empirical analysis of the perception of mobile website interfaces and the influence of culture. In: PPT@ PERSUASIVE, pp. 44–56 (2016)
13. Steers, R.M.: Introduction to Organizational Behavior. Goodyear Publishing Company, New York (1981)
14. Glen, S.: Wilcoxon signed rank test: definition, how to run (2020). https://www.statisticshowto.com/wilcoxon-signed-rank-test/. Accessed 19 July 2020
15. Sun, H.: Building a culturally-competent corporate web site: an exploratory study of cultural markers in multilingual web design. In: Proceedings of the 19th Annual International Conference on Computer Documentation, pp. 95–102 (2001)
16. Tourangeau, R., Couper, M.P., Conrad, F.: Color, labels, and interpretive heuristics for response scales. Public Opin. Q. **71**(1), 91–112 (2007)
17. Treven, S., Mulej, M., Lynn, M.: The impact of culture on organizational behavior. Manag. J. Contemp. Manag. Issues **13**(2 (Special issue)), 27–39 (2008)
18. Wieloch, M., Kabzińska, K., Filipiak, D., Filipowska, A.: Profiling user colour preferences with BFI-44 personality traits. In: Abramowicz, W., Paschke, A. (eds.) BIS 2018. LNBIP, vol. 339, pp. 63–76. Springer, Cham (2019). https://doi.org/10.1007/978-3-030-04849-5_6

Making Them Use It: User Perceptions that Determine the Acceptance of a Persuasive Interventions for Child Healthcare

Sitwat Langrial[1]([⊠]), Jaap Ham[2], and Fannah Al Fannah Al Araimi[3]

[1] Sur University College, Sur, Oman
Dr.Sitwat.Langrial@suc.edu.om
[2] Eindhoven University of Technology, Eindhoven, The Netherlands
j.r.c.ham@tue.nl
[3] Ministry of Health, Muscat, Oman

Abstract. Persuasive Technologies can cause behavior change for improving child health care. However, for persuasive technology to be effective, users have to accept it. We propose a model of determinants of users' acceptance of persuasive technologies that contains five constructs from the Unified Theory of Acceptance and Use of Technology (UTAUT), which were used as latent variables determining users' acceptance to use a persuasive intervention for child healthcare. A structured questionnaire was validated and completed by 133 participants to assess their perceptions. Results indicate that Perceived Usefulness, Content of Intervention and Perceived Credibility can have a significant influence on Intention to Use the Intervention. The result support our proposed model of determinants of acceptance of persuasive technology. The most important conclusion of this model is that when users perceive an intervention as being credible and useful, they are most motivated to accept and adopt it.

Keywords: Persuasive Technology Acceptance Model · Persuasive information systems · Intervention · Perceptions · Child health

1 Introduction

Childhood illness remains an on-going challenge in low and middle-income countries for both healthcare professionals and parents [1]. To address this challenge, the World Health Organization [2] introduced Integrated Management of Childhood Illness (IMCI) as a simple algorithm-based strategy. IMCI-trained healthcare practitioners are more likely to treat sick children in an effective and timely manner [3]. Surprisingly, IMCI strategy has not resulted in desired/expected outcomes as childhood mortality rates remain high despite its global acceptance and implementation [4].

Researchers highlight the importance of parents' knowledge and skills in child healthcare [5]. While healthcare professionals are primarily responsible for guiding the parents with regard to IMCI-recommended practices, in the current research we investigate whether parents' knowledge and skills can be improved by reaching them

© Springer Nature Switzerland AG 2021
R. Ali et al. (Eds.): PERSUASIVE 2021, LNCS 12684, pp. 207–214, 2021.
https://doi.org/10.1007/978-3-030-79460-6_17

directly through the use of Persuasive Technology (PT).The evident benefits of IMCI for child healthcare have already been reported including cost effective interventions, better case management, improved illness classification and enhancing skills to support a sick child [1]. However, it is unfortunate that limited resources, continuous training and even reluctance from some medical practitioners have resulted in lower acceptance rate of IMCI [1]. We believe that the use of PT can help us reach a larger number of target audience and help persuade them to learn and apply the IMCI-related skills in order to improve child health.

Earlier research shows that patients, healthcare professionals and healthcare information consumers can be reached through Information Systems [6]. We therefore argue that providing parents with IMCI-recommended healthcare practices through persuasive technologies can improve their knowledge and skills. Healthcare information and guidance can be provided to the target audience through web- or mobile-based interventions, social media and wearable sensor technologies.

Advances and acceptance of persuasive technologies open up new opportunities to reach a larger healthcare audience [7]. Information Systems that use persuasive strategies (e.g., argumentation) for behavior change are more commonly known as Persuasive Technologies [8]. Research of IMCI and child healthcare has not focused the impact of such technologies on improving child healthcare [9]. At the same time, there is a call for an urgent solution for persistently high child mortality rates. We propose that designing and delivering simple and effective interventions that could improve parents' knowledge and skills to provide immediate care to sick children is highly desirable. One way forward in this direction is the use of Persuasive Technology [8].

2 Persuasive Technologies and Information Systems

Persuasive Technologies [8] or Persuasive Information Systems is a vibrant and relatively new area of research that is receiving researchers' growing attention from across the world. These technologies and systems are developed with an aim to support people modify and/or improve their behaviors and lifestyles, for example, health-related behaviors, eating habits, having an active lifestyle and general well-being [10–12]. [12] proposed the Persuasive Systems Design Model (PSD model), which describes software features in four categories: Primary Task Support, User-System Dialogue Support, Credibility and Social Support [12].

Especially in low and middle-income countries, where child mortality is higher (see e.g., [1]), acceptance of health information systems is far less when compared with the USA, EU and UK [13]. Still, also in more affluent countries IMCI strategies are not always followed and child health can be improved (see e.g., [4]). Therefore, this study investigates (self-perceived) determinants of user acceptance of a persuasive intervention for child healthcare that uses IMCI guidelines as its fundamental components. Our research model draws components from the PSD Model [12] (including e.g., Perceived Credibility) and the Technology Acceptance Model (TAM) [14]. The Technology Acceptance Model (TAM) focuses on the importance of perceived usefulness of a technology and its likely influence on the intention to accept or use a given technology [14].

3   Methods

Participants were recruited at Sur, Sultanate of Oman in June 2019. Ethical approval was obtained prior to data collection. The ethical application form included details about the purpose of the study, information about perspective participants, research plan, sample of an informed consent form and other ethical aspects such as data integrity and confidentiality. The study had no physical or psychological implications on the participants. Informed consent was received prior to the collection of data. Participants were advised that there was no monetary reward for participation and that they were under no obligation to complete the questionnaires.

We developed a research framework of determinants we labelled the Persuasive Technology Acceptance (PTA Model) model. Following predefined constructs were used for developing the research model: Perceived Usefulness [14], Perceived Credibility [20], Content of Intervention [15], Perceived Persuasiveness [6] and Intention to Use the Intervention [14]. The model was designed using a simplistic approach to identify the likely impact of latent variables on the formative construct (Intention to Use the Intervention).

A paper-based questionnaire was distributed among the residents of Sur, Sultanate of Oman. Inclusion criteria for the study included 1) Regular use of mobile phone, 2) Having one or more children under the age of 5, 3) Signing the Informed Consent and 4) Voluntary participation in the study. Data were collected over a period of 4 days. The questionnaire included demographic questions and five-point Likert Scale items (ranging from Strongly Agree to Strongly Disagree). A total of 133 completed questionnaires were received without any missing values. Out of 133 participants (Response Rate 88.7%), a high majority were females (84.9%). Therefore, the study sample primarily represents educated females aged between 19 and 38. Participant characteristics are exhibited in Table 1.

Table 1. Participants' demographics.

Demographics	Values	Distribution
Gender	Male	20
	Female	113
Age	19-25	55
	26-31	22
	32-38	56
	39 and above	None
Education	Diploma	40
	Bachelor	70
	Graduate	23

The research model was analyzed using Smart Partial Least Square software version 3.2.5 (SmartPLS GmbH, Bönningstedt, Germany) [16]. We chose SmartPLS for data analysis because it helps in developing a predictive model rather than verifying an existing model or theory. In addition, Smart PLS is widely being used to understand human perception in a specific context [1]. For the analysis, we adopted a two-step approach i.e., assessing the reliability, and validity of the research model [17]. The constructs and their properties were examined through factor loadings, discriminant validity and internal consistency. In such an analysis, factor loadings and variances are examined to ensure convergent validity where factor loadings and internal consistency values above 0.700 are acceptable [17]. Further, Cronbach's alpha was used to verify the internal consistency of the items for each construct. We also used Fornell-Larcker criterion to determine discriminant validity between the constructs in the research model. There are some criticisms about employing Fornell-Larcker criterion; therefore, we also applied the Heterotrait-Monotrait (HTMT) ratios for the correlations [18]. Figure 1 exhibits the research model.

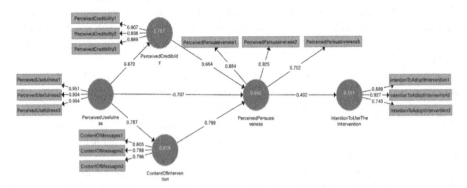

Fig. 1. The Persuasive Technology Acceptance Model

4 Results

Figure 1 shows the relationships between the studied constructs in the research model. Factor loadings and calculated variances for each item (per construct) were greater than 0.700 and 0.500 respectively. Findings confirm that all items in the research model loaded well. The Average Variance Extracted (AVE) values were above 0.635. Table 2 shows the composite reliability of the studied constructs. The discriminant validity of all correlations was below the desirable HTMT value of 0.90. Path coefficient analyses and outer loadings indicate that Perceived Usefulness (p < 0.001), Content of Intervention (p < 0.050), Perceived Credibility (p < 0.050) and Perceived Persuasiveness (p < 0.050) can have a significant influence on Intention to Use the Intervention. Also, the cross-loadings for all the items on their latent variables were larger than any other loading, showing reliability and validity of the constructs and the research model.

A relatively complex interrelation was observed in the studied constructs. There was a 75.5% and 61.9% variance in Perceived Credibility (PC) and Content of Intervention (PI) respectively. Both Perceived Credibility and Content of Intervention contributed to 64.2% variance in Perceived Persuasiveness (PP) leading to 16.1% variance in Intention

Table 2. Latent variables coefficients and correlations of the research model.

Studied Constructs	CR	CA	AVE	CoI	IUT	PC	PP	PU
COL	0.839	0.715	0.635	0.797				
IUT	0.891	0.836	0.732	0.525	0.856			
PC	0.936	0.898	0.831	0.724	0.595	0.912		
PP	0.879	0.79	0.71	0.724	0.402	0.628	0.843	
PU	0.943	0.909	0.846	0.787	0.675	0.87	0.499	0.92

CR= Composite Reliability; CA = Cronbach's Alpha; AVE = Average Variance Extracted; CoI = Content of Intervention; IUT = Intention to Use the Intervention; PC = Perceived Credibility; PP = Perceived Persuasiveness; PU = Perceived Usefulness

to Use the Intervention (IUT). Perceived Credibility (PC) and Content of Intervention (CoI) correlated strongly and contributed to higher Perceived Persuasiveness (PP). The R2 values for the studied constructs were: 1) 93.8 for Content of Intervention, 2) 91.9 for Perceived Credibility, 3) 45.6 for Perceived Persuasiveness and 5) 21.6 for Intention to Use the Intervention. While the constructs revealed a relatively low R^2 value for Intention to Use the Intervention, research indicates that low R^2 values cannot be overlooked [18], especially in research studies that aim to predict attitudes and intentions [19]. We therefore argue that even a relatively low R^2 value can be observed and noted as being significant. Based on the statistical findings, the research model is supported.

5 Discussion

Overall, all studied constructs showed significant variance predicting Intention to Use the Intervention: Users (parents) were more likely to use a persuasive intervention for child healthcare when they perceived the intervention as credible and having meaningful content (confirming earlier research, see [15]). Our findings add to the existing knowledge about IMCI especially by introducing a novel concept of reaching out the parents through persuasive information systems. Based on the statistical findings, it was observed that Perceived Credibility (PC) and Content of Intervention (CoI) contribute significantly to Perceived Persuasiveness (PP) of the intervention with a R^2 value of .642 which indicates the strength of the research model and a strong correlation between PC, CoI and PC. We propose that carefully designed persuasive information systems employed with simple software feature such as reminders [8] can help parents acquire child health care knowledge and skills as per IMCI guidelines.

This research extends our understanding of the determinants of acceptance of Persuasive Technology. The Persuasive Technology Acceptance Model proposed by [20] incorporates user-experience (UX) design attributes as determinants, and includes overlapping determinants (Perceived Usefulness, Perceived Credibility and Perceived Persuasiveness), additional determinants (Perceived Aesthetics and Perceived Usability) while not including Content of Intervention. Likewise, Ghazali and colleagues [21] tested a Persuasive Robots Acceptance Model in which comparable and additional determinants were incorporated. [21] suggests that different types of Persuasive Technologies (using different kinds of influencing strategies) might have different determinants of acceptance (perhaps even for different people, see [22]). Future research can combine these and other findings and extend the Persuasive Technology Acceptance Model.

The current research used a sample taken from a single educational institute, consisting mainly of females with higher education, making it hard to generalize the results. Also, although the statistical findings support the research model, there is a need for further investigation to confirm these findings. Future research can build on and extend the current work by assessing other forms of determinants and acceptance. That is, the current research focused on self-perceived determinants as these can be crucial for acceptance. Nonetheless, future research can investigate other types of determinants, such as determinants that users are unaware of, or social and system-related determinants. Likewise, current conclusions stem from a paper-based questionnaire, which might give insight in self-perceived determinants and self-perceived acceptance. However, future research can also investigate the role of these determinants (and others) for actual acceptance behavior or even usage behavior.

6 Conclusions

This research assessed determinants of user acceptance of a persuasive systems-based intervention for child healthcare. We proposed a model of Persuasive Technology Acceptance presenting determinants that were based on the Unified Theory of Acceptance and Use of Technology (UTAUT), testing it in an online study with 133 participants. Perceived Credibility (PC) and Content of the Intervention (CoI) were key contributors towards Perceived Persuasiveness (PP) leading to the action i.e., Intention to Use a child healthcare persuasive intervention. Findings support our model and indicate that users accept a persuasive intervention given that it is credible and has meaningful content.

When users accept an intervention as being credible and useful, it develops their intention to use it in real life. Thereby, the current research increased our understanding of the acceptance of persuasive technology – a crucial step for persuasive technology before it will be used and can effectively influence human behavior. This research contributes to the existing knowledge base in the health information systems research area by introducing a new model that focuses solely on the Acceptance of Persuasive Technologies. In future, we plan to continue working on the model by adding additional constructs to further strengthen the Persuasive technology Acceptance Model.

Acknowledgements. The authors would like to thank all participants for their valuable time and feedback that helped completion of this study.

References

1. Al-Araimi, F.A., Sitwat, U.L.: A hypothetical model to predict nursing students' perceptions of the usefulness of pre-service integrated management of childhood illness training. Sultan Qaboos Univ. Med. J. **16**(4), e469 (2016)

2. Goga, A.E., et al.: Results of a multi-country exploratory survey of approaches and methods for IMCI case management training. Health Res. Pol. Syst. **7**(1), 18 (2009)
3. Horwood, C., Voce, A., Vermaak, K., Rollins, N., Qazi, S.: Experiences of training and implementation of integrated management of childhood illness (IMCI) in South Africa: a qualitative evaluation of the IMCI case management training course. BMC Pediatr. **9**(1), 62 (2009)
4. Lange, S., Mwisongo, A., Mæstad, O.: Why don't clinicians adhere more consistently to guidelines for the integrated management of childhood illness (IMCI)? Soc. Sci. Med. **104**, 56–63 (2014)
5. Cooley, W.C., Sagerman, P.J., American Academy of Pediatrics and American Academy of Family Physicians: Supporting the health care transition from adolescence to adulthood in the medical home. Pediatrics **128**(1), 182 (2011)
6. Lehto, T., Oinas-Kukkonen, H., Pätiälä, T. and Saarelma, O.: Consumers' perceptions of a virtual health check: an empirical investigation. In: ECIS, p. 154 (2012)
7. DeRenzi, B., et al.: E-IMCI: improving pediatric health care in low-income countries. In: Proceedings of the SIGCHI Conference on Human Factors in Computing Systems, pp. 753–762. ACM, April 2008
8. Fogg, B.J.: Persuasive technology: using computers to change what we think and do. Ubiquity **2002**(December), 5 (2002)
9. Mitchell, M., Hedt-Gauthier, B.L., Msellemu, D., Nkaka, M., Lesh, N.: Using electronic technology to improve clinical care–results from a before-after cluster trial to evaluate assessment and classification of sick children according to Integrated management of childhood illness (IMCI) protocol in Tanzania. BMC Med. Inform. Decis. Mak. **13**(1), 95 (2013)
10. Angst, C.M., Agarwal, R.: Adoption of electronic health records in the presence of privacy concerns: the elaboration likelihood model and individual persuasion. MIS Q. **33**(2), 339–370 (2009)
11. Intille, S.S.: A new research challenge: persuasive technology to motivate healthy aging. IEEE Trans. Inf. Technol. Biomed. **8**(3), 235–237 (2004)
12. Oinas-Kukkonen, H., Harjumaa, M.: Persuasive systems design: key issues, process model and system features. In: Routledge Handbook of Policy Design, pp. 105–123. Routledge (2018)
13. Heeks, R.: Health information systems: failure, success and improvisation. Int. J. Med. Inform. **75**(2), 125–137 (2006)
14. Venkatesh, V., Davis, F.D.: A theoretical extension of the technology acceptance model: four longitudinal field studies. Manage. Sci. **46**(2), 186–204 (2000)
15. Langrial, S.U., Lappalainen, P.: Information systems for improving mental health: six emerging themes of research. Inf. Syst. (2016)
16. Henseler, J., Ringle, C.M., Sarstedt, M.: A new criterion for assessing discriminant validity in variance-based structural equation modeling. J. Acad. Mark. Sci. **43**(1), 115–135 (2014). https://doi.org/10.1007/s11747-014-0403-8
17. Anderson, J.C., Gerbing, D.W.: Structural equation modeling in practice: a review and recommended two-step approach. Psychol. Bull. **103**(3), 411 (1988)
18. Vinzi, V.E., Trinchera, L., Amato, S.: PLS path modeling: from foundations to recent developments and open issues for model assessment and improvement. In: Handbook of Partial Least Squares, pp. 47–82. Springer, Berlin, Heidelberg (2010). https://doi.org/10.1007/978-3-540-32827-8_3
19. Onditi, A.A.: Relationship between customer personality, service features and customer loyalty in the banking sector: a survey of banks in Homabay County, Kenya. Int. J. Bus. Soc. Sci. **4**(15) (2013)
20. Oyibo, K., Vassileva, J.: HOMEX: persuasive technology acceptance model and the moderating effect of culture. Front. Comput. Sci. **2**, 10 (2020)

21. Ghazali, A., Ham, J., Barakova, E., Markopoulous, P.: Persuasive robots acceptance model (PRAM): roles of social responses within the acceptance model of persuasive robots. Int. J. Soc. Robot. 1–18 (2020). https://doi.org/10.1007/s12369-019-00611-1
22. Masthoff, J., Grasso, F., Ham, J.: Special issue on personalisation and behaviour change. User models for motivational systems. User Model. User-Adapted Interact. 24 (2014)

Methods and Techniques

A Systematic Review of Persuasive Strategies in Mobile E-Commerce Applications and Their Implementations

Ashfaq Adib[(✉)] and Rita Orji

Faculty of Computer Science, Dalhousie University, Halifax, NS B3H 4R2, Canada
{ashfaq.adib,rita.orji}@dal.ca

Abstract. E-commerce applications are among the most popular category of applications in the market. Increasing popularity of these applications have raised many concerns of successful system design in this domain. Persuasive strategies play a vital role in interface design, similar to many other category of applications, e-commerce applications have also adapted to persuasive system design methods. This study focuses on analyzing some existing e-commerce applications to identify the persuasive strategies used with a view to understanding their effectiveness in e-commerce. Based on the analysis of 30 e-commerce applications, different implementation methods of many persuasive strategies were identified, where *Social Learning* and *Personalization* were the most implemented strategies. No significant correlation could be found between the number of strategies present and the ratings of the applications. Moreover, further analysis on the most popular and highly rated applications among the 30 applications surfaced some differences in the strategies applied while emphasizing the importance of applying persuasive strategies that are appropriate to the purpose of the application.

Keywords: Persuasive system design · E-commerce · Persuasive strategies

1 Introduction

The term "e-commerce" refers to conducting business over the internet [11]. In this technology-driven era, many tasks are now being done through the internet unlike before, it is not a surprise that shopping for clothes, shoes or even groceries are being carried out from home through some pressing of buttons. E-commerce has allowed businesses to grow, providing a platform for multinational operations and reaching out to people from around the world. It is not just about selling more products, businesses can now observe a customer's shopping behavior, implement targeted marketing and build a community of loyal customers all with the help of e-commerce.

Persuasive strategies are techniques that are employed in persuasive systems to motivate desired behaviours [9]. Persuasive strategies are employed in applications to motivate the users' towards a target behavior without coercion or

© Springer Nature Switzerland AG 2021
R. Ali et al. (Eds.): PERSUASIVE 2021, LNCS 12684, pp. 217–230, 2021.
https://doi.org/10.1007/978-3-030-79460-6_18

deception [5]. It is expected that e-commerce applications will use persuasive techniques for better system design and to achieve their system goals. As mentioned by Fogg [5], for a behavior to occur the person must have some level of motivation. The target behavior in e-commerce applications almost in all cases is to sell products. These strategies have also been applied in other domains of applications such as, mental health, diet, physical activity and fitness etc. [10] Our study focuses on persuasion in e-commerce applications.

In this study, we analyzed 30 e-commerce applications using the Persuasive Systems Design (PSD) model [8], which defines 28 persuasive strategies divided into 4 groups based on the motivation behind the applied strategy e.g. to help in the primary task of the system, to make use of social support etc. The aim of this study can be narrowed down into these research questions:

- What are the most common persuasive strategies in e-commerce applications?
- How are different persuasive strategies implemented in such applications?
- To understand the effectiveness of persuasive strategies in e-commerce, is there any relation between application's rating and popularity (reviews), and number of persuasive strategies used?
- What are the common strategies used in most successful e-commerce applications and how are they different from the others?

Our analysis showed that *Personalization* and *Social Learning* are the mostly used strategies in e-commerce, being present in 2/3rd of the applications. We also found that some strategies were implemented in a couple of different ways in the applications, especially *Tailoring* strategy- which had four different implementations. We further analyzed the most popular and highly rated applications among the 30 applications and found that *Tailoring* was the most implemented strategy among them. Detailed analysis of these popular applications surfaced that some strategies are more suitable for one purpose than the other, and appropriate implementation increases the effectiveness of the applied strategies.

2   Related Studies

Not many studies have been conducted in identifying the most effective and commonly used persuasive strategies in e-commerce applications. Adaji et al. [3] used Persuasive Systems Design (PSD) model to analyze persuasive strategies used in 10 popular e-commerce websites including Amazon, Ebay, Netflix etc. The most used persuasive feature that they found was Dialogue Support, which was present in all of the websites. They also found that all of the websites used Rewards, followed by Praise which was used in 90% of the websites. In paper [1], a successful e-commerce website- Amazon, was extensively analyzed to identify the applied persuasive strategies. Based on their findings, the perceived system credibility of the website had no influence on the participants to use the website. The study also stated that product reviews had the most impact on the perceived credibility of the website, which can be incorporated with the persuasive strategy "Social Learning".

The study conducted by Zhu et al. [13], provided two key elements on building trust in e-commerce: ability to tackle potential attacks and malicious behavior, and preservation of user privacy, which emphasize the implementation of System Credibility Support persuasive strategies. Zhao et al. [12] introduced personalising product information for better customer engagement. An experiment with participants from Amazon Mechanical Turk on their developed website showed significant increase in profit for sellers where the price of products were personalized to meet user's "Willingness to Pay" factor.

Adaji et al. [2] conducted an online survey on 244 participants recruited through Amazon's Mechanical Turk to find if persuasive strategies had any influence on healthy food shopping habits in e-commerce. The researchers considered Cialdini's [4] six influence strategies and found no correlation between them and building healthy food shopping habits. The researchers indicated that strategies like Scarcity may be effective in influencing the consumers purchase of goods such as, books, electronics etc. but they do not have any impact on encouraging the purchase of healthy foods. Another study [6], found that using tangible rewards (discounts, offers etc.) was more effective than intangible rewards (badges) in e-commerce applications to increase customer engagement. But intangible rewards offered more engagement than having no rewards.

In the study by Nkwo et al. [7], implementation of persuasive strategies from the PSD model were analyzed in two e-commerce applications- Amazon and Jumia. The researchers identified the presence of 17 strategies in their analysis. Among the strategies, both applications applied all of the strategies under the Dialogue Support category, which emphasises the importance of reminders, suggestions, praise and social roles in e-commerce applications. There were some differences too: strategies like simulation, social comparison, normative influence, and recognition were present in Amazon but not in Jumia. The researchers recommended that Jumia could benefit from adding these strategies in the application considering the success of Amazon in e-commerce domain.

There remains a need to analyze how different strategies are implemented in a wide variety of e-commerce applications. Also, observing the strategies present in popular applications in contrast with other applications is required to find if the popular applications are following different methods which make them successful. To achieve this, we extensively analyzed 30 e-commerce applications that include a variety of categories i.e. marketplace, food & drink, lifestyle and digital sales, and identified different implementation methods of the strategies. We then further analyzed the top 7 most successful applications among the 30 applications to find design implications for the developers to effectively use persuasive strategies in e-commerce.

3   Methodology

To answer the research questions stated in Sect. 1, some e-commerce applications were selected to be analyzed. The implementation method of the strategies were observed in order to understand how different applications aim to persuade the users. First, we selected 30 e-commerce applications for analysis. The selection process of the applications is described below.

3.1 Selection of Applications

We focused on mobile e-commerce applications for this study and selected 30 applications for analysis. Initially, two researchers identified most popular e-commerce applications. We browsed through different categories such as, shopping, lifestyle etc. in the Google Playstore and selected applications based on their popularity and rating. We collected information such as application's rating, number of reviews, last update date etc. during this process. The rating and number of reviews for each application was collected on April 12, 2020.

Table 1. Selected applications

Category	Avg. rating (Std. Dev.)	Avg. reviews (Std. Dev.)	Applications
Marketplace	4.18 (0.49)	1697794.38 (3576844.84)	Bestbuy, Kijiji, AliExpress, Flipkart, Newegg, eBay, Pickaboo, Daraz, Walmart, Amazon, Alibaba, Etsy, Canadian Tire, StockX, Gumtree, Evaly
Digital Sales	4.50 (0.27)	449390.75 (494959.37)	G2A, CeX: Tech, Steam, Audible
Food & Drink	3.74 (0.75)	589894.20 (988051.25)	Tim Hortons, Uber Eats, Second Cup, Starbucks, Skip The Dishes
Lifestyle	4.54 (0.37)	112142.20 (163900.95)	H& M, adidas, Wayfair, Sephora, IKEA

The collected applications were divided into four categories- marketplace, food & drinks, digital sales and lifestyle as shown in Table 1. The applications in the marketplace category offer a platform where various retailers or users can enlist their products for sale. The food & drink category has applications that sell food items either for a specific company or serves as a delivery system for restaurants. The applications in the digital sales category sell digital products i.e. video games or audio-books. The lifestyle category includes applications that are dedicated to selling one specific type of products such as clothes, cosmetics or furniture, generally for a specific company.

3.2   Coding Applications

To assess and identify the strategies, Persuasive System Design (PSD) model [8] was used in this study which includes a total of 28 persuasive strategies divided into four categories. The strategies and their categories will be discussed in details in the Results sections. Two researchers were involved in the coding process of the strategies. Initially, the selected applications were coded by the two researchers independently by identifying the persuasive strategies employed in the applications based on the definitions provided in the PSD model. After initial coding, the identified strategies were discussed between the researchers until both of the researchers reached an agreement on most of the coding. The remaining disagreements were discussed with fellow researchers from our university lab to correctly identify each of the strategies.

3.3   Analysis

To answer the research questions mentioned in Sect. 1, the coded strategies were analyzed as follows:

- First, the persuasive strategies and their implementations were identified.
- Second, Pearson's correlation analysis was performed to find any relation between the applications' effectiveness (ratings) and popularity (reviews), and number of persuasive strategies used.
- Finally, the most successful applications (based on ratings and no. of reviews) were further analyzed to identify the most effective strategies.

In the next section, we will discuss the results of our analysis.

4   Results

In this section the findings of our study will be discussed in detail. We will discuss the strategies that were identified along with their implementation methods.

4.1   Common Persuasive Strategies in E-Commerce Applications

As mentioned earlier, the PSD model has been used as a basis for identifying persuasive strategies in the applications for this study. Among the 28 strategies of that model, we found 21 strategies present in the applications. These 21 strategies were applied a total of 218 times among the 30 applications. The strategies identified and the number of applications they were applied in is shown in Fig. 1. As seen in the figure, the mostly used strategies were Personalization and Social Learning- being used in 20 out of the 30 applications. It is expected from e-commerce applications, since most of these applications focus on showing personalised contents to the user based on their search history or previous orders. Social Learning strategy was used mostly to inform users about products through

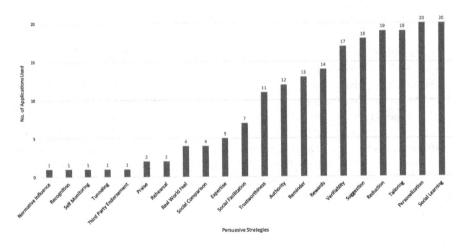

Fig. 1. Frequency of persuasive strategies in 30 e-commerce applications

other users' reviews, helping potential customers to buy the right product and bringing users together based on their common interests.

Many implementation methods of the strategies were identified during the analysis as shown in Table 2, 3, 4 and 5. Following the PSD model's four categories of strategies, we will describe our findings on the strategies identified and their implementation methods in detail below.

Primary Task Support: According to the PSD model, the main purpose of the strategies in this category is to assist the users in carrying out the main tasks in an application- which in case of e-commerce applications is purchasing products. The strategies identified from this category and their implementation methods have been demonstrated in Table 2. Two popular strategies from our analysis belong to this category- Personalization and Reduction. Personalization helps the user to easily find products that they are interested in while Reduction helps the user in going through the process of purchasing efficiently. Tailoring has also been applied many times in the applications, mostly achieved through supporting different languages. Rehearsal was an interesting strategy to find in the applications (Sephora and Wayfair), which used advanced augmented reality features to allow the users to try out products in real environments. Both of the applications that used this strategy were from the Lifestyle category.

Dialogue Support: The strategies in this category provide users feedback on their actions for an interactive experience with a view to helping them move towards their target behavior. These strategies and their implementations are shown in Table 3. Suggestion was among the mostly used strategies, unlike Personalization, these product suggestions are for all users in general, regardless of their shopping behavior. Rewards in the applications was implemented in different ways, but all of them were targeted towards the same outcome- saving

Table 2. Identified strategies in primary task support and their implementations

Persuasive strategy	Implementation	No. of applications used
Personalization	1. Product recommendations based on user activity	19
	2. Product recommendations based on user location	4
Reduction	1. Buy products by directly going to check-out	14
	2. Quickly order previous orders	6
	3. Find products by taking photo of an item/scanning QR code	5
Tailoring	1. Supports various languages/currencies	15
	2. View content based on user's gender or age	2
	3. View content based on user's culture or taste	3
	4. Content tailored for diet conscious user's i.e. showing calorie information, vegan/Halal tags etc.	5
Rehearsal	1. See how products would look like in a real environment through camera and augmented reality	2
Self Monitoring	1. Shows information on how long a user has used a product	2
	2. Shows information on amount of products sold over time	1 (StockX)
Tunneling	1. Provides step-by-step instruction on how to use a product	1 (Sephora)

money. Praise was only used twice, one of the applications was Sephora- which is expected in an application that sells cosmetics.

Social Support: The strategies in this category leverages the power of social influence in motivating the users to perform a target behavior; their implementations have been shown in Table 4. Although not many strategies from this category were identified, Social Learning was one of the most used strategies as shown in Fig. 1, being used in 20 applications. This strategy provides a platform for users to share their opinions on a product, enabling other interested users to learn about it. Normative Influence was present in one application- eBay, where the number of interested customers for a product is displayed. A major part of

Table 3. Identified strategies in dialogue support and their implementations

Persuasive strategy	Implementation	No. of applications used
Suggestion	1. Popular/featured/similar product recommendation	15
	2. Recommendation on a combination of products	3
Rewards	1. Get reward points/coins on product purchase	9
	2. Get discount on performing certain actions i.e. pre-ordering products, becoming a member, inviting friends to join etc	6
	3. User gets reward on his/her birthday	3
Reminders	1. Get notified on product sales, price changes or stock availability	13
Praise	1. Greet the user with compliments	2

Table 4. Identified strategies in social support and their implementations

Persuasive strategy	Implementation	No. of applications used
Social Learning	1. Learn about a product from user reviews	20
Social Facilitation	1. Show other users' purchase behavior e.g. others also bought, people also ordered etc	7
Social Comparison	1. See how other people are using a product	4
Normative Influence	1. Show the number of users that are interested in a particular product	1 (eBay)
Recognition	1. Display membership level i.e. gold/silver/bronze member	1 (AliExpress)

that application is bidding on products, thus, this strategy is very effective for the functionality of the application.

System Credibility Support: The System Credibility Support strategies increase the effectiveness of persuasion through making the applications seem more credible. Credibility is crucial for e-commerce applications, Especially for marketplace applications where various sellers are involved. Table 5 illustrates

Table 5. Identified strategies in system credibility support and their implementations

Persuasive strategy	Implementation	No. of applications used
Verifiability	1. Provide contact information of the store/manufacturer/product owner	17
Authority	1. Provide privacy policy and terms of use mentioning compliance with governing laws of a country	12
Trustworthiness	1. Provide assurance on purchases by highlighting money back guarantee or return policies	8
	2. Detailed description of product's ingredients or product's quality assurance	4
	3. Provide explanation of application's claims such as, low price guarantee, sustainable production etc	3
Expertise	1. Provide information of expert's involvement in application's contents i.e. beauty advisors, electronic technicians, athletes etc	6
Real-world Feel	1. Contact information of people behind the application	4
Third-party Endorsement	1. Show affiliation with British Red Cross as charity partner	1 (H& M)

the strategies applied from this category and their implementations. As expected, all of the marketplace applications applied at least one strategy from this category, with Verifiability being applied in 17 applications. Expertise was mostly found in applications from the Lifestyle category. The H&M application emphasizes their company's sustainable production policies throughout the application, for assurance they applied the Third-party Endorsement strategy which had a significant positive impact on the credibility of the application.

4.2   Relation Between Application's Popularity and Strategies Used

Measurement of popularity for the applications were considered based on the number of reviews that they received in the Google Playstore. Figure 2 shows a plot with number of reviews of an application and the number of strategies it applied. There seems to be a gradual increase in the number of strategies applied as the reviews increase, especially for applications with more than 100,000 reviews which might infer that popular applications tend to make use of as many strategies as possible. Pearson analysis between the two variables resulted in a coefficient, $r = 0.499$ and p value, $p = 0.005$. The low p value of less than 0.05 indicate a statistical significance of the correlation between the number of strategies employed and popularity of applications. An outlier in the graph is the application- Sephora, which is an application in the Lifestyle category that sells cosmetics. Their user group is typically smaller due to its focus on specific audience (with interest in cosmetic and beauty).

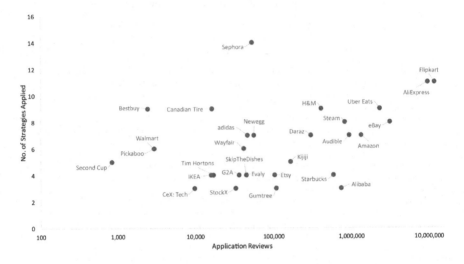

Fig. 2. No. of strategies applied and no. of application reviews

4.3 Relation Between Application's Rating and Strategies Used

As a measure of effectiveness of the applied strategies in application, application ratings were chosen since they reflect users' opinion on an application. The ratings were collected from Google Playstore. Pearson Correlation analysis between the ratings and number of strategies applied by the applications resulted in a coefficient, $r = 0.211$ and p value, $p = 0.263$. The low coefficient value proves that there is no significant relation between the application ratings and number of strategies applied. The p value also indicates that the correlation coefficient is not statistically significant considering the probability being greater than the conventional 5% ($p > 0.05$).

4.4 Detailed Analysis of the Top 7 Applications

To answer the last research question on finding common strategies among successful e-commerce applications and identifying any differences from the others; among the 30 applications we further analysed the most successful applications based on their rating and number of reviews. For our selection of top applications, we chose the ones that had a minimum of 4.5 rating among the top 10 most reviewed applications. This lead us to analyzing 7 applications. The strategies used in these applications are shown in Fig. 3.

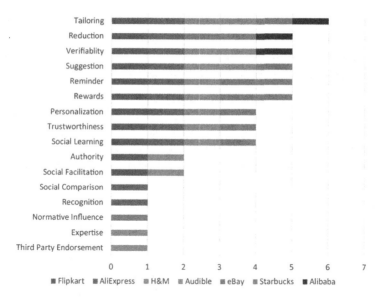

Fig. 3. Persuasive strategies identified in top 7 applications

Flipkart was the most reviewed application (11,595,361) with a rating of 4.5 which indicates that it is a very successful application with 11 persuasive strategies implemented, followed by Aliexpress with 9,563,727 reviews and 4.6 rating and 11 strategies used. These 2 applications have 9 strategies in common as shown in Fig. 3. Tailoring was found in 6/7 top applications, proving it's effectiveness in targeting users from different countries or cultures. Since these applications are very popular, having multiple languages and currencies support is crucial to their operation. Reduction, Verifiability, Suggestion, Reminder and Rewards were found in 5 of the top 7 applications. Three of these strategies are from Dialogue Support category, indicating the effectiveness of employing the strategies in this category to increase the interactivity of e-commerce applications. Personalization, Social Learning and Trustworthiness were found in 4 of the top applications. The other strategies were context specific for the application's purpose, i.e. normative influence in bidding feature of eBay, expertise on sustainable garment production of H&M etc. which added significant value to the purpose of these applications. Most used strategies among the 30 applications: Personalization and Social Learning (Fig. 1) were not the most used ones among the top applications, raising concerns about their effectiveness in e-commerce. Personalized contents and product reviews have become a norm in e-commerce applications, these aspects of e-commerce need to be further explored if they are still effective in encouraging purchase behavior or users overlook such content.

5   Discussion

In this study, we aimed to find how various e-commerce applications are using persuasive strategies to make more effective and usable applications. This section will discuss about the identified strategies and how they impact the design of e-commerce applications.

5.1　Strengths and Weaknesses of the Applications

Most applications in the marketplace category had the same pattern with an emphasise on personalized product suggestions throughout the interface. Although these are presented to help users, such suggestions crowded the interfaces of popular marketplace applications such as AliExpress, Flipkart, Amazon and Daraz which weakened their design. In contrary, Best Buy and Newegg had very simplistic design, offering a good navigational experience among the marketplace applications. Applications in the Lifestyle category had the most pleasing interface designs. These applications focus on fashion and latest trends, it was reflected in the unique and sophisticated design elements of their interfaces which was one of their strong suits. The Food & Drinks applications lacked having the option to review specific food items. However, these applications applied most effective ways of Tailoring by targeting specific user groups based on their dietary preferences rather than general country-based content tailoring seen in other applications. Some features that stood out among all the applications were the use of augmented reality in Sephora and Wayfair, and monitoring product usage information in Steam and Audible. Among the applications, Sephora had the most number of applied strategies (14), and it also stood out with unique features such as, trying out cosmetics using the camera, getting tips from beauty experts etc. It was also the highest rated application with a rating of 4.8/5. This application should be further analysed for it's success in applying so many strategies effectively.

5.2　Design Recommendations

The in-depth analysis of the top 7 applications surfaced the most effective strategies for e-commerce applications. Tailoring for different user groups plays a major role in the popularity of the application by making the system more usable by a variety of users. We suggest applications to include this strategy in their design, and if possible provide more refined tailoring as achieved in Food & Drinks applications e.g. considering specific group of individuals through having Halal, vegan options. Reduction was also a vital strategy in the top applications. Apart from the regular "Buy Now" feature found in most applications, we suggest offering more reduction techniques as AliExpress's product search through photo capturing feature. E-commerce applications should also employ Verifiability in their design, especially in marketplace applications. Successful applications like AliExpress, Flipkart and Alibaba heavily emphasize on the verification of the sellers in their systems and provide clear contact information of the sellers to the buyers. Also, some strategies are more suitable for one purpose than another, and should be employed in the applications accordingly e.g. provide experts' opinion if the system sells one specific type of product, get endorsements from relate parties if the system focuses on a specific domain etc. Most successful applications had unique strategies applied that suited their purpose as show in Fig. 3, which could be one of the reasons of their success. Overall, the strategies that were applied in at least 4 out 7 top applications from Fig. 3 can serve as a guideline for e-commerce application designers.

By considering the strengths and weaknesses of existing applications and design recommendations stated above, e-commerce developers can build effective and usable applications that will benefit both the users and companies.

6 Limitations

This study analyzed e-commerce applications to identify persuasive strategies and their implementations using the PSD model, however, there are many other models with different strategies that were not considered. Also, we did not order any product during our analysis; there are many steps that are crucial to these applications after the ordering process i.e. tracking products, cancelling orders etc. Moreover, we did not use these applications for a longer period of time, many systems adapt and change their interfaces based on user behavior which was not possible to observe during the short period of our study. These limitations can be addressed in future studies to further validate our findings and identify new recommendations.

7 Conclusion

We conducted this study to analyze various e-commerce applications and how persuasive strategies are being used in these applications. We found many interesting results such as, finding the mostly used strategies (Personalization and Social Learning) and finding no relation between application's effectiveness and number of strategies used but uncovering a correlation between their popularity and number of strategies used. We also highlighted the strengths and weaknesses of the applications and offered design recommendations by inspecting the most successful applications that might benefit the designers of such applications.

Acknowledgments. This research was undertaken, in part, thanks to funding from the Canada Research Chairs Program. We acknowledge the support of the Natural Sciences and Engineering Research Council of Canada (NSERC) through the Discovery Grant.

References

1. Adaji, I.: Towards improving e-commerce users persuasive technology. In: Proceedings of the 25th Conference on User Modeling, Adaptation and Personalization, UMAP 2017, pp. 318–321. Association for Computing Machinery, New York (2017). https://doi.org/10.1145/3079628.3079707

2. Adaji, I., Oyibo, K., Vassileva, J.: The effect of gender and age on the factors that influence healthy shopping habits in e-commerce. In: Proceedings of the 26th Conference on User Modeling, Adaptation and Personalization, UMAP 2018, pp. 251–255. Association for Computing Machinery, New York (2018). https://doi.org/10.1145/3209219.3209253

3. Alhammad, M.M., Gulliver, S.R.: Online persuasion for e-commerce websites. In: Proceedings of the 28th International BCS Human Computer Interaction Conference on HCI 2014 - Sand, Sea and Sky - Holiday HCI, BCS-HCI 2014, BCS, Swindon, GBR, pp. 264–269 (2014)

4. Cialdini, R.B.: Influence: Science and Practice, vol. 4. Pearson Education, Boston (2009)

5. Fogg, B.: A behavior model for persuasive design. In: Proceedings of the 4th International Conference on Persuasive Technology, Persuasive 2009. Association for Computing Machinery, New York (2009). https://doi.org/10.1145/1541948.1541999

6. Meder, M., Plumbaum, T., Raczkowski, A., Jain, B., Albayrak, S.: Gamification in e-commerce: tangible vs. intangible rewards. In: Proceedings of the 22nd International Academic Mindtrek Conference, Mindtrek 2018, pp. 11–19. Association for Computing Machinery, New York (2018). https://doi.org/10.1145/3275116.3275126

7. Nkwo, M., Orji, R.: Persuasion in ecommerce: a comparative analysis of western and indigenous African ecommerce. In: Proceedings of the Second African Conference for Human Computer Interaction: Thriving Communities, AfriCHI 2018, Association for Computing Machinery, New York (2018). https://doi.org/10.1145/3283458.3283516

8. Oinas-Kukkonen, H., Harjumaa, M.: Persuasive systems design: key issues, process model, and system features. Commun. Assoc. Inf. Syst. **24**(1), 28 (2009)

9. Orji, R., Oyibo, K., Lomotey, R.K., Orji, F.A.: Socially-driven persuasive health intervention design: competition, social comparison, and cooperation. Health Inform. J. **25**(4), 1451–1484 (2019)

10. Oyebode, O., Ndulue, C., Alhasani, M., Orji, R.: Persuasive mobile apps for health and wellness: a comparative systematic review. In: Gram-Hansen, S.B., Jonasen, T.S., Midden, C. (eds.) PERSUASIVE 2020. LNCS, vol. 12064, pp. 163–181. Springer, Cham (2020). https://doi.org/10.1007/978-3-030-45712-9_13

11. Singh, G., Kaur, H., Singh, A.: Dropshipping in e-commerce: a perspective. In: Proceedings of the 2018 9th International Conference on E-Business, Management and Economics, ICEME 2018, pp. 7–14. Association for Computing Machinery, New York (2018). https://doi.org/10.1145/3271972.3271993

12. Zhao, Q., Zhang, Y., Friedman, D., Tan, F.: E-commerce recommendation with personalized promotion. In: Proceedings of the 9th ACM Conference on Recommender Systems, RecSys 2015, pp. 219–226. Association for Computing Machinery, New York (2015). https://doi.org/10.1145/2792838.2800178

13. Zhu, Y., Yan, Z.: A survey on trust evaluation in e-commerce. In: Proceedings of the 9th EAI International Conference on Mobile Multimedia Communications, MobiMedia 2016, ICST (Institute for Computer Sciences, Social-Informatics and Telecommunications Engineering), Brussels, BEL, pp. 130–139 (2016)

Using Inspiration Cards for Designing Persuasive Technology to Improve Creative Situations

Max Jalowski(✉) ⓘ

Friedrich-Alexander-Universität Erlangen-Nürnberg (FAU), Chair of Information Systems
– Innovation and Value Creation, Lange Gasse 20, 90403 Nuremberg, Germany
max.jalowski@fau.de

Abstract. Persuasive technology is an established field of research that is applied in various domains. However, creative situations, collaborative, or knowledge-intensive processes are still underrepresented. Numerous established approaches exist for the design of persuasive technology. For this purpose, first applications for inspiration cards are already described in the literature. These serve as a source of inspiration in workshops and facilitate the communication between participants and designers. In this study, inspiration cards were used to facilitate the design of persuasive technology to improve creative situations. Applying a design science research approach, this study developed inspiration cards and a canvas. This artifact consists of 17 technology cards, 49 application cards, nine potentials cards and a canvas to structure the design process. The artifact was evaluated in a workshop in which a persuasive technology to support creative behavior in a creative situation was developed by the participants. The results advance the concept of inspiration cards for the design of persuasive technology, provides tools to better analyze a specific application context, that is, a creative situation, and may help promote the use of persuasive technology in an underrepresented field.

Keywords: Inspiration cards · Persuasive design · Creative situation

1 Introduction

Workshops are a widely used format for conducting collaborative processes. They are gaining more and more importance and are used by various organizations to carry out creative processes in groups. They are used, for example, to design new products, services, or business models. These creative processes are influenced by different characteristics, for example, cognitive abilities, knowledge, and intrinsic motivation on an individual level or the composition of a group and the task on a group level [1]. All these factors have an influence on creative behavior [1], which in turn, can be supported by persuasive technology [2]. Knowledge work and collaboration have been described as a challenging field for persuasive technology [3], but there are only a few studies addressing the use of persuasive technology in collaborative settings. Examples include user engagement in collaborative interaction [4], collaborative learning [5], and in virtual

© Springer Nature Switzerland AG 2021
R. Ali et al. (Eds.): PERSUASIVE 2021, LNCS 12684, pp. 231–244, 2021.
https://doi.org/10.1007/978-3-030-79460-6_19

teams [6]. Furthermore, there are various approaches to design persuasive technology, such as the eight-step design process [7] and persuasive system design [8, 9]. There has been some research regarding inspiration card-based approaches to the design of persuasive technology [10]. There are also preliminary works that have brought persuasive design principles into card format to be used in the technology design process [11]. These approaches address the design of persuasive technology in general. If one wants to develop a technology for a creative process, special points have to be considered because the use of a technology to support the participants is not yet widespread. Furthermore, there are special challenges and behaviors in collaborative and creative situations that should be considered when designing a technology [2]. For this purpose, the use of inspiration cards is suitable on three levels: (1) to identify and describe the challenges, (2) to select a suitable technology channel, and (3) to find generic application scenarios as a basis for developing an adapted persuasive technology. The present paper answers the following research question: *How can inspiration cards be applied to enable the design of persuasive technology to improve creative situations?*

2 Background

This section describes related work and background on the use of inspection cards, the design of persuasive technology, and the challenges presented in creative situations and how they can be addressed.

2.1 Inspiration Cards

Inspiration cards are a concept introduced by Halskov and Dalsgård [12] for use in the design process. Such a card contains an ID, a title, a description, an image, and some space for comments. The authors distinguish between different types of inspiration cards:

- Technology cards describe technologies in general or applications of a technology [12]
- Domain cards contain descriptions of the domain, for example, situations or people [12]

The cards are created by designers either in collaboration with domain experts or based on previous studies. They serve as inspiration in a workshop and facilitate communication between participants and designers [12]. As a method of application, the *inspiration card workshop* has been described as a means to develop new design concepts based on preliminary work in technologies and domains [12, 13]. Furthermore, it is possible to integrate other types of cards depending on the chosen concept [12].

The concept has been applied in several other studies; for example, in the form of 22 cards for communicating playful experiences. These can be used with two techniques: for brainstorming or in a scenario with a supporting game board [14, 15]. There are also preliminary works for the design of technologies, for example, with a set of 110 cards, a book, and a game board for the conception of the internet of things applications [16].

Existing research on persuasive technology has taken up the concept of inspiration cards. Davis [10] described an inspiration card workshop to generate ideas for new technologies to promote sustainable living. The technology cards were defined based on existing applications of persuasive technology. To define the persuasive features of a technology, Ren et al. [11] transformed the persuasive principles (cf. [8]) into cards for use in technology design workshops.

2.2 Canvases

A canvas is often used in design workshops to structure the process. Canvases are especially common in collaborative business model development. In this context, the Business Model Canvas is particularly well known. It is intended to facilitate understanding, discussion, creativity and analysis of business models [17]. It thus offers a means of visualization and can be seen as a tool that supports collaboration [18, 19]. A canvas can also be seen as a boundary object [18, 20] that helps to create a common understanding between different groups of people [21].

2.3 Designing Persuasive Technology

There are different approaches to designing technology; for example, classical software development processes using the waterfall model or more agile software development methods [22]. Also, research-oriented approaches like design science research [23] or participatory design [10, 24] can be applied. If a persuasive technology is to be developed, a special focus must be placed on behavioral change, for example by drawing on behavior theories [22].

A common approach in this context is the eight-step design process [7], which can be seen as best practice for the design of a persuasive technology. Especially relevant for this study are the following four steps: (3) find what prevents the target behavior, (4) choose a familiar technology channel, (5) find relevant examples of persuasive technology, and (6) imitate successful examples [7].

Research on *behavior change support systems* and persuasive system design puts more emphasis on the persuasion context. An accurate analysis of the persuasion context is important for successful behavior change, which can be analyzed in terms of intent, event, and strategy [9, 25]. Furthermore, 28 persuasive design principles are described in four categories to support the design and implementation of persuasive technology. The four categories are: (1) primary task support, (2) dialogue support, (3) system credibility support, and (4) social support [8, 9].

In addition to the approaches described above and the inspiration card workshop (cf. Sect. 2.1), there are other approaches to designing persuasive technology; for example, the integration of the persuasive system design model into a technology development process. The resulting persuasive technology design canvas contains three blocks: (1) analysis of the intention, (2) design of the content, and (3) design of the functionalities. In a co-creative session, participants can jointly develop a persuasive technology [22].

2.4 Challenges and Potentials in Creative Situations

The field of application for persuasive technology in this study were creative situations, Woodman et al. [1] describe them as "the sum total of social and environmental (contextual) influences on creative behavior" (p. 310). These influences consist of individual, group, and organizational characteristics. The focus of this study was on individual and group characteristics, in particular on cognitive abilities, intrinsic motivation, knowledge, group composition, task, and teamwork [1]. A previous study analyzed creative processes for potentials for persuasive technology and identified potentials on individual, group, and process levels [2]. Table 1 summarizes these potentials, which can serve as a starting point for designing a persuasive technology to support participants in creative situations.

Table 1. Potentials for persuasive technology on three levels as identified by [2].

Individual level	Potentials for persuasive technology
Ability	• Make non-routine behavior more simple and reduce physical effort and brain cycles • Structure and simplify the process • Sparks or facilitators as triggers • Present examples of what results might look like
Knowledge	• Increase knowledge about the tools used in the workshop • Provide facilitating triggers, including examples, support and explanations
Motivation	• Introduce a playful component or modern technologies • Track the progress of a workshop and show previous sub-results • Increase thematic interest
Group level	**Potentials for persuasive technology**
Composition	• Composition of the group as a success factor • Conduct self-tests before dividing into groups
Task	• Support the task by improving knowledge and ability • Better structuring or design of the task
Teamwork	• Capture the behavior of the group, e.g. discussions or passive participants, intervene through triggers • Increase involvement by supporting thematic interest • Introduce playful components to activate passive participants
General level	**Potentials for persuasive technology**
Time management	• Support a clear time management • Track speech times of participants
Task structuring	• Simplification of the task and division into subtasks • Guide through the task (tunneling)
Documentation	• Technology-supported documentation of the results • Influence on the outcome of a creative process during the process and in the follow-up

3   Research Design

To answer the research question, we followed the design science research methodology [26] to develop an artifact as a contribution to the knowledge base [27]. Design science research is popular in information systems research to create new and innovative artifacts [28]. Of the various approaches, this study chose a problem-centered approach [26] whose steps are described below.

Problem and Motivation. There is a lack of concrete approaches on how persuasive technology can be used in and designed for a challenging field, i.e. knowledge work and collaboration [3]. Previous research has provided approaches for how persuasive technology can be designed in general, and there are also first implementations for creative situations. However, there is no concrete approach to designing such a persuasive technology to improve a creative situation.

Objective. The artifact aims to develop inspiration cards that can be used together in a workshop to develop a persuasive technology to improve participant behavior in creative situations.

Design and Development. Building on existing design knowledge and on established approaches to the development of persuasive technology [7–9] and challenges in creative situations, as well as previous work on application scenarios for persuasive technology in design processes, 17 technology cards, 49 application cards, nine potentials cards, and one canvas were developed.

Demonstration and Evaluation. To demonstrate the artifact, it was applied in an artificial *ex ante* setting (cf. [29]). Afterwards a workshop was conducted to evaluate the artifact. Evaluation is a crucial part of a design science research approach and can be carried out regarding utility, functionality, and efficacy [28]. Evaluation can be artificial and naturalistic [30]. In this study, a naturalistic approach was chosen and the artifact was tested *ex post* in a real-word setting (cf. [29]) with users who wanted to design a persuasive technology (cf. Sect. 5).

Communication. The communication of the results is an important step in design science research [26] and takes place via this scientific contribution and further presentations at conferences.

4   Artifact Description: Inspiration Cards for Designing Persuasive Technology to Improve Creative Situations

The artifact consists of different subcomponents. As suggested by Halskov and Dalsgård [12], other types of inspiration cards were introduced. First, 17 technology cards were developed that named and described common persuasive technology platforms. The 49 application cards are used to select possible application scenarios. The nine potentials cards summarize common problems in creative situations that can be addressed by persuasive technology. The workshop process for designing the technology is structured via a canvas. The following sections describe the components.

4.1 Technology Cards

Technology cards are used to define the technology channel (cf. [7–9]) in such a way that it matches the participants of the creative situation. It should be chosen so that the participants are familiar with the technology to be developed. The cards are based on the extension of a previous study [31]. For this purpose, all papers of the PERSUASIVE conference since 2006 were analyzed; 449 different applications of persuasive technology were identified and then categorized into 17 technology platforms. Table 2 shows the technologies that were considered for the cards.

Table 2. Overview of existing persuasive technology platforms, extended based on [31].

Technology platforms	
Artificial intelligence & analytics	Physical tags
Augmented & Virtual Reality	Robotics
Collaboration Software	Sensors
Display & Stationary Computer	Smartphone & Mobile Device
Games	Speech, Sound & Video
Internet of Things	Wearables
Lights & Markers	Website & Web-based
Online Social Network/Social Software	Virtual Agent/Coach & Assistant
Persuasive Messages & Reminders	

Each technology card contains an ID, a title, a description of the technology, and an example of how it could be used. In addition, images are included to give an impression of how the technology would look or how it could be applied. Fig. 1 shows an example of a technology card.

4.2 Application Cards

Together with the potentials cards, the application cards represent the application domain. They are used to define possible implementations and should inspire the technology designers and facilitate the definition of the required features. The cards, like the technology cards, are based on an advancement of the scenarios described in Jalowski et al. [31]. Each card contains an ID, a title, and a description of how the scenario could be implemented. Furthermore, possible persuasive design principles (cf. [8, 9]) are mentioned and images are included to give an impression of how the application could look. Altogether there are 49 cards (IDs M1–M6, E1–E14, T1–T13, G1–G16), divided into four categories; there are scenarios that (1) help to create tangible things, (2) facilitate verbal communication, (3) encourage physical activity, and (4) support organizational processes. Depending on the size and objectives of the planned workshop, only appropriate categories should be chosen to reduce the number of application cards to be used.

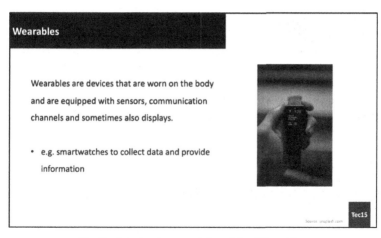

Fig. 1. A technology card describing *Wearables*.

In this study, each scenario was tailored to one technology, but in the future, could also be adapted for other technologies. The scenarios were designed to be as generic as possible and were based on sample implementations accessible via a QR code on the cards. Figure 2 shows an application card that describes a scenario to support general aspects. In a creative situation, technologies can be used to monitor progress and suggest further actions to the participants.

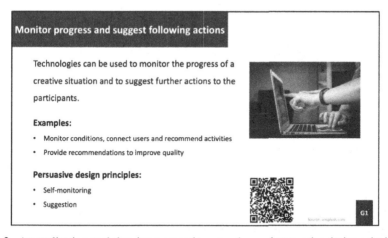

Fig. 2. An application card showing a scenario, examples, and persuasive design principles.

4.3 Potentials Cards

The potentials cards serve to better describe the application and persuasion context. There are nine potentials cards (IDs P1–P9) based on a study in which observations of workshops and interviews with workshop moderators and participants were conducted [2]. The cards are divided into three categories: individual, group, and general. Each category contains three components (see Table 1). Each card contains an ID, a title, a description of the component, possible starting points that suggest how a persuasive technology could be used, and an image to visualize the descriptions. The technology designer should identify behavioral patterns of the participants in relation to the respective components in order to design a technology based on them. Figure 3 shows an example of a potentials card.

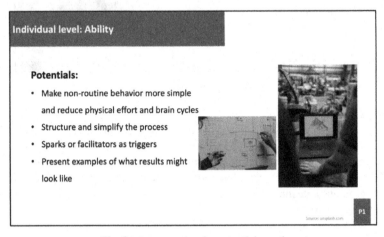

Fig. 3. An example of a potentials card.

4.4   Canvas

To facilitate the use of the inspiration cards, a canvas was developed to structure the design process. In a workshop for the design of a persuasive technology to improve a creative situation, the canvas should be placed on a wall. The technology designers can thus work together on planning the persuasive technology. The fields should be filled with sticky notes and the inspiration cards. Figure 4 presents a preview of the canvas.

The underlying process in this study is based on established methods, especially persuasive system design [8, 9] and the eight-step design process [7]. The design of the canvas follows a similar structure as other well-established canvases (cf. Sect. 2.2). The actual arrangement of the fields is based on the author's experience from a number of workshops structured by canvases. Furthermore, the designs were discussed with workshop facilitators and evaluated with participants (cf. Sect. 5). The following paragraphs describe the individual fields of the canvas.

First, the goal and topic of the workshop should be defined. Afterwards preconditions should be identified and noted. This includes the intent, the context and the strategy. First of all, the persuader should be identified; then, the intended outcome and change can be designed (cf. [8, 9]). The potentials cards (cf. Sect. 4.3) should then be used to identify problems and potentials in the creative situation to be improved. This should facilitate the definition of the use- and user-context (cf. [8, 9]). Based on this, the technology cards (cf. Sect. 4.1) are used to select one or more technologies that the participants are familiar with and that fit the defined context.

Once the preconditions have been set, the technology to be developed should be defined more precisely. The application cards (cf. Sect. 4.2) provide inspiration for possible implementations. By using the QR code to find examples, existing implementations can be imitated and adapted (cf. [7]). Based on selected application scenarios, basic features should be noted in the corresponding field and appropriate persuasive design principles should be chosen to better describe the persuasive component of the technology. Here, a combination with the *Perswedo* cards [11] is possible.

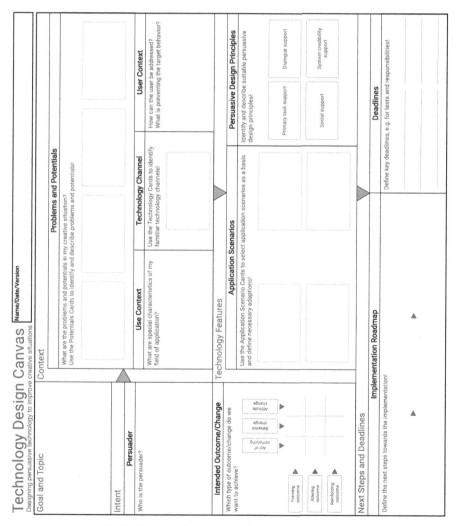

Fig. 4. Preview of the evaluated and improved canvas.

Finally, the roadmap should be defined and responsibilities determined: when will the implementation start? How and when can the implementation be tested and adapted? When could one start using the technology?

5   Demonstration and Evaluation

Demonstration and evaluation are important aspects of a design science research approach [26, 28]. The demonstration shows the applicability of the artifact. Therefore, it is applied to an existing persuasive technology. In a virtual setting, participants were asked to collaboratively work on requirements and challenges for the development of AI-based business models. They were supported by a persuasive technology that structured the task and divided it into subtasks (*reduction*), led through the process (*tunneling*), and provided messages with explanations and reminders (*reminders*). From a potentials card point of view, the technology primarily addressed the individual level, that is, cards P1–P3, the structure of the task (P8), and time management (P7). From a technology card perspective, a website (Tec16), persuasive messages, reminders (Tec9), and color markers (Tec7) were used. The following application scenarios were identified as the basis: involve passive people, provide triggers and reminders (G8), collaboration by supporting decision making and explaining or recommending actions (G12), show additional data or background information about certain items (G16), display the state of different tasks to motivate and influence participation (E3), show short text messages or explanatory sentences to start discussions (T3), supply triggers to motivate and remind participants (M5). Figure 5 shows screenshots of the described technology and three of the inspiration cards (P8, G8, G12).

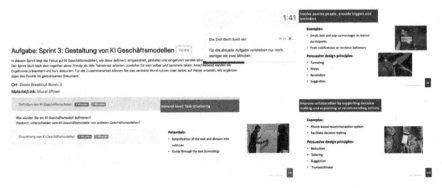

Fig. 5. Screenshots of the technology and a selection of suitable inspiration cards.

After the applicability of the artifact could be shown in an artificial *ex ante* setting [29], the artifact was applied in a real setting. An inspiration card workshop was held with the cards and the canvas presented in Sect. 4. The goal of the workshop was to design a persuasive technology that supports the development of an AI-based business model. This technology should also be applicable in a virtual creative process. The focus is especially on the individual support of the participants, who are usually not experts in business model development.

The inspiration card workshop was also conducted virtually, with participants taking part in a video conference and working in parallel on a virtual collaboration board. All potentials cards, all technology cards, and all general level application cards were present on the collaboration board. The participants were able to become familiar with the cards and drag them directly onto the canvas. Furthermore, virtual sticky notes were available to fill the fields of the canvas. Figure 6 shows a screenshot of the collaboration board.

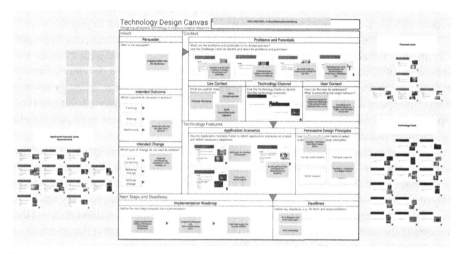

Fig. 6. Screenshot of the collaboration board after the evaluation workshop. The collaboration board and its built-in elements are under copyright of Conceptboard, conceptboard.com.

After the workshop, participants were asked whether the cards were helpful for understanding and designing the persuasive technology. The application cards, which provided clear examples of how persuasive technology could be used, were particularly highlighted. These served as an inspiration for the more precise design of the technology. Some of the participants were not experts in conducting workshops, and for these, the potentials cards were also helpful. More experienced participants remarked that the potentials were too generic and could not be used directly for the analysis of the existing creative setting. Furthermore, the technology cards in particular contained too few descriptions, which had to be adapted in a revised version (cf. Fig. 1). Based on the feedback of the participants and the reviewers of this paper, the canvas was also adapted slightly. Overall, the participants emphasized the applicability of the artifact, which could help facilitate the design of persuasive technology to improve participant behavior in creative situations.

6 Discussion and Conclusion

The results of this study have several contributions. First, the concept of inspiration cards is further elaborated in persuasive technology research and specialized and tailored to a specific application domain. Previous studies have introduced the concept and described first applications [10, 24] or supported a specific aspect of the persuasive design principles [11]. The artifact presented here combines the cards with a specific canvas to structure the technology design workshop. Furthermore, the findings offer the potential to support an underexplored field (i.e., knowledge work and collaboration [3]) and thus contribute to the development of new persuasive technology for this field. Creative situations are often knowledge intensive and are conducted in groups, so collaboration between the participants plays a major role. Through the concrete approach to technology development and the specific focus on the domain, the author hopes that the concepts will be taken up and new persuasive technology will be developed for this field, which can then provide a further contribution to research. From a design science research perspective, the artifact is an exaptation (cf. [27]) where known solutions (i.e., inspiration cards for the design of technologies) are applied to a new application field (i.e., creative situations).

Furthermore, the artifact builds on existing design methods for persuasive technology [7, 8, 22]. Thus, it contributes to the generation of new insights for these methods and their further application in a new field. Furthermore, the cards and the canvas help analyze the persuasion and the application context (cf. [8, 9]) more precisely and thus develop a more suitable persuasive technology. In particular, the potentials cards and the structure of the canvas come into account. The technology cards support the selection of a suitable technology channel (cf. [7–9]). The application cards support the identification and imitation of existing persuasive technology (cf. [7]).

Even though the concept described has a specific domain focus, many elements can be used to design persuasive technology in general without further adaptation. For example, the canvas and the technology cards would only need to be slightly adapted to increase their general applicability. The entire concept would then have to be evaluated on a larger scale. For practitioners, the artifact represents a good approach that is based on existing design methods (cf. [12]) to facilitate the development of a persuasive technology.

This paper has presented a novel approach to the development of persuasive technology for improving creative situations. The introduced artifacts consisted of 75 inspiration cards in three categories and a canvas to structure an inspiration card workshop. First applications show that, especially the application cards, support the technology design. By following established concepts of persuasive technology research, the ideas presented here can be combined with a variety of existing approaches as described above.

Limitations of the study primarily result from the low number of implementations and the fact that the COVID-19 pandemic has so far allowed only virtual workshops. However, the underlying concepts of the inspiration cards and the canvas have been presented and published in several scientific formats and discussed with practitioners, which underlines the relevance of the topic. Future work should focus on further implementations of the concepts in order to gain deeper insights for the design of persuasive technology to improve creative situations.

References

1. Woodman, R.W., Sawyer, J.E., Griffin, R.W.: Toward a theory of organizational creativity. Acad. Manag. Rev. **18**(2), 293–321 (1993)
2. Jalowski, M., Schymanietz, M., Möslein, K.M.: Supporting participants in creative processes: opportunities for persuasive technology in participatory design. In: Proceedings of the Forty-First International Conference on Information Systems 2020, India (2020)
3. Torning, K., Oinas-Kukkonen, H.: Persuasive system design: state of the art and future directions. In: Proceedings of the 4th International Conference on Persuasive Technology (2009)
4. Stibe, A., Oinas-Kukkonen, H.: Designing persuasive systems for user engagement in collaborative interaction. In: Proceedings of European Conference on Information Systems 2014 (2014)
5. Challco, G.C., Andrade, F., Oliveira, T., Isotani, S.: Towards an Ontological Model to Apply Gamification as Persuasive Technology in Collaborative Learning Scenarios. An. do XXVI Simpósio Bras. Informática na Educ. (SBIE 2015) (2015)
6. Peng, C.-H., Lurie, N.H., Slaughter, S.A.: Using Technology to persuade: visual representation technologies and consensus seeking in virtual teams. Inf. Syst. Res. **30**(3), 948–962 (2019)
7. Fogg, B.: Creating persuasive technologies: an eight-step design process. In: Proceedings of 4th International Conference on Persuasive Technology (2009)
8. Oinas-Kukkonen, H., Harjumaa, M.: A systematic framework for designing and evaluating persuasive systems. In: Oinas-Kukkonen, H., Hasle, P., Harjumaa, M., Segerståhl, K., Øhrstrøm, P. (eds.) PERSUASIVE 2008. LNCS, vol. 5033, pp. 164–176. Springer, Heidelberg (2008). https://doi.org/10.1007/978-3-540-68504-3_15
9. Oinas-Kukkonen, H., Harjumaa, M.: Persuasive systems design: key issues, process model, and system features. Commun. Assoc. Inf. Syst. **24**, 485–500 (2009)
10. Davis, J.: Generating directions for persuasive technology design with the inspiration card workshop. In: Ploug, T., Hasle, P., Oinas-Kukkonen, H. (eds.) PERSUASIVE 2010. LNCS, vol. 6137, pp. 262–273. Springer, Heidelberg (2010). https://doi.org/10.1007/978-3-642-13226-1_26
11. Ren, X., Lu, Y., Oinas-Kukkonen, H., Brombacher, A.: Perswedo: introducing persuasive principles into the creative design process through a design card-set. In: Bernhaupt, R., Dalvi, G., Joshi, A., K. Balkrishan, D., O'Neill, J., Winckler, M. (eds.) INTERACT 2017. LNCS, vol. 10515, pp. 453–462. Springer, Cham (2017). https://doi.org/10.1007/978-3-319-67687-6_31
12. Halskov, K., Dalsgård, P.: Inspiration card workshops. In: Proceedings of the 6th ACM Conference on Designing Interactive Systems - DIS '06, pp. 2–11. ACM Press, New York (2006)
13. Halskov, K., Dalsgaard, P.: The emergence of ideas: the interplay between sources of inspiration and emerging design concepts. CoDesign **3**(4), 185–211 (2007)
14. Lucero, A., Arrasvuori, J.: PLEX cards: a source of inspiration when designing for playfulness. In: Proceedings of the 3rd International Conference on Fun and Games - Fun and Games 2010, pp. 28–37. ACM Press, New York (2010)
15. Lucero, A., Arrasvuori, J.: The PLEX cards and its techniques as sources of inspiration when designing for playfulness. Int. J. Arts Technol. **6**(1), 22–43 (2013)
16. Mora, S., Gianni, F., Divitini, M.: Tiles: a card-based ideation toolkit for the Internet of Things. In: Proceedings of the 2017 Conference on Designing Interactive Systems, pp. 587–598. ACM, New York (2017)
17. Osterwalder, A., Pigneur, Y.: Business Model Generation: A Handbook for Visionaries, Game Changers, and Challengers. John Wiley, Hoboken, New Jersey (2010)

18. Eppler, M.J., Hoffmann, F., Bresciani, S.: New business models through collaborative idea generation. Int. J. Innov. Manage. **15**(6), 1323–1341 (2011)
19. Joyce, A., Paquin, R.L.: The triple layered business model canvas: a tool to design more sustainable business models. J. Clean. Prod. **135**(1), 1474–1486 (2016)
20. Hakanen, T., Murtonen, M.: Service business model canvas: a boundary object operating as a business development tool. Int. J. Ind. Syst. Eng. **9**(8), 2687–2692 (2015)
21. Star, S.L., Griesemer, J.R.: Institutional ecology, "Translations" and boundary objects: amateurs and professionals in Berkeley's museum of vertebrate zoology, 1907–39. Soc. Stud. Sci. **19**(3), 387–420 (1989)
22. Harjumaa, M., Muuraiskangas, S.: Building persuasiveness into information systems. Electron. J. Inf. Syst. Eval. **17**(1), 23–35 (2014)
23. Oyibo, K.: Designing culture-based persuasive technology to promote physical activity among university students. In: UMAP 2016 – Proceedings of 2016 Conference on User Modeling, Adaptation and Personalization, pp. 321–324 (2016)
24. Davis, J.: Early experiences with participation in persuasive technology design. In: PDC 2012: Proceedings of the 12th Participatory Design Conference, pp. 119–128 (2012)
25. Oinas-Kukkonen, H.: A foundation for the study of behavior change support systems. Pers. Ubiquit. Comput. **17**(6), 1223–1235 (2013)
26. Peffers, K., Tuunanen, T., Rothenberger, M.A., Chatterjee, S.: A design science research methodology for information systems research. J. Manage. Inf. Syst. **24**(3), 45–78 (2007)
27. Gregor, S., Hevner, A.R.: Positioning and presenting design science research for maximum impact. MIS Q. **37**(2), 337–355 (2013)
28. Hevner, A.R., March, S.T., Park, J., Ram, S.: Design science in information systems research. MIS Q. **28**(1), 75–105 (2004)
29. Sonnenberg, C., vom Brocke, J.: Evaluations in the science of the artificial – reconsidering the build-evaluate pattern in design science research. In: Peffers, K., Rothenberger, M., Kuechler, B. (eds.) DESRIST 2012. LNCS, vol. 7286, pp. 381–397. Springer, Heidelberg (2012). https://doi.org/10.1007/978-3-642-29863-9_28
30. Venable, J.: A framework for design science research activities. In: Proceedings of the 2006 Information Resource Management Association Conference (CD) (2006)
31. Jalowski, M., Fritzsche, A., Möslein, K.M.: Applications for persuasive technologies in participatory design processes. In: Oinas-Kukkonen, H., Win, K.T., Karapanos, E., Karppinen, P., Kyza, E. (eds.) PERSUASIVE 2019. LNCS, vol. 11433, pp. 74–86. Springer, Cham (2019). https://doi.org/10.1007/978-3-030-17287-9_7

Users Want Diverse, Multiple, and Personalized Behavior Change Support: Need-Finding Survey

Mina Khan[✉], Glenn Fernandes, and Pattie Maes

MIT Media Lab, 75 Amherst St., Cambridge, MA, USA
glennfer@mit.edu, pattie@media.mit.edu

Abstract. Behavior change research usually takes a theory-driven or application-specific approach. We took a user-centered view of real-world user needs and conducted a survey with 53 participants to investigate the overall behavior change goals and support preferences of everyday users. Our survey revealed three key themes. First, individual users have *multiple* behavior change goals, desired context types for behavior change reminders, and desired activities for self-tracking. Second, users have *diverse and personalized* desired actions, implementations, contexts, and reminders for their behavior change goals, as well as *diverse* preferences for behavior change support features and sensors. Third, users want to set custom *personalized* goals, reminder contexts, reminder messages, and even train custom machine learning models. Thus, users want multiple, diverse, and personalized behavior change support in the real world. We suggest a 'convergence with connection and customization' approach to meet the diverse, multiple, and personalized behavior change needs of everyday users.

Keywords: Persuasive technology · User survey · Need-finding · Self-tracking · Goals · Reminders · Sensors · Personalization

1 Introduction

Behavior change is a rich field of research and a burgeoning industry. While there are multiple behavior change theories and technologies, we take a user-centered view of real-world behavior change needs. In particular, our work investigates two questions – what are the behavior change goals of people and what type of behavior change support do people want?

While specific behavior change applications are common, real-world health and well-being is interconnected, e.g., as evident by the co-morbidity of diseases and the focus of lifestyle/preventive medicine on multiple health behavior change [19]. Also, research shows that behavior change is a holistic process [21]. Thus, we take the user as a unit and focus on the holistic needs of everyday users, instead of targeting a specific behavior, support technique, or population group.

© Springer Nature Switzerland AG 2021
R. Ali et al. (Eds.): PERSUASIVE 2021, LNCS 12684, pp. 245–255, 2021.
https://doi.org/10.1007/978-3-030-79460-6_20

We conducted a survey, N = 53 participants, to investigate the behavior change goals and support preferences of everyday users. Our results show that users have multiple, diverse, and personalized behavior change goals and support preferences – *Multiple:* Users have multiple behavior change goals (Q1), want to track multiple activities (Q10), and want support in multiple contexts (Q9); *Diverse:* Users have diverse behavior change goals (Q1), target actions (Q2), target implementations (Q3), target implementation contexts (Q4), and preferences for behavior change reminders (Q5) and sensors (Q8); *Personalized:* Users want to set custom personalized goals, intervention contexts, and intervention messages, and even train machine learning models on custom personalized data (Q7).

Our survey highlights multiple, diverse, and personalization behavior change needs of users. Self-guided change is the most common form of long-term maintained health behavior change [3] and we recommend a user-centered approach to address the multiple, diverse, and personalization behavior change needs of users to help translate behavior change research to the real world.

2   Related Work

There are several behavior change theories [6] and persuasive technologies that employ different theories and strategies [14,17]. There are also several commercial applications [15] and reviews of what users like in those applications [1]. While some technologies apply specific strategies, e.g., personal informatics [7] and just-in-time interventions [13], others focus on specific domains, e.g., mental health [2,11]. We take a user-centered approach to behavior change and focus on identifying the behavior change goals and support preferences of users, not on creating or evaluating different behavior change theories, systems, or techniques.

User-centered studies are common in behavior change, but are mostly focused on specific application areas or behavior change techniques and there is not much work on identifying the holistic everyday user needs. Some examples of user-centered studies for specific behavior change applications include applications areas like sustainable household recycling [4], self-monitoring at work [10], and smoking cessation using digital communities [12]. Users' contextual needs have also been studied for specific behavior change applications, e.g., diabetes management [20] and physical activity [5]. Finally, there are investigations into user preferences for different behavior change strategies, e.g., personalized goals setting [8], self-experimentation [9], and habit-formation contexts [18]. While these studies go into details of specific strategies or application domains, they do not account for the holistic behavior change needs of everyday users.

We take a user-centered approach towards holistic, not application or theory specific, user needs. The work we found closest to our work is Rapp et al.'s user interviews about 'how individuals live, account for, and manage life changes'

[21]. Our survey takes a similar user-centered approach to holistic behavior change, but we investigate what, when, and how the users would like to change, along with their desired behavior change support preferences, e.g., context-aware reminders, activities for self-tracking, sensors, personalization, and self-reflection notes. Thus, while Rapp et al. focus on the nature of behavior change, our work adds to their findings in terms of the behavior change support desired by users.

3 Survey Design

We identified three components of behavior change goals from previous behavior change literature: what (e.g., footsteps), how (number of footsteps), and when (e.g., after lunch). We also identified three types of support features: User tracking (including self-reflection, self-report, goal-tracking, sensor-based tracking, and self-tracking visualizations), reminder contexts, and reminder messages (including content and medium). Personalization is also a key theme in behavior change [15]. Based on the three components of behavior change goals and three types of behavior change support features, we designed a need-finding [16] survey to identify the behavior change goals (Q1–4) and support preferences (Q5–10).

The questions are in Table 1. We used common themes in Persuasive Technologies as the option categories [1,14,15,17]. *Q1 Goal categories:* fitness, diet, productivity, personal growth, mindfulness, calm, focus, mental health, sleep, meditation, healthy thought, healthy relationships, and other/add custom. *Q6 Overall support features:* daily activity tracking, context-aware reminders, machine learning support, self-reflection notes, and goal progress tracking. *Q7 Customization for personalization:* goals, reminder contexts, reminder messages, and machine learning models. *Q8 Sensing types:* camera, microphone, heart rate, motion, location. *Q9 Reminder Contexts:* specific times, enter/leaving locations, indoor locations, specific daily activities, physiology/emotions, self-identified thoughts, people/face, specific objects, and other/add custom. *Q10: Activities for self-tracking:* diet, physical activity, heart rate, work, phone usage, computer usage, self-reported thoughts, social interactions, sleep, other/add custom.

We shared our 'behavior change survey' via department email lists and social media, without any exclusion or inclusion criteria or compensation. We received 53 responses ($\mu = 29.5$ yrs, $\sigma = 11.0$ yrs; 21 males, 31 females, 1 unknown; 5 countries, including 3 USA states; 15 students, 24 professionals, 14 unknown).

Table 1. Survey questions about desired behavior change goals and support preferences

#	Questions	Response type
1	Behavior change areas: 12 categories + custom/other	Multiple select
-	Select One Target Behavior Change (Q2-5)	
2	What would you do?	Open-Ended
3	How would you do it?	Open-Ended
4	When would you do it?	Open-Ended
5	How would you remind yourself?	Open-Ended
6	Overall support features: 5 categories	Yes/No/Maybe each
7	Customized and personalized features: 4 categories	Yes/No/Maybe each
8	Sensors: 5 categories	Yes/No/Maybe each
9	Contexts for reminders: 8 Categories + custom	Multiple select
10	Activities for self-tracking: 9 Categories + custom	Multiple select

4   Results

The results for each survey question are below and the figures are in Appendix.

Q1. Behavior Change Categories: Each participant selected *multiple* categories, an average of 5.5 categories ($\sigma = 3.2$) out of 13: Fitness (64%), Diet (57%), Productivity (53%), Personal Growth (49%), Mindfulness (47%), Calm (42%), Focus (40%), Mental Health (40%), Sleep (38%), Meditation (38%), Healthy Thoughts (38%), Healthy Relationships (36%), and Other (4%). See Fig. 1.

Q2. What would you do?: The responses varied from health-related actions (e.g. weight loss, healthy eating, better sleep, and exercise) to learning-related goals (e.g., learn a new spoken or coding language) to mindfulness goals (e.g., "be more mindful so that I'm not distracted by initial struggles and stick to the self-development plan I've drawn out for myself", "Bring unconscious behaviors, patterns, thoughts to consciousness to be more aware in my relationships") and even broad goals ("giving my best effort"). The responses show that individual goals are *diverse* and *personalized* and even dynamic and exploratory, e.g., to "Live a FULL life". Figure 2 (left) shows the word cloud for the responses.

Q3. How would you do it?: The responses were *diverse and personalized.* For example, "practice mindfulness for a minute or two every few hours", "Meditate once every morning", "Journaling, noticing thoughts or behaviors", "Do 7-minute workouts", "Learning a few words a day", "Lay out a bowl and oatmeal", "sleep half an hour earlier" "Keeping fruits or nuts in bag", "Only opening max 2 tabs", etc. Even when users had similar goals (Q2), they had different desired implementations (Q3). Figure 2 (right) shows the word cloud for the responses.

Q4. When would you do it?: People chose *diverse and personalized* contexts, e.g., working, eating, meditating, exercising, reaching home, waking up, standing up, brushing teeth, doing my nails, sleeping, starting work, putting on night pajamas, answering text message, getting anxious, ordering food, reading messages, leaving home, etc. Figure 3 shows the word cloud for the responses.

Q5. How would you remind yourself?: Participants chose reminders using *diverse* mediums, with audio reminders (45%) being the most common one, followed by text (25%) and 'ambient' notes (14%), and rest 'none'. The participants also included *personalized* reminder messages. 25% responses also involved self-tracking goals and activities. Figure 3 shows the word cloud for the responses.

Q6. Overall Support Features: At least 50% said 'Yes' (N = No, M = Maybe, Y = Yes) to daily activity tracking (3N, 18M, 32Y), context-aware reminders (2N, 16M, 35Y), machine learning support (4N, 20M, 29Y), self-reflection notes (6N, 21M, 26Y), and goal-progress tracking (0N, 11M, 42Y). The preferences were *multiple and diverse*. The results are in Fig. 4.

Q7. Customization for Personalized Support: Over 50% said 'Yes' (N = No, M = Maybe, Y = Yes) to setting custom *personalized* goals (1N, 22M, 30Y), reminder contexts (2N, 19M, 32Y), reminder messages (3N, 17M, 33Y), and machine learning model training (4N, 21M, 28Y). The results are in Fig. 5.

Q8. Sensors: Over 50% said 'Yes' (N = No, M = Maybe, Y = Yes) to wanting heart rate (6N, 9M, 38Y) and physical activity (9N, 11M, 33Y), but not location (10N, 19M, 24Y), microphone (12N, 19M, 22Y), and camera (23N, 17M, 13Y). The preferences were *diverse* and *personalized*. The results are in Fig. 6.

Q9. Reminder Contexts: Each participant selected *multiple* desired context categories, an average of 2.5 categories ($\sigma = 1.4$) out of 9: specific times (68%), enter/leaving locations (42%), indoor locations (38%), specific activities, e.g., eating, meditating, etc. (38%), physiology/emotion (21%), self-reported thoughts (21%), people/face (15%), and specific objects, e.g., mug (13%). See Fig. 7.

Q10. Activities for Self-tracking: Each participant selected *multiple* activity categories, average of 5.4 categories ($\sigma = 2.4$) out of 10: Diet (73%), physical activity (83%), heart rate (61%), work (58.8%), phone usage (64.7%), computer usage (51%), self-reported thoughts (61%), social interactions (41%), sleep (53%), and other - meditation (2%), alcohol/cigarettes (2%), social (2%). See Fig. 8.

5   Discussion

We discuss the findings, recommendations, and limitations of our survey below.

5.1   Key Findings

Our survey showed that users want multiple, diverse, and personalized behavior change support. Users have *multiple* behavior change goals (Q1), desired context types for behavior change reminders (Q9), and desired activities for self-tracking (Q10). Also, users have *diverse and personalized* desired actions (Q2), implementations (Q3), contexts (Q4), and reminders (Q5) for their behavior change goals, as well as *diverse* preferences for behavior change support features (Q6) and sensors (Q8). Finally, users want to set *personalized* goals, reminder contexts, and reminder messages, and even train custom machine learning models (Q7).

5.2   Key Recommendations

Our findings about the *multiple, diverse, and personalized* behavior change needs of users raise three key questions: *Multiplicity:* Given the multiple behavior change goals and support preferences for each user, how do the goals and strategies interact with each other? *Diversity:* How do we support the diverse needs and goals of each user?; iii. *Personalization:* How do we enable personalization?. We have the following recommendations for the aforementioned questions.

Multiplicity: Research usually takes a reductionist perspective and considers different behavior change goals and strategies in isolation to measure their independent impacts. However, it is important to take a holistic perspective and rigorously understand the interplay of different behavior change goals and strategies in the real world, especially since behavior change is a holistic and connected process [21]. Data collection and processing would be helpful to track the interactions between different behavioral goals and strategies over time.

Diversity: Both our survey and previous research shows that users prefer variety [1], and thus, we recommend diverse functionality in each behavior change application. Given the diverse sensing, reminders, and activity tracking needs of users, we suggest an open-source modular platform for behavior change with diverse sensing, output, and machine learning capabilities. Different users, developers, and researchers can experiment with different elements of the platform, add new elements to it, and report their results in a standardized manner.

Personalization: We recommend customizability of behavior change applications to enable each user or researcher to select their desired behavior change support preferences. We also recommend the use of Artificial Intelligence to allow machines to learn the best personalized strategies for each user in a transparent and human-in-the-loop manner. Finally, we recommend n-of-1 testing to evaluate the holistic experiences of different users with behavior change applications.

We jointly call the above recommendations 'convergence with connection and customization' because building for diversity creates convergence of difference techniques, whereas multiplicity enables connection and personalization enables customization. We urge interdisciplinary researchers to consider the *multiple, diverse, and personalized* behavior change needs of users, especially with the above recommendations in mind, to meet the real-world user needs.

5.3   Key Limitations and Future Work

We note three key limitations of our survey and recommend related future work. *First,* what users want is not necessarily best for them, and what users think they want may not be what they actually want. Thus, we recommend further evaluating the efficacy and user experience of multiple, diverse, and personalized behavior change support. *Second*, we also recommend longitudinal studies to evaluate the efficacy and user experience of multiple, diverse, and personalized behavior change support as user preferences and experiences change over time, especially as users use the different behavior change support. *Third*, we recommend evaluating the emergent trends and correlations in the longitudinal studies of multiple, diverse, and personalized behavior change support to note if different user preferences and experiences converge over time.

6 Conclusion

We took a user-centered approach towards behavior change and surveyed the behavior change goals and support preferences of users. Our survey showed that the behavior change needs and support preferences of users are *diverse, multiple, and personalized*. In particular, users have multiple behavior change goals and also, diverse and personalized target actions, implementations, contexts, and reminders preferences for their goals. Also, users want diverse and personalized behavior change support, including for goal-setting, activity tracking, intervention contexts, sensors, and machine learning. Thus, in tandem with the existing theory-driven and application-specific approaches, we recommend a user-centered and holistic approach towards user's *diverse, multiple, and personalized* behavior change support preferences to meet the real-world behavior change needs of users.

Appendix: Survey Result Visualizations

We provide visualizations of the results of each of the questions.

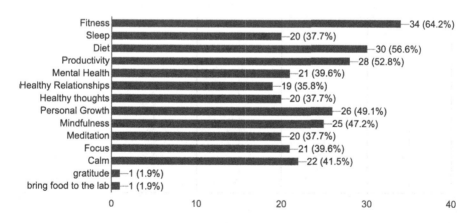

Fig. 1. Q1: Behavior change goal categories (Multiple select, 12 + other categories)

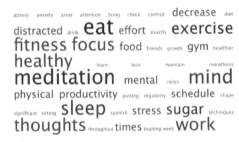

Fig. 2. Q2: What would you do? (Left); Q3: How would you do it? (Right)

become better changes constantly daily decrease distracted **eat** effort everyday everything **exercise fitness focus** food giving gym **healthy improve increase** life live maximal **meditation** mental miles **mind** module others person physical plan productivity putting refined schedule self-development **sleep** space start stick stop strengthen stress **sugar thoughts** times unconscious understand work

alarm **audio** breath calendar change computer control **deep** description done eat expecting goal **habit** hours ignore **intention** keep lets log marching **maybe** mediate meditate mental **morning** motivate needs **note notification phone** please practice prefer **reminder** seconds **simple** sound start **text** think thought today tried unrealistic ups wanted whatever **work** written

Fig. 3. Q4: When would you do it? (Left); Q5: How would you remind yourself? (Right)

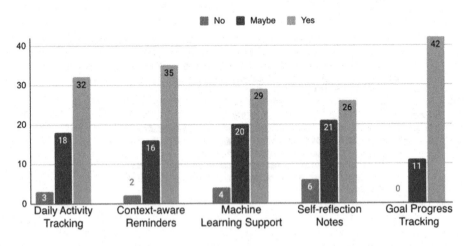

Fig. 4. Q6. Desired overall features for behavior change support

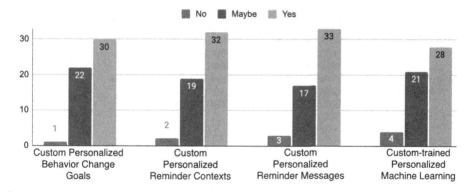

Fig. 5. Q7. Desired customization for personalized support

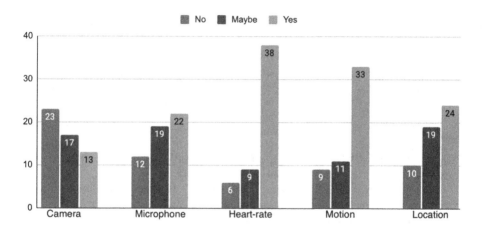

Fig. 6. Q8. Desired sensors

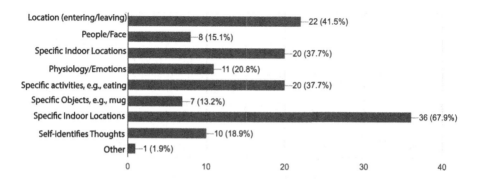

Fig. 7. Q9. Desired contexts for reminders

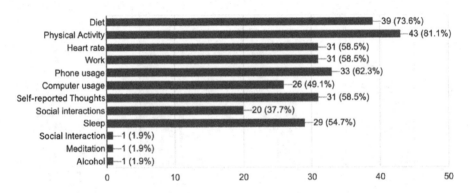

Fig. 8. Q10. Desired activities for self-tracking

References

1. Alqahtani, F., Orji, R.: Insights from user reviews to improve mental health apps. Health Inf. J. 1460458219896492 (2020)
2. Aung, M.H., Matthews, M., Choudhury, T.: Sensing behavioral symptoms of mental health and delivering personalized interventions using mobile technologies. Depress. Anxiety **34**(7), 603–609 (2017)
3. Bishop, F.M.: Self-guided change: the most common form of long-term, maintained health behavior change. Health Psychol. Open **5**(1), 2055102917751576 (2018)
4. Bremer, C.: Not (b)interested? Using persuasive technology to promote sustainable household recycling behavior. In: Gram-Hansen, S.B., Jonasen, T.S., Midden, C. (eds.) PERSUASIVE 2020. LNCS, vol. 12064, pp. 195–207. Springer, Cham (2020). https://doi.org/10.1007/978-3-030-45712-9_15
5. Choi, W., Park, S., Kim, D., Lim, Y.K., Lee, U.: Multi-stage receptivity model for mobile just-in-time health intervention. Proc. ACM Interact. Mob. Wearable Ubiquit. Technol. **3**(2), 39:1–39:26 (2019)
6. Davis, R., Campbell, R., Hildon, Z., Hobbs, L., Michie, S.: Theories of behaviour and behaviour change across the social and behavioural sciences: a scoping review. Health Psychol. Rev. **9**(3), 323–344 (2015)
7. Kersten-van Dijk, E.T., Westerink, J.H., Beute, F., IJsselsteijn, W.A.: Personal informatics, self-insight, and behavior change: a critical review of current literature. Hum.-Comput. Interact. **32**(5–6), 268–296 (2017)
8. Lee, J., Walker, E., Burleson, W., Hekler, E.B.: Understanding users' creation of behavior change plans with theory-based support. In: Proceedings of the 33rd Annual ACM Conference Extended Abstracts on Human Factors in Computing Systems, CHI EA 2015, pp. 2301–2306. Association for Computing Machinery, New York (2015). https://doi.org/10.1145/2702613.2732870
9. Lee, J., Walker, E., Burleson, W., Kay, M., Buman, M., Hekler, E.B.: Self-experimentation for behavior change: design and formative evaluation of two approaches. In: Proceedings of the 2017 CHI Conference on Human Factors in Computing Systems, CHI 2017, pp. 6837–6849. Association for Computing Machinery, New York (2017). https://doi.org/10.1145/3025453.3026038
10. Meyer, A.N., Murphy, G.C., Zimmermann, T., Fritz, T.: Design recommendations for self-monitoring in the workplace: studies in software development. Proc. ACM

Hum.-Comput. Interact. **1**(CSCW), 79:1–79:24 (2017). https://doi.org/10.1145/3134714

11. Mohr, D.C., Burns, M.N., Schueller, S.M., Clarke, G., Klinkman, M.: Behavioral intervention technologies: evidence review and recommendations for future research in mental health. Gener. Hosp. Psychiatry **35**(4), 332–338 (2013)

12. Myneni, S., Cobb, N., Cohen, T.. In pursuit of theoretical ground in behavior change support systems: analysis of peer-to-peer communication in a health-related online community. J. Med. Internet Res. **18**(2) (2016). https://doi.org/10.2196/jmir.4671. https://www.ncbi.nlm.nih.gov/pmc/articles/PMC4756252/

13. Nahum-Shani, I., et al.: Just-in-time adaptive interventions (JITAIs) in mobile health: key components and design principles for ongoing health behavior support. Ann. Behav. Med. **52**(6), 446–462 (2018)

14. Orji, R., Moffatt, K.: Persuasive technology for health and wellness: State-of-the-art and emerging trends. Health Inf. J. **24**(1), 66–91 (2018)

15. Oyebode, O., Ndulue, C., Alhasani, M., Orji, R.: Persuasive mobile apps for health and wellness: a comparative systematic review. In: Gram-Hansen, S.B., Jonasen, T.S., Midden, C. (eds.) PERSUASIVE 2020. LNCS, vol. 12064, pp. 163–181. Springer, Cham (2020). https://doi.org/10.1007/978-3-030-45712-9_13

16. Patnaik, D., Becker, R.: Needfinding: the why and how of uncovering people's needs. Design Manage. J. (Former Ser.) **10**(2), 37–43 (1999)

17. Pinder, C., Vermeulen, J., Cowan, B.R., Beale, R.: Digital behaviour change interventions to break and form habits. ACM Trans. Comput. -Hum. Interact. **25**(3), 15:1–15:66 (2018)

18. Pinder, C., Vermeulen, J., Wicaksono, A., Beale, R., Hendley, R.J.: If this, then habit: exploring context-aware implementation intentions on smartphones. In: Proceedings of the 18th International Conference on Human-Computer Interaction with Mobile Devices and Services Adjunct, pp. 690–697. ACM, September 2016

19. Prochaska, J.J., Prochaska, J.O.: A review of multiple health behavior change interventions for primary prevention. Am. J. Lifestyle Med. (2011). https://doi.org/10.1177/1559827610391883. https://journals.sagepub.com/doi/10.1177/1559827610391883. Publisher: SAGE PublicationsSage CA: Los Angeles, CA

20. Raj, S., Toporski, K., Garrity, A., Lee, J.M., Newman, M.W.: "My blood sugar is higher on the weekends": finding a role for context and lthe design of health Self-Management technology. In: Proceedings of the 2019 CHI Conference on Human Factors in Computing Systems, CHI 2019, pp. 119:1–119:13. ACM, New York (2019)

21. Rapp, A., Tirassa, M., Tirabeni, L.: Rethinking technologies for behavior change: a view from the inside of human change. ACM Trans. Comput. -Hum. Interact. **26**(4), 22:1–22:30 (2019)

Theory and Guidelines

Theory-Informed Design Guidelines for Shared Decision Making Tools for Health Behaviour Change

Cindel Bonneux[1]([⊠]), Gustavo Rovelo Ruiz[2], Paul Dendale[3], and Karin Coninx[1]

[1] Faculty of Sciences, HCI and eHealth, UHasselt-tUL,
Agoralaan, 3590 Diepenbeek, Belgium
{cindel.bonneux,karin.coninx}@uhasselt.be
[2] Expertise Centre for Digital Media, UHasselt-tUL,
Wetenschapspark 2, 3590 Diepenbeek, Belgium
gustavo.roveloruiz@uhasselt.be
[3] Faculty of Medicine and Life Sciences, UHasselt,
Agoralaan, 3590 Diepenbeek, Belgium
paul.dendale@uhasselt.be

Abstract. Recently, the design and development of persuasive applications to support behaviour change in healthcare have gained interest. However, achieving sustained behaviour change remains challenging. Shared decision making (SDM) is increasingly advocated for making preference-sensitive decisions. In SDM, the patient and caregiver combine the patient's preferences, values, goals, and context with the medical evidence and expert opinions to make an informed decision. The link between shared decision making and behaviour change has not yet been investigated thoroughly. Furthermore, there is little guidance on designing applications providing SDM support. In this paper, we focus on how SDM can help in achieving sustained behaviour change by presenting how SDM can bring in the caregiver perspective in the well-known, patient-oriented Fogg Behaviour Model. We propose seven principles to design a system aimed at supporting patients and caregivers during SDM encounters when making decisions regarding behaviour change. We conclude with an illustration of how our proposed design principles have been applied in two existing applications developed to support SDM for behaviour change.

Keywords: Shared decision making · Behaviour change · Design principles · Decision aids · Persuasion · eHealth

1 Introduction

Persuasive design focuses on attitude and behaviour change of users. As such, it can be used to incite new behaviours, or to change or reinforce existing ones [21]. Several theories and frameworks have been developed to inform the design of

© Springer Nature Switzerland AG 2021
R. Ali et al. (Eds.): PERSUASIVE 2021, LNCS 12684, pp. 259–274, 2021.
https://doi.org/10.1007/978-3-030-79460-6_21

persuasive applications, including the Fogg Behaviour Model [7], the Persuasive Systems Design Model [22], and the Behaviour Wizard Framework [8]. In the context of healthcare, persuasive design is often applied to help people adopting a healthier lifestyle. Examples include supporting people in smoking cessation, increasing physical activity, or eating healthier. However, achieving long-term health behaviour change remains challenging.

In chronic care, decisions often need to be taken on how to change the patient's lifestyle and habits. For example, when a person needs to lose weight, there are multiple possible behaviour changes: moving more, eating healthier, or a combination of both. When the patient decides to focus on moving more, there are again different options available e.g. increasing the daily step count, starting with a new sport, or joining a gym. It may not be feasible for a patient to go to a gym weekly (because of money, time, or travel restrictions), but the patient may want to start with a daily walk. For this type of situations, where there are at least two valid alternative treatment options and a trade-off has to be made by balancing pros and cons of each option, it is advocated that shared decision making should be used [30]. Shared decision making (SDM) combines the patient's personal preferences, values, goals, and context with the clinical evidence and expert opinions to make an informed decision [14,29]. A review on the effects of SDM [12] demonstrated that interventions showing an improvement in adherence, satisfaction, depression, and well-being all included treatment programs or contained multiple sessions. In all these interventions, patients had to make longer-term decisions and/or had a chronic disease. Despite these opportunities for SDM, there is limited research on using SDM in multiple patient and caregiver interactions [24] and the influence of SDM on behaviour change has not yet been investigated thoroughly.

To support caregivers in initiating a SDM process and help patients in stating their preferences in an encounter, different initiatives have been taken. Decision aids are tools (paper or digital) that support patients in SDM by making the decision explicit, offering information about the available options (and their pros/cons), and assisting in clarifying congruence between personal preferences/values and the decision. Numerous decision aids are being developed to support patients and caregivers in SDM. Using them leads to increased involvement in decision making, increased patient knowledge, and decreased decisional conflict related to feeling uninformed [27]. According to Hess et al. [10], the best moment to apply a decision aid depends on the nature of the decision to take. Depending on the decision at hand, the patient might be given a decision aid to review before the encounter, during the encounter, or at both time points. Using a decision aid during the encounter improves patients' knowledge and shows a trend towards better acceptability and less decisional conflict [11].

The International Patient Decision Aids Standards (IPDAS) Collaboration [6,13] defines a set of quality criteria for patient decision aids organized in ten dimensions. The quality criteria are rather generic and focus extensively on what information should be presented. The criteria can be used as a general guide for the design and development of a decision aid, since there are several criteria related to the development process, such as including needs assessment, review, and field testing with patients and caregivers. However, when looking at these criteria from an Human-Computer Interaction (HCI) point of view, we do not find any concrete guidelines on how to design patient decision aids. We can only find some rather general advice such as a patient decision aid should provide step-by-step decision making, support comparison of positive and negative features of the options, and include tools like worksheets or lists of questions to use when discussing the options. As a consequence, the criteria are too limited to be applied directly to design decision aids supporting a SDM conversation. Furthermore, the quality criteria focus on one-off decisions and do not explicitly take into account follow-up, revision and reversal of decisions in multiple encounters. In general, there has been little research from HCI point of view on how to design interactive decision aids to support the conversation during a SDM encounter. Given the growing number of decision aids being developed, there is an emerging need for concrete guidelines on how to design and evaluate interactive decision aids from an HCI point of view.

To address the aforementioned issues, we analyze existing frameworks and models for behaviour change and shared decision making from medicine and HCI. Based on our analysis, we argue that SDM can be used to achieve sustained health behaviour change. Bringing in the caregiver's perspective and striving for SDM can make patients feel better informed, more empowered, and as a result, more capable of achieving sustained behaviour change. The relationship between SDM and behaviour change has not yet been investigated thoroughly. We make this relationship more explicit and bring in the caregiver's perspective for behaviour change by mapping SDM on the well-known Fogg Behaviour Model [7]. Furthermore, we introduce seven design principles for designing systems to support SDM for behaviour change. Lastly, we illustrate the application of our design principles in two existing tools to be used during SDM encounters.

2 Bringing Together Shared Decision Making and Behaviour Change

In this section, we briefly describe some well-known frameworks and models for shared decision making and behaviour change from medicine and HCI. Furthermore, we describe the relationship between SDM and behaviour change. Lastly, we highlight the similarities between designing systems to support behaviour change and designing systems to support SDM for behaviour change and emphasize the added value of SDM.

2.1 Existing Models About Caregiver's Role and the Dialog Between Caregiver and Patient

The principles of SDM have been well-documented and described [18]. When striving for SDM, a consultation would go as follows. Patients and caregivers start by defining and/or explaining the patient's health problem that needs to be addressed. Caregivers present the available options and discuss pros and cons with the patient. Furthermore, caregivers elicit patient preferences and values and use their knowledge to make recommendations. The ability and self-efficacy of the patient are discussed to come up with a plan. During this process, both caregivers and patients check understanding of the information and provide further clarification when needed. Together, patients and caregivers select the best option (or decide to defer the decision) and arrange follow-up [18].

Elwyn et al. [5] describe three key steps of SDM for clinical practice: choice talk, option talk and decision talk. In the first step (i.e. choice talk) the caregiver ensures that the patient knows that reasonable options are available. During option talk, the caregiver focuses on explaining the available options in more detail. The consultation is ended with decision talk in which the patient and caregiver consider patient preferences and make the decision. Stiggelbout et al. [28] propose to have four steps for SDM by splitting decision talk in two separate steps (discussing patient preferences and making the decision), since it contains two quite distinct processes. We prefer to follow this approach of four steps for SDM as defined by Stiggelbout et al. since it makes the distinction between elicitation of patient preferences and making the decision more apparent.

As described above, most SDM models focus on the patient-caregiver diad. However, in the context of chronic care, it is important to recognize that often different stakeholders are involved including the patient, the informal caregivers, and different professional caregivers. For example, in the context of cardiac rehabilitation, there is a multidisciplinary team with dietitians, physiotherapists, psychologists, and cardiologists next to the general practitioner supporting the patient. Légaré et al. [16] defined the interprofessional SDM model (IP-SDM) comprised of three levels: the individual (micro) level and two (meso and macro) healthcare system levels. Their model was developed for primary care and as a consequence, highly applicable for chronic diseases.

It has been shown that decision aids improve patients' knowledge of the options and make patients feel better informed about what matters most to them [27]. However, there is often a mismatch between patients' preferences and caregivers' perceptions [4]. Therefore, Légaré et al. [15] suggest to target patients directly and not depend solely on caregivers' perception of the applicability of SDM. Furthermore, Elwyn et al. [5] propose to use decision aids during option talk. Patients and their caregivers are more likely to talk about a decision when using a decision aid [27]. Therefore, we focus in this paper on the design of digital, interactive decision aids that can be used during an encounter to facilitate shared decision making regarding health behaviour change. We refer to these interactive decision aids to be used during the SDM encounter as "SDM tools for behaviour change".

2.2 Existing Models About Designing for Behaviour Change

One of the most famous models for behaviour change is the Fogg Behaviour Model (FBM) [7], depicted in Fig. 1A. Fogg defines three factors for behaviour change to occur: (1) motivation, (2) ability, and (3) triggers. Assume a person needs to be more physically active to lose weight. For this behaviour change to take place, the person should have sufficient motivation, sufficient ability and an effective trigger. The person should be motivated to start exercising, but the person should also have the ability to do so. If the person does not have time to do sports or does not have money to pay a gym membership, this limits the person's ability. A possible trigger can be a doctor that tells the person that by being obese, he/she has an increased risk of cardiovascular disease. The FBM has been used extensively to inform the design of persuasive applications. However, the FBM focuses on the patient's perspective and does not take into account the caregiver's role. To add the caregiver's perspective and define the influence of SDM on behaviour change, we map SDM on the FBM in Sect. 2.3.

Oinas-Kukkonen et al. [22] describe the process to design and develop persuasive systems. First, it is crucial to understand the fundamental issues behind persuasive systems. Next, the designer analyzes the context for the persuasive system by recognizing the intent, event, and strategies for the use of a persuasive system. Finally, he/she designs actual system qualities for the new system. For this, the Persuasive System Design (PSD) Model suggests 28 design principles divided into four categories: primary task support, dialogue support, system credibility support, and social support. Examples of principles include personalization, simulation, self-monitoring, suggestion, and trustworthiness. The PSD principles are often applied in applications supporting health behaviour change and several of these principles are also applicable for the design of systems supporting SDM. Furthermore, the process to design and develop a persuasive system can be considered similar to the process to design a tool supporting SDM for behaviour change. This is discussed in more detail in Sect. 2.3.

2.3 Shared Decision Making for Behaviour Change

In this section, we investigate the relationship between SDM and behaviour change in more detail. The FBM [7] describes how to design systems to support behaviour change from a patient perspective. The FBM is illustrated in Fig. 1A. The patient icon (⚇) indicates the elements that refer to the patient's perspective. In this paper, we expand the FBM with the caregiver's role by showing how SDM can be mapped on the FBM in Fig. 1B. The caregiver icon (⚇) indicates the elements that we added to the FBM to define the caregiver's role.

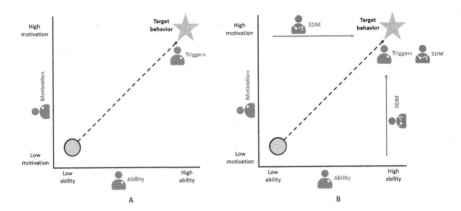

Fig. 1. A) The FBM that highlights the patient's perspective on designing for behaviour change. B) The relationship between shared decision making and behaviour change. Addition of the caregiver's perspective to the FBM. Based on the FBM [7].

As depicted in Fig. 1B, SDM leads to setting goals that are feasible and achievable. As such, SDM can increase a person's ability to perform the target behaviour. This increase in ability by SDM is denoted in Fig. 1B by the horizontal blue arrow. On the other side, SDM tends to increase motivation by making a public commitment. Also, social norms and social pressure (originating from the caregiver) can steer the patient's motivation to a higher level. The increase in motivation by SDM is denoted in Fig. 1B by the vertical blue arrow. Lastly, SDM can provide the necessary triggers for behaviour change by having a clear moment to reflect upon the behaviour change, state preferences, and make a decision and public commitment to work on it. This is illustrated by the label SDM next to triggers in Fig. 1B.

We illustrate this mapping of SDM on the FBM with an example. Assume a patient has a SDM encounter with a tobaccologist to discuss smoking cessation. The tobaccologist discusses with the patient the different options to quit smoking (e.g. medication, nicotine replacement therapy, individual or group counselling). Together with the tobaccologist, the patient decides to go for medication in combination with individual counselling. They discuss the patient's quit date and arrange a follow-up appointment. In this example, the tobaccologist helped the patient choosing a feasible quit date and a suitable combination of quit support (increase in ability). The patient made a public commitment by deciding together with the tobaccologist about smoking cessation and stating when he/she will quit smoking (increase in motivation). By having the encounter with the tobaccologist, the patient already set the first step in smoking cessation. Thinking about smoking cessation together with the tobaccologist and deciding on how to tackle it can initiate the patient's behaviour change (triggers).

We argue that SDM can help in increasing all three core components of the FBM. Nevertheless, we recognize that SDM does not solve all behaviour change challenges. SDM can be used to increase ability, enhance motivation and/or provide triggers, but this will not always be enough to achieve sustained behaviour change. We suggest that in those situations, a supporting, persuasive application that the patient uses while being at home can provide the necessary additional motivation, ability, and triggers.

The process to design a SDM tool for behaviour change is similar to the process described by Oinas-Kukkonen et al. [22] to design a persuasive system. First, the designer needs to understand the key aspects of shared decision making (e.g. the steps for SDM, the role of decision aids, and the quality criteria for decision aids). Next, the designer should analyze the SDM context. It is important to analyze the stakeholders in the decision-making process, the setting in which SDM will take place, and how much time will be available. Furthermore, it needs to be considered if the decision is a one-off decision or a decision about a long-term condition with multiple encounters in which the decision will be revised (i.e. chronic condition). Finally, the designer should define the actual system qualities for the new system. For this last phase, we propose seven design principles in Sect. 3.

3 Principles to Design SDM Tools for Behaviour Change

Based on our analysis of existing models, theories and frameworks and the relationship between SDM and behaviour change, we propose seven principles to design systems supporting shared decision making for health behaviour change. When reading these principles, imagine yourself designing a tool to support SDM for behaviour change (increase physical activity, eat healthier, or both) aiming at weight loss.

3.1 Give an Overview of the Current Status, the Target Situation, and the Available Options

The first step in the goal-setting and action-planning practice framework of Scobbie et al. [23] is goal negotiation. This step is devoted to showing where the patient is now and where the patient would like to get to in the future. In the context of behaviour change, two types of goals can be distinguished: 1) high-level, non-actionable outcome goals, and 2) lower-level, actionable behaviour change goals. When considering the example introduced above, the patient should lose weight and achieve a Body Mass Index of lower than 25 (outcome goal). To reduce weight, the patient can exercise, eat healthier, or can apply a combination of both (possible behaviour change goals). Assume the patient decides during the SDM encounter to focus on exercising (behaviour change goal). To achieve this, the patient can start a new sport, join a gym, or make a daily walk. When looking at this example, we can identify two times a set of available options: 1) possible behaviour change goals to achieve the outcome goal and 2) possible strategies to achieve the behaviour change goal. Both of these should be taken into account when designing a SDM tool for behaviour change.

The first step for SDM is for the caregiver to make clear to the patient that a decision has to be made, there are several options available, and the patient's opinion is important in choosing the best option [5,28]. When using a SDM tool for behaviour change, the tool should support the caregiver in conveying the current status, target situation, and available options to the patient. Therefore, a SDM tool should give an overview of this information, highlight the differences between the current status and target situation, and nudge the patient to reflect on the discrepancy between these two.

3.2 Encourage Collaborative Goal-Setting

According to the goal-setting theory of Locke and Latham [17], a specific, difficult goal leads to higher performance than urging people to do their best. The highest level of effort is achieved for tasks that are moderately difficult. Tasks that are very easy or very hard lead to the lowest effort. This is aligned with the reduction and tunneling principles of the PSD model [22]. When goals are difficult (which is often the case for behaviour change goals), commitment plays an important role. Two main factors contributing to goal commitment are: (1) the importance of goal attainment to the person, and (2) the belief that the person can attain the goal (self-efficacy). One possibility to enhance importance of goal attainment is by making a public commitment [17].

In the context of behaviour change, it is important to set specific, actionable goals. However, the outcome and behaviour change goals that the patient sets are often quite generic (e.g. losing weight until my Body Mass Index is below 25, eating healthier, or exercising more). When the patient sets such a goal, this goal should be paired with related, actionable goals (e.g. exercise 30 min per day, lower my daily calorie intake to 2000 kcal, or eat fish once a week) [19].

Shilts et al. [25] define 5 goal-setting types: self-set, assigned/prescribed, participatory/collaborative, guided, and group-set. In the context of SDM, participatory/collaborative and guided goal-setting are most interesting. In collaborative goal-setting, the goals are designed and chosen jointly by the caregiver and the patient, whereas in guided goal-setting, the caregiver proposes multiple goal choices and the patient chooses one of these. The effect of the goal source is an important factor to take into account [17]. Take the example of exercising more to reduce weight. When considering goal-setting, we could have collaborative or guided goal-setting together with a fitness expert or with a medical expert. Consolvo et al. [3] concluded that guided and collaborative goal-setting with a fitness expert are attractive to people. People desire to meet the fitness expert in person. They expect the expert to get to know their current abilities, constraints and long-term objectives before setting the goal, to follow-up on their progress, and adjust their goals over time. People not only find the options with a fitness expert appealing because of the expert's perceived knowledge and experience, but also the ongoing relationship. On the other side, people do not think of medical doctors to ask advice about physical activity. We can learn from the work of Consolvo et al. that patients prefer to take a decision regarding behaviour change together with a closer involved, specialized caregiver (e.g.

physiotherapist, dietitian, or psychologist) rather than with a medical doctor. A system should support the role of a medical doctor taking care of long-term follow-up on the process and the role of closer involved caregivers taking care of the daily activities, short-term feedback and follow-up.

Setting a goal collaboratively with a caregiver in a SDM encounter can help in setting a goal that is personalized, feasible and achievable. In the context of chronic diseases, the frequent encounters allow for follow-up and regular revisions of goals. SDM with a caregiver can be considered as such a public commitment. The patient feels social pressure to adhere to the goal. Furthermore, if there are follow-up SDM encounters in which they check progress and revise goals, this can provide extra motivation to adhere to the commitment since the patient will sit together with the caregiver later and will need to talk about his/her progress.

We suggest that during a SDM encounter a SDM tool should support the patient and caregiver in deciding first on a broader outcome or behaviour change goal (e.g. eating healthy). Next, the tool should guide them in setting specific, short-term goals that lead to achieving the behaviour change goal (e.g. eating 3 pieces of fruit daily). As such, a SDM tool for behaviour change should support the collaborative goal-setting of these short- and long-term goals. The tool should invite the patient and caregiver to discuss the patient's goals from a clinical point of view and assess how they match with the patient's preferences. The SDM tool should allow to record the mutually-agreed goals, so progress towards these goals can be assessed at follow-up encounters.

3.3 Support Making an Action Plan

After setting a goal, it is important to make a plan on how the patient will achieve the goal [23]. Planning is a mental simulation linking concrete responses to future events. It has been shown that planning is a powerful self-regulatory tool that can help to translate goals into behaviour. There are two types of planning: action planning and coping planning. Action planning refers to planning details of action implementation, whereas coping planning refers to defining detailed strategies to cope with expected obstacles and difficulties. It is suggested to include both these types of planning in interventions at different stages in health behaviour change [26]. When the goal is to exercise more, the action plan can be an exercise plan for next week. In the coping plans, the patient defines what he/she will do in case it is not possible to follow the exercise plan due to expected obstacles or difficulties. For example, when the patient planned to go for a run today but it is raining, he/she will go to the gym instead.

Another important aspect is the patient's self-efficacy, as it is an essential element of goal-setting and SDM [18]. When setting goals, it is important to assess the patient's confidence in achieving that goal. When the patient reaches the goal, this increases the patient's self-confidence about his/her ability to suc-cessfully achieve the target behaviour for this goal (or even a more difficult one) in the future [1,19].

A SDM tool for behaviour change should support the patient and caregiver in defining an action plan for the agreed behaviour change goal(s). The tool should provide support in constructing an action plan that is feasible for the patient and towards which progress can be followed up. The action plan should be recorded in the SDM tool, so the patient's adherence to the action plan can be assessed at follow-up encounters. Furthermore, importing the goals and action plans into a self-monitoring application can allow patients to follow-up on their progress and action plans between encounters.

3.4 Demonstrate the Effects of Behaviour Change

When looking at health behaviour change, people often know already what is the link between the cause and the effect and what are the benefits of making the behaviour change. For example, people know that you can improve your physical condition (effect) by going for a daily walk (cause) and they know that you will feel better (effect) by having a better physical fitness (cause). However, it is important to make this relationship between cause and effect explicit to a person from the start and to show you can succeed in achieving your targets. Having some examples and allowing patients to increase their self-understanding through small scale experiments is a key aspect of supporting positive behaviour change. It helps them in building a better model of how different activities and behaviours can contribute to their goal [19]. Simulation can be one approach to show the effect of behaviour change. An example is showing before-and-after pictures of people who have lost weight [22]. Allowing the patient to perform small scale experiments can also be linked with feedforward, e.g. by showing the effects of a specific action. An example can be showing how many calories will be burned by swimming for one hour.

During a SDM consultation, a SDM tool should support caregivers in demonstrating the effects of behaviour changes to their patients. The tool should let them collaboratively explore the effects of different actions. As such, the patient can improve his/her understanding of the different options and their effects. Having some visual representation of the data (e.g. before-after pictures, graphs, or pictographs) can help caregivers in conveying the information to the patient. Furthermore, references to literature can be included to increase the authority and credibility of the presented information.

3.5 Provide Suggestions or Tips

One of the key tasks of the caregiver in shared decision making is making recommendations for goals and how to achieve these to the patient, considering the patient's preferences and the clinical evidence [18]. In the PSD model, this can be linked to the principles personalization and suggestion [22].

Providing suggestions or tips as part of the system can help the caregiver during choice talk in making recommendations to the patient. Therefore, a SDM tool should provide suggestions or tips on how the patient can achieve the mutually-agreed goals by means of the action plans. The suggestions can be related to the action plan (e.g. getting suggestions about sports activities when making an exercise plan) or to the goals itself (e.g. recommended goals based on the patient's self-monitored behaviour). Furthermore, these suggestions and tips can be integrated into the demonstration of the effects of behaviour change. For example, when making a meal plan, the tool can recommend some healthy alternatives and show that these alternatives contain a lot less calories than the patient's current meals.

3.6 Enable Progress Follow-Up with Visual Elements

The last step in the goal-setting and action-planning practice framework of Scobbie et al. [23] is appraisal and feedback. This step includes evaluating the patient's performance in relation to the action plan and progress in relation to the goal. Self-monitoring apps are gaining interest to follow-up remotely on patient behaviour. In the PSD model, self-monitoring is described as keeping track of one's own performance or status to support the patient in achieving goals [22].

In the context of chronic care, the frequent encounters allow for progress follow-up. However, the huge amounts of information collected by means of self-monitoring applications can lead to information overload for caregivers. Therefore, it is important that SDM tools combine the collected information from self-monitoring applications in a meaningful way and present it in an appropriate format for discussion. Clear language and visualization of information are needed to support patients with varying levels of health literacy and digital literacy in understanding the presented information. In addition, SDM tools should provide a means to visualize the patients' adherence to the agreed action plans and their progress towards the mutually-agreed goals. Highlighting of important events and deviations from action plans can support caregivers in discussing progress and providing feedback. Showing the patient-collected data during the encounter does not only support caregivers in discussing the patient's progress, but also supports patients in reflecting on their behaviour and progress.

3.7 Give Feedback on Performance

Giving feedback to the patient is equally important as showing progress [23]. Providing feedback on performance can be linked to the principles praise and rewards from the PSD model [22]. To fulfill their role in SDM, caregivers should provide patients feedback on their performance and use the information provided by the system and by the patient to adjust the patient's goals and action plans accordingly. As such, it is a continuous process of refinement and updating of goals according to patient preferences and abilities.

When having SDM in chronic care, there are frequent encounters that allow for follow-up and feedback. During these SDM encounters, the SDM tool should support the caregiver in providing feedback to the patient. Colors, graphs, and icons can be used to give a concise and comprehensible overview of the information. Important events, achievements, or deviations from the plan should be highlighted to spark discussion.

4   Application of Our Design Principles

In this section, we demonstrate the feasibility of our suggested principles to design SDM tools for behaviour change through discussing some existing tools. We illustrate how these applications apply our proposed design principles.

In the context of cardiovascular disease (CVD) prevention, a huge amount of online CVD risk calculators are available [2]. Risk calculators can be used by patients at home prior to an encounter or during a SDM encounter with a healthcare professional to estimate a patient's CVD risk. The "What's your heart age?" risk calculator of NHS [20] is one example of a CVD risk calculator (Fig. 2). This risk calculator *gives an overview of the patient's current status, the target situation, and the available options to achieve the target situation* (Fig. 2A, C and D). The tool leverages the principle *demonstrate the effects of behaviour change* by allowing the patient to explore the effects of the possible behaviour changes (Fig. 2B). Furthermore, the tool gives some *suggestions* on how to achieve the goal in the form of simple steps to achieve the goal (Fig. 2C and D). These simple steps can *support making an action plan*. However, it is not possible to record the agreed goal(s) and associated action plan(s) in the tool. As a result, there is no possibility to *follow-up on progress* or *receive feedback on performance*. Also, there are no specific features or elements to encourage collaboration and spark discussion. The absence of these features can be attributed to the fact that a risk calculator is not designed specifically to be used during a SDM encounter. However, using a risk calculator during an encounter could support patients and caregivers in SDM.

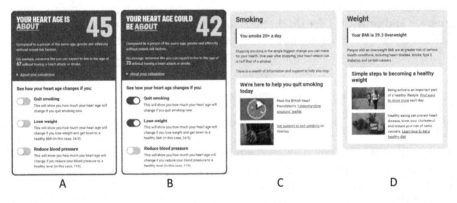

Fig. 2. Screenshots of the "What is your heart age?" risk calculator of NHS [20].

HealthDecision has developed several decision aids including some for SDM regarding behaviour change, such as their decision aid for hypertension [9] (Fig. 3). This decision aid *gives an overview of the current status, the target situation and the available options* (Fig. 3A, B and C). The tool allows the user to *demonstrate the effects of possible behaviour changes* by selecting the behaviour changes that the patient wants to make (Fig. 3A). The icon array depicting the patient's risk of a cardiac event (Fig. 3C) and the patient's estimated systolic blood pressure (Fig. 3B) are updated when different behaviour changes are selected. The tool provides *suggestions* which behaviour changes are possible to lower the patient's blood pressure (Fig. 3A), but does not provide specific tips on how to achieve the behaviour changes. Furthermore, there is also no *support in making an action plan.* Despite the decision aid is developed for discussion during a SDM encounter, there is no *support for recording the mutually-agreed goals, following up on progress,* or *giving feedback on performance.* This could be explained by the fact that it is an online, publicly available decision aid, which brings in issues related to storing sensitive patient data and protecting data privacy.

Our analysis of existing decision aids demonstrated how some of our proposed principles can be applied in the design of a SDM tool for behaviour change. It is not our intention to evaluate the chosen applications on their potential to achieve their goals, but to use them as illustrations of how our design principles can be applied. Both studied applications did not support recording of mutually-agreed goals, enable progress follow-up with visual elements, or give feedback on performance. This highlights possibilities for future research in these directions. Furthermore, there are still opportunities for improvement in encouraging collaborative goal-setting and supporting to make action plans. In general, we suggest to use all seven proposed design principles when relevant to guide the design and development of tools supporting SDM for behaviour change.

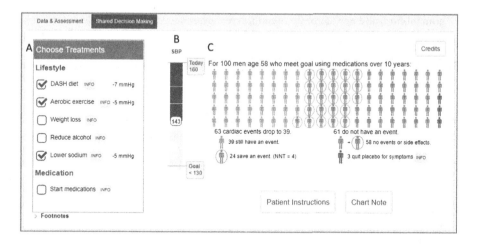

Fig. 3. Screenshot of the hypertension decision aid of HealthDecision [9].

5   Conclusion

Despite the increased attention for persuasive design and its application in the design and development of applications, achieving sustained behaviour change remains challenging. Shared decision making can be advocated as a means to increase the chances of success when making decisions regarding behaviour change. In this paper, we have made the relationship between SDM and behaviour change more apparent by mapping SDM on the Fogg Behaviour Model and adding the caregiver's role to this model. Furthermore, we proposed seven principles to design tools supporting SDM for behaviour change. Based on our design principles, we illustrated how two existing applications support SDM for behaviour change. There are still a lot of opportunities to enhance the support for discussion and collaboration during SDM. We hope that our proposed design principles can provide applicable guidelines to researchers and developers when designing SDM tools for behaviour change.

Acknowledgements. This research was funded by the Special Research Fund (BOF) of Hasselt University (BOF18DOC26) and the EU funded project H2020 IA CoroPrevention (848056).

References

1. Bandura, A.: Self-efficacy: toward a unifying theory of behavioral change. Psychol. Rev. **84**(2), 191 (1977)
2. Bonner, C., Fajardo, M.A., Hui, S., Stubbs, R., Trevena, L.: Clinical validity, understandability, and actionability of online cardiovascular disease risk calculators: systematic review. J. Med. Internet Res. **20**(2), (2018). https://doi.org/10.2196/jmir.8538
3. Consolvo, S., Klasnja, P., McDonald, D.W., Landay, J.A.: Goal-setting considerations for persuasive technologies that encourage physical activity. In: Proceedings of the 4th International Conference on Persuasive Technology, Persuasive 2009, pp. 8:1–8:8. ACM, New York (2009). https://doi.org/10.1145/1541948.1541960
4. Dierckx, K., Deveugele, M., Roosen, P., Devisch, I.: Implementation of shared decision making in physical therapy: observed level of involvement and patient preference. Phys. Ther. **93**(10), 1321–1330 (2013). https://doi.org/10.2522/ptj.20120286
5. Elwyn, G., et al.: Shared decision making: a model for clinical practice. J. Gener. Internal Med. **27**(10), 1361–1367 (2012)
6. Elwyn, G., et al.: Developing a quality criteria framework for patient decision aids: online international Delphi consensus process. BMJ **333**(7565), 417 (2006). https://doi.org/10.1136/bmj.38926.629329.AE
7. Fogg, B.J.: A behavior model for persuasive design. In: Proceedings of the 4th International Conference on Persuasive Technology, Persuasive 2009, Association for Computing Machinery, New York (2009). https://doi.org/10.1145/1541948.1541999
8. Fogg, B.J., Hreha, J.: Behavior wizard: a method for matching target behaviors with solutions. In: Ploug, T., Hasle, P., Oinas-Kukkonen, H. (eds.) PERSUASIVE 2010. LNCS, vol. 6137, pp. 117–131. Springer, Heidelberg (2010). https://doi.org/10.1007/978-3-642-13226-1_13

9. HealthDecision: Healthdecision (2020). https://www.healthdecision.org/tool#/tool/hypertension. Accessed 17 Oct 2020

10. Hess, E.P., Coylewright, M., Frosch, D.L., Shah, N.D.: Implementation of shared decision making in cardiovascular care past, present, and future. Circul.: Cardiovasc. Qual. Outcomes **7**(5), 797–803 (2014). https://doi.org/10.1161/CIRCOUTCOMES.113.000351

11. Jones, L.A., Weymiller, A.J., et al.: Should clinicians deliver decision aids? Further exploration of the statin choice randomized trial results. Med. Decis. Making **29**(4), 468–474 (2009). https://doi.org/10.1177/0272989X09333120

12. Joosten, E.A., DeFuentes-Merillas, L., De Weert, G., Sensky, T., Van Der Staak, C., de Jong, C.A.: Systematic review of the effects of shared decision-making on patient satisfaction, treatment adherence and health status. Psychother. psychosomat. **77**(4), 219–226 (2008)

13. Joseph-Williams, N., et al.: Toward minimum standards for certifying patient decision aids: a modified Delphi consensus process. Med. Decis. Making **34**(6), 699–710 (2014). https://doi.org/10.1177/0272989X13501721

14. Kon, A.A.: The shared decision-making continuum. Jama **304**(8), 903–904 (2010). https://doi.org/10.1001/jama.2010.1208

15. Légaré, F., Ratté, S., Gravel, K., Graham, I.D.: Barriers and facilitators to implementing shared decision-making in clinical practice: update of a systematic review of health professionals' perceptions. Patient Educ. Counsel. **73**(3), 526–535 (2008)

16. Légaré, F., et al.: Interprofessionalism and shared decision-making in primary care: a stepwise approach towards a new model. J. Interprof. Care **25**(1), 18–25 (2011)

17. Locke, E.A., Latham, G.P.: Building a practically useful theory of goal setting and task motivation: a 35-year odyssey. Am. Psychol. **57**(9), 705 (2002)

18. Makoul, G., Clayman, M.L.: An integrative model of shared decision making in medical encounters. Patient Educ. Counsel. **60**(3), 301–312 (2006). https://doi.org/10.1016/j.pec.2005.06.010. eACH Conference 2004

19. Medynskiy, Y., Yarosh, S., Mynatt, E.: Five strategies for supporting healthy behavior change. In: CHI 2011 Extended Abstracts on Human Factors in Computing Systems, CHI EA 2011, pp. 1333–1338. Association for Computing Machinery, New York (2011). https://doi.org/10.1145/1979742.1979770

20. NHS: What's your heart age? (2016). https://www.nhs.uk/conditions/nhs-health-check/check-your-heart-age-tool/. Accessed 17 Oct 2020

21. Oinas-Kukkonen, H., Harjumaa, M.: Towards deeper understanding of persuasion in software and information systems. In: First International Conference on Advances in Computer-human Interaction, pp. 200–205. IEEE (2008)

22. Oinas-Kukkonen, H., Harjumaa, M.: Persuasive systems design: Key issues, process model, and system features. Commun. Assoc. Inf. Syst. **24**(1), 28 (2009)

23. Scobbie, L., Dixon, D., Wyke, S.: Goal setting and action planning in the rehabilitation setting: development of a theoretically informed practice framework. Clin. Rehabil. **25**(5), 468–482 (2011)

24. Shay, L.A., Lafata, J.E.: Where is the evidence? A systematic review of shared decision making and patient outcomes. Med. Decis. Making **35**(1), 114–131 (2015)

25. Shilts, M.K., Horowitz, M., Townsend, M.S.: Goal setting as a strategy for dietary and physical activity behavior change: a review of the literature. Am. J. Health Promot. **19**(2), 81–93 (2004)

26. Sniehotta, F.F., Schwarzer, R., Scholz, U., Schüz, B.: Action planning and coping planning for long-term lifestyle change: theory and assessment. Eur. J. Soc. Psychol. **35**(4), 565–576 (2005)

27. Stacey, D., Légaré, F., et al.: Decision aids for people facing health treatment or screening decisions. Cochrane Database Syst. Rev. (4) (2017). https://www.cochranelibrary.com/cdsr/doi/10.1002/14651858.CD001431.pub5/full

28. Stiggelbout, A., Pieterse, A., Haes, J.D.: Shared decision making: concepts, evidence, and practice. Patient Educ. Counsel. **98**(10), 1172–1179 (2015). https://doi.org/10.1016/j.pec.2015.06.022

29. Stiggelbout, A.M., et al.: Shared decision making: really putting patients at the centre of healthcare. BMJ **344**, 28–31 (2012). https://doi.org/10.1136/bmj.e256

30. Wennberg, J.E., Fisher, E.S., Skinner, J.S.: Geography and the debate over medicare reform. Health Affairs, W96–W114 (2003). https://www.proquest.com/docview/204500754?pq-origsite=gscholar&fromopenview=true

Perceptions of Ethics in Persuasive User Interfaces

Christopher C. Branch, Catherine I. Beaton, Michael Mcquaid$^{(\boxtimes)}$, and Elissa Weeden

Rochester Institute of Technology, Rochester, NY 14623, USA
{cb3741,ciiics,mjmics,elissa.weeden}@rit.edu

Abstract. We explore the perceptions of the ethics of persuasive technology as applied to the design of user interfaces. We learn whether consumers of software see persuasion through technology as ethical, whether producers of software view the development of persuasive technology as ethical, and whether these opinions can be reconciled. This research consists of a review of relevant literature on the topic, a survey of software consumers, interviews with software producers, and an analysis of the data, resulting in conclusions intended to influence the responsible design of user interfaces in the future.

We find that persuasive technology is effective, that software consumers do not necessarily recognize persuasion when it is applied to them, and that they do not generally wish to be persuaded, unless they view the motivation of the persuader as being morally admirable. Software developers, on the other hand, do not intentionally behave unethically, but are open to the development of persuasive technology, and even deceptive technology, under some conditions.

Keywords: Ethics · Persuasive interfaces · Consumer perceptions · Software developer perceptions

1 Introduction

The study of user interface and user experience design is meant to help producers improve the user experience of hardware and software, but the definition of improved user experience is not always clear. In the case of persuasive technology, the user may have the experience of being persuaded to behave in a particular way, with the interface having been intentionally designed to obtain this result. This includes benign persuasion, such as persuasion to guide users in the most effective use of the technology, but also persuasion to influence users for the persuader's benefit.

Many software professionals design and implement interfaces that are persuasive or even deceptive for the persuader's benefit, rather than, or in addition to, the benefit of users. For example, persuasion can be used in web-based software to convince users to click on ads or links. It can be used in social media

© Springer Nature Switzerland AG 2021
R. Ali et al. (Eds.): PERSUASIVE 2021, LNCS 12684, pp. 275–288, 2021.
https://doi.org/10.1007/978-3-030-79460-6_22

software to increase the time people spend using the software. It can be used in social networking software to encourage users to invite or engage with others to attempt to increase the number of users. While the user may interpret the experience as positive, the truth is that users may not be aware of the persuasion having taken place. It is worthwhile to ask if persuasive design is an ethical use of technology.

The answer may depend on whether the intentions of the producer are seen as morally admirable, morally neutral, or morally questionable. Or it may depend on people's perception of having been deceived and their reaction to the deception, even if it was done in the service of a goal that is seen as morally admirable.

The perceptions of both consumers (users) of technology and producers (software development professionals) are of interest here. The first contribution of this research is to learn whether consumers see persuasion through technology as ethical, and if so, under what circumstances they are comfortable with it being applied. The second contribution is to learn whether software professionals view the development of persuasive technology as ethical, and if so, under what circumstances they are comfortable with developing it. Finally, we attempt to reconcile these opinions.

The remainder of this paper includes a brief assay of the background, a report on a survey of consumers, and a report on interviews with software developers.

2   Background

Reviews of the literature have been conducted in [13] and [21], both calling for more research into the ethics of persuasive technology. The more recent review, [13], studies [1,3,6,7,10,12,18] among other important sources. These date back to the 1999 introduction of the oft-cited Golden Rule of persuasive technology design, as well as including the main textbook for the topic, [7], by the coiner of "captology", as well as its critique in [1], and sophisticated definitions of voluntary persuasion, such as that tendered by [18]. Relevant work not covered in these reviews include [5] and [19] the latter advocating for *libertarian paternalism* in *nudges* or persuasive techniques to encourage people to act in their own best interest as judged by choice architects. Some prior work considers surveillance and persuasion. Leth Jespersen et al. in [15] believes the intent of a persuader should be made clear to avoid being cast as manipulation. Nagenborg [16] claims that persuasion is not unethical but sees potential ethical challenges in the way that data collected by surveillance is used to influence users. Barral et al. [2] go further, asserting that subliminal persuasion technology is ethical if it is consistent with participants' goals and intentions, although they leave open how the producer could possibly know the participants' goals and intentions. By contrast, Timmer et al. [20] consider transparency to be of critical importance, and propose methods such as value sensitive design and participatory design to maintain it, approaches also advocated by [6]. Other work such as [22] cast only a glance at ethics. A similarly brief discussion of ethics can be found in [14], along with the exhortation that ethical analysis of designs from behavioral economics would be a fruitful and important area for future work in HCI.

Kaptein and Eckles [11] explore the idea of persuasion profiles – adapting persuasive technology to individual differences in the effectiveness of a particular persuasion strategy. Tristan Harris [9] describes ways in which technology hijacks users' minds and persuades them to act in ways that benefit the technology company.

The term *dark patterns* was first coined in a blog post by Harry Brignull [4], and later defined in [8]. The dark patterns concept is closely related to the use of persuasive technology in an unethical way, as explored in this paper.

3   Survey of Software Consumers

3.1   Methodology

A survey, given to faculty, students, and staff at a U.S. higher education institution, investigated whether computer software users (consumers) recognize persuasion in software, whether they consider persuasion to be ethical, and if so, under what circumstances, and whether consumers are persuaded by interfaces designed to do so.

The first question presents a mockup of a user interface, Figs. 1 and 2, which differs among four conditions, selected randomly for each participant: a neutral design; a persuasive design with a morally admirable goal; a persuasive design with a neutral goal; and a persuasive design with a morally questionable goal. The following research question is addressed by this survey question:

RQ1: Are consumers persuaded using technology when the goal is (1) for their own benefit, (2) neutral, or (3) for the benefit of the producer?

The next two questions are intended to determine if consumers recognized the attempt at persuasion, if any, in the initial UI mockup, and whether the attempt was considered to be deceptive.

RQ2: Do consumers recognize persuasion using technology when the goal is (1) for their own benefit, (2) neutral, or (3) for the benefit of the producer?

RQ3: Do consumers consider persuasion using technology to be deceptive?

The next two questions were randomly assigned to experimental conditions B, C, or D. Each question is phrased to reveal the attempt at persuasion and the producer's motivation. Question X asks the participant to rate their view of the motivation on a seven-point Likert scale from *extremely morally admirable* to *extremely morally questionable*. Question Y asks the participant to rate their reaction to the persuasion on a seven-point Likert scale ranging from *extremely positive* to *extremely negative*.

RQ4: Do consumers consider persuasion using technology to be morally admirable when the stated goal is (1) for their own benefit, (2) neutral, or (3) for the producer's benefit?

RQ5: Do consumers consider persuasion using technology to be ethical when they consider it to be morally (1) admirable, (2) neutral, or (3) questionable?

Several demographic questions were included to check for whether responses differ based on age, gender, or education.

3.2   Results

We received 438 responses across the four variants the of the survey.

Fig. 1. Condition B (left) and Condition C (right)

To answer RQ1(1), we wanted to learn whether participants were persuaded by the user interface presented in condition B, shown in Fig. 1(left). By prominently displaying four items with photos as "Featured items," the intention was to persuade participants to choose one of these items rather than one of the less prominently positioned, text-only "Additional choices." Since the featured items were all fruits or vegetables, expected to be viewed as healthy snacks, while the additional choices included less healthy options, such as chocolate, baked goods and potato chips, this condition represented an attempt at persuasion with a motivation that would be considered morally admirable: to encourage healthy snacking.

There were 74 valid responses to this question, and of these, 53 chose one of the four featured items, while 21 chose one of the six additional choices. The expected proportion, if participants had an equal chance of selecting any item, would have been 29.6 and 44.4, respectively. A χ^2 test, $p < 0.001$, indicates that participants were persuaded by the interface. (Note that in all cases, $\chi^2 = \sum_{i=1}^{r} \sum_{j=1}^{c} (O_{i,j} - E_{i,j})^2 / E_{i,j}$.)

Participants were also asked whether they felt they were persuaded by the user interface, in order to address RQ2(1). In this case, the results were inconclusive, with 58 participants answering "Yes" and 43 answering "No," $p = 0.14$. We cannot determine whether participants were aware of having been persuaded by the interface mockup.

To answer RQ1(2), we wanted to learn whether users were persuaded by the user interface displayed in condition C, shown in Fig. 1 (right). Similarly to condition B, by prominently displaying two items with photos as "Featured items," the intention was to persuade participants to choose one of these items rather than one of the less prominently positioned, text-only "Additional choices." The difference in this condition was that all items in both the featured items and the additional choices categories were fruits or vegetables, and thus considered to be healthy choices, so the persuasion attempt here was intended to be morally neutral – with no obvious motivation on the part of the producer. The results here were that 44 participants chose one of the featured items, while 61 chose one of the additional choices – almost exactly the expected proportion, $p = 0.69$, and we cannot conclude that participants were persuaded by this mockup. The associated question to determine whether participants recognized the attempt at persuasion and address RQ2(2) was likewise inconclusive, with 54 participants responding "Yes" and 58 responding "No," $p = 0.71$.

Condition D was the final attempt at persuasion, an effort to answer RQ1(3) using the interface mockup shown in Fig. 2(left). Here the "Featured items" category contained exclusively items that would be considered less healthy alternatives, while the healthier items were all listed under "Additional choices." In this case, there were 83 valid responses, with 43 participants choosing one of the four featured items, while 40 selected one of the six additional choices. The χ^2 test, $p = 0.028$, indicates that participants were indeed persuaded by this mockup.

The question of whether participants recognized the persuasion, RQ2(3), is yet again inconclusive, with 59 answering "Yes" and 51 answering "No," $p = 0.45$.

Finally, condition A, shown in Fig. 2(right) was intended as a control condition, in which there was no attempt at persuasion. The snack choices were presented in alphabetical order, each with both a text label and a small photo of the snack. Healthy items were alternated with less healthy choices, with the expectation that users would choose the snack that they truly preferred, rather than being influenced by the UI. In fact, the results suggest that this was indeed the case. The χ^2 test, $p < 0.001$, reflects only the unlikelihood that the results would occur by chance.

In fact, on the question of whether participants felt persuaded by the interface, a significant result was found, with 23 of the 109 valid responses being "Yes" and 86 being "No," $p < 0.001$, indicating that participants recognized, correctly, that they were *not* being persuaded.

Fig. 2. Condition D (left) and Condition A (right)

To summarize, *when participants were presented with UI mockups intended to persuade them to choose a featured snack for their own benefit (condition B) or for the benefit of the UI producer (condition D), results suggest that the persuasion was effective. In the case of persuasion with a neutral motivation, we could not conclude from the results whether participants were persuaded or not. In all three experimental conditions, B, C, D, the question of whether participants recognized the persuasion was inconclusive. And in the control scenario, condition A, results show that participants were not systematically persuaded in any discernable way, and they correctly recognized the lack of persuasion in the UI.*

To answer RQ3, we asked participants whether or not they felt that the persuasion attempted by the UI mockup was deceptive. Since only conditions B, C, and D involved an attempt at persuasion, we consider only those responses, of which there were 323. These results consisted of 156 "Yes" responses and 167 "No" responses, $p = 0.54$, so we cannot conclude whether participants found any of these interface mockups to be deceptive. However, examining the results to this question for the control scenario, condition A, we find that only 12 participants answered "Yes" and 95 answered "No" to this question, $p < 0.001$, indicating that participants overwhelmingly recognized that this interface mockup was *not* intended to be deceptive. When contrasted with the inconclusive results in the three experimental conditions, it seems likely that more participants than would be expected found the interfaces to be deceptive, even if not to a statistically significant degree.

We turn next to the issue of whether participants considered the interfaces designed for persuasion to be ethical, when the attempt at persuasion and its motivation were revealed. For this we use the responses to questions previously denoted X and Y, which asked participants how they viewed the motivation of the producer and for their reaction to the attempt at persuasion, respectively.

For condition B, it was explained to participants that the motivation of the producer was for the benefit of the software consumer, in an effort to encourage the selection of healthy snacks. The answers to questions X and Y in this condition are used to address research questions RQ4(1) and RQ5(1), respectively. Of the 101 responses to question X, we discard the responses of the 22 participants who considered the producer's motivation to be morally neutral. Of the remaining 79 answers, 64 participants responded that the producer's motivation was extremely, moderately, or slightly morally admirable, while 19 responded that the motivation was extremely, moderately, or slightly morally questionable. The χ^2 test, $p < 0.001$, indicates that most participants found the motivation to be morally admirable. For question Y, there were 37 neutral responses, which we discard. Of the remaining 63 responses, there were 44 participants who reported their reaction to this attempt at persuasion to be extremely, moderately, or slightly positive, while 19 had reactions that were extremely, moderately, or slightly negative. The χ^2 test, $p < 0.001$, indicates that participants reacted positively to this attempt at influencing their choice.

For condition C, it was explained that the motivation of the producer was neutral, with no particular intent. The answers to questions X and Y in this condition are used to address RQ4(2) and RQ5(2), respectively. In this case, we are interested in the number of participants who viewed the persuasion attempt as morally neutral, as compared to those who found it to be morally admirable or morally questionable. Of the 113 responses to this question, 55 found the motivation to be morally neutral, while 58 participants chose one of the other six options on the Likert scale. The χ^2 test, $p < 0.001$, indicates that participants generally considered the motivation to be morally neutral. Similarly, for question Y, there were 49 participants whose reaction to the attempt at persuasion was neither positive nor negative (neutral), while 64 participants chose one of the six positive or negative responses, $p < 0.001$, indicating that participants in general had neither a positive nor negative reaction to the attempt at persuasion.

For condition D, we explained that the motivation of the producer was to benefit snack food manufacturers in an effort to sell snacks. The answers to questions X and Y in this condition are used to address RQ4(3) and RQ5(3), respectively. Of the 110 responses to question X, we discard the responses of the 31 participants who considered the producer's motivation to be morally neutral. Of the remaining 79 answers, 6 participants responded that the producer's motivation was extremely, moderately, or slightly morally admirable, while 73 responded that the motivation was extremely, moderately, or slightly morally questionable, $p < 0.001$, indicating that a large majority of participants found the motivation to be morally questionable. For question Y, we had 42 neutral responses, which we discard. Of the remaining 68 responses, 10 participants reported their reaction to this attempt at persuasion to be extremely, moderately, or slightly positive, while 58 had reactions that were extremely, moderately, or slightly negative. The χ^2 test, $p < 0.001$, indicates that most participants reacted negatively to this attempt at influencing their choice.

To summarize, *participants correctly recognize differing motivations as being morally admirable, morally neutral, or morally questionable, and they reacted positively to persuasive technology with a morally admirable motivation, negatively to persuasive technology with a morally questionable motivation, and neither positively nor negatively to persuasive technology with a morally neutral motivation.*

4 Interviews with Software Producers

4.1 Methodology

The interview attempts to learn whether computer software professionals (producers) consider the development of persuasive technology to be ethical, and if so, under what circumstances. The design of this interview reflects this goal, in the following ways:

The first four questions are intended to gather some background about the participants, including the software development roles they have performed, whether they ascribe to a particular moral framework, and, if so, which one, and whether they adhere to a formal code of ethics.

The next two questions (5 and 6) are intended to determine whether producers find it necessary to consider the ethical implications of their work, and if so, in what circumstances.

The next three questions (7 through 9) are intended to determine if producers have been involved in the development of software that they consider to be persuasive, and if not, whether they would consider doing so and why.

The final three questions (10 through 12) are intended to determine if producers have been involved in the development of software that they consider to be deceptive, and if not, whether they would consider doing so and why.

4.2 Results

Interviews were conducted with 12 participants, a convenience sample of the first author's professional contacts, who ranged in experience from 1.5 years up to 37 years in software development. All of the participants had performed multiple roles in their careers, with the largest number having been developers (11), followed by designers (6), and first line managers (6). Five participants had been software architects or second line managers, four had been testers, and three reported a role of junior/senior software engineer. The following roles were reported by one participant each: UX designer, tech lead, team leader, product owner, embedded real time developer, web developer, salesperson, director, and vice president.

Three participants answered "Yes" to indicate that they adhere to a formal code of ethics such as the ACM Code of Ethics. Five answered "No," and four answers were less straightforward. The answers overall suggest that some participants believed their behavior would be in agreement with a formal code of ethics, but since they could not claim to have read and agreed to the code, they could not be certain. For example, one participant answered "I think I do," but that "I can't say that I'm familiar with the details." Another responded "Not formally," and one pointed out that many companies have a formal code of ethics that one must agree to follow as a condition of employment.

On the question of whether participants had found it necessary to consider the ethical implications of their work, there was an even split, with six participants responding "Yes" and six responding "No." Of those who answered "Yes," there was little commonality among the responses, with each answer being a distinct situation.

The next several questions ask whether the participant has ever been involved in the development of persuasive technology and, if not, whether they would consider doing so, and why or why not. On the first question, six participants responded "Yes" and six responded "No." Most participants also expanded on their answer with details of the occasions, including positive or negative reactions. Of those who answered "Yes," there was one negative comment, a participant who "did not enjoy developing for a client that used such marketing techniques on a public facing web site."

The majority of the comments from those who answered "Yes" were positive, with participants emphasizing the use of persuasion as a means of guiding the user through the proper use of the software. One participant said that the goal is "designing systems that are easy to use and intuitive." Another expressed the intent to develop "software that creates triggers for people to react to things," adding that "we want to be persuasive, and enable people to accomplish tasks by providing triggers for them to do something in the software." There are "certain scenarios that we want people to accomplish," said one participant, and another claimed to be "trying to design software that persuades them through the proper way of using it ... we guide them through the use of the software."

Some participants in this category also expressed the opinion that "everything we do influences people," stating that "the way we design software is intended for the user to do something," and that "the way we lay things out is intended to influence the user's behavior; that's not done in a negative way." One participant concluded that "you can't avoid doing it, because otherwise you can't create a product." This echoes a statement from a user experience study where the authors "acknowledge the persuasive intent underlying all of design activity" [8].

One participant answered that "I don't think influencing behavior is intrinsically bad," and that "as long as the persuasiveness is in general beneficial to the user, is clearly spelled out, and can be configured, I don't have a problem with it," referencing [19] in support.

Of the six participants who answered that they had not been involved in the development of persuasive software, four said they would consider doing so, while two said that they would not consider doing so. Of the six participants who *had* previously been involved in the development of persuasive technology, four of them nevertheless volunteered a response to this question, with three of them saying "Yes," they would consider doing this (again) and the fourth answering "No." Of the seven participants who answered "Yes" or "Maybe," many provided conditions for their agreement. Three of them argued that it's reasonable and expected to use persuasion to encourage sales of the product, with one stating that "selling a product, I probably would," because "marketing products is a part of our culture." Another participant said that "as long as the behavior is ethical, it could be considered a type of sales," and the third said that "we want people to be engaged," and "we want people using the software," because "you want to sell a product you're making." The fourth participant expressed the opinion that "persuasive software is acceptable as long as it is developed to influence the user toward positive ethical outcomes."

Of the three participants who stated that they would not consider developing persuasive technology, two provided explanations for their reasoning. One participant referred to the use of loot boxes in video games, and expressed the opinion that "a lot of that software moves toward the predatory," further pointing out that these "technologies are drawing a lot from slot machines and the gambling industry," and are "targeting people who are making impulsive decisions." "We all have moments of poor impulse control," said this participant, and "I think targeting those people is unethical." Another participant implied that persuasion can be deceptive by its nature, stating that "as a customer I wouldn't want to be deceived in any way, so I do not want to contribute to that."

To summarize, *the majority of interview participants (nine out of twelve) consider it acceptable to be involved in the development of persuasive technology, at least under some conditions. The conditions varied among participants, and fell into three categories: guiding the user in the most efficient and effective use of the software itself, using persuasive technology as part of a sales or marketing effort, and persuading the user to do something that the participant would not find to be unethical.*

The final three questions were intended to learn the opinions of software professionals when it comes to deception in software. Of the 12 interview participants, two said that they had been involved in the development of deceptive software, while 10 responded that they had not. Of those 10, when asked if they would consider doing so, six answered "No," three answered "Yes" or "Maybe," and one offered no response. When asked why or why not, the two participants who had been involved in the past both expressed that they would prefer not to do so again, with one answering "I don't enjoy building sites that market products in a deceptive way," and the other stating that "I wouldn't want to use software that's deceptive. I want to understand and be able to trust what I'm working with, so I don't want to build software that others don't trust or can't rely on."

Of the six who said that they would not consider it, three of them provided their reasoning, with one saying "I would not like to do things to others that I would not like others to do to me." Another responded that "It feels like it's crossing a moral boundary," and the third answered "I think by nature that's dishonest, and I think that would do harm."

The three who answered "Yes" or "Maybe" explained their reasoning in several ways—two of them mentioned the software itself as a deciding factor, with one answering that "It depends on the nature of the intended software product," and another saying that "It would depend on the circumstance and the ultimate goal of it. If the proverbial good versus evil can be achieved, my morals would not prevent me from working on it if I believed it was for the greater good." Two of the three also mentioned personal circumstances, with one saying that "given some (extreme) preconditions, I'd consider it." The preconditions mentioned included the need for health insurance for a spouse's (but not the participant's own) serious condition. The other offered the opinion that "the world isn't black and white," but said that "the bar would be set pretty high. I don't think I would ignore that and just do it because it's a job."

In summary, *the majority of the interview participants (eight out of 12) do not consider it acceptable to be involved in the development of deceptive software. The minority who would consider it would do so only given certain conditions of the software or of their personal situations.*

5   Discussion

A major finding from the UI mockups presented in the survey was that in two of the three conditions in which persuasion was present, it was, in fact, effective at persuading the participants, regardless of whether the producer's motivation was intended to be positive or negative toward the participant. This finding is confirmed by the control scenario, in which no persuasion was present, as participants appeared to respond in accordance with their own natural preference, and not as a reaction to any systematic influence from the UI design. Additionally, although it was inconclusive whether participants recognized the attempts at persuasion in the conditions where persuasion was present, the lack of persuasion in the control condition was clearly identified.

The finding that persuasive technology really works is to be expected, but it's significant here because the persuasion used in this study was rudimentary—involving no more than prominent placement and the use of stock images for items that users were persuaded to choose. Modern software used in mobile applications and websites—especially online shopping, social media and networking applications—uses far more advanced approaches, including not only interactive graphics and language, but constructions such as false or hidden affordance, and sophisticated techniques such as providing the illusion of choice by presenting a limited set of menu options, providing intermittent variable rewards to encourage addiction, using norms of social approval and social obligation [9].

This is the point at which the perceptions of persuasion by software consumers and those of software producers have the potential to conflict. The majority of interview participants considered the development of persuasive technology to be acceptable under some conditions; in particular: when guiding the user in the most efficient use of the software, as part of a sales or marketing effort, or when the software producer does not consider the persuasion to be unethical. But as shown by [17], it can be all too easy for software producers to determine that their scenario falls into one of these categories. For example, much software is developed as part of an effort to make money for the developers. If the use of persuasion for sales and marketing is acceptable, then virtually anything the producer chooses to do in service of that goal becomes acceptable.

Among the survey findings were that while software consumers consider persuasion in general to be ethical, they react negatively to attempts to persuade them personally, particularly when the motivations of the producer are seen as morally questionable. Since the explicitly stated motivation of the morally questionable UI mockup variant in the survey was an attempt by a manufacturer to sell snacks, this appears to be in direct contradiction with the attitude of software producers that it is acceptable to use persuasion in the service of sales.

6   Conclusion

This paper has explored the perceptions of the ethics of persuasive technology, resulting in some significant findings:

Persuasive technology can work. Even the rudimentary attempts in the survey used in this study were shown to be effective.

Software consumers do not necessarily recognize persuasion, although they correctly identify cases where it is *not* present.

Software consumers do not wish to be persuaded, unless they view the motivation of the persuader as being morally admirable.

Software producers do not want to behave unethically, but they are largely open to the development of persuasive technology, and a minority would also not rule out the development of deceptive technology, as long as their personal moral boundaries are not crossed.

The academic literature on ethics in the use of persuasive technology needs expansion. Some significant work has been done to describe, analyze, and predict many aspects of persuasive technology, but often the ethical considerations have been given only secondary importance. In a few cases, authors have expressed strong opinions about the ethics of designing and developing software.

An important limitation of this study is that the survey respondents (not the interviewees) were all associated with a single higher education institution, so the findings may be related to level of education, cultural background, or economic class.

References

1. Atkinson, B.M.C.: Captology: a critical review. In: IJsselsteijn, W.A., de Kort, Y.A.W., Midden, C., Eggen, B., van den Hoven, E. (eds.) PERSUASIVE 2006. LNCS, vol. 3962, pp. 171–182. Springer, Heidelberg (2006). https://doi.org/10.1007/11755494_25

2. Barral, O., et al.: Covert persuasive technologies: bringing subliminal cues to human-computer interaction. In: Spagnolli, A., Chittaro, L., Gamberini, L. (eds.) PERSUASIVE 2014. LNCS, vol. 8462, pp. 1–12. Springer, Cham (2014). https://doi.org/10.1007/978-3-319-07127-5_1

3. Berdichevsky, D., Neuenschwander, E.: Toward an ethics of persuasive technology. Commun. ACM **42**(5), 51–58 (1999). https://doi.org/10.1145/301353.301410

4. Brignull, H.: Dark patterns: dirty tricks designers use to make people do stuff 08 July 2010. https://www.90percentofeverything.com/2010/07/08/dark-patterns-dirty-tricks-designers-use-to-make-people-do-stuff/. Accessed 29 Sep 2019, from 90 Percent Of Everything website

5. Cialdini, R.: Influence: the Psychology of Persuasion. Collins, New York (1984). NY, rev. edn

6. Davis, J.: Design methods for ethical persuasive computing. In: Proceedings of the 4th International Conference on Persuasive Technology, vol. 6, pp. 1–6 (2009). https://doi.org/10.1145/1541948.1541957

7. Fogg, B.: The ethics of persuasive technology. In: Persuasive Technology, pp. 211–239. Morgan Kaufmann (2003). https://doi.org/10.1016/B978-155860643-2/50011-1

8. Gray, C.M., Kou, Y., Battles, B., Hoggatt, J., Toombs, A.L.: The dark (patterns) side of UX design. In: Proceedings of the 2018 CHI Conference on Human Factors in Computing Systems - CHI, vol. 18, pp. 1–14 (2018). https://doi.org/10.1145/3173574.3174108

9. Harris, T.: How technology is hijacking your mind–from a former insider, 18 May 2016. https://medium.com/thrive-global/how-technology-hijacks-peoples-minds-from-a-magician-and-google-s-design-ethicist-56d62ef5edf3. Accessed 6 Apr 2019, from Medium website

10. IJsselsteijn, W., de Kort, Y., Midden, C., Eggen, B., van den Hoven, E.: Persuasive technology for human well-being: setting the scene. In: IJsselsteijn, W.A., de Kort, Y.A.W., Midden, C., Eggen, B., van den Hoven, E. (eds.) PERSUASIVE 2006. LNCS, vol. 3962, pp. 1–5. Springer, Heidelberg (2006). https://doi.org/10.1007/11755494_1

11. Kaptein, M., Eckles, D.: Selecting effective means to any end: futures and ethics of persuasion profiling. In: Ploug, T., Hasle, P., Oinas-Kukkonen, H. (eds.) PERSUASIVE 2010. LNCS, vol. 6137, pp. 82–93. Springer, Heidelberg (2010). https://doi.org/10.1007/978-3-642-13226-1_10

12. Karppinen, P., Oinas-Kukkonen, H.: Three approaches to ethical considerations in the design of behavior change support systems. In: Berkovsky, S., Freyne, J. (eds.) PERSUASIVE 2013. LNCS, vol. 7822, pp. 87–98. Springer, Heidelberg (2013). https://doi.org/10.1007/978-3-642-37157-8_12

13. Kight, R., Gram-Hansen, S.B.: Do ethics matter in persuasive technology? In: Oinas-Kukkonen, H., Win, K.T., Karapanos, E., Karppinen, P., Kyza, E. (eds.) PERSUASIVE 2019. LNCS, vol. 11433, pp. 143–155. Springer, Cham (2019). https://doi.org/10.1007/978-3-030-17287-9_12

14. Lee, M.K., Kiesler, S., Forlizzi, J.: Mining behavioral economics to design persua-sive technology for healthy choices. In: Proceedings of the SIGCHI Conference on Human Factors in Computing Systems, pp. 325–334 (2011). https://doi.org/10.1145/1978942.1978989

15. Leth Jespersen, J., Albrechtslund, A., Øhrstrøm, P., Hasle, P., Albretsen, J.: Surveillance, persuasion, and panopticon. In: de Kort, Y., IJsselsteijn, W., Midden, C., Eggen, B., Fogg, B.J. (eds.) PERSUASIVE 2007. LNCS, vol. 4744, pp. 109–120. Springer, Heidelberg (2007). https://doi.org/10.1007/978-3-540-77006-0_15

16. Nagenborg, M.: Surveillance and Persuasion, Ethics and Information Technology, Dordrecht, vol. 16 (2014). https://doi.org/10.1007/s10676-014-9339-4

17. Nodder, C.: Evil by Design: Interaction Design to Lead Us into Temptation. Wiley, Indianapolis, IN (2013)

18. Smids, J.: The voluntariness of persuasive technology. In: Bang, M., Ragnemalm, E.L. (eds.) PERSUASIVE 2012. LNCS, vol. 7284, pp. 123–132. Springer, Heidel-berg (2012). https://doi.org/10.1007/978-3-642-31037-9_11

19. Thaler, R.H., Sunstein, C.R.: Nudge: Improving Decisions About Health, Wealth, and Happiness. Penguin Books, New York (2009). Revised and expanded edn

20. Timmer, J., Kool, L., van Est, R.: Ethical challenges in emerging applications of persuasive technology. In: MacTavish, T., Basapur, S. (eds.) PERSUASIVE 2015. LNCS, vol. 9072, pp. 196–201. Springer, Cham (2015). https://doi.org/10.1007/978-3-319-20306-5_18

21. Torning, K., Oinas-Kukkonen, H.: Persuasive system design: state of the art and future directions. In: Proceedings of the 4th International Conference on Persuasive Technology. Persuasive 2009. Association for Computing Machinery, New York (2009). https://doi.org/10.1145/1541948.1541989

22. Tromp, N., Hekkert, P., Verbeek, P.P.: Design for socially responsible behavior: a classification of influence based on intended user experience. Des. Issues 27(3), 3–19 (2011)

The Fine Line Between Persuasion and Digital Addiction

Deniz Cemiloglu[1](✉), Mohammad Naiseh[1], Maris Catania[2], Harri Oinas-Kukkonen[3], and Raian Ali[4]

[1] Faculty of Science and Technology, Bournemouth University, Poole, UK
{dcemiloglu,mnaiseh}@bournemouth.ac.uk
[2] Kindred Group, Sliema, Malta
maris.bonello@kindredgroup.com
[3] Oulu Advanced Research on Service and Information Systems, University of Oulu, Oulu, Finland
harri.oinas-kukkonen@oulu.fi
[4] College of Science and Engineering, Hamad Bin Khalifa University, Doha, Qatar
raali2@hbku.edu.qa

Abstract. Digital addiction is becoming a prevalent societal concern and persuasive design techniques used in digital platforms might be accountable also for the development and maintenance of such problematic behavior. This paper theoretically analyses the relationship between persuasive system design principles and digital addiction in light of theories on behavioral and substance-based addictions. The findings suggest that some of the persuasive design principles, in specific contexts, may trigger and expedite digital addiction. The purpose of this paper is to open a discussion around the potential effects of persuasive technology on digital addiction and cater to this risk in the design processes and the persuasive design itself.

Keywords: Digital addiction · Persuasive system design · Addiction theory

1 Introduction

Digital addiction (DA) has emerged as an important research topic over the past few years due to its rising prevalence and public concern about the harmful consequences of excessive use of digital devices and services [1]. While there is no agreed definition or diagnostic criteria for digital addiction, different types of DA such as the internet, social media, and gaming addiction have started to be used and approaches to treat them were proposed [2, 3]. For example, Internet Gaming Disorder is stressed within the Statistical Manual of Mental Disorders (DSM-5) for further research [4]. In 2018, the World Health Organization recognized gaming disorder in its International Statistical Classification of Diseases [5].

Despite the lack of a common framework, research suggesting similarities between DA and behavioral and substance-based addictions [6–8] enabled articulating DA

© Springer Nature Switzerland AG 2021
R. Ali et al. (Eds.): PERSUASIVE 2021, LNCS 12684, pp. 289–307, 2021.
https://doi.org/10.1007/978-3-030-79460-6_23

through four main conceptualizations. The first focused on time spent on the device and/or platform and the usage style [9]. The second defined DA through DSM-V diagnostic criteria either within compulsive-impulsive spectrum or behavioral addiction [8, 10–12], which included symptoms like preoccupation, mood modification, conflict, tolerance, and withdrawal. The third defined DA through negative consequences brought to the subject's life [13] and the fourth defined DA as just a symptom of other more profound psychiatric conditions [14]. While such conceptualizations provide a general understanding of DA, the focus on symptoms in explaining DA limits the discussion to the individuals. As addiction is an interwoven connection developed with an entity, the nature of the entity also has an influence on the addictive behavior. This is especially true for DA, as the interactive, intelligent, and personalized nature of digital media make it more possible to attract attention and trigger and reinforce a problematic relationship with it [15]. Hence, software design shall be also studied when studying DA.

In the last two decades, the world economy started to move from a materials economy to an attention economy establishing a market where individual attention is a valuable resource [16]. As human attention is limited, interactive online platforms started to employ immersive and persuasive design techniques to engage users and increase business profit [17]. The use of persuasive design techniques in such platforms raised ethical concerns arguing whether software-mediated persuasion without user informed consent is ethical [18]. Moreover, it is argued that persuasive design techniques intended to increase user engagement or ease task completion for users may also be responsible of excessive usage and in some instances DA [15, 19, 20].

Understanding the relationship between DA and persuasive design techniques requires an investigation that goes beyond analyzing DA symptoms. That is, one needs to look at the etiological factors that give rise to addictive symptoms in the first place to see whether persuasive design techniques tap on similar mechanisms. Persuasive design techniques are designed to prompt behavioral, cognitive, psycho-social, and other psychological mechanisms to change a person's attitudes and behavior and, while doing so, they may trigger or expedite mechanisms related to addictive behavior. In this paper, we provide a concise review of theories of addiction (Sect. 2) and persuasive design principles [21] (Sect. 3) and the contribution of these principles, in certain contexts of use, to hosting and expediting DA and adding to the underlying causes and symptoms of it (Sect. 4). Finally, we discuss the findings and present directions for future work (Sect. 5).

2 Theories of Addiction

Many theoretical approaches and models have been proposed to explain the development, maintenance, and relapse of addiction. For a collection of reviews, see the work in [22–25]. Each approach highlights different underlying mechanisms in explaining addiction, and there is no single explanation dominating the field [22]. Moreover, the proposed theories and models are not mutually exclusive such that underlying mechanisms highlighted in one can be interrelated with another [24]. This view then suggests that the appearance and maintenance of addiction is a consequence of many integrated mechanisms, in which biological, personal, social, and environmental factors work together [23].

Since DA is argued to show similarities with behavioral and substance-based addictions [6–8], determining the etiological factors of addictive behavior can provide a good basis to compare between persuasive systems design principles and DA. Accordingly, we searched the literature for theories in addiction and grouped them under different categories. For the purpose of this paper, we grouped the theories according to eight factors contributing to addiction: biological, predisposition, learning, decision-making, motivation, self-regulation, psycho-social, and contextual. Due to space limitation, a summary is provided for each theory group.

Biological Theories. These theories postulate that addiction is mainly a 'brain disease' which results from a disorder in dopamine reward circuit and other circuits involved with conditioning, motivation, and executive functions [26]. It has been shown that drug ingestion activates similar reward circuits in the brain as natural rewards. The fast increase in neurotransmitters caused by drug intake compared to natural rewards may impair reward sensitivity to natural rewards and cause substance dependence [27]. While activation in the reward circuit helps explain initial drug-taking, activation in neural circuits related to motivation, memory, and executive functions help explain compulsion [28]. It has been suggested that improper regulation of dopamine and other neurotransmitters in the neural system reinforces learned associations, enhances the rewarding and motivational value of the substance, and reduces inhibitory control and this, in turn, leads to compulsivity and impulsivity [26].

Predisposition Theories. Individuals may hold certain dispositions which may increase their probability of developing addiction [29]. For example, genetic vulnerability could also arise from comorbid addictive disorders and psychiatric disorders [30] suggesting common causation such that the risk factors that give rise to each disorder may be related [31]. Certain personality traits such as approach-related traits that are associated with sociability, sensation seeking, and impulsivity or avoidance-related traits associated with neuroticism [29], stressful life experience [32], low life satisfaction [33], and socio-demographic characteristics such as education level, occupation, income level [34] may all have an influence on increasing the likelihood of developing addictive behavior.

Learning Theories. Addiction may arise as a learnt behavior through associations made between cues, reinforcements, and responses or through observing others. According to classical conditioning [35], addiction can be explained as a learned response produced when two stimuli are associated together. Addiction develops when the positive-reinforcing value of substance stimuli is implicitly associated with environmental stimuli as it predicts drug ingestion. Operant conditioning, on the other hand, explains addiction as a learned response produced when an association is made between a behavior and its outcome [36]. In time continuous pairing of addictive behavior and the positive outcome may cause the act to become automatic, hence once a goal-directed behavior may turn into a habit, an unconscious response which is no longer linked to the value of the outcome [37]. According to social learning theory, addiction is a learned response produced by observing others [38]. Addiction develops when one associates with peers that show addictive behavior, holds a positive definition of and a positive attitude towards addictive behavior, anticipates positive outcomes as in physiological effects and reaction from others, [39, 40].

Decision-Making Theories. Theories on decision-making suggest that individuals decide to engage in addictive behavior, and they base these decisions on cognitive processes. According to the dual-process theory [41], two different types of processing underlie decision-making: the intuitive which is the fast processing based on (heuristics) mental shortcuts, and the rational which is the slow processing based on reflective and deductive reasoning. While intuitive processing saves time and effort in decision-making, its heavy reliance on heuristics and its unconscious nature makes it susceptible to biases. From this perspective, addiction might arise from information-processing biases that favor the addictive behavior [42]. For example, Field et al. [43] showed that participants with high levels of cannabis craving were prone to attentional bias, that is, they were showing elevated attention to cannabis cues. Rational decision-making on the other hand is based on analytical processes where decision-makers come to a decision by calculating the cost and benefits of possible options and choose the one that is in their best interest [44]. The term rational here does not imply rationality but suggests that higher-order cognitive processes are involved in coming to that decision. From this perspective, addiction might arise when individuals deliberately assign more value to events that are closer in time while being fully aware of the consequences of the addictive activity in the short and long terms [45]. They may also do that due to missing or incorrect information [46], and when they rationalize their actions and beliefs in a way that favors addictive activity [47].

Motivation Theories. Motivation theories state that addiction may arise due to substance dependence serving as a method to fulfil different motives. Three different motives dominate the literature, (i) achieving pleasure [48], (ii) a means of self-medication, relief distress, meeting pre-existing psychological needs [49, 50], and (iii) fulfilling diverse needs such as social identity [51].

Self-regulation Theories. Self-regulation theories state that actions are goal-directed and feedback-controlled such that individuals exert self-control to override impulses and manage their behaviors [52]. In this light, it is suggested that addiction arises from a deficiency in self-control where sub-functions of self-control such as goal setting, self-monitoring, and action planning are individually or collectively impaired [53, 54]. One might be less likely to self-regulate against addiction if they hold conflicting goals (e.g. I don't want to be an addict versus I want to enjoy another drink), favor gratification goals over self-relevant goals [53], if they cannot monitor their consumption level due to internal distraction or external distractions [55], if they cannot translate their intention to quit to proper action plan [56] and if they do not believe that they are capable of resisting drinking [57].

Psycho-Social Theories. Psycho-social theories state that addiction may arise as a result of social connection and social influence [58]. People try to conform to social norms in order to secure social gains and avoid social losses [59] and two types of social norms influence behavior. The first is descriptive norms, the perception of how frequently the behavior is conducted by others and the second is injunctive norms, the perception of approval or disapproval of the defined behavior by others [60]. In this light, addiction may arise from the perception of a high frequency of addictive activities conducted by others and perceived approval of addictive activities within social settings [61]. The concept of identity, a person's sense of who they are could also be a facilitator of addiction [51]. Individuals with unmet identity needs may try to construct a sense of self by identifying with addictive activities due to its promise of belonging and respect. Moreover, increased consumption serving to meet identity needs may in time facilitate the individual to identify with the addict role [62].

Contextual Factors Theories. Theories on contextual factors state that vulnerability to addiction can be amplified by broader social environmental factors [63]. These factors could be grouped into three categories: micro-system and community factors, media and advertising factors, and policy and legislation factors. Each factor's influence on the development of addiction may be direct or indirect and is mainly mediated by the individual's characteristics [64]. Moreover, the contextual factors may work on their own or reinforce each other. For example, advertisements on alcohol could reinforce the social norms of drinking.

3   The Persuasive System Design

It has been suggested that user behavior in digital environments can be guided by persuasive systems which are defined as "computerized software or information systems designed to reinforce, change or shape attitudes or behaviors or both without using coercion or deception" [21]. Systems can persuade users through both human-computer interaction and computer-mediated communication in which persuasion occurs through other people using the system. Within their persuasive system design (PSD) model, Oinas-Kukkonen, Harjumaa [21] define four categories of design principle which enable a system to be persuasive at an operational level. These include (i) *primary task support*, design principles that support and ease conducting activities such as reduction and personalization, (ii) *dialogue support*, design principles that support the achievement of goals while using the system such as praise, rewards and reminders, (iii) *social support*, design principles that enable motivating certain action through social influence such as social learning and competition and (iv) *system credibility support*, design principles that make the system more trustworthy, thus more persuasive such as authority and third-party endorsement.

4   Persuasion and Digital Addiction

In this section, we analyses the association between PSD principles and DA in light of addiction theories discussed in Sect. 2. We define DA as relationships with technology that meets the diagnostic criteria of behavior addiction (conflict, tolerance, withdrawal symptoms, salience, and relapse) and associated with harm to the person's life. Such a relationship with technology may lead to a usage characterized by being obsessive, impulsive and excessive under the effect of immersion and pressure. This relation can be facilitated through the design and can be analyzed through the addiction theories. Here we have focused on the PSD principles and studied them in light of addiction literature for their potential to facilitate such a relation whether directly or indirectly.

We made an argument about an association between DA and PSD when we found literature to support it. Hence, we do not claim our pairing is comprehensive or that the association we depict is a confirmatory evidence. Our purpose is to shed light on the potential of PSD principles to facilitate DA in certain conditions related to users and their context. In reporting the relationship between PSD principles and DA, we differentiated between PSD principles that can be seen themselves as triggers for DA, on one hand, and design principles that can act as facilitators through triggering other cyber behaviors leading to DA. In addition, we considered both addictive actions, i.e. impulsive and hasty cyber actions and addictive behavior in terms of attitudes and habits towards technology. The findings are summarized in Table 1.

Table 1. PSD and DA relationship

PSD design principles	Theories of addiction
Primary task support	
Reduction	BT, SRT, LT, DMT
Personalization	SRT
Dialogue support	
Praise	LT, MT
Rewards	BT, LT, DMT
Reminders	SRT, LT, PST
Suggestions	LT, DMT
Liking	DMT
Social support	
Social learning	LT
Social comparison	PST
Normative influences	PST
Cooperation	PST
Competition	PST
Recognition	PST
System credibility support	
Authority	PST
Third-party endorsements	CFT

BT: Biological Theories. **LT:** Learning Theories. **DMT:** Decision-making Theories. **MT:** Motivation Theories. **SRT:** Self-regulation Theories. **PST:** Psycho-social Theories. **CFT:** Contextual Factor Theories.

4.1 Primary Support

Reduction. *A system that reduces effort that users expend with regard to performing their target behavior may be more persuasive.*

Biological Theories and Self-regulation Theories: Diminished Self-control. One way the reduction principle could directly relate to DA is through the concept of self-control. Neuroimaging studies showed that addicted individuals had significantly reduced activity in brain regions involved in self-control on tasks that involve response inhibition [65]. Similarly, self-regulation theories explained addictive behavior through one's inability to override impulse [66]. Thus, reducing the steps needed to perform an action may worsen an individual's ability to restrain from performing the action. For example, the ability to link one's credit card to his Android account may reduce the hassle of payment for content within freemium games to a single click. Such reduction principle can increase the likelihood of failing to suppress automatic buy responses and result in large debts, personal distress, and interpersonal conflict [67].

Learning Theories: Strengthened Cue-Outcome Association. Because reduction reduces the steps between cue and outcome, the increased proximity between the two can strengthen their association [68]. For example, the appearance of camera icon and ease of access within social media platforms reduces the effort to post photos. Thus, once a person is triggered by an external or internal cue, the ease in taking the action can possibly strengthen the association between posting photos and earning reward in the form of likes. The strengthened association in return can increase the likelihood of repeating the behavior. This example is supported in [69] where the reward and speed of reward play role in forming gambling addiction.

Decision-Making Theories: Biased Decision-Making. Reducing the steps in taking an action may speed up the decision-making process. In such cases, individuals may rely on intuitive processing as heuristics allow fast decision-making [41]. However, intuitive processing may make individuals prone to cognitive biases [70]. Biases such as the illusion of control (thinking one can influence the occurrence of an event) and gambler's fallacy (thinking one can predict the probability of an event) are found to be related to excessive gambling [71].

Personalization. *A system that offers personalized content or services has a greater persuasive capability.*

Self-regulation Theories: Diminished Self-control. Personalization may have an indirect relation to DA through the concept of self-control. Optimizing feeds based on individual interests may encourage individuals to continuously scroll through content and the spontaneous joy experienced while doing so may create a flow experience [72, 73]. The authors in [74] demonstrated that people with low self-control are more likely to experience greater flow and more likely to be addicted to the internet, mobile phones and video games. Since flow experience is associated with low self-control [74] providing a personalized content may then arguably tamper an individual's ability to apply self-control and this can, in turn, have an indirect effect on excessive usage.

4.2 Dialogue Support

Praise. By offering praise, a system can make users more open to persuasion.

Learning Theories: Reinforcement. The praise principle which can be in the form of word, image, symbols or sound may act like a positive reinforcement as it acknowledges the progress that has been made [75]. While one cannot argue the use of praise will directly lead to DA, sound and music used at online gambling and potentially gaming platforms such as encouraging statements, cheers, and claps may contribute to positive feelings about play and reinforce further rounds and hence loss of control over the play [69].

Motivation Theories: Fulfilling a Heterogenous Need. Praise may also have a negative effect on individuals who overuse digital platforms to promote their self-esteem [76]. For example, authors in [77] suggested that excessive gameplay may result from associations made between self-worth and an avatar's achievements. Thus, having the opportunity to promote self-esteem through the praises on the avatar may act as self-medication and prompt excessive play.

Rewards. Systems that reward target behaviors may have great persuasive powers.

Biological Theories: Dopamine Hit. Reward principle is believed to be one of the core factors in the development and maintenance of DA. Reward principle is thought to act directly on reward centers in the brain [78]. Each time a reward is received in the form of likes, game points, digital coins, the dopamine circuits in the brain get stimulated resulting in an increase in dopamine release along with other neurochemicals. In time the circuits become habituated to the dopamine, producing a need for higher stimulation which results in increased interaction with digital platforms [79]. This resembles the tolerance symptom of substance based and behavioral addictions.

Learning Theories: Reinforcement. Digital platforms provide multiple rewards in different forms and the association made between use and the positive outcome makes interaction with digital platforms more likely. For example, social approval attained within virtual gaming platforms may act as a social reward further reinforcing the behavior [77]. The reinforcing power of digital rewards increases if the rewards are delivered on a variable ratio schedule which has been proven to be effective in the gambling industry [80]. Rewards in digital platforms such as likes, mentions, game points represent an example of variable-ratio reinforcement due to their unpredictable nature of occurrence. The variable-ratio schedule of such rewards then promotes a high rate of usage as users aim to receive more positive outcomes [81].

Decision-Making Theories: Cost-Benefit Analysis. According to reflective decision-making theories, individuals apply cost-benefit analysis and select behaviors that are aligned with their self-interest [45]. While doing such analysis it is believed that individuals do temporal discounting in which they assign greater value to events that are closer in time and assign a lower value to future events. While such a tendency is generally not seen as irrational and problematic, problems may arise when the discounting curves get steeper which is typical in addiction [82]. Thus, the presence and the appeal of rewards in digital platforms may contribute to individuals assigning greater value to experiences they have in present, without focusing much on the negative effects in the long run, e.g. reduced academic performance.

Reminders. *If a system reminds users of their target behavior, the users will more likely achieve their goals.*

Self-regulation Theories: Diminished Self-control. Visual and/or audio alerts may act as external triggers and disrupt individuals from their primary goals making it difficult for them to disengage from digital platforms [83]. Notifications of friend requests, chat messages or comments may hinder self-regulation and this, in turn, can result in loss of control and preoccupation with digital platforms [84]. Preoccupation is one of the main symptoms of behavioral addiction [85]. However, the relationship between notification principle and DA is not as direct, as on the contrary notifications can also reduce preoccupation and repeated checks to see whether one received a new message or alert from the platform.

Learning Theories: Cue to Act and Reinforcement. The learned associations between signals and behavior may lead to habit formation such that signals trigger automatic responses without the awareness of the individual [86]. According to Fogg [87] one of the three important ingredients to initiate behavior is *trigger*. Thus, in the context of digital platforms, notifications may act as triggers that cue an action [88]. Notifications may also act like rewards as they are delivered with variable-ratio reinforcement. Each time a notification is received, a positive expectation may be linked to it causing a "high". If the expectation is not met, this might cause a craving for more [81]. This mimics the relationship between variable-ratio reinforcement on slot machines and excessive gambling [80].

Psycho-Social Theories: Social Pressure. Messages and notifications may also be indirectly linked to DA in cases where notifications are received from significant others. In a time where constant connection has become a social norm [89], notification signaling messages from others can make the receiver obliged to respond immediately so that they are not seen in a bad light [90]. As a result, this social pressure might cause people to be preoccupied with social media platforms and neglect their other priorities. The ubiquity of networks that enables notifications to be received wherever and whenever also has the potential to increase this pressure. While social media messaging features such as delivery and read reports and the two ticks indicating that, may help reduce such preoccupations, in some contexts they might worsen the situation e.g. when the sender gets anxious if the receiver reads the message but does not reply [91, 92].

Suggestion. *Systems offering fitting suggestions will have greater persuasive power.*

Learning Theories: Cues for Act and Reinforcement. Just as notifications, suggestions may act as cues for action. While reminders are more about predefined tasks, suggestions are more about exploration and new actions. Consequently, algorithmic suggestions optimized by data characterizing individual interest may promote prolonged digital consumption where success in previous suggestions reinforces further user engagement [93].

Moreover, in addition to the content, the timing and framing are significantly important for the success of suggestions and can be highly optimized through the power of usage data and AI [94].

Decision-Making Theories: Biased Decision-Making. Artificial intelligence (AI) explanations provided with system suggestions for the purpose of transparency may also indirectly relate to DA. Presenting personalized explanations or explanations that use social proof for content suggestions may trigger biases that favor the addictive behavior. For example, explanations expressing why a video content is suggested (e.g. because your friends viewed it or because your age group viewed it) may activate bandwagon bias [95] which is a mental shortcut for acting in compliance with others and this can imply the correctness of prolonged engagement.

Liking. *A system that is visually attractive for its users is likely to be more persuasive.*

Decision-making Theories: Biased Decision-making. According to Cialdini [96] liking is one of the six persuasive strategies that can be used to influence and persuade people. One way liking might persuade people is through activating the halo effect bias which is a mental shortcut for judging a trait, e.g. look and attractiveness, in a good light [97]. Similar to the influence of attractive presentation of alcohol through advertisements and product placements [98], visually attractive software, e.g. the online gambling products, may trigger such bias and motivate engagement [99]. In support of this argument, Vaghefi et al. [100] stated that system design which is visually attractive is one of the causes explaining prolonged use which suggests a potential indirect link between liking principle and DA.

4.3 Social Support

Social Learning. *A person will be more motivated to perform a target behavior if they can use a system to observe others performing the same behavior.*

Learning Theories: Social Learning Social learning principle may indirectly relate to DA as being able to observe the relationship between other people's actions and related consequences may reinforce one to model similar behavior to acquire similar outcomes [101]. The authors of [102] found that individuals with game addiction were friends with people who also showed excessive gameplay and suggested that DA could be a result of modelling deviant peers. For example, observing social media influencers getting attention and affection from followers in the form of likes and shares may reinforce others to imitate similar online activity for social reward and this learnt behavior may transform into excessive social media use in time.

Social Comparison. *System users will have a greater motivation to perform the target behavior if they can compare their performance with the performance of others.*

Psycho-Social Theories: Social Comparison: The use of social comparison principle within digital platforms enable individuals to learn about other people's abilities and performances. Such information may increase the likelihood of DA especially for individuals who are high on social comparison orientation (SCO) [103, 104]. Because digital platforms are novel platforms with endless social comparison information, individuals high on SCO who base their self-evaluation on comparisons with others may spend longer hours in such platforms than intended in an attempt to decrease the uncertainty they feel regarding their self-concept [103].

Normative Influence. A system can leverage normative influence or peer pressure to increase the likelihood that a person will adopt a target behavior. Provides normative information on the target behavior.

Psycho-Social Theories: Normative Influence: This principle may indirectly relate to DA through descriptive norms and injunctive norms as people choose to behave in ways that are common and seen appropriate [60]. For example, Netflix's Top 10 most-watched video list within your country, updated regularly, can reinforce further usage as descriptive norms and may be seen as implying correctness of the behavior of watching more content. This influence could be coupled with social comparison, in which individual's asses themselves by how well their actions fit with others. In the Netflix example, this could refer to how up to date the user feels compared to his/her peers in terms of knowing the latest movies and documentaries. Another way normative influence principle may have a moderate effect on DA is through injunctive norms which refers to the perception of approved behaviors by others [105]. Injunctive norms act as building blocks of social relationships [60] and because digital platforms enable people to observe and interact with each other, injunctive norms could be easily formed and transferred in this medium. For example, peer pressure on excessive internet usage and fast responses may reinforce others to comply with the behavior. This is because not complying with expectations may mean loss of connection with peers [106]. As a result, digital interactions can become a salient part of the individual's life and dominate their minds.

Cooperation. A system can motivate users to adopt a target attitude or behavior by leveraging human beings' natural drive to cooperate.

Psycho-Social Theories: The Need to Belong and Peer Pressure: Cooperation principle introduced in some digital platforms may indirectly relate to DA as it generates user commitment to others online. For example, in massively multiplayer online role-playing games (MMORPG) cooperation with others is essential to progress as some missions are designed to be accomplished by group work [107]. Thus, the feeling of responsibility to the group and the peer pressure may reinforce gamers to play more and increase their playtime [12, 108]. Such a feeling of responsibility may cause preoccupation with the virtual world and increase individual's likelihood of giving up offline activities. This is supported by participant responses in [12] who felt committed to their friends and could not leave them alone in accomplishing a game task.

Competition. A system can motivate users to adopt a target attitude or behavior by leveraging human beings' natural drive to compete.

Psycho-Social Theories: Normative Influence and Comparison: Competition is based on self-progress in which individuals are driven by a unidirectional upward push to meet target performance and/or protect one's authority against others [109]. Accordingly, the presence of information on the number of likes, followers on social media platforms, or points, and achievements through badges of leader boards in games may trigger social comparison and encourage competition. Moreover, certain personality traits such as extraversion, assertiveness [110] and narcissism [111] may make individuals prone to competition and increase their engagement with digital platforms. In support, participants in [112] stated that they viewed competition as trigger for addiction.

Recognition. *By offering public recognition for an individual or group, a system can increase the likelihood that a person/group will adopt a target behavior.*

Psycho-Social Theories: Identity: The use of the recognition principle at digital platforms may indirectly relate to DA especially for individuals with low self-esteem. This is because individuals with low self-esteem might be using digital platforms to promote and enhance their self-concept which they find harder to do at offline settings [77, 113]. Thus, the respect and reputation that these people receive from social media and gaming platforms in the form of likes, points, awards may help individuals to avoid negative feelings and satisfy their self-esteem needs which in turn can explain their overuse.

4.4 System Credibility Support

Authority. *A system that leverages roles of authority is more persuasive.*

Psycho-Social Theories: Normative Influence. Influencers can be perceived as authority figures of social media platforms and promotions run by these platforms (e.g. YouTube Creator Awards) may encourage such perception. Technology companies can rely on celebrities and influencers for promoting new features in the apps and games which can act as a trigger for using them by users in a hasty style and without thinking of consequences. For example, when live streaming is presented with a demo showing a celebrity using the features, concerns like privacy and risks become lesser in comparison to the normative influence that demo has created.

Third Party Endorsements. *Third-party endorsements, especially from well-known and respected sources, boost perceptions on system credibility.*

Contextual Factor Theories: Advertisements. Marketing activities may reinforce vulnerability to DA as over-use of digital experiences may be portrayed in a favorable way through advertisements and product placements. This influence may come about in two ways, first advertisements may reinforce popular culture norms and second advertisements may act as cues for addictive activity [98, 114].

5   Conclusion

The present paper is one of the first attempts to examine the relationship between persuasive design techniques and DA. From the discussion, we can hypothesize that certain

PSD principles such as reduction, reward and social comparison may have a more direct effect on DA and other principles such as personalization and liking may have a more moderating effect. However, the differentiation made between direct and moderating effect of PSD principles should be treated as hypotheses that need to be addressed in future research. Overall, the purpose of this paper is not to argue causation but rather to open a discussion around the potential effects of PSD principle on DA in certain context and modality of usage. The paper does not discuss whether PSD principles trigger, worsen or contribute to DA. It is also possible that the relationship between persuasive design techniques and DA might also be explained by additional factors given that the digital products hold unique characteristics in comparison to addictive substances, e.g. their intelligent, interactive, personalized, and real-time nature. Nevertheless, analyzing the potential role of persuasive design in triggering and/or expediting DA from the lens of addiction theories is a start to discuss behavioral, cognitive, psycho-social, and other psychological mechanisms that may be involved in the development and maintenance of addictive behavior in the digital space. Identifying such mechanisms can also facilitate developing frameworks to design for responsible addictive technology through proactive (e.g. psychometric tests) and reactive measures (e.g. self-regulation tools).

Acknowledgments. This work has been partly supported by Kindred Group – Division of Responsible Gaming and Research, through a match-funded PhD project titled "Responsibility by Design: the Case of Online Gambling".

References

1. Cheng, C., Li, A.Y.-L.: Internet addiction prevalence and quality of (real) life: a meta-analysis of 31 nations across seven world regions. Cyberpsychol. Behav. Soc. Netw. **17**(12), 755–760 (2014). https://doi.org/10.1089/cyber.2014.0317
2. Winkler, A., Dörsing, B., Rief, W., Shen, Y., Glombiewski, J.A.: Treatment of internet addiction: a meta-analysis. Clin. Psychol. Rev. **33**(2), 317–329 (2013). https://doi.org/10.1016/j.cpr.2012.12.005
3. Gioia, F., Boursier, V.: Treatment of internet addiction and internet gaming disorder in adolescence: a systematic review. In: Multifaceted approach to digital addiction and its treatment. pp. 157–176. IGI Global (2019). https://doi.org/10.4018/978-1-5225-8449-0.ch008
4. American Psychiatric Association: Diagnostic and statistical manual of mental disorders (DSM-5®). American Psychiatric Pub (2013)
5. World Health Organization: ICD-11 for mortality and morbidity statistics (2018) (2018)
6. Kuss, D.J., Griffiths, M.D.: Internet and gaming addiction: a systematic literature review of neuroimaging studies. Brain Sci. **2**(3), 347–374 (2012). https://doi.org/10.3390/brainsci2030347
7. Olsen, C.M.: Natural rewards, neuroplasticity, and non-drug addictions. Neuropharmacology **61**(7), 1109–1122 (2011). https://doi.org/10.1016/j.neuropharm.2011.03.010
8. Young, K.S.: Internet addiction: the emergence of a new clinical disorder. Cyberpsychol. Behav. **1**(3), 237–244 (1998). https://doi.org/10.1089/cpb.1998.1.237
9. Johansson, A., Götestam, K.G.: Internet addiction: characteristics of a questionnaire and prevalence in Norwegian youth (12–18 years). Scand. J. Psychol. **45**(3), 223–229 (2004). https://doi.org/10.1111/j.1467-9450.2004.00398.x

10. Block, J.J.: Issues for DSM-V: Internet addiction. Am. J. Psychiatry **165**(3), 306–307 (2008). https://doi.org/10.1176/appi.ajp.2007.07101556

11. Beard, K.W.: Internet addiction: A review of current assessment techniques and potential assessment questions. CyberPsychol. Behav. **8**(1), 7–14 (2005). https://doi.org/10.1089/cpb. 2005.8.7

12. Beranuy, M., Carbonell, X., Griffiths, M.D.: A qualitative analysis of online gaming addicts in treatment. Int. J. Ment. Heal. Addict. **11**(2), 149–161 (2013). https://doi.org/10.1007/s11 469-012-9405-2

13. Lemmens, J.S., Valkenburg, P.M., Peter, J.: Development and validation of a game addiction scale for adolescents. Media Psychol. **12**(1), 77–95 (2009). https://doi.org/10.1080/152132 60802669458

14. Kardefelt-Winther, D.: The moderating role of psychosocial well-being on the relationship between escapism and excessive online gaming. Comput. Hum. Behav. **38**, 68–74 (2014). https://doi.org/10.1016/j.chb.2014.05.020

15. Ali, R., Jiang, N., Phalp, K., Muir, S., McAlaney, J.: The emerging requirement for digital addiction labels. In: Fricker, S.A., Schneider, K. (eds.) REFSQ 2015. LNCS, vol. 9013, pp. 198–213. Springer, Cham (2015). https://doi.org/10.1007/978-3-319-16101-3_13

16. Goldhaber, M.H.: The attention economy and the net (1997). https://doi.org/10.5210/fm.v2i 4.519

17. Hogan, E.A.: The attention economy: understanding the new currency of business. In. Academy of Management Briarcliff Manor, NY 10510 (2001). https://doi.org/10.5465/ame. 2001.5898765

18. Atkinson, B.M.C.: Captology: a critical review. In: IJsselsteijn, W.A., de Kort, Y.A.W., Midden, C., Eggen, B., van den Hoven, E. (eds.) PERSUASIVE 2006. LNCS, vol. 3962, pp. 171–182. Springer, Heidelberg (2006). https://doi.org/10.1007/11755494_25

19. Alrobai, A., Phalp, K., Ali, R.: Digital addiction: a requirements engineering perspective. In: Salinesi, C., van de Weerd, I. (eds.) REFSQ 2014. LNCS, vol. 8396, pp. 112–118. Springer, Cham (2014). https://doi.org/10.1007/978-3-319-05843-6_9

20. Kuonanoja, L., Oinas-Kukkonen, H.: Recognizing and mitigating the negative effects of information technology use: a systematic review of persuasive characteristics in information systems. In: Müller, S.D., Nielsen, J.A. (eds.) SCIS 2018. LNBIP, vol. 326, pp. 14–25. Springer, Cham (2018). https://doi.org/10.1007/978-3-319-96367-9_2

21. Oinas-Kukkonen, H., Harjumaa, M.: Persuasive systems design: key issues, process model, and system features. Commun. Assoc. Inf. Syst. **24**(1), 28 (2009)

22. West, R.: EMCDDA insights: models of addiction. Publications Office of the European Union. Luxemburg (2013)

23. West, R.: Theories of addiction. Addiction **96**(1), 3–13 (2001). https://doi.org/10.1046/j. 1360-0443.2001.96131.x

24. Kovac, V.B.: The more the 'Merrier': a multi-sourced model of addiction. Addict. Res. Theory **21**(1), 19–32 (2013). https://doi.org/10.3109/16066359.2012.691581

25. Elster, J., Skog, O.-J.: Getting Hooked: Rationality and Addiction. Cambridge University Press, Cambridge (1999)

26. Volkow, N.D., Wang, G.-J., Fowler, J.S., Tomasi, D., Telang, F.: Addiction: beyond dopamine reward circuitry. Proc. Natl. Acad. Sci. **108**(37), 15037–15042 (2011). https://doi.org/10. 1073/pnas.1010654108

27. Volkow, N.D., Fowler, J.S., Wang, G.J.: Role of dopamine in drug reinforcement and addiction in humans: results from imaging studies. Behav. Pharmacol. **13**(5), 355–366 (2002)

28. Volkow, N.D., Fowler, J.S.: Addiction, a disease of compulsion and drive: involvement of the orbitofrontal cortex. Cereb. Cortex **10**(3), 318–325 (2000). https://doi.org/10.1093/cer cor/10.3.318

29. Munafo, M.R., Zetteler, J.I., Clark, T.G.: Personality and smoking status: a meta-analysis. Nicotine Tobacco Res. **9**(3), 405–413 (2007). https://doi.org/10.1080/14622200701188851
30. Goodman, A.: Neurobiology of addiction: an integrative review. Biochem. Pharmacol. **75**(1), 266–322 (2008). https://doi.org/10.1016/j.bcp.2007.07.030
31. Kendler, K.S., Prescott, C.A., Myers, J., Neale, M.C.: The structure of genetic and environmental risk factors for common psychiatric and substance use disorders in men and women. Arch. Gener. Psychiatry **60**(9), 929–937 (2003). https://doi.org/10.1001/archpsyc.60.9.929
32. Keyes, K.M., Hatzenbuehler, M.L., Hasin, D.S.: Stressful life experiences, alcohol consumption, and alcohol use disorders: the epidemiologic evidence for four main types of stressors. Psychopharmacology **218**(1), 1–17 (2011). https://doi.org/10.1007/s00213-011-2236-1
33. Zullig, K.J., Valois, R.F., Huebner, E.S., Oeltmann, J.E., Drane, J.W.: Relationship between perceived life satisfaction and adolescents' substance abuse. J. Adolesc. Health **29**(4), 279–288 (2001). https://doi.org/10.1016/S1054-139X(01)00269-5
34. Pennanen, M., et al.: Smoking, nicotine dependence and nicotine intake by socio-economic status and marital status. Addict. Behav. **39**(7), 1145–1151 (2014). https://doi.org/10.1016/j.addbeh.2014.03.005
35. Pavlov, I.P.: The work of the digestive glands. Charles Griffin (1902)
36. Skinner, B.F.: Science and human behavior. Simon and Schuster (1965)
37. Wood, W., Rünger, D.: Psychology of habit. Ann. Rev. Psychol. **67** (2016). https://doi.org/10.1146/annurev-psych-122414-033417
38. Bandura, A.: Social cognitive theory: an agentic perspective. Ann. Rev. Psychol. **52**(1), 1–26 (2001). https://doi.org/10.1146/annurev.psych.52.1.1
39. Akers, R.L., Krohn, M.D., Lanza-Kaduce, L., Radosevich, M.: Social learning and deviant behavior: a specific test of a general theory. In: McCord, J., Laub, J.H. (eds.) Contemporary Masters in Criminology, pp. 187–214. Springer, Boston (1995). https://doi.org/10.1007/978-1-4757-9829-6_12
40. Akers, R.L., Cochran, J.K.: Adolescent marijuana use: a test of three theories of deviant behavior. Deviant Behav. **6**(4), 323–346 (1985). https://doi.org/10.1080/01639625.1985.9967683
41. Evans, J.S.B.T.: Dual-processing accounts of reasoning, judgment, and social cognition. Ann. Rev. Psychol. **59**, 255–278 (2008). https://doi.org/10.1146/annurev.psych.59.103006.093629
42. McCusker, C.G.: Cognitive biases and addiction: an evolution in theory and method. Addiction **96**(1), 47–56 (2002). https://doi.org/10.1046/j.1360-0443.2001.961474.x
43. Field, M., Mogg, K., Bradley, B.P.: Cognitive bias and drug craving in recreational cannabis users. Drug Alcohol Depend. **74**(1), 105–111 (2004). https://doi.org/10.1016/j.drugalcdep.2003.12.005
44. Scott, J.: Rational choice theory. Understand. Contemp. Soc.: Theories Present **129**, 671–685 (2000)
45. Becker, G.S., Murphy, K.M.: A theory of rational addiction. J. Polit. Econ. **96**(4), 675–700 (1988). https://doi.org/10.1086/261558
46. Orphanides, A., Zervos, D.: Rational addiction with learning and regret. J. Polit. Econ. **103**(4), 739–758 (1995). https://doi.org/10.1086/262001
47. Fotuhi, O., Fong, G.T., Zanna, M.P., Borland, R., Yong, H.-H., Cummings, K.M.: Patterns of cognitive dissonance-reducing beliefs among smokers: a longitudinal analysis from the International Tobacco Control (ITC) four country survey. Tob. Control **22**(1), 52–58 (2013). https://doi.org/10.1136/tobaccocontrol-2011-050139
48. Everitt, B.J., Robbins, T.W.: Neural systems of reinforcement for drug addiction: from actions to habits to compulsion. Nat. Neurosci. **8**(11), 1481–1489 (2005). https://doi.org/10.1038/nn1579

49. Baker, T.B., Piper, M.E., McCarthy, D.E., Majeskie, M.R., Fiore, M.C.: Addiction motivation reformulated: an affective processing model of negative reinforcement. Psychol. Rev. **111**(1), 33 (2004). https://doi.org/10.1037/0033-295X.111.1.33
50. Khantzian, E.J.: The self-medication hypothesis of substance use disorders: a reconsideration and recent applications. Harv. Rev. Psychiatry **4**(5), 231–244 (1997). https://doi.org/10.3109/10673229709030550
51. Walters, G.D.: Addiction and identity: exploring the possibility of a relationship. Psychol. Addict. Behav. **10**(1), 9 (1996). https://doi.org/10.1037/0893-164X.10.1.9
52. Carver, C.S., Scheier, M.F.: On the Self-regulation of Behavior. Cambridge University Press, Cambridge (2001)
53. Webb, T.L., Sniehotta, F.F., Michie, S.: Using theories of behaviour change to inform interventions for addictive behaviours. Addiction **105**(11), 1879–1892 (2010). https://doi.org/10.1111/j.1360-0443.2010.03028.x
54. De. Ridder, D.T.D., Lensvelt-Mulders, G., Finkenauer, C., Stok, F.M., Baumeister, R.F.: Taking stock of self-control: a meta-analysis of how trait self-control relates to a wide range of behaviors. Pers. Soc. Psychol. Rev. **16**(1), 76–99 (2012). https://doi.org/10.1177/1088868311418749
55. Baumeister, R.F., Vonasch, A.J.: Uses of self-regulation to facilitate and restrain addictive behavior. Addict. Behav. **44**, 3–8 (2015). https://doi.org/10.1016/j.addbeh.2014.09.011
56. Webb, T.L., Sheeran, P., Luszczynska, A.: Planning to break unwanted habits: habit strength moderates implementation intention effects on behaviour change. Br. J. Soc. Psychol. **48**(3), 507–523 (2010). https://doi.org/10.1348/014466608X370591
57. Oei, T.P., Baldwin, A.R.: Expectancy theory: a two-process model of alcohol use and abuse. J. Stud. Alcohol **55**(5), 525–534 (1994). https://doi.org/10.15288/jsa.1994.55.525
58. Kobus, K.: Peers and adolescent smoking. Addiction **98**, 37–55 (2003). https://doi.org/10.1046/j.1360-0443.98.s1.4.x
59. Asch, S.E.: Studies of independence and conformity: I. A minority of one against a unanimous majority. Psychol. Monogr.: Gener. Appl. **70**(9), 1–70 (1956). https://doi.org/10.1037/h0093718
60. Cialdini, R.B., Trost, M.R.: Social influence: Social norms, conformity and compliance. In: The Handbook of Social Psychology, 4th edn., vol. 1–2 pp. 151–192. McGraw-Hill, New York (1998)
61. Borsari, B., Carey, K.B.: Descriptive and injunctive norms in college drinking: a meta-analytic integration. J. Stud. Alcohol **64**(3), 331–341 (2003). https://doi.org/10.15288/jsa.2003.64.331
62. Dingle, G.A., Cruwys, T., Frings, D.: Social identities as pathways into and out of addiction. Front. Psychol. **6**, 1795 (2015). https://doi.org/10.3389/fpsyg.2015.01795
63. Smedley, B.D., Syme, S.L.: Committee on capitalizing on social science and behavioral research to improve the public's health. Promoting health: intervention strategies from social and behavioral research. Am. J. Health Promot. **15**(3), 149–166 (2001)
64. Chaloupka, F.J.: Contextual factors and youth tobacco use: policy linkages. Addiction **98**, 147–149 (2003). https://doi.org/10.1046/j.1360-0443.98.s1.10.x
65. Goldstein, R.Z., Volkow, N.D.: Drug addiction and its underlying neurobiological basis: neuroimaging evidence for the involvement of the frontal cortex. Am. J. Psychiatry **159**(10), 1642–1652 (2002). https://doi.org/10.1176/appi.ajp.159.10.1642
66. Baumeister, R.F., Heatherton, T.F.: Self-regulation failure: an overview. Psychol. Inq. **7**(1), 1–15 (1996). https://doi.org/10.1207/s15327965pli0701_1
67. Weinstein, A., Maraz, A., Griffiths, M.D., Lejoyeux, M., Demetrovics, Z.: Chapter 98 - compulsive buying—features and characteristics of addiction. In: Preedy, V.R. (ed.) Neuropathology of Drug Addictions and Substance Misuse, pp. 993–1007. Academic Press, San Diego (2016). https://doi.org/10.1016/B978-0-12-800634-4.00098-6

68. Molet, M., Miller, R.R.: Timing: an attribute of associative learning. Behav. Proc. **101**, 4–14 (2014). https://doi.org/10.1016/j.beproc.2013.05.015

69. Parke, J., Griffiths, M.D.: The Role of Structural Characteristics in Gambling, pp. 211–243. Elsevier, New York (2007)

70. Kahneman, D.: Thinking, Fast and Slow. Macmillan (2011)

71. Chóliz, M.: Cognitive biases and decision making in gambling. Psychol. Rep. **107**(1), 15–24 (2010). https://doi.org/10.2466/02.09.18.22.PR0.107.4.15-24

72. Csikszentmihalyi, M., Csikzentmihaly, M.: Flow: The psychology of optimal experience, vol. 1990. Harper & Row, New York (1990)

73. Webster, J., Trevino, L.K., Ryan, L.: The dimensionality and correlates of flow in human-computer interactions. Comput. Hum. Behav. **9**(4), 411–426 (1993). https://doi.org/10.1016/0747-5632(93)90032-N

74. Khang, H., Kim, J.K., Kim, Y.: Self-traits and motivations as antecedents of digital media flow and addiction: the Internet, mobile phones, and video games. Comput. Hum. Behav. **29**(6), 2416–2424 (2013). https://doi.org/10.1016/j.chb.2013.05.027

75. Gable, R.A., Hester, P.H., Rock, M.L., Hughes, K.G.: Back to basics: rules, praise, ignoring, and reprimands revisited. Interv. Sch. Clin. **44**(4), 195–205 (2009)

76. Mei, S., Yau, Y.H.C., Chai, J., Guo, J., Potenza, M.N.: Problematic Internet use, well-being, self-esteem and self-control: data from a high-school survey in China. Addict. Behav. **61**, 74–79 (2016). https://doi.org/10.1177/1053451208328831

77. Sioni, S.R., Burleson, M.H., Bekerian, D.A.: Internet gaming disorder: social phobia and identifying with your virtual self. Comput. Hum. Behav. **71**, 11–15 (2017). https://doi.org/10.1016/j.chb.2017.01.044

78. Han, D.H., Lee, Y.S., Yang, K.C., Kim, E.Y., Lyoo, I.K., Renshaw, P.F.: Dopamine genes and reward dependence in adolescents with excessive internet video game play. J. Addict. Med. **1**(3), 133–138 (2007). https://doi.org/10.1097/ADM.0b013e31811f465f

79. Cash, H., Rae, C.D., Steel, A.H., Winkler, A.: Internet addiction: a brief summary of research and practice. Curr. Psychiatry Rev. **8**(4), 292–298 (2012). https://doi.org/10.2174/157340012803520513

80. Griffiths, M.: Fruit machine gambling: the importance of structural characteristics. J. Gambl. Stud. **9**(2), 101–120 (1993). https://doi.org/10.1007/BF01014863

81. Berthon, P., Pitt, L., Campbell, C.: Addictive de-vices: a public policy analysis of sources and solutions to digital addiction. J. Public Policy Mark. **38**(4), 451–468 (2019). https://doi.org/10.1177/0743915619859852

82. Ainslie, G., Monterosso, J.: Chapter 2 - hyperbolic discounting as a factor in addiction: a critical analysis. In: Vuchinich, R.E., Heather, N. (eds.) Choice, Behavioural Economics and Addiction, pp. 35–69. Pergamon, Amsterdam (2003). https://doi.org/10.1016/B978-008044056-9/50043-9

83. Du, J., Kerkhof, P., van Koningsbruggen, G.M.: Predictors of social media self-control failure: immediate gratifications, habitual checking, ubiquity, and notifications. Cyberpsychol. Behav. Soc. Netw. **22**(7), 477–485 (2019). https://doi.org/10.1089/cyber.2018.0730

84. LaRose, R., Lin, C.A., Eastin, M.S.: Unregulated Internet usage: addiction, habit, or deficient self-regulation? Media Psychol. **5**(3), 225–253 (2003). https://doi.org/10.1207/S1532785XMEP0503_01

85. Alavi, S.S., Ferdosi, M., Jannatifard, F., Eslami, M., Alaghemandan, H., Setare, M.: Behavioral addiction versus substance addiction: correspondence of psychiatric and psychological views. Int. J. Prev. Med. **3**(4), 290 (2012)

86. Limayem, M., Hirt, S.G., Cheung, C.M.K.: How habit limits the predictive power of intention: the case of information systems continuance. MIS Q. 705–737 (2007). https://doi.org/10.2307/25148817

87. Fogg, B.J.: A behavior model for persuasive design. In: Proceedings of the 4th international Conference on Persuasive Technology (2009). https://doi.org/10.1145/1541948.1541999
88. Osatuyi, B., Turel, O.: Tug of war between social self-regulation and habit: explaining the experience of momentary social media addiction symptoms. Comput. Hum. Behav. **85**, 95–105 (2018). https://doi.org/10.1016/j.chb.2018.03.037
89. Ames, M.G.: Managing mobile multitasking: the culture of iPhones on stanford campus. Paper Presented at the Proceedings of the 2013 Conference on Computer Supported Cooperative work, San Antonio, Texas, USA (2013). https://doi.org/10.1145/2441776.2441945
90. Kalman, Y.M., Rafaeli, S.: Online pauses and silence: chronemic expectancy violations in written computer-mediated communication. Commun. Res. **38**(1), 54–69 (2011). https://doi.org/10.1177/0093650210378229
91. Alutaybi, A., Arden-Close, E., McAlaney, J., Stefanidis, A., Phalp, K., Ali, R.: How can social networks design trigger fear of missing out? In: 2019 IEEE International Conference on Systems, Man and Cybernetics (SMC), 6–9 October 2019, pp. 3758–3765 (2019) https://doi.org/10.1109/SMC.2019.8914672
92. Alutaybi, A., Al-Thani, D., McAlaney, J., Ali, R.: Combating fear of missing out (FoMO) on social media: the FoMO-R method. Int. J. Environ. Res. Public Health **17**(17), 6128 (2020). https://doi.org/10.3390/ijerph17176128
93. Gomez-Uribe, C.A., Hunt, N.: The Netflix Recommender System: Algorithms, Business Value, and Innovation. J ACM Trans. Manage. Inf. Syst. **6**(4), Article 13 (2016). https://doi.org/10.1145/2843948
94. Siles, I., Espinoza-Rojas, J., Naranjo, A., Tristán, M.F.: The mutual domestication of users and algorithmic recommendations on Netflix. Commun. Cult. Critique **12**(4), 499–518 (2019). https://doi.org/10.1093/ccc/tcz025
95. Navazio, R.: An experimental approach to bandwagon research. Public Opin. Q. **41**(2), 217–225 (1977). https://doi.org/10.1086/268376
96. Cialdini, R.B.: Harnessing the science of persuasion. Harv. Bus. Rev. **79**(9), 72–81 (2001)
97. Nisbett, R.E., Wilson, T.D.: The halo effect: evidence for unconscious alteration of judgments. J. Pers. Soc. Psychol. **35**(4), 250–256 (1977). https://doi.org/10.1037/0022-3514.35.4.250
98. Sulkunen, P.: Images of addiction: representations of addictions in films. Addict. Res. Theory **15**(6), 543–559 (2007). https://doi.org/10.1080/16066350701651255
99. Fogg, B.J.: Persuasive technology: using computers to change what we think and do. Ubiquity **2002**(December), 2 (2002). https://doi.org/10.1145/764008.763957
100. Vaghefi, I., Lapointe, L., Boudreau-Pinsonneault, C.: A typology of user liability to IT addiction. Inf. Syst. J. **27**(2), 125–169 (2017). https://doi.org/10.1111/isj.12098
101. Bandura, A.: Social Learning Theory. Prentice-Hall (1977)
102. Gunuc, S.: Peer influence in Internet and digital game addicted adolescents: is internet/digital game addiction contagious. Int J High Risk Behav Addict **6**(2), e33681 (2017). https://doi.org/10.5812/ijhrba.33681
103. Vogel, E.A., Rose, J.P., Okdie, B.M., Eckles, K., Franz, B.: Who compares and despairs? The effect of social comparison orientation on social media use and its outcomes. Pers. Individ. Differ. **86**, 249–256 (2015). https://doi.org/10.1016/j.paid.2015.06.026
104. Yang, C.-C.: Instagram use, loneliness, and social comparison orientation: interact and browse on social media, but don't compare. Cyberpsychol. Behav. Soc. Netw. **19**(12), 703–708 (2016). https://doi.org/10.1089/cyber.2016.0201
105. Cialdini, R.B., Reno, R.R., Kallgren, C.A.: A focus theory of normative conduct: recycling the concept of norms to reduce littering in public places. J. Pers. Soc. Psychol. **58**(6), 1015 (1990). https://doi.org/10.1037/0022-3514.58.6.1015

106. Wang, Y., Wu, A.M.S., Lau, J.T.F.: The health belief model and number of peers with internet addiction as inter-related factors of internet addiction among secondary school students in Hong Kong. BMC Public Health **16**(1), 272 (2016). https://doi.org/10.1186/s12889-016-2947-7

107. Yee, N.: The psychology of massively multi-user online role-playing games: motivations, emotional investment, relationships and problematic usage. In: Schroeder, R., Axelsson, A.-S. (eds.) Avatars at Work and Play: Collaboration and Interaction in Shared Virtual Environments, vol. 34, pp. 187–207. Springer, Dordrecht (2006). https://doi.org/10.1007/1-4020-3898-4_9

108. Klemm, C., Pieters, W.: Game mechanics and technological mediation: an ethical perspective on the effects of MMORPG's. Ethics Inf. Technol. **19**(2), 81–93 (2017). https://doi.org/10.1007/s10676-017-9416-6

109. Festinger, L.: A theory of social comparison processes. Hum. Relat. **7**(2), 117–140 (1954). https://doi.org/10.1177/001872675400700202

110. Fong, M., Zhao, K., Smillie, L.D.: Personality and competitiveness: extraversion, agreeableness, and their aspects, predict self-reported competitiveness and competitive bidding in experimental auctions. Pers. Individ. Differ. **169**, 109907 (2021). https://doi.org/10.1016/j.paid.2020.109907

111. Luchner, A.F., Houston, J.M., Walker, C., Alex Houston, M.: Exploring the relationship between two forms of narcissism and competitiveness. Pers. Individ. Differ. **51**(6), 779–782 (2011). https://doi.org/10.1016/j.paid.2011.06.033

112. Hussain, Z., Griffiths, M.D.: The attitudes, feelings, and experiences of online gamers: a qualitative analysis. CyberPsychol. Behav. **12**(6), 747–753 (2009). https://doi.org/10.1089/cpb.2009.0059

113. Gonzales, A.L., Hancock, J.T.: Mirror, mirror on my Facebook wall: effects of exposure to Facebook on self-esteem. Cyberpsychol. Behav. Soc. Netw. **14**(1–2), 79–83 (2011). https://doi.org/10.1089/cyber.2009.0411

114. Martin, I.M., et al.: On the road to addiction: the facilitative and preventive roles of marketing cues. J. Bus. Res. **66**(8), 1219–1226 (2013). https://doi.org/10.1016/j.jbusres.2012.08.015

Defining Features of Behavior Design

Considering Context

Sandra Burri Gram-Hansen[(✉)]

Department of Communication and Psychology, Aalborg University, Aalborg, Denmark
burri@hum.aau.dk

Abstract. Since the early recognition of Persuasive Technologies, the notion of digital design with the intent to influence and change attitudes and behaviors has evolved tremendously. Digital influence and behavior design is now recognize in a variety of theoretical and methodological approaches, and behavior design is continuously influencing more complex application domains. With the development of the field emerges a need for clearer understanding of these different design approaches, their possibilities and limitations, in order for designers to identify and apply the best approach depending on the intent and context. In this paper, we discuss some of the primary overlaps between Nudging and Persuasive Design. Moreover, we point towards research in neuroscience in order to highlight a potential need to reconsider central elements of persuasive design, such as efficient praise and rewards. The aim of the paper is to contribute to the ongoing discussion about the role of behavior design in digital media, and the ethical considerations that emerge from this domain.

Keywords: Persuasion · Nudging · Behaviour design · Digital pollution · Ethics

1 Introduction

In this paper, a discussion of the similarities and differences between nudging and persuasive design, potential overlaps and diverse areas of application for these two approaches to behaviour design direct the paper towards a discussion of ethical considerations and the need the further development of the persuasive technology field. Whilst Nudging and Persuasive Technology both emerge from similar theoretical foundations - in particular, social psychology and digital design, this paper suggests that ethical, and methodological differences, as well as diversity in the users' realisation processes, constitute subtle differences, which are important to consider if new solutions are to be efficient. In a time where the vast majority of interactive technologies are designed to influence users, understanding the possibilities and limitations of different approaches is essential to designers who wish to provide affective technologies with respect for the intended use contexts and overall intention of the technology itself.

When research and practice in persuasive technologies emerged in early 2000, the notion that technologies were more than simple tools, was novel and ground breaking. Since then, with the progression of social media, smart applications and complex organizational systems, the understanding that technologies are far beyond simple tools, is

© Springer Nature Switzerland AG 2021
R. Ali et al. (Eds.): PERSUASIVE 2021, LNCS 12684, pp. 308–319, 2021.
https://doi.org/10.1007/978-3-030-79460-6_24

more generally accepted. As users, we appreciate that technologies make life easy for us, and consequently we accept that the technologies (and as such the designers) make decisions for us which we would previously have paid more attention to. For instance, we embrace the help we can receive about spelling and grammar, and in return blindly accept that our way of communicating potentially becomes more systematized and less creative [1].

With the introduction of Persuasive Technology Fogg exposed a previously unnoticed development in HCI, comprised by the transition of technologies functioning as tools, to also being a facilitator of mediation and social interactions with the potential to influence the user's attitude and behaviour [2]. Since then, and in particularly during the past decade, the world has witnessed a massive transformation both technological and design wise, resulting in a much wider range of behaviour change systems.

In 2009 Thaler and Sunstein introduced Nudging [3], as a slightly similar approach to behaviour change, but also in areas such as learning [4, 5] and mediation of cultural heritage [6], digital solutions are being designed with clear intentions of influencing the users' attitudes or motivating them to change behaviour either momentarily or continuously. Likewise, the majority of leisure technologies such as games and social media are increasingly applying behaviour change principles in their designs. Designing with the intent to change has become an ambition across a wide range of different application contexts, yet persuasive technology and nudging distinguish themselves by not being domain specific but rather applicable in a wide variety of different situations.

With this swift development in the way we design and apply technologies, understanding the subtle yet significant nuances of different approaches to behaviour design is crucial not only to designers but also to end users. For designers, understanding the variances between different approaches to behaviour change is fundamental for choosing the right approach for a specific problem. For users, understanding different ways a technology has the potential to influence them, ensures a transparency and enables the users to stay in control of the technology. It is with this at mind, that we argue that ethics remains essential to both research and practice in behaviour design, and that ethics is a defining element of persuasive design.

In this paper, theories of nudging and persuasive design are outlined, in order to discuss their theoretical relations as well as their potential and limitations in different application domains. To further nuance the discussion, perspectives from neuroscience with particular attention towards the impact of digital resources and the dangers of digital disturbance are included. As such, these outlines also include ethical considerations related to changing people's behaviour. The aim of the paper is to contribute to the ongoing theoretical discussion regarding the potential of persuasive technologies in relation to other approaches to behaviour design.

This paper supports previous arguments, that ethics should be considered a defining feature of persuasive design, not simply in theory but also in practice. In order to exemplify some of the fundamental distinctions of persuasion, nudging is presented as an alternative approach to behaviour design, with different ethical implications, as well as different potential concerning application domains. The neuroscientific perspective aims to highlight practical implications of digital technologies provide recommendations for future research and practical consideration within persuasive design.

As the digital realm is increasingly influencing both private and professional practices, more and more things may be seen as a product of design, and design itself a particular type of communication. Designs are created with a specific intention in mind, and through e.g. shapes, colours and areas of application, the intended use is communicated to the user. It is with this in mind that neuroscience is identified as a relevant perspective to the further development of the PT field. When PT was initially introduced, much research focused on translating the principles of the physical world into corresponding digital designs. However, recent studies in neuroscience indicate that the impact of physical interaction does not correspond directly to efforts made through technology. Consequently, design as a type of communication may potentially call for a language of its own – particularly if communication is to be both affective and effective.

2   Nudging vs. Persuasion, a Few Distinctions

Fogg's original research [7] on the potential of persuasive technologies comprised novelty and foresight in several ways. Not only did it draw attention towards design features and principles which when applied in a structured and considered manner had the potential to influence the users', but more importantly it very early on identified a new tendency in the design of digital resources and in the application of interactive systems. Although Fogg's research in persuasive technology is acknowledged as a novel perspective on the potential of interactive technologies, his work was soon followed by Thaler and Sunstein's introduction of another approach to behaviour change designs; Nudging [3].

Similar to persuasive design, nudging is based on years of research in social psychology, and with the introduction of digital nudging [8], the distinctions between these different approaches to behaviour design has become even more of a grey area. Nudging is argued to facilitate behaviour change by organizing the context in a manner by which some choices are made more obvious than others. The approach draws upon what Kahneman refers to as fast thinking [9] and which is described by Thaler and Sunstein as the automatic system of information processing [3]. Kahneman's theories are not distinctly related to nudging, as they have also been discussed and related to persuasion e.g. in The Elaboration Likelihood Model (ELM) [10]. However, it is the discussion about automatic and reflective systems, which provide the first indication of a distinction between persuasion and nudging.

Humans are argued to subject to irrational behaviour, which stems from two kinds of thinking. In short, these two ways of processing information gives name to dual-process theory that describes their modes of operation. Stanovich and West conceptualizes the two processes as systems, labelling them System 1 and System 2 - or in Thaler and Sunstein's terms: The Automatic System and The Reflective System, respectively. Individuals utilise both systems when processing information and making decisions. Whereas System 1 operates in an intuitive, automatic, fast, and largely unconscious and, thus, effortless manner, System 2 process information consciously in a controlled, slow, and effortful way. The automatic system operates in an intuitive, automatic and mostly unconscious manner, without rational processing of the situation. Hence, nudges are solely efficient within the context where they are applied, and do only motivate momentary behaviour change. Nudging frames choices by organising the context in a specific way to make some decisions more appealing than others. This means making some choice options seem more significant than others do. Nudging overcomes the bounded rationality of an individual by designing an environment that intervenes in the perception as well as the decision-making. It manages to do so since a nudge always targets and motivates automatic behaviour, but rarely encourages deliberate choices. - In short, a nudge can only change behaviour momentarily since the effect only pertains to the specific context of the nudge.

The distinction between automatic and reflective systems becomes relevant, as it also relates to a particularly important difference between nudging and persuasion. Distinctions that are subtle, yet important when aiming to choose the appropriate strategy in a given behaviour design context.

As is the case in nudging, persuasion constitute an approach to design with the intent to change the user's behaviour. Throughout the past decade, the notion of persuasive technologies and persuasive design has been explored from the perspectives of several well-established research fields, including computer science, social psychology and classical rhetoric. Although persuasion as a concept lacks an unequivocal definition, important distinctions have been suggested.

The point has been made that persuasion is a process rather than a momentary influence [11, 12] that persuasion is a more transparent and reflective concept than the rhetorical peithenanke [13] and that ideally the goal of persuasion is for the persuasive initiative to become redundant [14]. In a critical review of Fogg's original work [15], Atkinson argued that in order for persuasive technologies to be ethical, some level of transparency is required, in the sense that the users must be informed about the persuasive intention of the technology. A point also supported by Berdichevsky and Neuenschwander [16].

Considering the above, it may be argued that while nudging predominantly targets the automatic system, persuasion contrarily targets the reflective system. Users are not to be manipulated or led blindly into a particular behaviour. Rather they are to actively and willingly engage in a behaviour change process. As such, persuasive design distinguishes itself from more behaviouristic approaches to behaviour design, by facilitating an already agreed upon change. An agreement, which is also the foundation of achieving not only behaviour change but also a change of attitude.

Pointing towards differences between nudging and persuasion does not intend to promote one approach over the other. Rather, the goal of the above perspectives, as well as the following, is to point towards distinctions that may be relevant when selecting the appropriate approach to a behaviour design. For instance, it may be argued that persuasive initiatives with the intent to motivate users to sort their waste, have potentially little effect compared to nudging if the persuasion context is a busy pedestrian street in a city, where people pass by swiftly and without particular attention to their surroundings. In this particular example, a simple nudge guiding the user to the correct bin is likely more appropriate. Likewise, nudging may have limited potential if the intended behaviour change is related to lifestyle, such as healthier eating habits or a more environmentally friendly approach to waste management. In such cases, in order for the behaviour change to become permanent, there is a likely need for both transparency and recognition that change takes time.

In consideration that attitudes and behaviours are now being influenced through most types of technology design, a growing challenge for behaviour designers is to identify and apply the right approach to ensure the most efficient result. Any type of behaviour design entails knowledge about different methods and the implications they may have. In other words, designers should know when and how to change what. Different approaches to behaviour design ('how') excel at changing specific behaviours ('what') at specific times and in specific contexts.

3   Ethics as a Defining Feature of Persuasion

In line with the argument that persuasion calls for transparency remains a distinct focus on the ethical demand of persuasion, which may be further elaborated upon by reference to the rhetorical understanding of persuasion, and the notion of Kairos.

Persuasion itself has been suggested to distinguish itself as a more ethical approach than the more forceful or potentially deceptive and manipulative peithenanke [17]. Peithenanke is not by definition unethical, but rather a recognition of influential strategies that are not transparent, and which present the truth in a more decorative manner. Gram-Hansen et.al. referred to Chocolate covered broccoli as a way of describing the approach, which may for instantly appear in marketing strategies [13].

Another often-referenced rhetorical concept is Kairos, which comprises the opportune moment for a persuasive initiative to take place. Kairos is most often referred to as timing; however, the concept combines the appropriate time with considerations regarding the appropriate place and manner of the action. As is the case with the rhetorical appeals; logos, pathos and ethos, the three dimensions are inseparable and must all be considered and balanced in accordance with the persuasive intention [18, 19]. With a distinct focus on appropriateness, Kairos not only facilitates reflections regarding the intended use context and e.g. timing and location specifics within the persuasive systems. It also provides important indications regarding the ethical and methodological perspectives related to persuasive design.

The notion of appropriateness itself underlines the importance of ethical reflections, as that which is appropriate in one situation may not be in another. In relation to persuasive design, this leads to the understanding that persuasive initiatives that are efficient in one context may not be so in another. Persuasive initiatives must be designed in consideration of the intended use context and in the appropriate manner as perceived by the user. A potential implication of this is that participatory design or similar approaches to user-centered design, may be a requisite to persuasive design, due to the element of appropriate manner. Whilst designers may be able to determine the appropriate time and place for a persuasive initiative to take place, the appropriate manner is based on the user's understanding of the context. As a result, users must be considered throughout the design process, and acknowledged as experts equally to the designers [12].

In comparison, nudging [20], does not disregard ethics, however, it does not share the perspectives on transparency as opposed to coercion. As the approach targets the previously mentioned automatic system, there can be little expectation towards the user making reflective decisions. Consequently, ethics is very often brought into consideration, simply by ensuring that users are not forced into only one possible action. While the desired behaviour may be the most obvious choice, there will always be a way around, or a chance to opt out.

Subtle as these differences may be, they are essential when considering the appropriate method for a design, as it indicates that while nudging may be highly appropriate in situations, which call for very little cognitive action by the user, it does not necessarily support long-term changes. E.g., Nudging may be the by far most appropriate solution in a busy shopping centre, where users pass by with little though about their surroundings, but less appropriate for a smart installation in an office or home, where the technology is meant to facilitate long-term change.

4 Mapping Out the Differences?

The new range in behaviour design approaches as well as new application domains, call for a far stronger awareness regarding the previously mentioned questions about what to influence, how to do at when to do it. Acknowledging that while for instance Persuasive technology and Nudging share some common background, they do also have important differences which make them either more or less suitable as a method, depending on the intention and on the application context. While persuasion and nudging are currently be the dominant approaches, it is likely that the future will give reason to also include other techniques with similar yet subtle differences. For instance, digital learning has the potential to influence both the attitudes and behaviours of the learners, however with equally delicate differences both in theory and in practice [21]. Learning designs have the potential to change attitude and behaviour; however, it is also quite possible to learn something but not change either one. Moreover, learning does not necessarily provide the same level of voluntariness as argued to be essential in persuasion. Students may be motivated by different learning designs, but the process of getting the students to engage in a learning process may not be force-free but simply mandatory [12]. While learning may have previously been considered somewhat domain specific, developments in both the traditional educational system as well as e.g. work place education, gives reason to consider digital learning as one of the potential future contributors to behaviour design both theoretically and methodologically.

Establishing an overview of different approaches to behaviour design has to some extent, already previously been approached by Fogg, in terms of a behaviour grid mapping out 15 different ways for behaviour change to take place [22]. The Behavior grid was initially subject to much critique, as it also suggested that persuasive principles could be mapped to the different types of behaviour change, thus easing the process of identifying which persuasive initiatives would be efficient to a given intention. In spite of this critique, the mapping of different types of behaviour change does hold potential as a tool for reflecting upon the intention of a design, and subsequently the choice of appropriate method. As such, the grid may be used to facilitate the dialogue about e.g. nudging vs persuasive design as well as areas where the two approaches may benefit from being applied in combination.

As visualized in Fig. 1, Fogg's Behavior Grid does provide designers with a framework for reflections regarding different approaches to behaviour design, based on the intended outcome. Extending the previous sections overview of nudging and persuasion,

Fig. 1. Fogg's behaviour grid with indications of persuasion and nudging

nudging is identified as what Fogg refers to as Dot behaviour, while persuasion with its distinct focus on continuous behaviour change is identified as Path behaviour. Moreover, what Fogg refers to as a Span behaviour may potentially comprise designs that target the grey area where nudges are no longer sufficient, yet the need is not for a continuous behaviour change. Such would for instance be the case for some patients recovering from injury, and find themselves in a strict rehabilitation regime for a shorter or longer period.

If extending the framework, the behaviour grid would benefit greatly from including other approaches to behaviour design (e.g. learning) and more importantly an overview of the ethical implications of the different behaviour design methods. As previously stated, ethics appears to be a distinguishing concept between at least nudging and persuasion, and in some areas, also digital learning.

Most importantly however, a further development of the framework would provide behaviour designers with a much-needed overview of the possibilities and limitations of different approaches to behaviour design. While the rhetorical notion of Karis may indicate that persuasion calls for User centered and possibly participatory approaches to the design process, Nudging may comprise a more expert driven approach. Maslow argued that "if all you have is a hammer, then everything appears to be a nail" [23]. With the development in digital resources and the recognition of different approaches to behaviour design applied, it appears timely to move beyond the hammer and identify these as different tools in a larger behaviour design toolbox.

5   Considering the Nature of the Mind

While the introduction of persuasive technologies focused on transforming physical experience and solutions into digital counterparts, recent studies strongly indicate that the future of persuasive technologies calls for more than digitalization of the physical realm. As we learn more about the influence of digital resources, it becomes evident that efficient persuasive technologies of the future may require reconsideration of fundamental persuasive principles.

Adding not only to the ethical discussions regarding behaviour design but also to the distinctions between persuasion and nudging, Rashid and Kenner approaches behaviour change technology from a biological and neuroscientific perspective, pointing towards the influence technology has on our hormone levels and consequently our ability to act rationally in a digital age [24].

Pointing towards resent and ongoing studies, Rashid and Kenner argue that the rapid digital development is showing consequences for the human brain, for instance concerning production of dopamine molecules. Dopamine is generally described as a neurotransmitter, a hormone that influences our desires, motivation and attention, which is released in response to different inputs and influences our emotions. The human mind strives for pleasure and dopamine is released on the expectation of rewards. While unfortunate implications of dopamine influence include addiction, the release of dopamine also influences more general senses of joy, such receiving a compliment, being acknowledged at work, or winning a game. Unfortunately, one of the observations made when exploring digital influence from a biological perspective indicates that the dopamine release becomes less if the joyful interaction takes place online, compared to real life interactions. Praise given face to face by far exceeds the pleasure of receiving a friendly text message [24].

A second important observation addressed by Rashid, relates to the previously mentioned automatic and reflective systems [9], and more distinctly towards the balance between them. Rashid argues that the automatic system is by far the most dominant – potentially being applied for as much as 90% of the time, leaving as little as 10% for reflective thoughts. The automatic system is not a challenge in itself – it is rather beneficial that we do not need to think much about breathing. What is however, a challenge is the potential of digital resources enabling the automatic system to take up even more of our time, such as the case appears to be with the mobile phone.

In 2007, Fogg argued that the mobile phone had the potential to be the most important platform for behaviour design, not only due to the technological potential, but also due to our emotional connection to our mobile phones [25]. The perspectives presented by Fogg were once again early indications of new tendencies, and have in more recent studies been elaborated upon by Jane Vincent, who argues on the unique emotional relation between users and their mobile phones [26]. We bring our phones everywhere, personalize them and share our most precious content with them, and in return, they comprise the one technology that enables us to almost anything, including finding our way, shopping and finding information for both work and entertainment. When Fogg initially addressed mobile persuasion, the world was only witnessing the early days of smartphones. A decade down the way, the smartphone has become a natural companion for both children and adults in most areas of the world. Moreover, personalization has shifted from being a manner of expressing oneself to the world through covers and select ringtones, to something far more personal and private, were the mobile phone contains all things near and dear to us, such as pictures of our loved ones.

The challenge in this development however, remains that the vast majority of actions taken via the mobile phone is done automatically, rather than reflective. Playing games and surfing social media is with the mind set to auto pilot [24]. Rashid refers to this as digital pollution and argues that users of digital media must become more aware of the way they are being influenced by technologies. Particularly to ensure that they have the ability to identify digital influence and actively decided whether it is desired or not. Rather than arguing that all technology is evil, he recommends a stronger awareness amongst users, so that they remain in power of the technology and in control of when to apply it and when to switch it of or simply go offline.

6 So What Does This Mean for Behaviour Design?

The observations presented by Rashid are relevant not only with regards to distinguishing different approaches to behaviour design from each other, but also in relation to a further development of the persuasive technology field and the development of persuasive systems.

Previous research within the persuasive technology community has included studies on areas such as praise and rewards. Providing the user with positive feedback and rewards for completing or engaging in specific tasks is a recognized way of sparking motivation both in games and in behaviour design systems in general. As mentioned, the release of dopamine hormones motivate humans to enjoy acknowledgement and strive for pleasure. If recognizing that the dopamine levels differ between physical and digital interaction, future research may need to include exploring new ways of providing praise and rewards through digital media. Potentially to the extent where computer mediated communication is recognized as an entirely different way of communicating, compared to those in the physical realm. The need to consider computation a fourth language in line with spoken, written and mathematic languages is already suggested within computational thinking, and as a result, researchers are suggesting a stronger need for computational empowerment amongst children and young adults. Where previous divides have been identified between users of technology and non-users, this perspective is no longer relevant. Rather, the divide is seen between those who are users and those who are able to apply technologies critically and constructively [27].

This challenge becomes even more apparent when also considering the notion of digital pollution and the very limited time during which we are reflective. In a future where digital pollution is unlikely to become less, designers appear to face a significant challenge praise and rewards that do not simply drown in the noise, but rather stand out and trigger the desired production of dopamine.

Also in a wider scale, the implications of fast and slow thinking or automatic and reflective systems is important to consider when choosing the right approach for influencing a given behaviour. As mentioned, previous research has suggested that while nudging targets the automatic system, persuasion aims at influencing the user through the reflective system. With transparency and ethics continuously mentioned as fundamental features of persuasion, persuasive systems must to some extent aim to ensure these very features. However, in a digitally polluted reality, it is not sufficient that the designer provides information regarding the system and the intended outcomes reflective user engagement is a necessity for transparency to be implemented in practice.

7   Future Research

In this paper, I have sought to highlight some of the subtle differences between persuasive technology and nudging, and based on this, point towards some of the challenges designers face in current state of digital behaviour design. Very few answers have been provided and even fewer solutions. Rather, this paper has aimed at contributing to the ongoing discussion of the possibilities and limitations of persuasive technologies. That being said, the main points to take away should include the following:

1. Similar to most other approaches to behaviour design, Persuasive Design and Nudging represent individual approaches to behaviour design, with multiple overlaps but also with clear and important distinctions. In order for design practitioners to identify the appropriate design approach, a nuanced understanding of the intended type of influence, and its correspondence with the intended context is necessary.
2. Users are different and contexts change – there is no such thing as a "one fits all" solution. Direct transition cannot be made from the physical to the digital context, and within the digital realm, solution from one domain cannot be transferred directly to another.
3. Ethical considerations remain a defining concept of persuasive design, comprising not only a strength to this behaviour change approach, but also some limitations. While design solutions may be transferrable, they may not be ethical in a new context, and consequently, ethical reflections must remain at the core of persuasive design theory as well as in practice.
4. The majority of language are living and constantly developing. In order for persuasive technologies to remain efficient, keeping up with this development in theory as well as in practice, is essential. Neuroscience indicates that the digital realm may call for a language of its own. If recognising design as a particular type of communication, research in Persuasive technology must remain focused on identifying and developing affective principles in areas such as digital social support.

As mentioned, during the past decade, the world has witnessed a transition in the way in which technologies are designed, which make it continuously harder to identify different approaches to behaviour design and to tell them apart. Where Fogg was early to identify these new tendencies, the development in digital media during the past decade have led to the dawn of many other approaches to design, which all hold the potential to intentionally influence the users. In an age where UX designers ensure easy navigation for even very young users, and where interactive technologies are continuously being applied in new domains, it becomes increasingly more difficult to navigate through the digital realm.

This challenge is relevant not only to the designers who strive to create systems that are efficient and engaging, but also the end users who potentially loose autonomy because of digital pollution and lack of transparency.

Persuasive technologies has often been related to classic and digital rhetoric. At its core, rhetoric is the art of winning over ones audience by beautiful and affective argumentation [28]. However, even the most affective arguments fail their purpose if they drown in a digitally polluted world. In consideration of the studies presented by

Rashid and Kenner, in particularly the suggestion that the automatic system is taking up increasingly more space in the human brain, behaviour designers and in particular persuasive designers appear to be facing new challenges in terms of simply catching the user's attention at a reflective level. This challenge becomes even more essential when also considering the argument that users do not have the same hormonal reactions to digital influence as they do to physical interaction.

In order to meet these new challenges, designers must become equipped to navigate in a growing toolbox of behaviour design methods and frameworks. Entangled the different approaches may appear, they do also have distinctions which may help indicate situations where they are particularly relevant to apply or particularly likely to fail. Picking the right method for the job should be a first step for designers who wish to make themselves heard above the digital pollution.

Moreover, by reference to the already ongoing discussions in Computational Thinking, future research in persuasive technology and persuasive design may benefit from considering design a 4th language, and more thoroughly explore what implications this may have. Much has already been learned from classical rhetoric, and much can yet be derived from this field. However, in consideration that future generations will be computationally empowered, there may be a need to expand the range of persuasive principles and our understanding of multimodality.

References

1. Twersky, E., Davis, J.: "Don't say that!" In: de Vries, P.W., Oinas-Kukkonen, H., Siemons, L., Beerlage-de Jong, N., van Gemert-Pijnen, L. (eds.) PERSUASIVE 2017. LNCS, vol. 10171, pp. 215–226. Springer, Cham (2017). https://doi.org/10.1007/978-3-319-55134-0_17
2. Fogg, B.: Persuasive Technology, Using Computers to change what we Think and Do. Morgan Kaufmann Publishers, Massachusetts (2003)
3. Thaler, R., Sunstein, C.R.: Nudge: Improving Decisions About Health, Wealth, and Happiness. GBR: Penguin Books, London (2009).Rev. and expanded ed.
4. Gram-Hansen, S.B.: Persuasive designs for learning - learning in persuasive design: exploring the potential of persuasive designs in complex environments. Aalborg Universitetsforlag, pp. 181 (2016)
5. Glasemann, M., Kanstrup, A.M., Ryberg, T.: Making chocolate-covered broccoli: designing a mobile learning game about food for young people with diabetes. In: DIS 2010 Proceedings of the 8th ACM Conference on Designing Interactive Systems. ACM, New York (2010)
6. Gram-Hansen, S.B., Gram-Hansen, L.B.: Motivating the Interest in Danish Literature with Mobile Persuasive Learning. In: Behringer, R. (ed.) IWEPLET, ECTEl 2013, Paphos, Cyprus (2013)
7. Fogg, B.: Persuasive Computers, Perspectives and Research Directions. In: CHI. ACM Press, New York (1998)
8. Weinmann, M., Schneider, C., Vom Brocke, J.: Digital Nudging. Social Science Research Network, Mexico (2015)
9. Kahneman, D.: A perspective on judgment and choice: mapping bounded rationality. Am. Psychol. 58(9), 697–720 (2003)
10. O'Keefe, D.J.: The Elaboration Likelihood Model. In: Dillard, J.P., Shen, L. (eds.) The Persuasion Handbook, SAGE, Thousand Oaks (2013)

11. Miller, G.R.: On being persuaded, some basic distinctions. In: Dillard, J.P., Pfau, M. (eds.) The Persuasion Handbook, Developments in Theory and Practice, Saga Publications, London (2002)
12. Gram-Hansen, S.: Persuasive Designs for Learning, Learning in Persuasive Design. Ph.D.-serien for Det Humanistiske Fakultet, Aalborg Universitet. Aalborg Universitetsforlag (2017)
13. Gram-Hansen, S.B., Rabjerg, M.F., Hovedskou, E.K.B.: What Makes It Persuasive? Springer International Publishing, Cham (2018)
14. Spahn, A.: And lead us (Not) into persuasion...? Persuasive technology and the ethics of communication. Sci. Eng. Ethics **18**(4), 633–650 (2011)
15. Atkinson, B.M.C.: Captology: a critical review. In: Persuasive Technology 2006. ACM, New York (2006)
16. Berdichevsky, D., Neuenschwander, E.: Towards an ethics of persuasive technology. Commun. ACM **43**, 51–58 (1999)
17. Ehninger, D.: Contemporary Rhetoric: a Reader's Coursebook. Scott, Foresman and Company, Glenview, IL (1972)
18. Benedikt, A.F.: On doing the right thing at the right time. In: Sipiora, P., Baumlin, J.S. (eds.) Rhetoric and Kairos, Essays in History, Theory and Praxis, State University of New York Press, Albany (2002)
19. Kinneavy, J.L.: Kairos in classical and modern rhetorical theory. In: Sipiora, P., Baumlin, J.S. (eds.) Rhetoric and Kairos, Essays in History, Theory and Practice, State University of New York Press, Albany (2002)
20. Hansen, P.G., Jespersen, A.M.: Nudge and the manipulation of choice: a framework for the responsible use of the nudge approach to behaviour change in public policy. Eur. J. Risk Regul. EJRR **4**(1), 3–28 (2013)
21. Illeris, K.: How We Learn - Learning and Non-Learning in School and Beyond. Routledge (2007)
22. Fogg, B.: The Behavior Grid: 35 Ways Behaviour Can Change. In: Persuasive 2010. ACM: Copenhagen, Denmark (2010)
23. Maslow, A.H.: The Psychology of Science. Harper & Row, New York (1966)
24. Rashid, I., Kenner, S.: Offline - Free your mind from Smartphone and Social Media stress. Wiley, Hoboken (2018)
25. Fogg, B., The Future of Persuasion is Mobile. In: Fogg, B., Eckles, D. (eds.) Mobile Persuasion, 20 Perspectives on the Future of Behavior Change. Stanford Captology Media, Palo Alto (2007)
26. Vincent, J.J.K.: Technology and policy. Emot. Attach. Mob. Ph. **19**(1), 39–44 (2006)
27. Caspersen, M., Nowack, P.: Computational thinking and practice - a generic approach to computing in Danish high schools. In: ACE 13 Proceedings of the Fifteenth Australian Computing Education Conference. ACM (2014)
28. Lindhardt, J.: Retorik. Rosinante (2003)

Are User Manuals Obsolete with Persuasive Systems?

Eunice Eno Yaa Frimponmaa Agyei$^{(\boxtimes)}$ and Harri Oinas-Kukkonen

University of Oulu, Oulu, Finland
eunice.agyei@oulu.fi

Abstract. Ensuring that users can successfully perform their primary tasks and achieve their behavioral goals is critical for the success of persuasive system. Are user manuals needed to achieve this goal? In this paper, we sought to understand the role of end-user documentation for persuasive systems. 50 persuasive apps from the Google Play Store were analysed to determine the importance of user manuals or guides for persuasive health apps. Although based on a small data set, our results show that in most cases persuasive systems need user documentation and hence we encourage developers of such systems to allocate resources for creating quality documentation for their users.

Keywords: User documentation · User manual · Persuasive systems design · Persuasive systems · Self-explanatory user interface

1 Introduction

User documentation such as user manuals, instruction sheets, quick reference guides, and troubleshooting keys are types of documentation aimed at helping users to use an information system [1]. They are used to provide information on what, when, and how to do something with a given system [2]. There exist a variety of user documentation genres including online forums, feature guides, Frequently Asked Questions (FAQ), and web-based tutorials [3]. User documentation as communication tool can enhance the value of an application to the user which in turn may improve user satisfaction [4]. Explanations provided to support the use of interactive systems have yielded benefits such as increased task completion rate [5], a reduction of computer usage anxiety [6], an increase in user satisfaction with the system [7], and better usability [8]. Despite these benefits of user documentation, often little effort, time and budget are devoted to it [9].

While the purpose of user manuals (whether in print, online, within software, on external device) is to enable people achieve their goals when using information systems, they often fail to do so. Research has shown that many end-users do not like to read user manuals [10] and this is attributed to the fact that users may often be overwhelmed by the amount of information they need to read and assimilate before using the software system [11, 12]. As a result, they skip over to sections that deals with the task they want to accomplish, skip over-explanations, prematurely ignore actions that they deem irrelevant to the tasks they want to achieve, forgo the user manual entirely and rely on

© Springer Nature Switzerland AG 2021
R. Ali et al. (Eds.): PERSUASIVE 2021, LNCS 12684, pp. 320–327, 2021.
https://doi.org/10.1007/978-3-030-79460-6_25

from previous experience with other software systems instead of reading the provided manual. These user attitudes result in gaps in knowledge and skills required to attain the desired goal with the software [11, 12]. In addition, users are challenged with the need to 'multi-task' (i.e., read, follow the detailed instructions, and perform the tasks with the software). This type of multi-tasking requires the user to shift their gaze periodically from the manual to the software and vice versa. This may create a discontinuity that could lead to errors which hinders the user from achieving the intended results and may leave them perplexed about their results, and what to do next [11]. The task of developing user manuals can be daunting because the quality of the user documentation matters. Quality concerns the worth of the information content delivered to users and its aesthetics as described by [13] as well as the resources allocated to it.

The advances in the computer technology has made it possible to design apps to influence and motivate people adopt new behaviour such as exercising. *Persuasive systems* (PS) are "computerized software or information systems designed to reinforce, change or shape attitudes or behaviors or both without using coercion or deception" [14]. It may be easily assumed and perhaps even taken for granted that systems such as these do not need any user guides as they are so engaging *per se*.

In this paper, we seek to investigate the relevance of end-user documentation for persuasive systems and how they can be made feasible to support users. The paper is structured as follows. Sections 2 addresses the dual connection between end-user documentation and persuasive systems. We analyze the need for end-user documentation for persuasive systems and vice versa. Section 3 presents the study setting and results are presented in Sect. 4. Finally, Sect. 5 discusses the results and conclusion.

2 Dual Connectivity Between End-User Documentation and Persuasive Technologies

End-User Documentation for Persuasive Technologies. End-user documentation are often dismissed as irrelevant because of two popular clichés; a "well designed software needs no documentation" [15] and users do not read user manuals [16]. To counter these, firstly, it is important to note that bad software designs do exist in the real world and that people will refer to manuals if there is the need to [17]. Also, the complex and interactive features in persuasive systems necessitate the need for user manuals to improve their usability [9]. People conduct internet-based searches to obtain help with using a software. A quick google search (on 28.10.2020) produced 73,100,000 search results in 0.67 s for the phrase, *"how to use fitbit"*, a leading persuasive system for physical activity self-monitoring (See Fig. 1). This backs the claim that persuasive systems, among other software systems, require user manuals to support users achieve their goals. Help resources such as webpages, images and video tutorials among others were retrieved and were produced by the Fitbit company and other third-party entities such as bloggers and social media influencers. Figure 2 shows an of example user documentation available online to help users achieve their goals and the genuine need for them.

User-developed manuals differ from the vendor-developed manuals because they are more action-oriented, customized to the specific tasks, user roles, and are often shorter than those produced by the vendors according to a study by [18]. While this study was inconclusive on which of these manual types is better, it highlights the difference in user support needs and hence these findings can inform the design of end-user documentation resources.

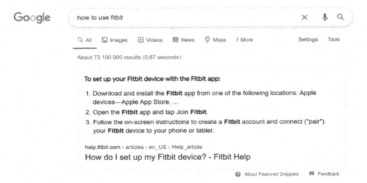

Fig. 1. Example of the need for user documentation for persuasive systems.

Fig. 2. Fitbit's official help functionality.

Although user documentation is a useful source of support to the user, their scope may be limited due to not being dynamic or contextual enough to answer some of the questions users may have [19]. In recent years, there has been a move towards embedding instructions in the user interface also known as self-explanatory user interface (SEUI) or instructional user interface to improve user experience [5, 20, 21]. Embedding instructions in the UI possess the capability to guide an end-user to interact with the system by providing information regarding the rational of the UI (e.g. the purpose of a menu item, its current state and how the state can be changed) [22] while the user is interacting with it. The goal of SEUI is to generate dynamic help systems (e.g., help message, prompts) to guide the user to perform tasks. Often these dynamic help systems are not only aware of the context of use but also the user's current task, the structure of the UI and how the UI is presented to the user [22]. They may possess the ability to reason on the application state and generate useful and valuable explanations to support the user fulfil their task.

User documentation (e.g. interactive tutorials) is used for onboarding users to an application and hence are needed for first time users to discover, learn, and engage with system functionalities, as well as to help them to achieve their goals in a timely manner [23]. This helps users to form a mental model of the application and informs their decision to use or ignore it. Also, a user documentation is an important marketing tool [24]. [25] recommends evaluating the quality of it before purchasing the software product to determine the true value of the app. It can be considered a part of the software package and its presence demonstrates professionalism and orientation of the software towards users. As a marketing tool, it can also be used to stimulate the interest of users [26].

Persuasive Technologies for End-User Documentation. End-user support documentation is key to the successful implementation and realization of the benefits of information systems [18]. Although user documentation is an auxiliary for persuasive technologies, it has to be feasible to the user in order to support the user accomplish the tasks that ultimately influence their habits, behaviours, or attitudes. To make user documentation more feasible, there is a need to determine when a persuasive system needs an end-user documentation.

3   Research Setting

Research Question. Persuasive technology includes a wide variety of technologies (e.g., web apps and mobile apps) which are available on platforms such as Android, and iOS. In this paper, we investigate and analyse persuasive apps that run on the Android platform to determine if such systems need a user manual or not. We assume here that the apps designed for a certain purpose, used by a certain group of people, produced by a company of a certain size, with certain a complexity/size of the app can mandate the need for a user documentation. The following questions guided this research:

1. Do persuasive apps published on the Google Play Store require developers to upload an end-user documentation?
2. Does the purpose/category/ user type (e.g., patients) of a PS mandate an end-user documentation?
3. Does the size of producers and resources available for a PS mandate a user documentation?
4. Does the complexity and size of a PS call for an end-user documentation?

Inclusion Criteria and Data Extraction. Apps included in the analysis had to be published in English and available on the Android platform for free. Each app was installed on an Honor 8, an android phone that runs Android 7 operating system. Data collected included the rank of the app, total ratings, average ratings, name of the app, purpose of app, type(s) of user documentation, nature of user interface, location of the user documentation, website of the app, size of the company that produced the app, which is measured by the number of employees, the install size of the app as an indicator of the size/complexity of the app, and the category of the app (i.e., Health and fitness/Medical).

Data Source. A total of 50 apps were included in the study from the health and fitness and medical categories on Play Store. We initially collected 500 health and fitness mobile apps on the 26.11.2020 from an Android app ranking website which uses the total number of app reviews as a criteria to grade apps [27]. Out of this, we selected the top 20 and bottom 15 apps to provide a broad overview of the apps within the category (most rated vs least rated). Concerning the medical category, we retrieved 15 mHealth applications listed on databases for European digital app because the apps categorized as medical by [27] were not appropriate for this review. Ten of the 15 apps were selected from the "my Health apps" repository [28] while the other five (5/10) apps from the "mHealth hub" repository [29, 30].

4   Results

Characteristics of Studies. 45/50 were listed as health and fitness apps and the remaining (5/50) as medical apps. The apps were developed for self-management of health condition (13/50), fitness tracking (10/50), weight tracking (5/50), period (i.e., menstrual cycle) tracking (4/50), sleep monitoring (3/50), drinking water tracking (2/50), medication adherence (2/50), disease monitoring (1/50) and elderly care (1/50) purposes. The type of user documentation varied. User documentation was available for 39/50 apps which were located in the app (30/50), on the company's website (20/50), or some online resource (1/50). The companies behind these apps were classified as micro, small, medium or large using the Organization for Economic Co-operation and Development classification system for companies with a slight modification to the boundaries corresponding to less than 10 employees, between 11 and 49, 50–200 and 201 or more respectively [31]. The size of company was not available for 13 out of 50 apps. The size of the apps ranged from 3.8 to 483 megabytes. The total and average ratings were available for (49/50) which indicates the perceived quality of the app [32].

When a User Documentation is Needed. We found that apps uploaded on the app store are required to include descriptions of the app. These descriptions tells the user what the app is for and qualify as a minimum level of user documentation (compare [1, 2]). However, the amount of information in the app descriptions varied and hence may not be enough to provide the needed support. We identified other forms of user documentation such as FAQs. All the apps evaluated had user interfaces that are self-explanatory or intuitive. Also, the apps that were listed in the medical category had user documentation(s) other than the descriptions on the Google Play store. It is important to note that apps declared 'medical' on the app store does not necessarily mean that they are 'medical apps' according to the Medical Device Regulation definitions [33] or used by patients. As such, we cannot conclude if a user documentation is needed for medical apps or not. Some apps (11/50) in the health and fitness category did not have any additional documentation. These includes four (4/11) fitness apps, two (2/11) sleep monitoring apps, two (2/11) weight tracking apps, one (1/11) activity tracking app, one (1/11) period tracking and one (1/11) self-management of health condition apps did not have any other documentation apart from the descriptions on the app store.

Different types of user manuals were produced by companies of varying sizes and available for users in the app, website, and online resources. The size of the company is associated with the amount of resources (e.g. finance and human) available and that can be allocated for creating a user documentation [34]. Our analysis shows that all the companies of small (n = 5) and large (n = 5) sizes produced other forms of user documentation apart from the descriptions on the Play Store. Majority of the micro-sized (n = 12/15) and medium sized (n = 6/15) companies also provided other forms of user documentation in addition to descriptions on the Play Store. The ability of micro-sized companies to provide additional documentation is indeed promising if we consider the amount of resources (i.e., <10 employees) that may be available for a user documentation.

We found that both the smallest (3.8 megabytes) and biggest app (483 megabytes) sizes had other forms of user documentation in addition to the minimum level of user documentation (i.e., descriptions on the Play Store). This finding gives an indication that the size of the app does not excuse the need for a user documentation. As such the availability of these end-user documentations is indeed commendable. Also, we identified that some apps (9/50) that possessed high average ratings (i.e., >4 <5) did not have any other documentation apart from the minimum level of user documenta-tion (i.e. app descriptions on Play Store) which suggests that there is no correlation between user documentation and user ratings. This finding is contrary to the research by [35] who investigated troubleshooting comments embedded in user reviews of apps listed on the Play Store. They found out that when developers responded and supported users to solve the problems users faced, user ratings of the app improved subsequently. Such troubleshooting activities reveal the need for apps to have troubleshooting con-tent embedded in its user documentation or a separate troubleshooting user guide. This need further validates the importance of a user documentation. We believe that a user documentation that contains guides for troubleshooting is a proactive way to support multiple users to use an app instead of the passive approach via user reviews which calls for one-to-one troubleshooting activities. Providing a user documentation with the necessary information shows professionalism. In the absence of an official user manual to support users, third-party manuals made available by other app users, bloggers, or social media influencers can serve as an alternative source of user documentation for PSs especially those that are popular with many users (See Fitbit example in Sect. 2).

5 Conclusion and Discussion

In this paper, we discussed the need and relevance of end-user documentation for persua-sive systems. We analyzed 50 persuasive mobile apps. Our results give an indication that a user documentation(s) is relevant for persuasive systems. Although user documentation can be challenging to create due to limited resources, some micro and small companies identified in this study provided user documentation(s), which shows that it is possible to create a user manual regardless of the size of the company. The cliché that users do not read user manuals does not excuse the need to create one because users will consult it when they are stuck. As a PS developer, you want your users to be able to perform tasks that lead to behaviour change and not quit because they are unable to use the app due to poor-quality documentation or the lack thereof. Also, they can take advantage of the Play Store app descriptions (i.e., 80 and 4000 characters for short and full descrip-tions respectively) to document how their apps can be used. These descriptions can be considered as the minimum level of user documentation and together with intuitive user interfaces may provide enough support to the user. This research is a first and small step towards investigating whether user documentation is needed for persuasive systems or not. We call for more research into this topic. Future studies should investigate the impact of the type and quality of a user manual may have on task completion rates, app ratings, and perceived quality of the app. We encourage persuasive system developers to create suitable level of user documentation to support its users.

References

1. Souza, R., Oliveira, A.: Guide automator: continuous delivery of end user documentation. In: Proceedings - 2017 IEEE/ACM 39th International Conference on Software Engineering: New Ideas and Emerging Results Track, ICSE-NIER 2017, pp. 31–34 (2017)
2. Mcarthur, G.R.: If Writers Can't Program and Programmers Can't Write, Who's Writing User Documentation? (1986)
3. Earle, R.H., Rosso, M.A., Alexander, K.E.: User preferences of software documentation genres. In: SIGDOC 2015 - Proceedings of the 33rd Annual International Conference on the Design of Communication, pp. 1–10 (2015)
4. Torkzadeh, G.: The quality of user documentation: an instrument validation. J. Manag. Inf. Syst. 5(2), 99–108 (1988)
5. Myers, B., Weitzman, D.A., Ko, A.J., Chau, D.H.: Answering Why and Why Not Questions in User Interfaces (2006)
6. Moore, B.Y.: Computer anxiety's impact on computer user documentation (2000)
7. Gemoets, L.A., Mahmood, M.A.: Effect of the quality of user documentation on user satisfaction with information systems. Inf. Manag. 18(1), 47–54 (1990)
8. Chaudhuri, N.B., Dhar, D.: Self-explanatory interface: embedding visual and aural syntax to improve usability. Procedia Comput. Sci. 171, 1898–1907 (2020)
9. Amalfitano, D., Fasolino, A.R., Tramontana, P.: Using dynamic analysis for generating end user documentation for Web 2.0 applications. In: Proceedings - 13th IEEE International Symposium on Web Systems Evolution, WSE 2011, pp. 11–20 (2011)
10. Laue, R.: Anti-patterns in end-user documentation. In: ACM International Conference Proceeding Series, vol. Part F132091, pp. 1–11 (2017)
11. Vanasse, H.D., Stolovitch, S.: The paradox of user documentation: useful, but rarely used. Perform. Instr. 28(7), 19–22 (1989)
12. Carroll, J., Rosson, M.: Paradox of the active user. Undefined (1987)
13. Kahn, B.K., Strong, D.M., Wang, R.Y.: Information Quality Benchmarks: Product and Service Performance (2002)
14. Oinas-Kukkonen, H., Harjumaa, M.: Persuasive systems design: key issues, process model, and system features. Commun. Assoc. Inf. Syst. 24(1), 485–500 (2009)
15. Van Loggem, B.: User documentation: the cinderella of information systems. In: Advances in Intelligent Systems and Computing. vol. 206 AISC, pp. 167–177 (2013)
16. Rettig, M.: Nobody reads documentation. Commun. ACM 34(7), 19–24 (1991)
17. Van Loggem, B., Lundin, J.: Interaction with user documentation: a preliminary study. In: ACM International Conference Proceeding Series, pp. 41–46 (2013)
18. Shachak, A., Barnsley, J., Tu, K., Jadad, A.R., Lemieux-Charles, L.: Understanding end-user support for health information technology: a theoretical framework. Inform. Prim. Care 19(3), 169–172 (2012)

19. García Frey, A., Calvary, G., Dupuy-Chessa, S., Mandran, N.: Model-Based self-explanatory UIs for free, but are they valuable? In: Kotzé, P., Marsden, G., Lindgaard, G., Wesson, J., Winckler, M. (eds.) INTERACT 2013. LNCS, vol. 8119, pp. 144–161. Springer, Heidelberg (2013). https://doi.org/10.1007/978-3-642-40477-1_9
20. Lim, B.Y., Dey, A.K., Avrahami, D.: Why and why not explanations improve the intelligibility of context-aware intelligent systems (2009)
21. Purchase, H.C., Worrill, J.: An empirical study of on-line help design: features and principles. Int. J. Hum. Comput. Stud. **56**(5), 539–567 (2002)
22. Frey, A.G.: Self-explanatory user interfaces by model-driven engineering. In: EICS2010 - Proceedings of the 2010 ACM SIGCHI Symposium on Engineering Interactive Computing Systems, pp. 341–344 (2010)
23. Strahm, B., Gray, C.M., Vorvoreanu, M.: Generating mobile application onboarding insights through minimalist instruction. In: DIS 2018 - Proceedings of the 2018 Designing Interactive Systems Conference, pp. 361–372 (2018)
24. Gastegger, M.: Maintenance of technical and user documentation
25. Pakin, S.: Evaluate user documentation before you buy the software. IEEE Trans. Prof. Commun., **PC-24**(2), pp. 75–78 (1981)
26. Synko, A., Peleshchyshyn, A.: UDC 004.91 Software development documenting-documentation types and standards
27. List of Android Most Popular Google Play Apps | androidrank.org. https://androidrank.org/android-most-popular-google-play-apps?start=1&sort=0&price=all&category=HEALTH_AND_FITNESS. Accessed 26 Nov 2020
28. myhealthapps.net - apps tried and tested by people like you. http://myhealthapps.net/. Accessed 28 Nov 2020
29. European mhealth hub | Health apps repositories in Europe. https://mhealth-hub.org/health-apps-repositories-in-europe. Accessed 28 Nov 2020
30. NHS Apps Library - NHS. https://www.nhs.uk/apps-library/. Accessed 28 Nov 2020
31. Entrepreneurship - Enterprises by business size - OECD Data. https://data.oecd.org/entrepreneur/enterprises-by-business-size.htm. Accessed 27 Nov 2020
32. Noei, E., Syer, M.D., Zou, Y., Hassan, A.E., Keivanloo, I.: A study of the relation of mobile device attributes with the user-perceived quality of Android apps. Empir. Softw. Eng. **22**(6), 3088–3116 (2017). https://doi.org/10.1007/s10664-017-9507-3
33. Medical devices | European Medicines Agency. https://www.ema.europa.eu/en/human-regulatory/overview/medical-devices. Accessed 29 Nov 2020
34. Churchill, N.C., Lewis, V.L., The Five Stages of Small Business Growth
35. Hassan, S., et al.: Studying the Dialogue Between Users and Developers of Free Apps in the Google Play Store

Author Index

Printed in the United States
by Baker & Taylor Publisher Services